GODS AND GODDESSES

of Greece and Rome

Marshall Cavendish
Reference
New York

Other Marshall Cavendish Offices:

Marshall Cavendish International (Asia) Private Limited, 1 New Industrial Road, Singapore 536196 ● Marshall Cavendish International (Thailand) Co Ltd. 253 Asoke, 12th Flr, Sukhumvit 21 Road, Klongtoey Nua, Wattana, Bangkok 10110, Thailand ● Marshall Cavendish (Malaysia) Sdn Bhd, Times Subang, Lot 46, Subang Hi-Tech Industrial Park, Batu Tiga, 40000 Shah Alam, Selangor Darul Ehsan, Malaysia.

Marshall Cavendish is a trademark of Times Publishing Limited.

All websites were available and accurate when this book was sent to press.

Library of Congress Cataloging-in-Publication Data

Gods and goddesses of Greece and Rome.
    p. cm.
  Includes bibliographical references and index.
  ISBN 978-0-7614-7951-2 (alk. paper)
1. Gods, Greek. 2. Goddesses, Greek. 3. Gods, Roman. 4. Goddesses, Roman. 5. Mythology, Greek. 6. Mythology, Roman.
  BL783.G63 2012
  398.20938'01--dc22

                                                    2011006780

Printed in Malaysia

15 14 13 12   2 3 4 5

Marshall Cavendish
Publisher: Paul Bernabeo
Project Editor: Brian Kinsey
Production Manager: Michael Esposito
Indexer: Cynthia Crippen, AEIOU, Inc.

CONTENTS

INTRODUCTION

Tales of gods and goddesses have gripped the imagination of mere mortals from the time of the earliest known civilizations and have served to explain the beliefs, practices, and customs of those civilizations. While each civilization has developed its own system of deities and mythologies, some of the most prominent among the gods and goddesses from around the world and throughout time have continued to be the gods and goddesses of ancient Greece and Rome.

The ancient Greeks were polytheists, meaning that their worship involved many gods, not just one. The family of Greek gods evolved over the course of many centuries, often merging with similar deities from neighboring regions, but the great pantheon of gods now associated with Mount Olympus dates from roughly the fifth century BCE. The 12 gods of the Olympian family were Zeus, Hera, Poseidon, Athena, Apollo, Artemis, Aphrodite, Hermes, Demeter, Dionysus, Hephaestus, and Ares. The Greek gods were almost all fully human in form, and although the gods were immortal, they possessed many mortal traits, such as jealousy, anger, and lust. The Greeks believed that the gods could have a profound effect on the lives of mortals, so worship of the gods (including prayers, sacrifices, and festivals) was an important element in the daily lives of the Greeks who wanted to avoid the wrath of the gods.

The religion of pre-Christian Rome was also polytheistic. As with the Greeks, the Romans developed their pantheon over time and incorporated deities from other cultures, including Greece. In fact, many of the principle gods of the Roman pantheon bear more than a slight resemblance to the Greek gods. Apollo was incorporated into the Roman pantheon with the same traits and the same name as in Greece. Other Roman deities share the same traits as the Greek gods but have different names. For example,

Greece's Athena and Rome's Minerva are both known as the goddess of wisdom, arts and crafts, and war. Still, Rome's pantheon is not an exact duplicate of the Greek pantheon. For example, Saturn, Rome's god of agriculture, may have emerged from Etruscan culture north of Rome on the Italian peninsula. Also, while almost all Greek gods were human in form, some of the lesser gods and goddesses of Rome represented abstractions, such as harmony, health, and dutifulness. This difference in the nature of the gods has been proposed as one reason why there are fewer stories attached to some of the lesser Roman deities than to the lesser Greek deities.

The 76 articles in *Gods and Goddesses of Greece and Rome* represent the most well-known deities from those two civilizations. Included for discussion are the significance of given deities, and the forms of worship associated with the deities. The abundant illustrations in this volume represent centuries of artistic interpretations of the gods and goddesses and their mythologies. Each article includes a bibliography and a selection of cross-references to related articles. At the end of the volume is a pronunciation guide, a list of the major pantheons, resources for further study, and an index.

Although the articles in this volume should appeal to the general reader, they were written with high school students in mind, especially those who may find themselves in classes ranging from history and literature to art and music, where mythology plays a part. These articles illumine subjects that continue to reemerge in modern culture.

Additional information about Greek and Roman mythology is available in the single-volume *Heroes and Heroines of Greece and Roman*, the 11-volume set *Gods, Goddesses, and Mythology*, and the online *Gods, Goddesses, and Mythology* database at www.marshallcavendishdigital.com.

CONTRIBUTORS

Laurel Bowman
University of Victoria, Canada

Anthony Bulloch
University of California, Berkeley

Andrew Campbell
London, UK

Alys Caviness
Noblesville, Indiana

Kathryn Chew
California State University, Long Beach

Anna Claybourne
Edinburgh, UK

Peter Connor
London, UK

Barbara Gardner
Mendocino, California

Daniel P. Harmon
University of Washington

Karelisa Hartigan
University of Florida

Kathleen Jenks
Hartford, Michigan

Leslie Ellen Jones
Santa Monica, California

Deborah Lyons
Johns Hopkins University

Jim Marks
Spokane, Washington

James M. Redfield
University of Chicago

Carl Ruck
Boston University

Feyo Schuddeboom
Hilversum, Netherlands

Brian Seilstad
Lutherville, Maryland

Blaise Staples
Hull, Massachusetts

Kirk Summers
University of Alabama

ACHELOUS

In Greek mythology, Achelous was a river god. He was the son of Oceanus and Tethys and the eldest of 3,000 brothers. His union with one of the Muses produced the Sirens, alternatively known as the Acheloiades ("daughters of Achelous"). His name means "he who washes away care."

The Achelous River is the largest natural fresh waterway in Greece. It rises on Mount Pindus and flows in a southerly direction, forming the boundary between Acarnania and Aetolia. Finally, it flows into the Ionian Sea opposite the Echinades islands. The Achelous River is about 130 miles (210 km) in length.

Below: This mask of Achelous was sculpted in Greece during the classical period, probably about 470 BCE.

It is said to have been formed by the tears of Niobe, who fled to Mount Sipylon after the deaths of her husband, Amphion, and her six or seven children.

From the earliest times Achelous was worshiped throughout Greece as a great river god. He was honored with sacrifices and invoked in prayers. Achelous was the personification of, and a byword for, all freshwater. Roman poet Virgil (70–19 BCE) used the term *Acheloia pocula* ("cups of Achelous") to refer to water in general.

The story of a wrestling match between Achelous and Heracles over the latter's bride, Deianeira, is often depicted in ancient art. Achelous was initially overpowered by Heracles, but the river god turned himself into a raging bull. Heracles then broke off one of his horns with a great show of force. Achelous later recovered this horn from Heracles by giving him in return the horn of Amaltheia, the Greek equivalent of the cornucopia (horn of plenty). According to Roman poet Ovid (43 BCE–17 CE), in a somewhat different version, the Naiads received the horn that Heracles took from Achelous and changed it into the horn of plenty.

Achelous in art
In Greek art Achelous is depicted with the lower body and horns of a bull, and the face and torso of a man. He appears frequently in Greek vase painting, where he is shown wrestling with Heracles. He is also found in Greek sculpture, especially in the so-called nymph reliefs—the small carvings dedicated to the water goddesses and the god Pan. These effigies usually show the nymphs dancing in a line in a cave. In most cases only the bearded face of Achelous with his horns is shown at the side of the scene. Achelous also appears in Roman mosaics, although far less frequently than in Greek art.

FEYO SCHUDDEBOOM

Bibliography
Bulfinch, Thomas. *Bulfinch's Mythology.* New York: Barnes & Noble, 2006.
Ovid, and A. D. Melville, trans. *Metamorphoses.* New York: Oxford University Press, 2008.

SEE ALSO: Oceanus; Pan.

ANEMOI

The Anemoi were mythological beings that personified the winds. They were worshiped by ancient Greeks and Romans, who believed that the Anemoi were the children of Eos, goddess of the dawn.

Above: *This photograph shows three of the eight Anemoi depicted around the top of the Tower of Winds at the Roman Forum in Athens, Greece.*

The Greeks regarded the winds—*anemoi*, the plural of *anemos*—as divine beings. Greek poet Homer (c. ninth–eighth century BCE), who is credited with having composed the epic poems the *Iliad* and the *Odyssey*, identifies four chief winds, each of which corresponds to one of the four cardinal points of the compass: Boreas (the north wind), Eurus (the east wind), Notus (the south wind), and Zephyrus (the west wind). Hesiod (fl. 800 BCE), author of *Theogony*, which along with Homer's epics forms the basis of most modern knowledge of Greek mythology, describes these four winds as the children of Astraeus, a Titan, and Eos, goddess of the dawn. Hesiod distinguishes Boreas, Eurus, Notus, and Zephyrus from the destructive storm winds, which were children of the giant serpent Typhon. The four main winds were venerated because they could be beneficent to all humans, particularly to sailors, whom they could help on voyages, and farmers, to whom they could bring advantageous weather.

The four winds were rarely depicted in Greek art. One exception is a comical illustration of Boreas on a vase found near Thebes in Boeotia, Greece. The vase shows the hero Odysseus as a pudgy old man, sailing over the sea on a raft made of wine amphoras and using Poseidon's trident to catch a fish. To the right of the painting is Boreas, the north wind, blowing with round cheeks to help Odysseus on his way. Both figures are identified by inscriptions.

Roman wind

By contrast, the winds are frequently shown in Roman art, especially in mosaics. The winds are usually identifiable by their winged heads with open mouths and inflated cheeks. Sometimes they also have wings on their shoulders, as on the Tower of the Winds at the Roman Forum in Athens. There eight winds are represented—in addition to the four already mentioned are Kaikias (the northeast wind), Apeliotes (the southeast wind), Lips (the southwest wind), and Argestes or Sciron (the northwest wind).

In European paintings of the Common Era, the winds appear in numerous works. Among the most famous examples are two canvases by Italian artist Sandro Botticelli (1445–1510): *Primavera* ("Spring") and *The Birth of Venus*. In the former, Zephyrus grabs the fleeing nymph, Chloris, who is transformed into Flora, goddess of spring and flowers. In the latter, Zephyrus gently blows ashore the goddess of love, Venus (the Roman equivalent of the Greek Aphrodite), who stands naked in a gigantic seashell.

FEYO SCHUDDEBOOM

Bibliography

Hesiod, and M. L. West, trans. *Theogony* and *Works and Days*. New York: Oxford University Press, 2008.

Homer, and Robert Fagles, trans. *The Iliad* and *The Odyssey*. New York: Penguin, 2009.

SEE ALSO: Eos; Typhon; Venus.

APHRODITE

Above: This Greek bas-relief was sculpted in about 460 BCE. It depicts the birth of Aphrodite from the sea.

In Greek mythology, Aphrodite was the goddess of love. Beautiful and alluring, she had many lovers, including Adonis and the war god Ares. Her husband was Hephaestus, who was both ugly and lame. Aphrodite was the mother of Eros, who became her male counterpart.

A ncient authors give varying accounts of the manner of Aphrodite's birth. Most say that she was born from the body of Uranus, the sky god, after he was dismembered by his usurper, Cronus. When the genitals of Uranus fell into the sea at Cytherea, a small

Ionian island on the southwest tip of the Peloponnese, Aphrodite sprang from his seed and arose from the foam. The Greek word *aphros* (the etymological root of *Aphrodite*) means "foam."

Early exploits
From Cytherea, Zephyr (the west wind) carried Aphrodite to Cyprus, where she was cared for by the Horae (the seasons), who dressed her in exotic clothing and taught her how to behave seductively. She became the glamorous goddess of sensual love and allurement, and, as such, she took on the Graces as her companions. The magic girdle that she wore was said to inspire love in human hearts. What made Aphrodite irresistible to males was that she embodied the unsurpassed combination of aesthetic beauty

and divine power. She never hesitated to use the latter, and she sometimes went beyond the bounds of propriety. Her only concern was to strike passion into the hearts of gods, humans, and animals alike; she gave no thought to the cost to the parties concerned. Because the goddess was born on Cytherea and reared on Cyprus, she is commonly called either the Cytherean Aphrodite or the Cyprian Aphrodite.

Aphrodite's exploits were invariably erotic in nature, and there were numerous scandalous stories about her. Homer—a Greek epic poet of the ninth or eighth century BCE—tells of her nocturnal affair with Ares (Mars) while her husband, the blacksmith Hephaestus (Vulcan), was working at his forge. Hephaestus had won Aphrodite's hand in marriage after setting a trap for Hera, the wife of Zeus, and holding her for ransom. Aphrodite always despised her

Left: This is the face of Aphrodite as imagined by a Greek bronze sculptor of the third century BCE.

Above: This painting by Tintoretto (c. 1518–1594) is entitled Vulcan Surprises Venus and Mars. *At right, Mars can be seen hiding under the bed. Vulcan, Venus, and Mars were the Roman equivalents of the Greek Hephaestus, Aphrodite, and Ares, respectively.*

husband and much preferred the handsome and impulsive Ares, the god of war. In order to conduct their affair in perfect secrecy, Aphrodite and Ares employed a sentry named Alectryon (the Greek word for "rooster"), who was supposed to warn them when day was breaking, because it was at dawn that Hephaestus returned home from his smithy. One morning, however, Alectryon fell into a deep slumber and failed to sound the alarm. The sun god Helios, who saw everything on the earth beneath him, caught the couple in each other's arms and immediately told Hephaestus. The blacksmith god then set a trap for his unfaithful wife and her lover—he rigged up an invisible net above their bed that ensnared them when they next lay together. Some cuckolded husbands seek violent retribution, but Hephaestus took his revenge through ridicule. The following morning, he called all the other gods to come and see his wife and Ares in this compromising position and to witness his wife's infidelity. The Olympian gods laughed heartily, and Hermes reportedly exclaimed to Zeus: "I wish I could get caught in such a trap!"

Always passionate, always indiscreet, the powers that Aphrodite embodied are some of the most important components of human existence. Sappho (fl. c. 610–580 BCE), a female poet of the Greek island of Lesbos, wrote a beautiful verse in which she invoked Aphrodite for aid in her time of desperate love. She asks Aphrodite, the "weaver of ruses," to swoop down in her chariot drawn by sparrows to be her "helper in battle," the only one who can give her the charms needed to woo the object of her desire.

The legend of Pygmalion

Many of the myths surrounding Aphrodite illustrate the complexity of love, how it brings beauty to our lives, but how it also causes confusion and distress. Love is indiscriminate, touching gods and humans alike; it comes unexpectedly and deserts those it has visited as quickly as it came; its power knows no limits. In *Metamorphoses* Roman poet Ovid (43 BCE–17 CE) recounts the legend of Pygmalion, which brings together many of these elements in a single story. Pygmalion was a mythical king of Cyprus and an accomplished sculptor. Witnessing with disgust his female subjects selling their bodies to men, he vowed that he himself would never marry and never get involved with women. He lived alone. While carving an ivory statue of a maiden, whom he named Galatea, he fell in love with it. It

Symbols of Aphrodite

The myrtle was Aphrodite's sacred tree, the rose her sacred flower, and the dove her sacred bird. According to one version of the legend of her birth, the goddess was hatched from a dove's egg that had fallen into the Euphrates River in west Asia. When Aphrodite's son Aeneas was looking for the key to the underworld, it was a dove that showed him the Golden Bough. Aeneas immediately recognized the influence of his mother. Aphrodite is also strongly associated with seashells (a reference to the traditional account of her birth), and she is often depicted holding an apple, the prize she won in the Judgment of Paris.

was, after all, perfect in every way—beautiful, modest, and virginal. In the secret recesses of his palace, Pygmalion began to caress the statue and kiss it, and he even led himself to believe that it was responding. He brought her presents of flowers, precious stones, and clothing; paid her compliments; and courted the statue as if it were a living girl. His mind became so confused that he felt the statue had become his lover. He took her to his bed and addressed her as darling, but deep in his heart he knew that

she was not living, so his frustration grew. When the festival of Aphrodite came around, and all the people of Cyprus were celebrating by sacrificing snow white heifers and burning incense, Pygmalion too made an offering and prayed to Aphrodite that she would grant his wish that he could marry his ivory girl. Aphrodite heard Pygmalion's prayer and turned the ivory statue into a living, breathing girl who was able to return his kisses and feel his caress. Pygmalion was overjoyed that at long last Aphrodite had provided him with a perfect mate. Aphrodite then blessed the union of the couple with a daughter named Paphos, who founded the city in Cyprus named for her, which became sacred to the worship of Aphrodite.

This story has remained popular through the ages and has been retold many times, most notably in *Pygmalion* (1912) by Irish playwright George Bernard Shaw (1856–1950), and in *My Fair Lady* (1956), a musical by Frederick Loewe (1901–1988) and Alan Jay Lerner (1918–1986). In 1964 the latter was a film. Directed by George Cukor (1899–1983), it starred Rex Harrison (1908–1990) and Audrey Hepburn (1929–1993). In both

Below: This Roman floor mosaic in the House of Dionysus in Paphos, Cyprus, dates from the third century CE. It depicts Hippolytus and Phaedra.

these later retellings of the legend, the king is a professor of phonetics; the object of his love is a common flower girl whom he teaches to speak properly.

Aphrodite and Adonis

In another ancient legend, Aphrodite herself falls in love with a vegetation deity known as Adonis. This story links Aphrodite with both fertility in general and, in particular, the principle that life and death operate cyclically, with the continuation of each dependent on that of the other. The story of Aphrodite and Adonis has parallels with that of the Sumerian deities Dumuzi and Inanna.

The story goes that Theias, king of Syria, had a daughter named Myrrha who was very beautiful. Because Myrrha's mother boasted that the girl was more beautiful than Aphrodite herself, the goddess took revenge by inspiring the young woman with incestuous feelings toward her father. With the help of her nurse, Myrrha managed to deceive her father into thinking that she was his longstanding mistress. Theias unwittingly visited his own daughter in bed, so that on 12 successive nights the two were lovers. On the last night, Theias discovered the trick and was so filled with anger and hatred that he went after his daughter with a knife. He would have killed her, but the gods took pity on Myrrha and transformed her into a myrrh tree.

Ten months after the transformation, the bark of the tree split open, and out came a marvelous baby who was named Adonis. Aphrodite loved the child, secretly giving it to Persephone, the goddess of the underworld, for care and safekeeping. The problem was that Persephone, too, was smitten with love for Adonis, and she did not want to give the child back. Aphrodite and Persephone wrangled over Adonis, and the ensuing fight threatened to disrupt the peace of the gods. Zeus was called on to judge their rival claims. He ruled that the boy must spend one third of the year on earth with Aphrodite, one third of the year in the underworld with Persephone, and the other third in any manner he chose. Adonis spent his free time hunting, ignoring Aphrodite's warnings not to pursue big game. One day he was gored by a wild boar. As Adonis lay bleeding to death, Aphrodite swooped down in her chariot, held his body in her arms, and declared that every year a memorial ceremony should be held to honor the beautiful boy, and that his blood should be turned into the flowers of spring. The anemone bloomed at her command. Thereafter, to celebrate the beautiful Adonis as the god of vegetation, the women of ancient Greece, particularly in the region of Adonia, would plant seeds in a shallow tray, adding warm water to make the seeds grow quickly. Soon after the seeds sprouted in this way, the plants would die, whereupon the women would tear their hair, beat their breasts, and wander about, lamenting the death of Adonis.

Hippolytus and Phaedra

The story of Hippolytus illustrates that the demands of Aphrodite cannot be ignored. Hippolytus was the son of Theseus and the Amazon Hippolyta. When Hippolytus was still a teenager, Theseus took a new wife, a young woman named Phaedra, whom he had met long before in Crete while fighting the Minotaur. When Theseus was away, Hippolytus continued doing what he loved best: paying homage to Artemis, the virgin goddess of hunting. The problem was that whenever he was out chasing game, he was neglecting Aphrodite. Phaedra, meanwhile, cared more for Aphrodite than for any other deity, and the goddess used her as an instrument of revenge on Hippolytus by causing the queen to fall in love with her stepson. When Phaedra confessed her feelings to Hippolytus, he rejected her advances. She was so ashamed that she hanged herself, but she left a suicide note stating that Hippolytus had tried to rape her. When Theseus returned home, he found the note and his dead wife and became enraged at Hippolytus. Theseus did not want to kill his own son, however, so he sent him into exile. As Hippolytus was driving away, Theseus could no longer control himself, and he called on Poseidon to help him punish Hippolytus. Poseidon immediately sent a monster up from the sea, which frightened the horses, causing Hippolytus to fall out of his chariot. The boy became entangled in the reins and was dragged across the rocks to his death. According to some versions of the myth, Artemis then had Asclepius, the god of medicine and the

Children of Aphrodite and Ares

Aphrodite had three children by Ares: two sons, Deimos and Phobos, and a daughter, Harmonia. The first two children traditionally appeared in battles to cause havoc in the ranks of enemy soldiers. Their names have now been given to the two moons of the planet Mars. Harmonia married Cadmus, a Phoenician prince who came to Boeotia. Together they founded the royal house of Thebes. They had a son, Polydorus, who succeeded to his father's throne, and four daughters, one of whom was the sea goddess Ino. Another was Semele, who became the mother of Zeus's son Dionysus, the Greek god of wine.

APHRODITE

The Venus de Milo

One of the most famous of the many artistic representations of Aphrodite is the ancient statue commonly known as the Venus de Milo. This is a misleading name, however, because the statue dates from a time before the Roman civilization could have influenced the place in which it was found, the Greek Cycladean island of Melos. *Milo* is the French version of the Greek Melos, and the former has been widely adopted because the statue is now housed in the Louvre, a museum in Paris. The statue should properly be—but only sometimes is—called the Aphrodite of Melos.

Discovered in 1820, the statue, which stands about six foot (2 m) tall, is now thought to have been sculpted between 110 and 88 BCE. The identity of the artist is unknown, but from the style it is clear that he was influenced by the work of Praxiteles (370–330 BCE). The masterpiece was purchased in the 19th century by the marquis de Rivière, the French ambassador to the Ottoman Empire, and presented to King Louis XVIII, who donated it to the Louvre.

The arms are broken off, and the mystery of their original position has always fascinated scholars and critics. Some have claimed that Aphrodite was holding a shield to look at her reflection; others, that she was spinning thread; a few, that the statue never had any arms at all.

Left: After Leonardo da Vinci's Mona Lisa, *the so-called Venus de Milo is the most popular permanent exhibit at the Louvre in Paris, France.*

son of Apollo, bring Hippolytus back to life, after which Artemis took him to Italy to serve in her temple.

The story of Hippolytus is notable for its portrayal of the rivalry between Aphrodite, who represents indiscriminate lust, and Artemis, who stands for young, virginal unmarried women, and wants sex only to be a part of adulthood and proper marriage. In *Hippolytus*, Greek playwright Euripides (c. 486–c. 406 BCE) has Artemis utter the following words to the dying Hippolytus: "You will not be unavenged, for Aphrodite will find that the angry shafts she hurled against you for your piety and innocence will cost her dearly. I will wait until she loves a mortal next time, and with this hand, with these unerring arrows, I will punish him." As it turned out, the mortal lover in question was Adonis.

The women of Lemnos

Phaedra was no more than a pawn for Aphrodite when she tried to punish Hippolytus for paying the goddess insufficient attention. Aphrodite would not be neglected. The women of the island of Lemnos were to learn this to their cost when Aphrodite punished them for not honoring her cult. She made them so malodorous that their husbands abandoned them and went to Thrace in search of new mates. When the men returned with their new wives, the Lemnian women killed the men, condemning themselves to live without male companionship until the Argonauts appeared and helped them to repopulate their society.

The Judgment of Paris

While Aphrodite punished those who tried to ignore her, those who were completely devoted to her were also often the victims of misfortune—it was hard to get the right balance. The classic illustration of this point is the story of the Trojan prince Paris, whose preference for Aphrodite caused the Trojan War and the annihilation of his father's city. The tragedy began when Hermes appeared before Paris while he was tending his flock and invited him to adjudicate in a dispute between Hera, Athena, and Aphrodite. The three goddesses were vying jealously for possession of a golden apple that bore the inscription, "To the fairest." The fruit was part of a ruse devised by Eris (Strife) at the wedding of Thetis and Peleus.

In an effort to sway the judgment of Paris, each goddess tried to bribe him: Hera offered him world sovereignty, Athena wisdom and military prowess, and Aphrodite the most beautiful woman in the world. Paris unheroically awarded the golden apple to Aphrodite, who in turn offered him Helen. Paris took his prize back home to Troy, but his new bride was already married to Menelaus. As a result of this abduction, Agamemnon mustered a Greek army for an assault on Troy.

Below: The Judgment of Paris *by German painter Anselm Feuerbach (1829–1880) shows Hera, Athena, and Aphrodite with the Trojan prince.*

Helen was herself a keen follower of Aphrodite. In her early days at Sparta, before her marriage to Menelaus, she became famous for an incident that occurred during a rite of passage. In the Spartan town of Therapne young girls took part in races and dances in a grove of plane trees along the riverbank. Helen was so superior to all the hundreds of other women present, especially in regard to her beauty, that from then on, subsequent generations of young girls would lay lotus flowers at the feet of the plane trees in her memory. There in the groves of Therapne a cult developed in which Helen embodied one of the most important qualities of Aphrodite. The only account we have of the ritual performed in that sanctuary appears as an anecdote in the work of Greek historian Herodotus (c. 484–425 BCE). According to him, the Spartan king Ariston married a woman who had been the ugliest of children. As a child, Ariston's wife was taken regularly to the temple of Helen by her nurse until one day the goddess appeared to the nurse and caressed the child's head. From that moment, the little girl's appearance changed completely. From the homeliest of little girls, Helen created the most beautiful woman in all of Sparta, and, similar to Paris's abduction of Helen, Ariston deceived her first husband, a Spartan aristocrat, and eventually married her.

In this story, Helen appears as the goddess who gives beauty to female children, not for its own sake but for the sake of marriage. For women in ancient Greece, the passage from ugliness to beauty represented the transition from childhood to nubility. Thus the Helen venerated in Therapne was not the model of a married woman. Neither

Above: The Temple of Aphrodite in the ancient Greco-Roman city of Aphrodisias in modern Turkey now lays in ruins.

was she the equal or rival of Hera, who guaranteed the bonds of legal marriage. Instead, Helen appeared as an adult woman whose beauty, like that of Aphrodite, inspired sexual attraction. In the Greek conception of marriage, a beautiful woman played an essential role. Helen at Therapne was the incarnation of an adult woman whose perfect beauty placed her on the threshold of marriage.

Other forms of worship

Some Greeks regarded Aphrodite as a goddess of the sea from which she had sprung. Spartans and Thebans worshiped her as a goddess of war because of her connection with Ares. In general, however, Aphrodite was venerated as a goddess of fertility, so most of her rites focused on that aspect of her power. At Paphos, for example, Aphrodite was worshiped in a stone sanctuary shaped like a cone—the cone was a well-established symbol of fertility, and it appeared on many Roman coins. The votive offerings found at Paphos connect Aphrodite to the Semitic goddess Astarte or the Babylonian Ishtar. According to Greek historian Strabo (c. 64 BCE–23 CE), the priestesses in the temple of Aphrodite on the acropolis at

Corinth—nearly a thousand of them—were all prostitutes. Not everyone believes this account, but it is known that in both Greece and Rome prostitutes looked to Aphrodite as their patron goddess. The Athenians worshiped Aphrodite as a goddess "in the gardens" because she made the ground fertile for the growth of herbs and flowers. They also worshiped her in a festival known as the Arrephoria, which involved young girls between the ages of 7 and 11, and so may have been another initiation rite marking their transition from childhood to maturity. It is also apparent from votive offerings in sanctuaries all over Greece that women viewed Aphrodite as the goddess responsible for stimulating their sexual powers. These offerings were often figurines of birds, fruit, or phalluses.

KIRK SUMMERS

Bibliography
Homer, and Robert Fagles, trans. *The Iliad*. New York: Penguin, 2009.
Ovid, and A. D. Melville, trans. *Metamorphoses*. New York: Oxford University Press, 2008.

SEE ALSO: Ares; Artemis; Asclepius; Athena; Cronus; Eros; Graces; Helios; Hephaestus; Hera; Hermes; Persephone; Poseidon; Thetis; Uranus; Zeus.

APOLLO

The ancient Greeks worshiped Apollo for his provision of light, music, and harmony, as well as his punishment for wrongdoing and the protection of crops and animals. He was a powerful deity, whom mortals and immortals alike regarded with awe.

Apollo was one of the 12 major Olympian deities. He was the son of Zeus, king of the gods, and Leto, the daughter of the Titans Coeus and Phoebe. Zeus's wife, Hera, was jealous of Leto and barred her from giving birth to Apollo and his twin sister, Artemis, on firm land. Consequently, both children were born on the floating island of Delos, which Zeus then fixed to the seabed. The island in the Aegean Sea became an important shrine to Apollo for ancient Greeks and Romans.

With the exception of Hera, all the Olympian deities attended Apollo's birth. The goddess Themis fed the baby nectar and ambrosia, and Zeus presented him with a swan-drawn chariot. Hephaestus, the blacksmith of the gods, gave the baby one of his most important attributes, a bow and arrows. Within days the baby had grown into a strong and handsome youth, personifying the Greek ideal of *kouros* (male beauty).

Founding Delphi

At Zeus's urging, the young Apollo left Delos to find a site where he could establish an oracle, a shrine where a prophet revealed the plans of the gods to mortals. Apollo found such a place on the slopes of Mount Parnassus, overlooking the Gulf of Corinth, where the serpent Python guarded an oracle sacred to its mother, the earth goddess Gaia. The serpent had destroyed the surrounding countryside, killing people and flocks. Apollo struck Python dead with his bow and arrows and founded his own oracle. His shrine came to be known as Delphi because of his association with *delphinos* (dolphins).

Above: A mosaic depicting Apollo, riding in his sun chariot, by 19th-century Italian Giovan Battista Giorgi. Apollo is framed by the symbols of the nine Muses.

17

According to one story, Apollo found priests for his new oracle by taking on the form of a dolphin and diverting a Cretan ship, originally bound for Pylos. The crew landed at Delphi, where they became the god's servants.

Apollo's founding of his oracle at Delphi reflects the change in beliefs that occurred in Greece between the second and first millennia BCE, when sky gods brought by northern settlers replaced the previously dominant earth, or mother, goddess figure. The goddess Gaia and her offspring Python represented chthonic (earthbound) forces: Apollo's slaying of Python suggests a break with the worship of such deities. However, the myth also symbolized reconciliation with these older forces. After Python's death, Apollo underwent a period of purification in recognition of having killed Gaia's representative. Some accounts tell of Apollo undergoing this purification in the Vale of Tempe in Thessaly, a region in northeast Greece.

Every eight years a festival known as the Stepterion was celebrated at Delphi to commemorate Apollo's slaying of Python and his purification. During the festival a young boy would reenact Apollo's deed and would be temporarily banished to Tempe. According to legend, Apollo marked Python's death in two further ways: by founding the musical and athletic contests of the Pythian Games at Delphi, and by naming the prophetess at his oracle the Pythia.

Different names

Apollo had a great number of roles, many of which were reflected by different names. For instance, he was the god of healing, sometimes referred to as Paeon, as well as the god of light, whom the Greek poet Homer (c. ninth–eighth century BCE) first described as Phoebus Apollo (meaning "Shining Apollo"). After the fifth century BCE he came to be identified with the sun god Helios. Other names for Apollo reflected his status among rural people as a god who protected crops

Origins of the Apollo Cult

Apollo was not of Greek origin. Some scholars have suggested that he was first worshiped in Asia Minor (present-day Turkey), while others have identified him with the Egyptian god Horus. There is also a suggestion that his cult was brought to Greece by traders from Cyprus. Apollo entered the Greek pantheon of gods and goddesses at a relatively late stage. Lists of deities found on stone tablets at Knossos on the island of Crete from around 1400 BCE and Pylos in Greece from around 1200 BCE do not include his name, although they mention deities such as Zeus and Athena. However, by the time Homer wrote his epic poem the *Iliad* (dated to the ninth or eighth century BCE), Apollo was established as a major figure in Greek mythology. He occurs frequently in Homer's account of the Trojan War.

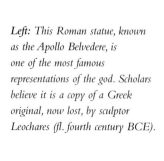

Left: This Roman statue, known as the Apollo Belvedere, is one of the most famous representations of the god. Scholars believe it is a copy of a Greek original, now lost, by sculptor Leochares (fl. fourth century BCE).

and livestock. Examples of these names include Alexikakos ("averter of evil"), Nomius ("shepherd"), and Lyceius, probably because people believed Apollo protected their flocks from *lykoi* (wolves).

God of music; god of order

The Greeks also worshiped Apollo as the god of music, poetry, and the arts. He presided over contests between the nine Muses, the patron goddesses of singing, dancing, poetry, and other forms of expression. One of Apollo's main attributes, alongside the bow, was the lyre, a stringed instrument similar to a small harp. Some sources suggest that the lyre was given to Apollo at his birth by Zeus, along with a chariot driven by swans. Other versions say that it was invented by Apollo's half brother Hermes, the messenger of the gods. According to this version, when the cunning Hermes was an infant, he stole 50 of Apollo's cattle and drove them backward to confuse anyone who followed their tracks. Apollo knew his half brother had committed the crime, but he was so charmed by the lyre, which Hermes had just invented, that he allowed the infant god to keep the animals in return for the instrument.

Below: The remains of the oracle at Delphi, where ancient Greeks consulted the Pythia. In 1987 Delphi was named a World Heritage Site by the United Nations Educational, Scientific and Cultural Organization.

The Importance of Delphi

Delphi was the site of the greatest oracle in the ancient world. People traveled from all over the Mediterranean to consult it on private and public matters. The Greeks believed that Delphi stood at the center of the world, a position marked by a stone called the omphalos (navel). The shrine's early buildings were destroyed by a combination of earthquake and fire, and most of its present-day remains date from the fourth century BCE.

On days of consultation, the oracle's prophetess, the Pythia, chewed laurel leaves before sitting on a tripod placed over a crack in the earth. Fumes from this crack sent the Pythia into a trance, during which people believed she spoke Apollo's words, which concerned Zeus's plans for mortals. Visitors were brought in one by one to present their questions. Words or even noises uttered by the Pythia were interpreted by priests, who wrote down her prophecies in verse form.

From the sixth century BCE the oracle at Delphi was so important that it was consulted by politicians on questions of government policy, particularly when one state planned to colonize another. Its status declined, however, during the Roman Empire and sank even lower when the Romans adopted Christianity as the imperial religion in the fourth century CE. The Roman emperor Theodosius closed the oracle in 385 CE.

Above: Apollo as Victor, Sitting on the Dragon *by German artist Sebastian Schütz (c. 1595–c. 1631). Behind Python's tail, to Apollo's left, is Eros, the god of love.*

Apollo played his lyre and danced at the banquets of the gods, bringing order and harmony to the heavens.

As an extension of the notion of Apollo ensuring order on Olympus, the Greeks regarded the god as the guarantor of civic harmony, providing laws by which humans could live together in peace. He stood for the Greek ideals of moderation and reason, demonstrated by the phrases on the wall of the oracle at Delphi: "Nothing in excess" and "Know thyself." Apollo was also regarded as the deity who made humans aware of their own guilt, and purified them of it. This judgmental aspect, together with his role in foretelling the plans of the gods through his oracle, left many people in awe of Apollo. This awe extended to the other gods: sources relate that only his parents, Zeus and Leto, could endure his presence.

Avenging and punishing

In a number of myths, Apollo's role was to avenge any offense against his honor or to prevent mortals and other beings from overstepping the boundary separating them from the gods. In one story Apollo plotted with the other Olympian deities Poseidon, Hera, and Athena to bind Zeus in chains and suspend him in the heavens, a plan prompted by the king of the gods' increasingly arrogant behavior. When Zeus discovered the conspiracy, he made Apollo and Poseidon—disguised as men—build the city walls of Troy for its king, Laomedon. However, when the gods' term of service was done, Laomedon refused to pay them the agreed fee and even threatened to cut off their ears and sell them as slaves. Once he had regained his divine form, Apollo sent a terrible plague to Troy as retribution.

In another myth, Zeus killed Apollo's son Asclepius, the god of healing, because he used his knowledge of medicine to bring a dead man to life. Zeus struck the god with one of his thunderbolts because he feared that Asclepius's powers might lead humankind to become immortal and compete with the gods. In revenge, Apollo killed the Cyclopes, the giant one-eyed craftsmen who made Zeus's thunderbolts. In his anger Zeus considered hurling Apollo into Tartarus, the worst part of the underworld, but instead decided to punish him with a year's servitude to a mortal. Apollo went to Thessaly, where he served King Admetus as a shepherd. In contrast to Laomedon, Admetus treated his divine servant well. In return, Apollo helped the king complete a task set by King Pelias of Iolcus and so win the hand in marriage of Pelias's daughter, Alcestis.

Two other myths involving Apollo's honor and his ability to mete out harsh punishments center around musical contests. In one story, the flute-playing satyr, or spirit, Marsyas challenged Apollo to see who was the better musician. When Apollo had proved he was superior, he punished Marsyas by tying him to a tree and skinning him alive. Another musical contest was held between Apollo and Pan, the half-man, half-goat god of shepherds and flocks. After both deities had performed, the mountain god Tmolus judged Apollo the winner. The mortal king Midas of Phrygia, however, who had observed the performances, declared that Pan was the better player. Outraged, Apollo gave Midas the ears of a donkey.

Apollo and the Trojan War

Apollo's role in the Trojan War further demonstrated his concern to avenge those who offended his honor. Apollo's wrath at his treatment by King Laomedon at Troy might have suggested that he would favor the Greeks in their 10-year-long battle against the Trojans, whose prince Paris had abducted Helen, wife of the Greek king Menelaus of Sparta. Instead, however, the god came to the assistance of the Trojans. The reason Apollo favored Troy lay in the Greeks' sacking of the island of Chryse and capture of Chryseis, the daughter of Chryses, a priest of Apollo. Chryseis was given to Agamemnon, the Greek commander, as a war prize. When the girl's father begged for her release, Agamemnon refused. In his epic the *Iliad*, Homer describes the refusal as an insult to Apollo, who sent a plague to infect the Greek camp. Agamemnon subsequently released Chryseis, but by then Apollo was committed to the Trojans.

Left: Apollo and Daphne *by Italian sculptor Gian Lorenzo Bernini (1598–1680). Daphne, who turned into a laurel tree after being chased by the god, was one of Apollo's many unsuccessful romances.*

Apollo played a crucial role in the deaths of the Greek champions Patroclus and Achilles. Patroclus stood in for his companion Achilles when Achilles refused to fight for the Greeks after Agamemnon replaced his war prize, Chryseis, with Achilles' concubine, but when Patroclus went into battle, Apollo stripped him of his breastplate, helmet, and shield, leaving him defenseless before the Trojan warrior Hector, who killed him. Patroclus's death spurred Achilles to rejoin the war and slaughter Hector and many other Trojans, but the Greek became another victim of Apollo's intervention. Paris, the brother of Hector, aimed an arrow at Achilles, and the god made sure it hit its target. In one version of the story, this target was Achilles' heel, the only part of his body not to have been made invulnerable by the warrior's mother, the sea goddess Thetis.

Apollo's love affairs

Apollo had numerous love affairs with both women and men, but many of them ended unsuccessfully, often with the lover's death or metamorphosis. In revenge for teasing Eros, the god of love, Apollo was cursed with an unrequited passion for the nymph Daphne. Apollo chased Daphne for a long time, but as he was about to catch her, she prayed to her father, the river god Peneius, to change her shape so that she could escape. Peneius transformed her into a laurel tree. Apollo responded by making the laurel his sacred tree—its leaves were used in the Pythia's rituals at Delphi.

On at least three occasions Apollo gave women gifts for returning his favors, but each time the act had tragic consequences. The god seduced Cassandra, daughter of King Priam of Troy, by teaching her the art of prophecy, but once taught she refused his advances. In response, he punished her by ensuring that no one would ever believe her prophecies. Meanwhile, to ensure the affections of the nymph Sinope, daughter of the river god Asopus, Apollo promised her whatever she wanted—he then had no choice but to grant her wish to remain a virgin forever. Apollo also granted the wish of the prophetess the Sibyl of Cumae to live for a thousand years in return for becoming his mistress. However, the Sibyl forgot to ask for her body to remain young, and she withered away to become an old crone.

In his love affairs with young men, Apollo fared no better. He accidentally killed the beautiful Hyacinthus with a discus as they were playing; from the youth's blood sprang

Right: The remains of the Temple of Apollo in Rome, built for the emperor Augustus in the first century BCE. The emperor dedicated the temple to the god after a military victory.

Apollo in Roman Mythology

The cult of Apollo was introduced at a very early date to Italy, where the god was worshiped mainly as deity of medicine and healing. A temple to Apollo Medicus (Apollo the Healer) was dedicated in Rome in 433 BCE, following a serious epidemic. In addition, the Vestal Virgins, the sacred priestesses who served the Roman goddess Vesta, prayed to Apollo for his help in matters of healing. In later centuries Apollo came to be seen as a divinity who interceded between the Roman people and Jupiter, king of the Roman gods. The first Roman emperor, Augustus (63 BCE–14 CE), adopted Apollo as his protector. In 28 BCE Augustus built a temple to Apollo on Rome's Palatine Hill, in gratitude for victory over the Roman leader Mark Anthony and the Egyptian queen Cleopatra at the Battle of Actium three years earlier.

Apollo in the Modern World

The figure of Apollo has been enormously influential in Western art and thought. Since the 19th century the god has been seen as a symbol of humankind's ability to overcome earthly restrictions. German philosopher Friedrich Nietzsche (1844–1900) developed this notion in his book *The Birth of Tragedy from the Spirit of Music* (1872). Nietzsche contrasted Apollo's qualities of reason and restraint with the irrationality and passion of Dionysus, the Greek god of wine and Apollo's half brother. He argued that Greek tragedy emerged out of the fusion of Apollonian and Dionysian qualities.

Apollo's association with the human spirit of adventure led to the use of his name for the 1960s' U.S. moon-landing project, which was named the Apollo Program. The program's first manned space-flight took place in 1968, when the spacecraft *Apollo 7* made a 163-orbit journey with a full crew of three astronauts. The next year, *Apollo 11* landed on the moon, and millions of people watched on television as astronaut Neil Armstrong became the first human to walk on the moon's surface. It is fitting that Apollo, who communicated between the heavens and earth via his oracle, should have been linked with the lunar mission.

Left: The Saturn V rocket launches the spacecraft Apollo 11 *in 1969. The program was one of 17 space missions named for the Greek god.*

the hyacinth flower. The youth Cyparissus was so distraught when he accidentally killed his favorite deer that he begged Apollo to make his tears flow eternally. The god transformed his lover into a cypress tree, which, because its sap resembled tears, became a symbol of mourning.

In spite of these frustrated romances, Apollo had many children with goddesses, nymphs, and mortal women. With Thalia, the muse or goddess of comedy, he fathered the sacred dancers known as the Corybantes. The nymph Dryope gave birth to his son Amphissus, who established the ancient city of Oeta. Appropriately for the founder of the Delphic oracle, Apollo also fathered a number of prophets, including Aristaeus, born to the huntress Cyrene, and Iamus, born to Poseidon's daughter Evadne.

Apollo's favorite and most famous son, the god of medicine, Asclepius, was the product of yet another unhappy affair. Apollo fell in love with the princess Coronis, and she became pregnant with the god's child. Before the baby was born, however, Coronis slept with a man named Ischys. Enraged, Apollo killed her. Then, as her body was about to be consumed by the flames of the funeral pyre, he lifted Asclepius from her womb.

Apollo in art

Surviving artworks from ancient Greece and Rome commonly depict Apollo as a beautiful, beardless youth, and either naked or wearing robes, and holding either a lyre or a bow. One of the most famous classical representations of

Above: The Flaying of Marsyas by Titian (c. 1489–1576). Apollo, with violin, is shown at left; Titian depicted himself in a toga, on the right; and next to him is the god Pan, carrying a bucket of water.

the god is the sculpture in the Temple of Zeus, built around 460 BCE in the sanctuary of Olympia, near the western coast of the Peloponnese peninsula. The sculpture of Apollo watches over the battle between the centaurs, and the Lapiths, whose king, Ixion, was said to have been their father. Apollo has also featured strongly in art since the Renaissance of the 15th and 16th centuries, when artists began to take more interest in the classical world. Popular subjects included Apollo's chasing of the nymph Diana, depicted by French painter Nicolas Poussin (1594–1665), among others; and Apollo in the company of the Muses, portrayed by French painter Claude Lorrain (1600–1682) and German painter Hans Holbein the Younger (c. 1497–1543). While Apollo has usually been portrayed in art as the embodiment of inspiration, harmony, and order,

some artists have also depicted his cruel nature, for example Italian painter Titian (c. 1489–1576), in his *The Flaying of Marsyas*. This painting—which inspired the 2002 sculpture *Marsyas* by British Indian Anish Kapoor—reminds us that the god had a dark side that contrasted with his brilliantly shining one, just as his symbol of the bow contrasted with that of the lyre.

PETER CONNOR

Bibliography

Barber, Antonia. *Apollo and Daphne: Masterpieces of Greek Mythology.* Los Angeles: John Paul Getty Museum, 1998.

Homer, and Robert Fagles, trans. *The Iliad.* New York: Penguin, 2009.

Howatson, M. C. *The Oxford Companion to Classical Literature.* New York: Oxford University Press, 2005.

SEE ALSO: Artemis; Asclepius; Gaia; Helios; Hermes; Jupiter; Leto; Muses; Vesta; Zeus.

ARES

Strong, muscular, tall, and often cruel, Ares, the Greek god of war, was the most despised of all the Olympians. However, despite the low opinion the gods and the Greeks had of him, Ares did feature in two myths that provided enduring lessons in morality and honor. These were his love affair with the goddess Aphrodite and his alleged murder of Poseidon's son Halirrhothius.

Ares was the son of Zeus and Hera, the king and queen of the gods, although one version of Ares' birth has it that Hera conceived the god of war when she touched a flower. For the ancient Greeks, Ares was the personification of war, strife, and brute force. Despite his belligerence, he was often romantically involved, especially with Eos, goddess of the dawn, and Aphrodite, goddess of love, beauty, and marriage. Aphrodite was also the wife of Ares' crippled half brother Hephaestus, god of fire and metalworking.

The bloodthirsty god

References to Ares in Greek mythology depict him as always overeager for war and the first Olympian to join in a battle among mortals. In combat Ares usually wore a gleaming helmet and armor, carried a sword, and rode in a chariot. He was often accompanied by his

Left: The Ares Ludovisi *sculpture is a Roman copy of a Greek original. It is an unusually relaxed portrayal of the young war god.*

Above: Venus and Mars, Victory and Cupid *by the Italian painter Paris Bordone (1500–1571). Ares' Roman equivalent, Mars, was a popular subject for Renaissance artists.*

sister Eris, the goddess of strife; his sons Deimos, who symbolized fear and terror, and Phobos, who represented panic; and Enyo, a bloodthirsty war goddess. It was told that during a battle Ares would roam the field looking for the bloodiest fights to join, rarely caring on whose side he fought.

Many Greek myths describe Ares as despised by both mortals and most of the gods; even his own parents, Zeus and Hera, did not like him. In the *Iliad*, an epic poem by Homer (c. ninth–eighth century BCE), Zeus says to Ares, "Most hateful to me are you of all gods on Olympus, for ever is strife dear to you and wars and fighting."

Stories of Ares

Ares was the main character in very few Greek myths. However, he did play a small but significant role in many other myths and legends. In the story of Cadmus and the founding of Thebes, for example, the dragon that guarded the spring near where Cadmus was to build the new city was either the servant of Ares or an offspring. One version of the myth has it that for slaying the dragon Cadmus had to pay homage to Ares for eight years.

Hippolyte, the queen of the Amazons, was said to wear a belt, or girdle, that was a gift to her from Ares. The belt was meant to symbolize the queen's power, and the Greek hero Heracles successfully stole it from her as one of his 12

labors for the king Eurystheus. Another famous Greek legend involved the hero Jason, who, along with the Argonauts, went on an epic quest for the Golden Fleece. It hung in an oak grove in Colchis that was dedicated to Ares, guarded by a dragon that never slept. Jason was only able to obtain the fleece with the help of the sorceress Medea, who was the granddaughter of Helios the sun god.

Ares performed an unusual role in the myth of Sisyphus and Thanatos, god of death. After Sisyphus had told Asopus, a river god, that Zeus had stolen his daughter, Aegina, Zeus sent Thanatos to take Sisyphus away. In the underworld, however, Sisyphus tricked the god of death and tied him up. As long as Thanatos was unable to reach the land of the living, no one died on earth. This angered the gods, and they sent Ares to solve the problem.

Ares' first act was to release Thanatos. He then captured Sisyphus, who was still in the underworld, and delivered him to the god of death. Thinking he had solved the problem and pleased the other gods, Ares returned to Olympus, but Sisyphus tricked death again and ended up living to a ripe old age.

Ares in Sculpture and Painting

In art, Ares was depicted as a handsome, often youthful warrior. Most representations of him were sculptures rather than paintings, and in these he was usually shown wearing a helmet and holding a spear, shield, and sword. Sometimes he was even depicted wearing an aegis (a special goatskin cloak or breastplate honoring Zeus and Hera), but in literature and paintings it was his rival Athena who was more often associated with the aegis.

One of the most famous representations of Ares is a sculpture known as the Ares Borghese. The work, carved around 125 CE, acquired its name in the 18th century when it was purchased by a member of the Borghese family, a powerful Roman dynasty. It stands at over 6 feet (2 m) and shows the war god as young and nude, wearing nothing but his war helmet. Today the sculpture is housed in the Louvre in Paris.

Paintings of Ares are few, but the Roman equivalent, Mars, was a popular subject of many artists. Two of the many paintings of Mars show the god of war as young and handsome, highlighting the deity's virility. The exploits of Venus (Aphrodite) and Mars (Ares) inspired paintings such as Jacques-Louis David's *Mars Disarmed by Venus and the Graces* (c. 1824), which shows a mature god of war, draped in a bloodred cloak, lounging with Venus. *Mars and Venus Caught in the Net* (1536) by Maerten van Heemskerck shows the lovers trapped in Vulcan's (Hephaestus's) net, dragged before the gods.

Left: The Ares Borghese was carved in the second century CE, but historians believe it was based on a fifth-century-BCE Greek original.

Other views of Ares

Ares had some very contradictory characteristics. Depending on the myth, he could appear either strong or weak, stupid or intelligent, mean or noble, and immature or resolute. For example, he was too weak to stop the twin giants Ephialtes and Otus, who attacked Olympus in an attempt to overthrow Zeus. The giants tied up Ares in brass chains and forced him into a jar, where he stayed for 13 months before being rescued by Hermes, the messenger of the gods.

Ares' meaner nature was revealed in some versions of the story of the death of Adonis. Loved by the goddess Aphrodite, Adonis was a handsome mortal who had the bad luck to incur the jealousy of Ares. A few sources record that Ares, angry at Aphrodite's love for Adonis, transformed himself into the boar that gored Adonis to death.

Ares was also an amorous god. His many lovers included Aglaurus, who was either a nymph or an Athenian princess, and the goddesses Aphrodite and Eos. In one myth

Aphrodite grew so angry at Eos for making love to Ares that she cast a spell forcing Eos always to fall in love with someone new, never settling with one god or mortal.

In another myth Aphrodite's husband, Hephaestus, suspected that his wife was unfaithful. To catch her and her lover, he forged a metal net so thin it was invisible to all but Hephaestus, and so strong that not even the gods could break free of it. He placed the metal net around Aphrodite's bed to entrap whoever joined her there. Ares and Aphrodite were caught, and Hephaestus dragged them before the other gods, seeking justice for his betrayal and humiliation. However, the gods just roared with laughter at the two hapless lovers. Ares appeared wanton and foolish, incapable of extricating himself from the snare and from the ridicule of the gods.

The Trojan War

The Trojan War, the legendary conflict between the Greeks and the Trojans, was the subject of many myths in ancient Greece. In these myths all the gods used their respective powers to help or hinder either the Greeks or the Trojans. Accounts of his involvement in the Trojan War depict Ares as untrustworthy and immature. The god of war promised both Athena and Hera, queen of the gods, that he would side with the Greeks, but he broke his promise and sided with Aphrodite, who was aiding the Trojans. Hera and Athena vowed to punish Ares for his broken promise.

During the battle Ares was a fearsome sight. According to one source even the fierce Greek hero Diomedes shuddered at the sight of the bloodstained god and cried out to the Greek soldiers to retreat from the battlefield. It was then that Hera asked Zeus if she could drive Ares from the battlefield. Zeus agreed. Hera joined Diomedes in the battle and urged him to strike at Ares. Diomedes hurled his spear at the god of war. The spear was guided by the angry Athena, Ares' half sister, who was invisible even to the gods because she was wearing the Helmet of Hades. The injured Ares cried out loudly and rushed back to Olympus, where Paeon, god of healing, tended his wound.

After Paeon's treatment Ares returned to the battlefield outside the walls of Troy. Knowing that Athena had aided Diomedes, Ares attacked her. According to Homer, Athena was at first surprised that Ares would even attempt to challenge her, but she quickly shook off the attack and threw a giant boulder at Ares, knocking him to the ground.

Ares had been a bitter rival of Athena for many years before the start of the Trojan War. Whereas Ares relied on his brute force when fighting, Athena used skill, intelligence, and cunning to earn her victories. As a result,

Children of Ares

Ares had many children with goddesses, nymphs, and mortal women. His most famous son was Diomedes—not the Greek hero of the Trojan War, but the king of the Bistonians of Thrace and the owner of horses that ate human flesh. Heracles, the Greek hero famous for his 12 Labors, was charged with bringing the flesh-eating horses to Mycenae, but Diomedes refused to give up the animals, so Heracles fed the king to the horses. Heracles also killed another of Ares' sons, Cycnus. Cycnus challenged Heracles to a duel, but the Greek hero defeated him. During the battle Ares tried to intervene on the side of Cycnus, but Heracles wounded him as well as killing Cycnus.

Most of Ares' children were bloodthirsty and heartless, like their father, and several met violent deaths. Phlegyas, for example, had a daughter named Coronis. Coronis was seduced by Apollo, god of the sun and the arts. Phlegyas became so angry that he torched Apollo's temple at Delphi. In revenge Apollo sent Phlegyas to the underworld.

Below: This 1865 painting by Gustave Moreau (1826–1898) shows Ares' son Diomedes being attacked by flesh-eating horses.

Enyo and Bellona

Enyo was a Greek goddess of war and waster of cities, but she was a minor Olympian and had no extensive mythology of her own. She was most often depicted as the daughter of Ares, but occasionally as his mother or his sister. She was often depicted as covered in blood and looking violent. According to Homer, Enyo sided with Ares during the Trojan War, but when the city of Troy finally fell and the Trojans were slaughtered by the Greeks, Enyo danced herself into a frenzy "like a hurricane" at all the spilled blood. Enyo the war goddess should not be confused with Enyo of the Graeae. The Graeae were three old women, or crones, who were born with gray hair and were the sisters of the Gorgons; they were not related to Ares.

Enyo's Roman equivalent was Bellona, a goddess of war and a favorite of Roman soldiers. She was far more prominent in the Roman pantheon than Enyo was among the Greek gods. The Romans built a temple to Bellona in the Campus Martius ("field of Mars"), a place outside the gates of Rome. The Senate greeted foreign ambassadors at the temple. They also met with Roman generals there before they entered the city on their victory march known as the triumph.

Bellona was originally called Duellona, and some scholars believe that the Romans could have based her on an Etruscan deity whose characteristics were merged with those of the Greek Enyo. According to legend she accompanied Mars into battle, just as Enyo did with Ares, and was variously depicted as either Mars's wife, sister, or daughter. Artistic representations of Bellona usually have her holding a sword and wearing a helmet. She is also often armed with a spear and a torch.

Left: Peter Paul Rubens (1577–1640) painted a portrait of Marie de Médicis, queen of France, as the Roman goddess Bellona.

Athena was far more honored by the ancient Greeks than Ares. In further contrast, Athena never relished the prospect of war, but once the fighting started she devised a strategy that attempted to achieve a quick victory with minimal bloodshed. Away from the battlefield Athena missed no opportunity to humiliate Ares, whom she viewed as slow-witted. At the same time, just the sight of Athena sent Ares into a violent rage.

Origin and legacy

Some scholars believe that the concept of Ares did not originate in Greece but that the Greeks adopted him from Thracian mythology. Thrace was an ancient civilization that occupied the territory north of the Aegean Sea. Today

Thrace forms a region that includes parts of Greece, Bulgaria, and Turkey. Both the ancient Greeks and Romans thought of Thrace (known as Thracia in Latin) as a country made up of fierce warriors. It is unclear whether the Thracian Ares was as battle-hungry and capricious as the Greek Ares, but in the Roman pantheon, Mars, who was modeled on Ares, was depicted as having more maturity and intelligence than the Greek deity.

Mars was originally an earth god and a god of spring, fertility, and growth. For some reason he eventually became associated with death and ultimately was viewed only as the Roman god of war. The Romans wrote far more positively of Mars than the Greeks did of Ares. In the *Aeneid*, an account of the founding of Rome by the poet Virgil (70–19 BCE), Roman warriors die gladly upon "Mars' field of renown." The soldiers worship Mars rather than fear and detest him. The Romans held festivals and built temples to honor him. With the significant exception of the Areopagus (Hill of Ares), located west of the Acropolis in Athens, the ancient Greeks barely acknowledged Ares in any public or tangible way. Other than the Areopagus, there was only one temple dedicated to Ares in all of Athens and only a single spring consecrated to him near Thebes.

Right: This Roman bust of Ares depicts a slightly older god of war than is usual. The Gorgon breastplate worn by this Ares was more commonly associated with Athena.

A god on trial

The Areopagus was where criminal trials were held. It was named for Ares because, according to legend, he was the defendant in the first trial held there. When Halirrhothius, Poseidon's son, attempted to rape Alcippe, Ares' daughter by Aglaurus, Ares saw the attack and killed Halirrhothius. In retribution, Poseidon, god of the sea, demanded that Ares be tried for murder. At the Areopagus Ares pleaded his case before 12 Olympian gods who acquitted him.

Works by some of the major dramatists and writers of ancient Greece, including the playwright Euripides (c. 484–406 BCE), refer to this myth. Ares' trial on the Areopagus can be seen as a legal commentary about justifiable homicide. The 12 Olympian gods summed up their verdict by saying that it was wrong for Ares to have committed murder, but in this case the murder was justified because the god of war was defending his daughter's honor.

This was a rationale that would have resonated with the ancient Greeks, and similar kinds of justification have formed the basis for many legal decisions in the modern world. For instance, defendants on trial for murder are often acquitted if a jury can be persuaded to see the killing as morally justified. In ancient Greek and many modern Western courts, such justifications could include self-defense, the defense of property, or the defense of loved ones. It is perhaps ironic that a character as loathsome as Ares could stand for a legal code so commonly recognized.

ALYS CAVINESS

Bibliography

Bulfinch, Thomas. *Bulfinch's Mythology.* New York: Barnes & Noble, 2006.

Graves, Robert. *The Greek Myths.* New York: Penguin, 1993.

Hamilton, Edith. *Mythology.* New York: Grand Central, 2011.

Homer, and Robert Fagles, trans. *The Iliad.* New York: Penguin, 2009.

Howatson, M. C. *The Oxford Companion to Classical Literature.* New York: Oxford University Press, 2005.

SEE ALSO: Aphrodite; Athena; Eos; Hephaestus; Hera; Hermes; Mars; Paeon; Phobos; Poseidon; Zeus.

ARTEMIS

The Greek goddess Artemis (known to the Romans as Diana) was the daughter of Zeus (the ruler of the gods) and Leto, and the twin sister of Apollo. She was primarily the goddess of hunting. Wilderness, mountains, forests, and uncultivated lands were sacred to her, as were the young, and unmarried women.

Below: This painting by Italian artist Giovanni Battista Pittoni (1687–1767) shows Artemis surrounded by her attendant nymphs after Actaeon has been torn to pieces by his dogs.

Artemis was usually depicted as a young woman of marriageable age, dressed as a hunter, wearing a short tunic and sandals, with a quiver of arrows on her back, and carrying a bow. In literature she was often described as being accompanied by nymphs, with whom she danced and hunted in the mountains, far from the cities of mortals. She was thought of as an aloof goddess, bloodthirsty and quick to anger, whom it was dangerous to annoy or even to approach too closely.

Artemis was worshiped from very early times. Her name may appear on tablets from Bronze Age Greece (second millennium BCE), on which was written a script called Linear B that has only recently been fully deciphered. There is also evidence that her origins lay farther east than Greece. Her name is found among the gods of the Lydians of Anatolia (part of modern Turkey), who worshiped her as

"Artimus," and the Lycians of southwest Asia Minor (modern Turkey), who called her Ertemis. She was often shown in art accompanied by lions, which were also associated with cultures east of Greece, particularly, with the great goddess Kybele (or Anahita). The poet Homer, who wrote the *Iliad* and the *Odyssey* around 850 BCE, called Artemis the "mistress of animals," a title given to various West Asian goddesses, including the Assyrian Ishtar.

Powers at birth

Artemis was usually said to have been born to the goddess Leto on the island of Delos. According to Apollodorus, who collected and wrote down many Greek myths in the second century BCE, Artemis was midwife at the birth of her twin brother Apollo immediately after her own birth. Callimachus, a Greek poet of the third century BCE, says that the pregnancy and birth of Artemis gave Leto no pain, unlike the birth of Apollo. Whether because of her own painless birth or her help as a midwife, Greek women worshiped Artemis as a goddess of childbirth.

In Callimachus's "Hymn to Artemis," the goddess asked her father, Zeus, to allow her never to marry, to carry a bow and arrows, and to wear a short tunic that would allow her to hunt. She also asked for 60 young nymphs, around nine years of age, to serve as her companions, and another dozen, of marriageable age, to serve as her handmaids and keep her hunting dogs and clothes in order. Both of these age groups were important in the worship of Artemis in classical Greece.

Chased by gods and mortals

Artemis, like Athena, was a virgin goddess. Unlike Athena, however, Artemis found herself the constant object of male attention. She was depicted as an attractive, healthy girl, and therefore greatly sought after by men, who invariably died when they pursued her. Artemis shot and killed the giant Orion, a great hunter, for example. Some sources, such as Callimachus, say that Orion wanted to marry her. Other accounts say that she attacked him because he tried to rape her.

According to the Roman poet Ovid (43 BCE–17 CE) in his poem *Metamorphoses*, Actaeon was another hunter who died through the actions of Artemis. He stumbled upon her bathing in a stream with her nymphs and

Right: The Greek goddess Artemis was taken up by the Romans and renamed Diana. This Roman statue shows her with her hunting dogs, reaching for an arrow.

inadvertently saw her naked. To punish him, Artemis turned him into a stag and then set his dogs on him. They chased him and then ripped him to pieces, egged on by Actaeon's own friends, since he was unable to speak to tell them who he was.

The chorus of Artemis

Groups of young women dancing and singing in a chorus were a common feature of festivals in classical Greece. Such groups aroused keen male interest, since women lived largely segregated lives, and public festivals were one of the few opportunities young men had to inspect their

future wives. Artemis's companions, the nymphs, were a reflection of this social reality in that they were described as persistently subject to male attentions, which were usually more successful than those received by the goddess herself. Thus Helen, who would cause the Trojan War, was said to have been kidnapped by Theseus from the chorus of Artemis. When the goddess Aphrodite disguised herself as a mortal in order to seduce the mortal Anchises, she told him that she had been dancing in the chorus of Artemis when the god Hermes had carried her off.

Often the attendant maiden's story had a tragic ending. Britomartis, a favorite companion of Artemis, threw herself off a cliff into fishermen's nets to escape a rape attempt by King Minos of Crete. She was turned into a sea goddess. In another story Zeus fell in love with Artemis's attendant Callisto. According to Ovid, Zeus disguised himself as Artemis in order to get close enough to Callisto to rape her. When Callisto's pregnancy was discovered, Zeus's enraged wife, Hera, turned Callisto into a bear. Apollodorus says that Artemis then shot her down as a wild beast, and the baby in her womb was rescued by the god Hermes. Ovid says that, after giving birth to Zeus's son, Callisto lived as a bear for years, until her son, Arcas, who had been raised by humans, met her in the forest, was terrified by her, and was about to kill her. Zeus saved him from the crime of killing his mother by turning them both into constellations, Big Bear and Little Bear (Ursa Major and Ursa Minor).

Artemis's favorites

From time to time Artemis made a favorite of a mortal, usually a young woman in her train. Callisto was one; Britomartis, Procris, Anticleia (the mother of Odysseus), and Atalanta were others. Eventually they were all forced to leave Artemis's band of maidens because they were married, raped, or, in the case of Britomartis, committed suicide to avoid rape.

One man, Hippolytus, was also a favorite of Artemis. He hunted with her and was permitted to hear her voice, although he was never allowed to see her. His story also ends tragically. Out of devotion to Artemis, Hippolytus refused to marry or have anything to do with mortal women. Aphrodite, the goddess of love, was angry at his neglect of her, so she set in motion a train of events that led to his death. Artemis mourned Hippolytus but could do nothing to protect him, because, as she explained, the gods never opposed each other directly over mortals; all she could do was promise to kill Aphrodite's next favorite, whoever he might be.

The fullest account of this story is in the tragedy *Hippolytus*, by Euripides (c. 484–406 BCE).

Sacrifice to Artemis

Several Greek myths link Artemis with human sacrifice. The story of the sacrifice of Iphigeneia is the best known. It illustrates Artemis's touchy pride and fierce temper. Iphigeneia was the eldest daughter of Agamemnon, the leader of the Greek forces at Troy. While he was waiting for his soldiers to gather at the harbor at Aulis, Agamemnon shot a deer and boasted that not even Artemis could have made a better shot. Artemis took offense and sent an opposing wind that held the boats in harbor. She demanded as a price for a favorable wind the sacrifice of Agamemnon's daughter Iphigeneia, and Agamemnon complied.

Euripides' play *Iphigeneia at Aulis* tells how at the last moment Iphigeneia was miraculously replaced on the altar by a doe. According to Euripides, Artemis transported Iphigeneia to barbarian Tauris, on the Black Sea, where she became a priestess of Artemis at a temple that practiced human sacrifice.

The Greeks believed that the Taurians sacrificed humans to Artemis, and the inhabitants of Patrae told the second-century Greek writer and traveler Pausanias that at one time they had sacrificed a youth and a maiden every year to Artemis, but they had stopped the practice around the time of the Trojan War, about 1,300 years before. In fact, all of the stories about Artemis and human sacrifice are derived from preexistent Bronze Age myths. There is no archaeological evidence that the Greeks ever made human sacrifices to Artemis. Instead, game animals—such as deer, boars, gazelles, and bear and wolf cubs—were commonly sacrificed to her, as were goats. The inhabitants of Patrae in classical times held an annual festival in which game animals were burned alive to the goddess.

Artemis the nurse and protector

In her role as a goddess of childbirth, children and fertility came under Artemis's influence. Diodorus Siculus, a Roman–Greek historian of the first century BCE, tells us that Artemis was called Kourotrophos, or "child-rearer," because of her importance in the nursing and healing of the young. Groups of Athenian girls, at about the age of seven, were dedicated to the worship of Artemis in her temple at Brauron, near Athens, in a ceremony that involved games and races, at which the girls dedicated their childhood toys to the goddess.

Artemis was also protective of young animals. In one version of the sacrifice of Iphigeneia, Artemis demanded her sacrifice because she was angry at Agamemnon, who had been promised victory at Troy only if he slaughtered a pregnant hare. This anger would be expected in a hunting goddess, since no good hunter kills a pregnant animal.

If a woman was said to have been "killed by the arrows of Artemis," as Andromeda says of her mother in Homer's *Iliad*, it meant that she had died of disease. Artemis's influence in matters of fertility, her quick temper, and her power over diseases afflicting women are all shown in the story of Niobe. According to Homer, Niobe bore 12 children, while other sources say that she gave birth to up to 20. She boasted that she had done better than Leto, who had borne only Apollo and Artemis. To punish Niobe, Apollo set out to kill all of her sons, and Artemis to kill all of her daughters. Only one daughter and one son survived, after praying to Leto. Niobe turned to stone in grief.

Artemis in the arts

The tragic stories of the humans who associated with Artemis have inspired many artists. Titian (c. 1489–1576) painted the death of Actaeon, Diana (Artemis) and Actaeon, and Diana and Callisto; Rembrandt (1606–1669) depicted Diana bathing with her nymphs. The composers Charpentier, Cavalli, and Rameau wrote operas based on the myths of Actaeon, Orion, and Hippolytus. The American playwright Eugene O'Neill (1888–1953) adapted the story of Hippolytus in *Desire Under the Elms* (1924).

LAUREL BOWMAN

Bibliography

Euripides, and P. Burian and A. Shapiro, eds. *The Complete Euripides,* 5 vols. New York: Oxford University Press, 2009–2010.

Ovid, and A. D. Melville, trans. *Metamorphoses.* New York: Oxford University Press, 2008.

SEE ALSO: Apollo; Diana; Leto; Zeus.

Artemis and Childbirth

Childbirth in the ancient world was much more dangerous than it is today. Artemis was the goddess of women's diseases, especially those associated with childbirth, and women approaching childbirth would pray to Artemis not to kill them during the birth, but assist them to have an easy and successful labor. If an Athenian woman died in childbirth, her friends or family would dedicate to Artemis clothing the dead woman had woven herself but never worn, at the temple at Brauron. It may seem odd that Artemis, the virgin goddess, would have also been the goddess of childbirth, but women at the threshold between maidenhood and marriage were sacred to her, and childbirth, as one of the main markers dividing virgins from wives, thus fell under her sphere of influence.

Below: Worship of Artemis continued for thousands of years. This temple to her in Jordan survived until the second century CE.

ASCLEPIUS

Asclepius was the Greek god of healing and had sanctuaries throughout the Hellenistic world. People who were sick and did not want to go to a local doctor could go to one of the cool and pleasant places sacred to the god and seek a cure for their illnesses.

According to legend, Asclepius was the son of the god Apollo and a mortal woman, Coronis. However, his mother did not remain faithful to her divine partner. When a crow spied Coronis with a mortal lover, he flew to Apollo and reported what he had seen. Apollo became angry and asked his sister Artemis to kill Coronis. Coronis, who was still pregnant, died, but Apollo did not want his son to perish. He snatched the baby from Coronis's burning body and gave him to the wise centaur Cheiron to raise. It is said that Cheiron taught Asclepius the arts of medicine. In time Asclepius joined his father at Epidaurus in central Greece.

Although this is the most famous story of Asclepius's birth, other versions report that Coronis abandoned her newborn baby in shame on the mountain at Epidaurus. Goats nursed the child and a herd dog guarded him. When a local shepherd discovered the baby, lightning flashed about the child's head, and the shepherd left the infant to be raised by the goats and dog, under the protection of Apollo.

Apollo had many responsibilities, so Asclepius soon took charge of health and healing. However, as time went on, he became almost too clever at his work.

Asclepius cast out

One day Asclepius brought a dead hero back to life, allowing him to live longer than his fated destiny. Zeus, angry at this bold deed, blasted Asclepius down to the underworld. However, the world needed the god of healing, so Zeus restored the demigod to the upper world, where he stayed.

Using a walking stick with a serpent coiled around it and accompanied by a sacred dog, Asclepius traveled throughout Greece, curing the patients who came to the groves and medicinal springs where his sanctuaries had been established.

Asclepius was often assisted in his healing arts by three of his five daughters. The eldest, Hygieia, was best known; from her name comes our word *hygiene*. His other daughters were Iaso, whose

Left: Asclepius leans on his staff, around which a snake is twisted —this is now the symbol of the American Medical Association.

Above: *A relief carved in the fifth century BCE shows Asclepius healing a patient, helped by his daughter Hygieia, right, while others wait for treatment.*

name comes from a Greek verb meaning "to heal," and Panacea, whose name became the word *panacea*, which means "cure-all."

The sanctuaries of Asclepius

The most famous real-life sanctuary of Asclepius was at Epidaurus near the eastern coast of the Peloponnese (southern Greece). In the sacred area, entered by an elaborate gateway, were a temple to the god, the dormitory (*abaton*) where the patients slept, houses for priests and temple attendants, a large dining hall, and a hotel. There was also a mysterious round building known as a *tholos*. This beautifully decorated building had a circular maze in its basement. It is believed that the sacred snakes of the god were kept there until they were released to visit patients.

At Epidaurus and the god's other holy places, the patients were cured in a notable way. After bathing, singing hymns, and watching a dramatic story of the god's actions, they went to the *abaton* to sleep. It was believed that either the god or his snake visited the patients in their dreams, either curing their illness at once or telling them what to do to become healthy again.

At Epidaurus there was also a grand theater, where hymns and pageants for the god were sung and performed. Even today this theater, the best preserved in Greece, is used every summer for performances of ancient Greek tragedies and comedies. Asclepius also had large sanctuaries at Rome, Kos, Pergamum, and Athens. The sanctuary at Rome was established on Isola Tiberina, an island in the Tiber River, in 293 BCE after a plague attacked the city. To this day there are archaeological remains of a healing sanctuary on the island; a modern hospital stands above them.

Kos was the island where Hippocrates, the Father of Medicine, had his medical school, but Asclepius was also worshiped there. The connection between Hippocrates and Asclepius can still be recognized today. Every doctor must learn the Hippocratic Oath, and every U.S. doctor can be a member of the American Medical Association (AMA), whose symbol is a staff with a serpent coiled around it— the walking staff of Asclepius and his sacred snake.

Because of his healing powers and the legends of his life, Asclepius was one of the Greek gods who was worshiped long into the Christian era. His followers saw similarities between the stories of his birth and powers and those of Jesus Christ and could see no reason to change their beliefs. Finally, Christian churches were built to healing saints on the sites of the ancient temples to Asclepius; thus the old god was buried beneath the new religion.

KARELISA HARTIGAN

Bibliography
Graves, Robert. *The Greek Myths*. New York: Penguin, 1993.
Howatson, M. C. *The Oxford Companion to Classical Literature*.
    New York: Oxford University Press, 2005.

SEE ALSO: Apollo; Zeus.

ATE

Ate was a mischief-making goddess who, the ancient Greeks believed, drove mortal men to folly and self-destruction. She was thrown out of Olympus, home of the gods, by her father, Zeus, who was angry at her rebellious behavior.

Ate was the goddess of discord and delusion. She was expelled from the home of the gods because she clouded Zeus's mind when he made Eurystheus a king instead of Heracles. There is a hill in Phrygia named for Ate, and it was believed to have been the spot where she landed when Zeus threw her out of Olympus.

Ate inspired infatuation, bringing mortal men under the power of women and clouding their judgment. During the Trojan War, for example, Agamemnon, king of Mycenae, took the mistress of his finest warrior, Achilles, as his own. Later he blamed Ate for his actions.

Origin of Ate

Ate's origin goes back some five thousand years, to when patriarchal tribes invaded the lands of the goddess-worshiping peoples of the Mediterranean. They substituted their sky gods for the mother goddess who, it was believed, had embraced both life and death. After the belief in sky gods took over in Europe, however, many maternal deities lost their creative qualities and came to represent death. The goddess Ate was one of them. The Greeks feared the goddesses they had displaced, such as Ate, and perhaps thought that ancient earth deities like her wanted to avenge their lost power.

Occasionally in Greek drama and mythology, Ate had a role of enforcing moral conduct. She was a variant of the Furies, who hounded men to madness if they broke sacred family laws; and like the Furies, she avenged crimes against her Olympian relatives.

Parallels to Ate also exist in other cultures. In Norse mythology, for example, Brynhild, the Valkyrie, was a daughter of Odin and visited warriors about to die on the battlefield. Her disobedience to her father was one of the reasons for Ragnarok, the ruin of the Norse gods.

BARBARA GARDNER

Left: This painting by German artist Johann Heinrich Tischbein (1722–1789) depicts the moment Achilles nearly draws his sword on Agamemnon, only to be stopped by the cloudy figure of the goddess Athena. According to the myth, the goddess Ate prompted Agamemnon to start the dispute.

Bibliography
Bulfinch, Thomas. *Bulfinch's Mythology.* New York: Barnes & Noble, 2006.
Homer, and Robert Fagles, trans. *The Iliad.* New York: Penguin, 2009.

SEE ALSO: Furies; Nemesis; Zeus.

ATHENA

Athena, the favorite daughter of Zeus, was the Greek goddess of wisdom, crafts, and war. Some say she created the bridle, showed men how to make and use a plow, and invented the trumpet. She was the guiding deity of Athens and gave the olive tree as a gift to the city. The owl was her favorite bird, and she is often shown with a coiled snake at her feet. Her cult came to Rome from Etruria, where she was called Minerva.

According to most sources of Greek mythology, Athena was born from the head of Zeus, ruler of the gods, and she was always his favorite daughter. One myth says that Zeus had been told that his first wife, Metis, goddess of intelligence, was destined to have a child who would eventually overthrow him, just as he had overthrown his own father, Cronus. To prevent this, Zeus swallowed Metis. (Other versions of Athena's birth claim that she had no mother and that she, not Metis, was the goddess of wisdom.) Then one day Zeus had an extremely painful headache and asked the Olympians to help cure it. Some versions of the story report that Prometheus, a Titan, stepped forward to strike the royal head with an ax; others say it was Hephaestus, god of metalwork and fire. When Zeus's head was split, Athena sprang forth wearing full battle armor and helmet, holding her spear in one hand and shield in the other (see box, page 39). In that account and others of the goddess of war, Athena was described as appearing with bright eyes flashing and her armor

Right: Athena's helmeted head is all that remains of this mid-second century CE Greek statue.

gleaming. Another source says that when she made her first appearance in front of the Olympians, all nature responded to her, the earth shook and the seas rose in huge waves, until the sun god, Helios, stopped his chariot and made the world stand still to honor the new goddess.

Athena was often called Pallas Athena (see box, page 40). Some sources claim that Pallas was the name of a favorite friend of Athena's—in one version her lover—whom she killed accidentally, and so out of guilt and grief she adopted Pallas's name as part of her own. Another name the Greeks added to hers was Tritogeneia. According to the Greek poet Hesiod, who lived around 800 BCE, *Tritogeneia* meant "she who was born on the banks of the river Triton," but the relevance of the name is unclear.

The defeat of Typhon

In one early Greek myth Athena showed her courage above all other gods when she single-handedly defended Mount Olympus, the home of the gods, when it was under threat from Typhon. Typhon was the largest, strongest, and most frightening monster on earth, and when he tried to climb Mount Olympus, all the other gods fled in terror. Only Athena remained, battling the monster while at the same time goading her father, Zeus, into action. Eventually Zeus regained his courage and returned to the battleground, striking the monster with his thunderbolts. Then Athena (or Zeus, depending on the version) threw Mount Etna on top of Typhon, crushing the monster underneath. It was believed that the volcanic rumblings of Etna were the moans of Typhon (or Cronus, according to some versions.)

The contest with Arachne

Zeus's favorite daughter shared many of the interests and abilities of her father. Yet very much unlike her lascivious father, Athena was not linked romantically to any other Olympian deity, nor did she have sexual relations with mortal men. She always remained a virgin goddess.

Athena, although goddess of war, also cared for the concerns of women, especially their important skill of weaving. It was believed that Athena would carefully guide a woman's hand as she wove the clothes for her family. Yet Athena was also vain about her own weaving and did not tolerate being challenged.

One young girl, Arachne, made the mistake of thinking that she was better at the loom than Athena, so she challenged the goddess to a weaving contest. Athena easily won the competition and to teach the arrogant girl a lesson, she changed Arachne into a spider, who would spend the rest of her days weaving webs. From this myth comes the modern classification name for spiders, *arachnids*.

Athena's Battle Dress

During times of peace Athena usually wore a peplos, the same type of garment the other Olympian goddesses wore. When a war or battle began, however, she put on her armor, which included a helmet, and picked up her spear or lance and a shield made from the tough skin of the giant Pallas. It was the same battle dress she had worn when she emerged from her father's skull.

In addition to the regular battle dress, she also wore Zeus's aegis, a goatskin cloak or breastplate with gold tassels. According to one version, the aegis would conjure storms and thunder when shook. Some descriptions of the aegis have it that in the center was embroidered the head of a Gorgon, a female monster with snakes for hair. Others claim that it was Athena's shield, not the aegis, that bore the image of a Gorgon's head. She also had another weapon in her arsenal. Because Athena was Zeus's favorite daughter, he allowed only her to summon his mighty thunderbolts during battle. However, she usually relied on her own strategic cunning and finesse to win her fights.

Left: Pallas Athena in her full battle dress is the subject of this 17th-century painting. The work has been attributed to Rembrandt.

Origins of Pallas Athena

As with most Olympian gods, Athena originated in cultures outside the Greek mainland. Early archaeological evidence shows that Athena's prototypes were mostly bird and snake goddesses. One of the earliest prototypes of the Greek Athena was a Minoan, or Cretan, snake goddess who was the patron of many female domestic skills, such as weaving, pottery making, and cooking. It is also thought that the Minoan priestesses of Athena were expert snake handlers. Athena's close association with snakes was maintained in early Athens, where an Athena figurine found in a tomb had snakes for arms, leading some scholars to assert that at one time Athena was considered a snake goddess of the underworld. Neith was an early snake goddess from Egypt, who was closely associated with vultures, as was Athena, and oversaw domestic skills. A third influence was the Canaanite deity Anat, again a snake goddess. The ancient Libyans of north Africa also had a goddess of snakes, death, and sun. The Libyan Pallas was a cattle deity and a war goddess. She was said to have been born from Lake Tritonis, near one of the areas believed to have been the home of the Amazons. Her worship was brought to the Greek islands by the Libyans as they emigrated across the Mediterranean sea. The Hellenes brought her to Athens around 800 BCE, where she merged with Athena.

Athena in battle

When a war began, Athena's attention focused on the soldiers, especially those who fought most heroically or were the leaders of the armies. Several heroes gained Athena's particular affection and assistance. For example, when Orestes, son of Agamemnon (king of Mycenae and leader of the Greek forces in the Trojan War), was on trial for killing his mother, Clytemnestra, who had murdered Agamemnon, Athena voted that Orestes be pardoned. The goddess argued that the father is the most important parent, so Orestes' crime was not as bad as that of Clytemnestra.

In Homer's *Odyssey* (c. 850 BCE), Athena most admired the hero Odysseus. Although the goddess could not spare him from the dangers Poseidon put in his way, she did make sure Odysseus survived them. When at last she revealed to him who she was and what she had done for him, she also told him why she cared for him. "You are so careful, your mind is so clever, Odysseus, and so I have always looked after you." Then the goddess helped her hero return safely to his palace in Ithaca.

Aiding Heracles

A third hero Athena assisted was Heracles. As a son of Zeus and the mortal Alcmene, Heracles had some divine blood (ichor) in his veins and superhuman strength. Nevertheless, he still needed the help of Athena, because Hera, wife of

Left: A Roman statue of Athena wearing her battle helmet and aegis, with the Gorgon's face on her left shoulder. Her spear is missing.

Below: Dating from around 1430, this painted plate depicts a contemporary version of Paris judging the beauty contest between the goddesses Hera, Athena, and Aphrodite.

Zeus and the queen of the gods, was jealous of Alcmene and made sure that Zeus's son by her suffered. Hera arranged for Heracles to act as a servant to King Eurystheus of Tiryns and Mycenae. Eurystheus forced Heracles to complete 12 Labors. Athena could not stop Hera's plans for Heracles any more than she had been able to overcome Poseidon's obstacles against Odysseus. However, she made sure Heracles successfully completed all of Eurystheus's tasks. In reference to the story, many vase paintings of Heracles show Athena by his side. In the myth of Heracles' mortal death and ascension to Mount Olympus, it was Athena who served him wine.

Judgment of Paris and the Trojan War

The goddess Athena played a central role in an important Greek legend, the story of the Trojan War. The story began with an episode of jealousy, vanity, and desire known as the Judgment of Paris. Zeus chose Paris, a prince of Troy who was considered the handsomest man in the world, to judge a beauty contest between Athena, Hera, and Aphrodite, goddess of love. Another version of the episode did not include Zeus but had Eris, goddess of strife, throwing the Apple of Discord to the goddesses. A message on the apple said that it was to be awarded to the fairest of all the goddesses. Together the three goddesses called on Paris to decide who most deserved the apple. While Paris was deliberating, Athena promised Paris wisdom and military skill if he chose her as the most beautiful, Hera offered the rule of a mighty kingdom, and Aphrodite told him that the most beautiful mortal woman in the world would be his if he voted for her. For Paris, Aphrodite's offer was the most tempting, so he chose the goddess of love as the winner. From that moment on both Hera and Athena vowed to harm Paris and Troy.

Although Aphrodite kept her word and introduced Paris to Helen, the most beautiful woman, one large problem remained. Helen was married to Menelaus, king of Sparta.

Above: Athena featured in vase paintings, such as on this amphora made in the sixth century BCE. The Gorgon is depicted on Athena's shield.

The only way Paris would be able to have Helen was to steal her from Sparta. Paris's abduction of Helen sparked the Trojan War, an epic conflict between Greece and Troy that lasted 10 years. The war split the Olympians between those gods that supported the Trojans, such as Ares and Aphrodite, and those that intervened on behalf of the Greeks, including Hera and Athena. A few gods remained neutral or acted arbitrarily, most notably Apollo and Zeus.

Athena stepped in on the side of the Greeks at several crucial times. One example was when Achilles, the Greeks' best warrior, was about to draw his sword on his ally Agamemnon, Greek king of Mycenae and brother of Menelaus. Achilles was angry because the Greek leader had insulted him. Just as Achilles was about to draw his sword, Athena stood invisible behind him and caught hold of his hair. In the *Iliad* she says, "I have come to stop your anger. Do not take your sword in your hand. You may abuse him with words but do not fight him." Achilles obeys. He goes on to slay many Trojans, most famously their champion Hector, the brother of Paris.

Athena and the fall of Troy

Athena played another important role in the fall of Troy. She helped the Greek carpenter Epeios build the Trojan Horse. Odysseus is said to have had the idea of the large wooden horse, but it was Epeios, aided by Athena, who actually constructed it. The wooden horse was left as a gift to the Trojans, who, thinking the Greeks had given up the war and left, wheeled it into the city. That night the few Greek soldiers who were hiding in the horse's belly emerged from the structure and opened the city's gates. The Greek army quickly returned, captured Troy, and killed nearly all the men, including Paris, who died from a poisoned arrow.

While Troy was under siege and the Greeks were pillaging, Ajax of Locris (also known as Ajax the Lesser; not to be confused with Ajax of Salamis, a Greek hero of the war) pursued the cursed soothsayer Cassandra, Priam's daughter, into Athena's temple. The frightened girl clung to the deity's image, but Ajax pulled her away and raped her. Athena determined he would suffer for his sexual violation of her temple. Ajax managed to survive the stormy seas she sent to hinder his trip home, and standing on a cliff he boasted that he had overcome the storm and conquered both Athena and Poseidon. At once the sea god sent an earthquake that split the cliff from the land, plunging Ajax into the waves and drowning him.

Patron of Athens and Bearer of Olive Oil

When Athens wanted a guiding deity, two Olympians, Poseidon and Athena, vied for the position. Poseidon struck the earth with his trident and a horse sprang forth (some versions have him bringing forth a saltwater spring). Athena touched the ground with her spear and an olive tree grew. The Athenians decided that the hilly countryside had no fields for horses and that the olive tree was the better gift. It was from that moment, according to legend, that Athena became the patron of Athens; in return the Athenians adopted the owl, Athena's symbol, as their own.

Athena's gift of olive oil became one of the most important products in the ancient world and helped to make Athens wealthy. Women used it in their face and body creams and perfumes, for burning in lamps, and in cooking. It was used by men in their athletic competitions. They would put oil on their bodies before their contests, then at the end scrape off the oil and sand with a special curved bronze tool called a strigil. Large jars, known as amphoras, of olive oil were given as prizes in athletic contests held annually in Athens. Olive oil also formed part of the healing lotions Greek warriors used after battle.

Right: Athenians stamped an owl on their coins in honor of their patron, Athena. This Athenian coin was made in the sixth century BCE.

Worship of Athena

Athena was worshiped in temples all over the Greek world, but her most famous sanctuary was the Parthenon, named for Athena's cult, Parthenos, meaning "Athena the Virgin." The Parthenon was built atop the Acropolis in Athens. Most Greek cities had an acropolis, which was a high fortified compound usually in the center of a city, inside which religious rituals took place and where, it was believed, the gods came to dwell. It was also where the citizens retreated during a siege. The acropolis in Athens is the best known, mainly because of the Parthenon. An earlier temple to Athena on the Acropolis had been burned during the Persian invasion of Greece in 480 BCE, and the Parthenon replaced that temple.

The political force behind the building of the Parthenon was Pericles (c. 495–429 BCE), the architects were Ictinus and Callicrates, and the artistic supervisor was the sculptor Phidias (or Pheidias; c. 490–430 BCE). Together these men were responsible for the construction of one of the world's most important and influential buildings. The Parthenon, built entirely of marble, was designed in the Doric style of architecture, the simplest of the classical orders, or styles of building, and constructed between 447 and 432 BCE. The outside of the Parthenon has a colonnade of 8 columns along the front and back and 17 along each side. On the

west, or back, pediment (the triangular section shaped by the roof above the columns) were sculptures of Athena and Poseidon offering their gifts to the Athenians (see box): the olive tree grows before Athena, a horse prances by Poseidon. On the east pediment the sculpture showed Athena being born from the head of her father, Zeus, while all the gods and goddesses watch the event. Phidias designed these and the other sculptures on the temple, which are now in the British Museum, London, England.

Around the wall of the temple itself, inside the colonnade, ran a long series of marble figures. They represented the citizens of Athens at the Panathenaea, a festival in honor of Athena held in the city every spring. Also shown were the gods and goddesses whom the citizens believed came to their ceremonies.

Statues of Athena

Inside the Parthenon stood a giant statue of Athena also designed by Phidias. Covered in gold and ivory, the statue was 36 feet (11 m) tall and showed the goddess wearing a peplos, the aegis, and an elaborate helmet; she held a spear in one hand and a statuette of the goddess of victory, Nike, in the other. Beside her was her shield with the Gorgon's head at its center, an owl, and the sacred snake. The citizens of Athens made sacrifices to their goddess on the altar in front of the temple, but they went into the Parthenon to worship before the giant statue of Athena. Another statue of the goddess stood in the center of the hill. Made of bronze, the deity's spear was so large and gleamed so brightly in the sun that, according to legend, it could be seen by sailors far out at sea.

A second, smaller temple was built at the western edge of the Acropolis. This one was also dedicated to Athena, but this time for her role as goddess of Athenian victory. The Nike temple is in the Ionic style (slightly more ornate than Doric) and has columns only on its front and back. On the protective wall setting of the temple was carved an image of the goddess untying her sandals, a symbolic message to the Athenians that she would always protect their city.

At the north side of the Acropolis stands a third temple. It is called the Erechtheum and was dedicated to the deities Athena and Poseidon, and to two mythic kings of Athens, Cecrops and Erechtheus. The interior held the tombs of these kings and a lamp lit with special olive oil. The east porch was dedicated to Athena, and inside stood the oldest statue of the goddess on the Acropolis. This simple wooden statue was believed to have fallen from the sky to Athens.

On the south side of the Erechtheum is another small porch also sacred to Athena. There the columns are in the form of six maidens bearing baskets on their heads. These statues, called caryatids, represent the women who carried gifts for the goddess in an annual but secret ceremony. Today the caryatids are housed in a museum for protection, and

replicas of the maidens support the porch roof. A porch on the north was dedicated to the god Poseidon. The Athenians believed that it protected the mark made by his trident when he created the horse as his offering to them. In an enclosure on the west flourished the olive tree given by Athena as her gift to the people of Athens.

KARELISA HARTIGAN

Right: This 19th-century color illustration is an artist's impression of the giant statue of Athena by the Greek sculptor Phidias. The original statue was gold and ivory and stood in the center of the Parthenon. In her left hand Athena holds a statue of Nike, the deity of victory.

Below: The Parthenon, a temple to Athena, was built in Athens in the mid-fifth century BCE and is considered one of the world's great structures.

Bibliography
Bulfinch, Thomas. *Bulfinch's Mythology.* New York: Barnes & Noble, 2006.
Homer, and Robert Fagles, trans. *The Iliad.* New York: Penguin, 2009.

SEE ALSO: Aphrodite; Ares; Hera; Nike; Poseidon; Typhon; Zeus.

ATLAS

Atlas was a Titan who was forced by the Greek god Zeus to bear the weight of the heavens on his shoulders. The image of him struggling under his great burden is still familiar today, mainly because of his widespread depiction in art.

The Titans included the children of Uranus and Gaia, the primordial god and goddess, as well as some of their grandchildren. Atlas's father was Iapetus, one of the six sons of Uranus and Gaia, and his mother was Clymene. His brothers included Prometheus and Epimetheus. They were respectively the fathers of Deucalion and Pyrrha, the only survivors of the great flood sent by Zeus to exterminate the human race. Atlas was thus uncle to the parents of the whole race of mortals.

The children of Atlas

Although his brother Prometheus was a more prominent benefactor of the human race, bringing fire to the world, Atlas also had close links to humankind. The ancient Greeks believed that about one third of the great dynasties of Greece were descended from a group of seven of his daughters, including the ruling families of Troy, Sparta, Mycenae, and Thebes. These daughters were collectively known as the Pleiades. Through one of these daughters, Maia, Atlas was the grandfather of the god Hermes, and several others of the Pleiades either married or bore children by the gods Zeus, Poseidon, and Ares.

Another batch of Atlas's daughters, the Hyades, were nurses to the god Dionysus. Later sources say that Atlas was also the father of the Hesperides, a group of nymphs who lived on an island at the end of the world. In the *Odyssey*, meanwhile, Homer (c. ninth–eighth century BCE) writes that Atlas was the father of Calypso, the nymph with whom Odysseus stayed on his way back to Ithaca.

Long before mortals were created, the Titans, under the leadership of Cronus, defeated their father Uranus and took over the universe. The Titans were in turn deposed by Cronus's son Zeus and Zeus's siblings, known as the Olympians for their home on Mount Olympus. The war that the Olympians waged against the Titans was known as the Titanomachy. The struggle between the two rival powers lasted for 10 years, and after he had led his forces to victory, Zeus cast the Titans down to Tartarus, the deepest part of the underworld.

For Atlas, however, Zeus reserved a special fate. Because of Atlas's great size and strength, Zeus made the Titan stand in the far west, beyond the Mediterranean Sea, holding the heavens on his broad shoulders. Atlas was destined to bear the weight of the heavens for all eternity. Because of his fate, his name is sometimes interpreted as meaning "the Bearer" or "the Endurer."

Atlas and Heracles

The best-known myth involving Atlas also featured the Greek hero Heracles. To make amends for an earlier crime, Heracles was forced to serve Eurystheus, the king of Tiryns and Mycenae, for 12 years. Eurystheus ordered Heracles to carry out the famous 12 Labors of Heracles.

One of Heracles' Labors was to bring King Eurystheus the golden apples of the Garden of the Hesperides. The tree bearing the golden apples had been a gift from Gaia to Hera, queen of the gods, when she married Zeus. The tree was guarded by a dragon. On his way to the Garden of the Hesperides, Heracles came across Atlas's brother Prometheus. After Heracles shot the eagle that Zeus had sent to torment him, Prometheus advised Heracles that Atlas, the father of the Hesperides, was best suited to retrieve the apples.

Heracles eventually found the Titan, who agreed to help him. However, someone would have to hold up the heavens while Atlas was away. That burden fell to Heracles, who was aided by the goddess Athena. Atlas retrieved the apples. He enjoyed the freedom from having to carry his great load so much that he told Heracles he would gladly take the golden apples to Eurystheus himself. However, Heracles easily tricked Atlas into returning to his position

Right: The Italian artist Giovanni Francesco Barbieri, also called Il Guercino (1591–1666), painted this version of Atlas holding the heavens. The heavens are depicted in the form of a globe.

by asking him to help for a moment while he adjusted the pillow he was using as a pad for his shoulders. When Atlas took the weight of the heavens from him, Heracles stepped away to leave the Titan to bear the weight for all eternity.

The Atlas Mountains

Today Atlas is also identified with a large mountain range that runs through present-day Morocco, Algeria, and Tunisia in north Africa. In ancient times, the Atlas Mountains formed a famous, almost impenetrable barrier between the Mediterranean coastal region and the Sahara Desert inland. As early as the fifth century BCE, the Greek historian Herodotus referred to the Atlas Mountains as the "pillars of heaven." The mountain range begins in the west of Morocco, near the Atlantic coast. To the ancient Greeks, this would have been the very end of the world, where Atlas would have been made to stand by Zeus.

Another legend tells a different version of how Atlas was turned into stone, however. According to the Roman poet Ovid (43 BCE–17 CE), the hero Perseus stopped in the land of the Hesperides after successfully decapitating the Gorgon Medusa, whose glance turned people to stone. He asked the region's king, Atlas, for hospitality. However,

an ancient prophecy had said that a son of Zeus was destined to steal the golden apples, so Atlas turned Perseus away. In response to this insult, Perseus took Medusa's head from his wallet. Even dead, the Gorgon turned King Atlas into a stone mountain.

Links with Atlantis

Atlas was also associated with the fabled land of Atlantis. The Greek philosopher Plato (c. 428–c. 348 BCE) recounted in two of his later works, *Timaeus* and *Critias*, that 9,000 years before there had existed a huge island paradise in the far west, way beyond the Pillars of Heracles (the modern Strait of Gibraltar). The island continent was called Atlantis and, according to Plato, was rich in natural resources. On it lived a people ruled by a dynasty of kings descended from the god Poseidon. According to Plato, the civilization there became very advanced and built an empire that extended from the far west into the Mediterranean, as far as today's Italy and Egypt. Plato's tale also described how the first inhabitants of Atlantis were an

Below: The snow-capped peaks of the Atlas Mountains in northern Africa. The mountains have long been associated with the Titan.

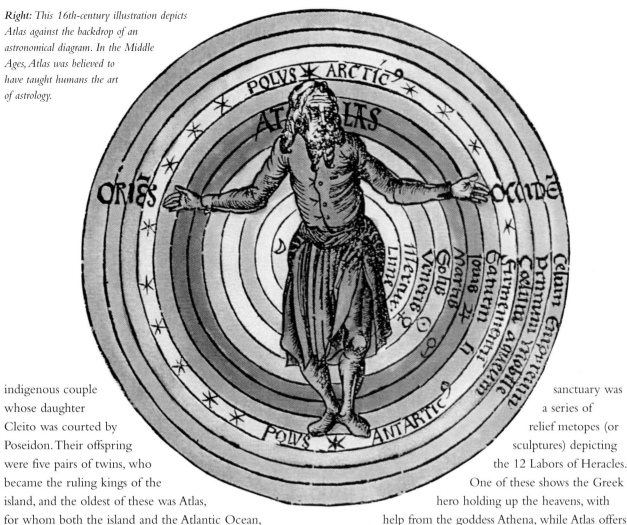

Right: This 16th-century illustration depicts Atlas against the backdrop of an astronomical diagram. In the Middle Ages, Atlas was believed to have taught humans the art of astrology.

indigenous couple whose daughter Cleito was courted by Poseidon. Their offspring were five pairs of twins, who became the ruling kings of the island, and the oldest of these was Atlas, for whom both the island and the Atlantic Ocean, were named. (Today, most scholars believe that the Atlantis myth was based on the volcanic eruption of the Mediterranean island of Thera around 1600 BCE.)

Atlas depicted in art

Over the centuries Atlas has been a popular subject for painters and sculptors. Among several significant works that depict him is *Atlas* by the 17th-century Italian artist Giovanni Francesco Barbieri. The painting shows a powerful and muscular Atlas bending under the weight of the great globe that he is holding up. Atlas is depicted in a similar pose in the Farnese Atlas, which is housed at the National Archaeological Museum in Naples. This is probably the most famous statue of Atlas and dates from the second century CE. It is possibly a Roman copy of a Greek statue. The statue features the earliest known depiction of a celestial globe, a map of the heavens in globe form.

The myth of Heracles and Atlas is depicted in several famous works of art from ancient Greece. One example was found in the Temple of Zeus in Olympia, the site of the ancient Olympic Games. In the middle of the temple's

sanctuary was a series of relief metopes (or sculptures) depicting the 12 Labors of Heracles. One of these shows the Greek hero holding up the heavens, with help from the goddess Athena, while Atlas offers him the apples of the Hesperides.

From Atlas's role as bearer of the heavens on his shoulders come several modern uses of the word *atlas*. Using the word *atlas* to denote a collection of maps comes from the practice of using a picture of the Farnese Atlas bearing the world (the orb of heaven that he carries being mistaken for Earth) as a frontispiece to collections of maps. The practice was made popular by the famous 16th-century geographer Mercator. In anatomy the atlas is the top cervical vertebra, which supports the skull, while in architecture an atlas is a male figure used as a column to support a roof or balcony.

ANTHONY BULLOCH

Bibliography

Bulfinch, Thomas. *Bulfinch's Mythology.* New York: Barnes & Noble, 2006.

Ovid, and A. D. Melville, trans. *Metamorphoses.* New York: Oxford University Press, 2008.

SEE ALSO: Athena; Cronus; Gaia; Poseidon; Prometheus; Titans; Uranus; Zeus.

ATTIS

Attis was a Phrygian fertility god whose death and resurrection were commemorated every year by the Phrygians, and later the Romans, to celebrate the start of spring. In most mythologies there are tales of gods or goddesses who were worshiped in order to ensure good harvests every year, but in most cases they are characterized as female. Attis was depicted as a beautiful—and sometimes as an effeminate—male.

The story of Attis (also spelled Atys) was set in Phrygia (modern-day Anatolia, which forms part of central and western Turkey). It has many parallels with the tale of the Greek Adonis, although there are several versions of the birth, loves, and death of Attis. One element is consistent: Attis came back to life.

Tales of birth and love

One account of the birth of Attis describes his mother as Nana, a water nymph. Nana, a virgin, placed on her breast a pomegranate from a tree that was created from the blood of the male sexual organs of Agdistis, a hermaphrodite. (Some versions suggest that an almond was used; according to other accounts, Nana ate the fruit.) There are also myths that describe Attis as the son of Cybele, the mother of the gods. Although it is not clear how he was conceived, no intercourse was involved. It is even possible that Cybele and Agdistis were one and the same character.

Whatever the circumstances of his birth and parentage, in every version of the story Attis grew into a pretty young man (he was sometimes described as effeminate) and became a shepherd. Because of his beauty Cybele grew obsessed with him. When the shepherd fell in love with a nymph, a curse was placed on him, which caused him to go insane and castrate himself. It is sometimes told that Cybele cast the spell to prevent Attis from ever loving anyone else.

One version gives Cybele a more active role. After she had cast her spell, Attis ran wildly through the woods, eventually falling into a drunken sleep. While he was asleep Cybele tied

Right: A marble bust of Attis shows him wearing a Phrygian cap. This soft, close-fitting felt headwear was later worn by freed slaves in Rome as a symbol of their liberty.

Right: This silver-and-gold plate shows Attis and Cybele riding in a procession, surrounded by dancers. It was made in Italy in the fourth century CE and was used to make offerings to the gods.

Attis's penis to her own foot. When he woke and tried to run, his penis was torn off and he soon died.

Violets sprang from Attis's blood, and the gods brought him back to life, never to age or decay. In some versions Attis was transformed into a pine tree, and pine trees played an important role in his worship. (In a few versions Attis, like the Greek Adonis, was killed by a wild boar, but while violets sprang from Attis's blood, in Adonis's case it was buttercups.) The resurrection of Attis symbolized the start of spring.

Introduction to Rome

The Phrygian myth of Attis and Cybele was introduced to Roman society around 204 BCE, when Rome was under threat from the Carthaginian general Hannibal (247–183 BCE). To boost Roman morale the authorities took advantage of a prophesy claiming that bringing Cybele to Rome would eventually force the retreat of Hannibal. A Roman envoy was sent to Phrygia to retrieve an ancient black stone that was said to embody the mother of the gods. The stone was housed in the temple of Victory on Rome's Palatine Hill. Within a year Hannibal was forced to return to Carthage.

Over the following two to three centuries the importance of Attis as a fertility god spread throughout the Greek and Roman worlds, and Attis was invested with celestial and solar attributes, eventually becoming a symbol of immortality. At the same time a cult grew around the myth of Attis. The priests of the cult were known as the Galli, and they supposedly castrated themselves in a fit of orgiastic frenzy during a special initiation ritual—although it is possible that they merely drew blood. The tale of a young man who fell into such a frenzy of devotion and castrated himself is told in a poem by the Roman poet Catullus (c. 84–54 BCE).

The worship of Attis's sacred pine tree, with the god's effigy bound to its trunk, was incorporated into the established religion of Rome and celebrated as a festival that began on March 22 and lasted several days. On March 23 there was an extended period of mourning. On the following day, the spring equinox, the resurrection of Attis was commemorated during the festival of Hilaria (Joy). This was a time of carnival and masquerading. Two days later the whole festival came to a close with a solemn procession to the waters of the Almo stream.

There was also a more private celebration that included a sacramental meal and an initiation ritual held on the Vatican Hill (the site of St. Peter's Basilica) in which a bull was slaughtered over a grating, beneath which the initiates were bathed in the fresh blood. Similar rites were performed in Gaul (modern France) and in Germany.

CARL RUCK

Bibliography

Frazer, James George. *The Golden Bough.* New York: Oxford University Press, 2009.

Wiseman, T. P. *Catullus and His World: A Reappraisal.* Cambridge, MA: Cambridge University Press, 1985.

SEE ALSO: Demeter; Mars; Quirinus.

BACCHUS

Originally Bacchus was an alternative name in ancient Greece for Dionysus, the god of wine. Later the Romans used Bacchus as their own god of wine and revelry, but he was a combination of the Greek Dionysus and an ancient Italian wine god named Liber. In Rome the worship of Bacchus formed the center of a dangerous underground cult that was brutally suppressed in the second century BCE.

The son of Jupiter and Semele, the Roman deity Bacchus was god of wine and ecstasy. It was believed he released people from the worries of daily life and brought a sense of personal freedom and happiness. However, there was always an element of danger in the freedom and debauchery associated with Bacchus. If people lost their inhibitions at the expense of their ability to reason, there was no telling what they might do. One example is the story of Pentheus, king of Thebes, and his mother, Agave, known from the ancient drama *Bacchants* (or *Bacchae*) by Euripides (c. 484–406 BCE). Agave (or Agaue), under the influence of Bacchus, was roaming in the mountains when she thought she saw a lion. In a frenzy she killed the beast. When she finally came to her senses, she discovered that she had in fact killed her own son, Pentheus.

Bacchus was usually depicted wearing a wreath of ivy, or occasionally grape vines, around his head. Among his other attributes were wine cups and animal skins, particularly fawn and panther. Sometimes he carried a large wand called a thyrsus, which was a fennel stalk or staff with ivy wound around the top. He often traveled in the company of satyrs and bacchants (or maenads), who were his followers. Satyrs were mythological creatures that usually

Left: This statue titled Bacchus *by Michelangelo was sculpted when the artist was 21 years old. It became the model for later representations.*

had the waist and legs of a goat and the arms and upper body of a man. Bacchants were women who participated in Dionysian rites and revelry. Together the satyrs and bacchants represented the unrestrained forces of nature. Sometimes the god Pan was also included in their company, although he was originally not connected to Bacchus.

Roman worship

In the official state religion of the Romans, Bacchus played only a minor role (unlike that of Dionysus in Greece), so important sanctuaries of Bacchus were few. There were, however, secret rituals known as Bacchanalia that were especially popular in the south of Italy and were originally held only for women.

The Bacchanalia, or Bacchic Mysteries, were Greek in origin, descended from seasonal festivals called Dionysia. At the core of the Roman Bacchanalia were secret rituals celebrated in private. The exact nature of the rituals are not known because the initiates were sworn to secrecy, but it was popularly believed that sexual orgies were included. What is known, however, is that the ritual included the drinking of wine and that it held out the promise of a happy afterlife to anyone who participated.

In 186 BCE a scandal concerning the Bacchanalia unexpectedly led to the suppression of the cult in Rome (see box). The Bacchic cult centers were closed down, with the exception of some venerable ancient shrines. Thousands of worshipers were persecuted. Many fled to the countryside; those who stayed behind were put to death. For more than a century the followers of Bacchus had to hold their meetings in secret, outside the city of Rome. It was not until the time of Julius Caesar (100–44 BCE) that the private worship of Bacchus was officially authorized again.

Representations of Bacchus

In Greek art the god of wine was usually portrayed as a bearded man, although he sometimes appeared beardless. In Roman art Bacchus was more commonly portrayed as a clean-shaven young man. In later art, from the Renaissance

Above: A sixth-century BCE pottery painting by Exekias shows the god of wine making vines spring from his boat's mast while sailing.

Scandalous Bacchanalia

In 186 BCE there was a great scandal in Rome concerning the Bacchanalia. A young nobleman named Publius Aebutius almost became the victim of a violent type of Bacchic cult. After the death of his father, his mother had remarried an immoral man who squandered almost the entire estate of his stepson, who was still underage. The mother and stepfather then decided to get rid of Aebutius by having him initiated into a dangerous Bacchic cult. Tradition has it that the young man was saved by his girlfriend, Hispala, who had accompanied Aebutius's mother to this particular cult on earlier occasions. She had seen things there that had terrified her, and she warned Aebutius that he would suffer an unspeakable fate, perhaps even death, if he joined the group. Aebutius went to the authorities with Hispala, who gave key evidence about the nature of the Bacchanalia. The matter was brought before the Senate, which immediately passed a law prohibiting the Bacchanalia.

Bacchus in Pompeii

In 79 CE Mount Vesuvius erupted, covering the neighboring town of Pompeii under a thick layer of volcanic ash. Because the ash layer was airtight, many objects and wall paintings were preserved until excavation work began in the mid-18th century.

In the House of the Centenary (so called because it was excavated in 1879, eighteen hundred years after the eruption), a wall painting (below) shows a landscape with Bacchus standing at the foot of Vesuvius as the volcano may have looked before the eruption. In the painting, the lower part of the mountain is covered with vineyards, and Bacchus is depicted as a giant bunch of grapes with human arms, head, and feet. With his right hand he pours wine to a panther; in his left hand he holds a thyrsus.

In the Villa of the Mysteries, built between 70 and 60 BCE, there is a room decorated on three walls with scenes relating to the Mysteries of Bacchus. The exact meaning of the scenes remains unclear. The central scene on the back wall shows the god himself lying in the arms of Ariadne. To the right a kneeling woman is about to uncover a secret object hidden in a winnowing basket.

Below: Bacchus and Mount Vesuvius, *a fresco painting from the House of the Centenary, Pompeii. The depiction of the god of wine as a bunch of grapes is rare but clearly shows who the subject is.*

Above: This 19th-century painting, titled Bacchanal, *by Lawrence Alma-Tadema (1836–1912), is the artist's impression of a Roman bacchanal, or drinking party.*

(15th and 16th centuries) onward, he was often depicted as a fat drunkard, the personification of excess.

In sculpture perhaps the most influential piece is Michelangelo's statue *Bacchus* (1496–1497), where the deity appears as a drunken adolescent. The depiction and pose of Michelangelo's Bacchus served as an example to many later sculptors of the character. In painting, Bacchus was often accompanied by a merry group of satyrs and bacchants. Many times he was paired with Ariadne, whom he consoled after she was abandoned by Theseus. The motif of the bacchanal (drinking party) was also common. Titian (c. 1489–1576) was the Renaissance standard-bearer of

mythological art, and he created the prototype for Bacchus and many other Greek and Roman mythological characters. Titian's *Bacchanal* and *Bacchus and Ariadne* (both 1522–1523) are two famous examples that were models for later painters of mythological scenes, such as Peter Paul Rubens (1577–1640) and Nicolas Poussin (1594–1665).

Bacchus and Christianity

In Christian art and literature Bacchus was sometimes regarded as a prefiguration (early form) of Christ. Like Christ, Bacchus was the son of a god and a mortal woman and extended the promise of a blissful afterlife. A floor mosaic in Cyprus shows a scene that looks similar to the familiar scene of the Virgin Mary holding the young Jesus, commonly referred to as the Madonna and Child. Instead of the Madonna in the mosaic there is Hermes (Mercury in Rome), who, according to legend, took the infant deity to be raised by bacchants. The infant Bacchus is depicted, like Jesus, with a halo around his head.

Early Christian art also made ample use of Bacchic symbolism, attaching new meaning to old symbols. The grapevines that had for centuries decorated Roman tombs as a symbol of everlasting life came to be used as a symbol for the Christian afterlife. An early example of this is found in the Santa Constanza in Rome, which was built between 337 and 361 as a mausoleum for Constantia, the daughter of Rome's first Christian emperor, Constantine the Great (who ruled 306–337). One of the ceiling mosaics in the mausoleum shows a large portrait of Constantia surrounded by swirling vines and men harvesting grapes, and her sarcophagus is decorated with cupids harvesting grapes.

FEYO SCHUDDEBOOM

Bibliography

Bulfinch, Thomas. *Bulfinch's Mythology.* New York: Barnes & Noble, 2006.

Euripides, and P. Burian and A. Shapiro, eds. *The Complete Euripides.* New York: Oxford University Press, 2009–2010.

Fleming, Stuart. *Vinum: The Story of Roman Wine.* Glen Mills, PA: Art Flair, 2001.

Howatson, M. C. *The Oxford Companion to Classical Literature.* New York: Oxford University Press, 2005.

SEE ALSO: Dionysus; Faunus; Pan.

CRONUS

In Greek mythology Cronus was the youngest of the Titan children of the creator deities Uranus and Gaia. He dethroned his father as ruler of the universe but was himself overthrown by his own mighty children, the Olympians, led by Zeus.

The creation story in Greek mythology begins with Uranus (Heaven or Sky) fertilizing Gaia (Earth) by raining on her. As Uranus's wife, Gaia then gave birth to many beings, most important the one-eyed giants named the Cyclopes; worker giants called the Hecatoncheires, each with a hundred hands; and the humanoid Titans, which were a primeval race of intelligent giants. Cronus was the youngest Titan.

Uranus grew jealous of his children and, according to Hesiod's *Theogony*, written in the eighth century BCE, he forced them back into the body of Gaia. The pain of having to carry her grown children inside her was too great for Gaia, and she called on them for help in overthrowing Uranus. Only Cronus was brave enough to volunteer. Gaia released Cronus, who armed himself with a sickle and hid when his father next visited his mother. At the right moment Cronus castrated Uranus and threw his genitals into the sea. According to one source, out of the foam produced by Uranus's genitals grew Aphrodite, goddess of love and beauty. Rendered powerless, Uranus relinquished his throne to Cronus, but not before warning him that he too would be defeated by one of his own children.

As the new ruler of the universe, Cronus freed the other Titans, the Cyclopes, and the Hecatoncheires and married his sister Rhea. He soon grew convinced, however, that the others were intent on removing him from power, so he imprisoned them again, despite Gaia's protests.

Left: Saturn Devouring a Son *(about 1636), by Flemish painter Peter Paul Rubens, was commissioned by King Philip IV of Spain for his royal hunting lodge. Saturn was the Roman name for Cronus.*

Cronus's paranoia was not abated by imprisoning his siblings, and when Rhea became pregnant, Cronus recalled Uranus's final warning. Rhea was about to give birth to the first Olympian, Hestia, who would become the goddess of the hearth. As soon as Hestia was born Cronus snatched her away from Rhea and swallowed her whole. When Rhea was next pregnant, this time with the goddess Demeter, Cronus again swallowed the newborn baby. Three more times Rhea gave birth and Cronus devoured the children in order to eliminate any threat to his power.

When Rhea was pregnant for the sixth time, she turned to Gaia for help, and the two came up with a scheme to save the next baby. First Rhea hid from Cronus—some sources say that she sought refuge in a cave on the island of Crete; others claim that she went to the rough hill country of Arcadia—and gave birth to Zeus. She then handed the baby to two nymph sisters, Adrasteia and Ida, who would nourish him on the milk from Amaltheia, a goat deity. Once Rhea knew her baby was safe, she wrapped a stone in swaddling clothes, returned to Cronus, and gave it to him. Thinking it was the newborn baby, he swallowed it. It has been suggested by historians that the subjugation of Rhea to Cronus and of Gaia to Uranus reflects the more malevolent, sky-god traditions of peoples who over centuries gradually invaded mainland Greece and merged uneasily with the region's earlier inhabitants.

Zeus's revenge

When Zeus grew up, he and Rhea devised a plan for rescuing his siblings. Together they made Cronus's favorite honeyed drink, but secretly added mustard and salt to it. When he gulped it down, the sickening mixture made him vomit. He heaved up the stone he had thought was his last child; then he vomited up the other five children, who by now were fully grown.

These children, the Olympians, immediately declared war on Cronus. Zeus and his siblings joined forces with many of the Cyclopes and Hecatoncheires. Cronus had powerful allies too. Most of the Titans and the river goddess Styx sided with him. The Cyclopes fashioned thunder and lightning into potent weapons for Zeus.

The war raged for a decade before Cronus was finally deposed and banished with his Titan allies. Some say they were imprisoned in the underworld realm of Tartarus, guarded by the Hecatoncheires. Roman writer Plutarch

Right: Saturn Devouring One of His Children *(1821–1823), by the Spanish painter Francisco Goya (1746–1828), was most likely based on the 17th-century painting by Rubens (opposite).*

POLIDORO DA CARAVAGGIO INVENTORE

Gio. Bat. Galestruzzi fece 1

Above: This 17th-century engraving is copied from an artwork depicting Uranus being castrated by his son Cronus. Gaia, Uranus's wife and the mother of Cronus, stands behind Cronus.

(c. 46–120 CE), however, wrote that Cronus was banished to the Isle of the Blessed, near Britain. Other accounts state that Zeus made Cronus ruler of Elysium, the fabled place where the souls of dead heroes lived.

Cronus and the Golden Age

There are some versions that depict the reign of Cronus as a golden age when all creatures lived in harmony with nature and each other. This different depiction of Cronus may have come from an ancient pre-Greek Cronus who was a grain deity in an era when wars were less common. The ancient Greeks believed that the Golden Age was a benevolent time for mortals, where there was no need for swords or weapons of any kind, abusive language was never spoken, and neither punishment nor retribution were ever considered. Even animals were kind to each other. It was a time when the universe revolved backward and the world was a paradise of abundance, where streams flowed full of milk and honey, and no one knew hunger. In many ways the Golden Age of Cronus was similar to the biblical Garden of Eden.

During the reign of Cronus, women did not give birth; humans rose out of the earth, and were thus said to be autochthonous. Because no one had parents, there were naturally no families. The humans of the Golden Age not only talked to each other but also spoke to and learned from all kinds of animals. Although the autochthons were

The Olympians' Revulsion at Eating Children

Cronus was not the only character in Greek mythology who ate his own children. There are other Greek myths in which a father serves up his children as a horrifying meal for others. The most infamous of these stories was that of Tantalus, a wealthy king who was said to be a son of Zeus. He was popular with the Olympian deities and frequently dined with them. One day, wondering if they were as all-knowing as they claimed to be, Tantalus had his infant son Pelops butchered and made into a stew. Then he invited the gods to dinner.

The goddess Demeter, still dazed with grief over the loss of her daughter Persephone to Hades, barely realized what she was doing when she began to eat. The other gods shrank back in shock and revulsion, for they had immediately understood the nature of the meat. They swiftly restored the poor infant to life and, since Demeter had already swallowed the tiny left shoulder blade, they replaced it with ivory. As for Tantalus, the gods sent him to the depths of gloomy Tartarus, where he remained "tantalizingly" (the word comes from his name) close to a refreshing pool of water and perfectly ripe, juicy fruits. Thus, the punishment of Tantalus was to go mad with thirst and hunger in the middle of an abundance he could never have. The severity of the punishment indicates the revulsion felt by the Olympians in the face of such child abuse. This is all the more understandable when one remembers that they too had been victims of such abuse by Cronus.

mortal, for them death came like a pleasant sleep without pain or fear.

The Golden Age ended when Zeus defeated Cronus. In one version of the fate of Cronus that relates to the story of the Golden Age, Cronus was placed by Zeus in a secret place where he lay sleeping, protected by women until the time was right for him to wake again and reign over another golden age.

Origins of Cronus

Most scholars agree that *Cronus* is a pre-Greek word, but where it came from is less clear. There is also disagreement concerning the origins of the character of Cronus. One speculation is that the Greek Cronus was adapted from the Phoenician god Moloch, who also devoured children.

Another theory is that Cronus may have been a pre-Greek deity who taught people the use of honey and was connected with grain. Evidence for this comes in part from the only important ritual associated with him in Greek times, the Cronia, a July harvest festival honoring Cronus and Rhea. The festival was held mainly in Athens; in Thebes, where it included a music contest; and on the island of Rhodes. It was a lively celebration that blurred social distinctions between master and slave and placed all celebrants on an equal footing. Evidence from Rhodes suggests that the ritual may have included human sacrifice. There was an instance when a condemned criminal, drugged with wine, was sacrificed outside the city gates at the shrine of Artemis Aristobule.

Right: This Roman sculpture depicts the moment when Rhea gives Cronus a rock wrapped in a blanket, which he believes to be the infant Zeus. Cronus swallows the rock without noticing the trick.

In addition to the Cronia, a ritual was held every spring in Athens, during which Cronus was honored with a sacrificial cake. At the spring equinox in Olympia, his priests offered sacrifices on a nearby hill named for him, and in summertime the people of Cyrene wore crowns of fresh figs and celebrated Cronus as the vegetation god who had taught them about fruits and honey.

Wars among the gods

Incidents of deities fighting each other, episodes known as cosmic wars, such as the usurpation of Uranus by Cronus and the battle between Cronus and his children the Olympians, are frequently found in world mythologies.

Above: The infant Zeus being secretly raised by the nymphs and reared on milk from the goat deity Amaltheia. According to legend, when Zeus dethroned Cronus and became ruler of the gods, he showed his thanks to the goat by making her the star Capella in the constellation Auriga.

Such struggles are usually interpreted as evidence of an older culture or religious tradition whose adherents were often demonized by the usurping, new culture or religion. For example, in addition to the cosmic wars of Greek myth, similar battles occur in ancient myths of India between the *ashuras* (demons), who were identified by their mothers' surnames, and their younger siblings, the *devas* (shining ones), gods who were identified by their fathers' surnames. The battles between the *ashuras* and the *devas* have been seen by some scholars as a metaphor for the historical conflict between an older, matriarchal culture in parts of India and an invading patriarchal culture.

Similarly, Celtic mythology includes the story of the Battle of Moytura, where an ancient race of dark, brutal, misshapen giants called the Fomorii were defeated by invading, handsome deities known as the Tuatha De Danaan. Another example, from Babylonian mythology, is the battle between the mother of the gods, an evil she-dragon named Tiamat, and the young champion deity called Marduk. Tiamat tried to destroy the gods but Marduk defeated her. After his victory Marduk was made the chief deity of the Babylonian pantheon. In Aztec mythology the young god of war, Huitzilopochtli, defeated his older warrior sister, Coyolxauhqui, and 400 brothers.

Cronus in art

The Romans adopted many of the characteristics and stories of Cronus for their ancient Italian deity Saturn, and because of the impact that the Roman empire had on the Western world, many Greek myths and characters that became the subject of works of art were titled by their Roman names. Perhaps the most famous painting of Cronus or Saturn is *Saturn Devouring One of His Children* by Francisco Goya (1746–1828), Spain's most influential artist of the late 18th and early 19th centuries. By the mid-1780s Goya had become one of the leading painters at the royal court in Madrid, where he studied many of the Old Masters.

Cronus, Philyra, and Cheiron

Cronus mated not only with Rhea. He also had a child with a young water maiden named Philyra, one of the countless daughters of Cronus's eldest Titan brother, Oceanus. Philyra was unwilling to be part of such a union with her uncle and fled. Cronus changed himself into a stallion and raced after her. When he caught her they mated, and the infant she bore was the centaur Cheiron, part horse and part man.

Appalled by a child she found hideous, Philyra begged the gods to free her from having to rear such an abomination. They heard her pleas and changed her into a peaceful, honey-sweet linden (lime) tree. The young Cheiron was emotionally wounded by his mother's desertion. He could have turned angry and belligerent, like the other centaurs, but instead he grew up to be gentle, caring, and wise in the arts of medicine, music, herbs, ethics, and archery.

Stepbrother to the Olympians, Cheiron was perhaps the wisest of them all. He became a surrogate parent and teacher to boys who grew up to be among Greece's greatest mythic heroes, including Heracles, the physician Asclepius, Achilles, Jason, Aeneas, and others. Even the god Apollo is said to have been his student for a brief time.

In another version Philyra did not detest her son, nor was she transformed into a linden tree. Instead she lived with Cheiron in his cave on Mount Pelion, enjoying her son's kindness and wisdom. Cheiron was eventually made into the constellation Sagittarius by Zeus.

Above: This painting by Italian artist Parmigianino (1503–1540) shows Cronus transformed into a horse to catch Philyra.

Some art historians believe that Goya's inspiration for his painting of Saturn was an early 17th-century painting of the same subject by the great Flemish artist Peter Paul Rubens (1577–1640). Around 1636, Rubens, who was a favorite of the kings of both Spain and England, was commissioned by King Philip IV of Spain to paint some 60 oil sketches based on Ovid's *Metamorphoses*. Despite his old age and ill health, Rubens completed the commission within a couple of years, and the paintings were hung at the Torre de la Parada, the royal hunting lodge outside Madrid. His *Saturn Devouring a Son* is from that series.

Comparing masterpieces

Although both Goya's and Rubens's paintings of Saturn eating his child are disturbing, each treats the subject matter differently. Rubens's Saturn is a one-dimensional monster who appears as if he were out on a stroll and had stopped momentarily to wolf down a child in the same way that he might wolf down a pastry. There is anguish in the painting, which comes solely from the face of the poor child.

Goya's *Saturn*, on the other hand, is far more complicated and nightmarish. Toward the end of his life, when the painting was made, Goya was profoundly deaf, a widower, and had retired from public life. During this lonely time he painted for his own home a series of works that have little tonal contrast and are overwhelmingly dark in color and theme. The series is known as Goya's "black paintings," of which *Saturn* is the most famous. Many interpretations have been applied to the painting, from a political commentary on Spain during the Napoleonic era to a lament for the death of the artist's own children—his wife had numerous miscarriages and stillbirths, leaving only one son surviving out of around 20 pregnancies—yet no definitive explanation exists. What is clear is that Goya's *Saturn* is not without emotion. By covering the lower portion of his face, it is arguable that the eyes of Saturn express very human emotions such as pain, shock, and despair. As with all truly great art, Goya's *Saturn* allows viewers to see a part of themselves in the painting, a part some viewers might rather leave unacknowledged.

KATHLEEN JENKS

Bibliography

Hesiod, and M. L. West, trans. *Theogony* and *Works and Days*. New York: Oxford University Press, 2008.

Howatson, M. C. *The Oxford Companion to Classical Literature*. New York: Oxford University Press, 2005.

SEE ALSO: Aphrodite; Demeter; Furies; Gaia; Hestia; Oceanus; Saturn; Titans; Uranus; Zeus.

CUPID

Cupid was the Roman god of love. Also known as Amor, he was the Roman counterpart of the Greek god Eros. His name was derived from the Latin *cupido*, meaning "desire."

Cupid was the son of Venus, goddess of love. Some accounts give his father as Mercury, the winged messenger of the gods, while others say that Cupid was the result of Venus's love affair with Mars, god of war. The Romans usually depicted him as a winged child, or baby, carrying a bow and a quiver full of arrows. He was also occasionally depicted as a beautiful adolescent, with or without wings. Sometimes he was shown wearing armor. This may be a reference to his paternity, or to draw a parallel between warfare and love, or to suggest the invincible power of love.

From his birth Cupid was an essential part of Venus's retinue, firing his arrows to inflame both men and women with passion. Since Venus (the Roman counterpart of the Greek goddess Aphrodite) was a notoriously jealous and spiteful goddess, it is not surprising that Cupid was portrayed as a willful and mischievous child, delighting in the complications that sometimes arise from sudden passion. However, unlike his mother, he was more often playful than malicious, although in some stories he did show a spiteful side.

According to the Roman poet Horace, Cupid's arrows were sharpened on a grindstone dampened with blood. In myth, Cupid had two different kinds of arrows. His leaden arrows filled their target with a fugitive, sensual desire that merely needed to be satisfied, while his golden arrows inspired a more spiritual and lasting love. In Shakespeare's play *A Midsummer Night's Dream*, Hermia makes a promise to her lover Lysander: "I swear to thee, by Cupid's strongest bow,/By his best arrow with the golden head,/By the simplicity of Venus' doves,/By that which knitteth souls and prospers loves."

Left: Cupid (1807) by Denis-Antoine Chaudet (1763–1810) holds a butterfly by its wings. The butterfly may symbolize Psyche or the torment Cupid brings to the human soul.

Cupid is a Romanized version of the Greek god Eros, but he lacks much of the latter's elemental energy. According to Hesiod's *Theogony*, Eros was present at the creation of the world and was one of the first beings. For the Greeks, therefore, Eros was not just the god of sensual or romantic love, he was also a primordial force without which life itself was not possible. This Greek sense of the immense power of Eros as a creative principle, which could wreak havoc as easily as it brings harmony, is almost entirely absent from the figure of Cupid as imagined in Roman and later times.

Cupid and Psyche

The most famous myth about Cupid is the tale of Cupid and Psyche, as told by the Roman writer Lucius Apuleius (c. 124–c. 170 CE) in his *Metamorphoses* (also known as *The Golden Ass*).

Psyche was one of three daughters of a king and queen. All three were fair, but Psyche's beauty was so astonishing that people flocked to marvel at her and sing her praises. As they did so they forgot to worship Venus, and her temples and altars were neglected. The goddess was enraged and determined to punish Psyche for her presumption. She called her son Cupid and ordered him to punish Psyche by making her fall in love with an unworthy being. However, when Cupid saw Psyche he was so struck by her beauty that he fell in love with her himself.

Psyche's two sisters married, but Psyche remained single. It seemed that, while everyone admired her, no mortal fell in love with her. This distressed both Psyche and her parents. They consulted an oracle who told them to take her to the top of a high mountain, where a monster would take her for its wife. Although her parents were devastated, Psyche decided to submit to her fate.

As she waited fearfully for the monster to arrive, she was lifted into the air by Zephyr, the west wind, who placed her in a flowery grove, where she fell asleep. On waking, she discovered that she was near a marvelous palace, which was far richer and more beautiful than any earthly one.

A disembodied voice spoke in her ear. It told her that the palace belonged to her and that invisible servants would obey all her commands. After bathing and eating, she went to bed. In the night someone whom she knew was her husband came to her, but she could not see him. Night after night her husband continued to come, but he always arrived in the dark and left before dawn.

Psyche fell in love and begged her husband to reveal himself to her. He refused, asking why she needed to see him: did she doubt his love? Psyche was calmed, but despite

---

Cupid and Ovid

There are numerous references to Cupid and his escapades in Latin poetry and literature. The great poet Ovid, writing at the time of Emperor Augustus (63 BCE–14 CE), features Cupid in his witty and cynical manual of seduction, *The Art of Love*, and in his famous poem *Metamorphoses*.

In *The Art of Love* Cupid is characterized as a willful child: "Cupid indeed is obstinate and wild,/A stubborn god; but yet the god's a child:/Easy to govern in his tender age."

In *Metamorphoses* Cupid plays a crucial role in Ovid's version of the tale of Daphne and Apollo (Roman, Phoebus): "Daphne, the daughter of a River God/was first beloved by Phoebus, the great God/of glorious light. 'Twas not a cause of chance/but out of Cupid's vengeful spite that she/was fated to torment the lord of light."

Phoebus mocks Cupid as a mere boy using the bow and arrow that are the preserve of men and gods, but Cupid is confident in his own power and takes his revenge for the god's mockery: "To him, undaunted, Venus' son replied;/'O, Phoebus, thou canst conquer all the world/with thy strong bow and arrows, but with this/small arrow I shall pierce thy vaunting breast.'"

Cupid fires an arrow of desire into the breast of the god, and an arrow inspiring loathing into Daphne's. The god pursues the unwilling nymph, who escapes only when her prayers are answered and she is transformed into a laurel tree.

Ovid's work has influenced many authors, including Milton and Shakespeare. Mythological allusions in the writings of the Renaissance period and modern times are often traceable to the Roman poet.

---

her love for her husband she felt increasingly sad at the thought of her parents and sister. Finally, she persuaded her reluctant husband to allow her sisters to visit her.

The sisters were consumed with envy when they saw Psyche's palace and its riches. They feigned concern, saying that she might be married to the monster the oracle had predicted, and they eventually persuaded her that she must discover her husband's true shape.

At their prompting, Psyche took to bed with her a knife to kill the monster and an oil lamp. She leaned over her husband to discover his face and found not a monster, but a beautiful, winged young man. As she gazed adoringly at him, a drop of oil fell from the lamp in her trembling hand and awoke him. Without a word, her husband flew away. Psyche tried to follow but fell to the ground. Her husband returned to tell her that he was the god of love, and that although he would not punish her for her lack of trust, he would have to leave her forever. Psyche went to her sisters, who pretended to grieve but secretly hoped to become Cupid's new wife. They jumped from mountains, expecting the west wind to bear them off, but instead they were dashed to pieces on the rocks. Psyche wandered the earth, forlornly searching for Cupid. She met the goddess Ceres (Demeter), who told her that there was no remedy but to beg Venus's forgiveness. At her temple, Venus received her angrily, and set her to various difficult and dangerous trials. Psyche succeeded in completing all the tasks because animals and plants pitied her plight and helped her.

Below: Cupid and Psyche, *painted by English painter John Roddam Spencer Stanhope (1829–1908). The god was originally sent to punish Psyche, but fell in love with the beautiful mortal and eventually wed her.*

The suspicious Venus gave Psyche one final task: she had to descend to hell and bring back in a box some of the beauty that only Ceres' daughter Persephone could bestow. Again Psyche despaired, but again she received unexpected help: the tower from which she intended to throw herself spoke and gave her instructions on how to fulfill the task. There was only one condition—Psyche must not look inside the box.

Persephone gave Psyche the box and she hurried back. Once again, her curiosity got the better of her and she opened the box. However, it did not contain beauty, but sleep. Psyche immediately fell into a deep sleep.

Cupid, meanwhile, had recovered from the wound caused by the hot oil. He longed for Psyche and began looking for her. When he found her sleeping he gathered up the sleep from her eyes and replaced it in the box so that she could give it to Venus.

Above: Venus Blindfolding Cupid *(c. 1565), painted by Venetian artist Titian (c. 1489–1576). Venus is being watched by two nymphs.*

While Psyche hastened toward Venus, Cupid flew up to heaven and begged Jupiter to help him. Jupiter persuaded Venus to forgive Psyche and Cupid. Psyche was brought up to heaven, where she was given a cup of ambrosia to make her immortal. She and Cupid were united in marriage, and in time she bore him a daughter named Pleasure.

Meaning of the myth

Apuleius's account is the only written source for the story of Cupid and Psyche, but it was depicted in earlier wall paintings and other images, which suggests that Apuleius was embellishing a much earlier and possibly widespread myth. In these images Psyche is often shown as a winged girl playing with Cupid. In Greek, *psyche* means both "soul" and "butterfly."

The myth may be an allegory about the struggle of the soul, the reflection of pure beauty, which is chained to the earth by its base passions—in particular, curiosity. Only after undergoing various difficult trials can the soul support the sight of pure beauty. And it is love (as embodied by Cupid) that helps the soul to reach its goal—the divine world of ideas.

Cupid in modern times

Today Cupid is one of the best-known of the ancient mythological figures. He has featured in visual art and in poetry from ancient times to the present.

In painting, from the Renaissance on, Cupid is shown either as a beautiful, winged youth accompanying his mother Venus or firing his mischievous arrows, or as a winged cherub, equally mischievous but more sentimental. In early Renaissance allegorical paintings Cupid is sometimes shown in almost devilish guise as a warning against the temptations of the flesh.

In modern times Cupid has entirely lost any powers suggestive of the sacred or the divine. Instead he is invoked as an aid to sentimental love in popular music, portrayed as a Kewpie doll or greeting card figure, and incorporated into the domain names of Internet dating agencies.

PETER CONNOR

Bibliography

Burr, Elizabeth, trans. *The Chiron Dictionary of Greek and Roman Mythology: Gods and Goddesses, Heroes, Places, and Events of Antiquity.* New York: Chiron Publications, 1994.

Craft, M. Charlotte. *Cupid and Psyche.* New York: William Morrow and Company, 1996.

SEE ALSO: Aphrodite; Eros; Jupiter; Venus.

DEMETER

Demeter was the goddess of corn and cultivation, and as such one of the most important deities in the Greek pantheon. The central story in Demeter's mythology involves the abduction of her daughter and its implications for the earth's harvests.

In Greek mythology the goddess Demeter was one of the original 12 Olympians and a sister of Zeus. As part of her duties, she ensured that the earth was fruitful and watched over the growth of crops. She also taught Triptolemus of Eleusis the secrets of cultivation so that he could in turn teach the rest of the world how to farm. To honor the goddess, the ancient Greeks performed two different rituals: the Thesmophoria festival, in which only women participated, and the Eleusinian Mysteries, which was a secret ceremony that in part may have reenacted the story of Demeter's search for her daughter Persephone, also known as Kore ("the Girl").

The abduction of Persephone

Most stories about Demeter concern the myth involving her search for and reunion with her favorite daughter, Persephone. One day Persephone, the daughter of Zeus and Demeter, was gathering flowers with her companions in the fields of Sicily, when suddenly the ground near them opened up. Hades, ruler of the underworld and Persephone's uncle, emerged from the gaping hole riding in a golden chariot. He seized the young goddess. Persephone cried out, but only three deities heard her: Helios, the sun god, who always saw everything; Hecate, the mysterious goddess of the dark side of the moon; and Demeter, who rushed to help her daughter but was too late.

Demeter wrapped a black veil over her head, threw a dark cloak over her shoulders, and roamed the earth looking for Persephone. She continued her search for nine days, carrying torches (a symbol of both funerals and mystery rites), until finally she consulted her other daughter, Hecate, who admitted that she too had heard Persephone's cry but did not know who took her. Together the goddesses conferred with Helios. He pointed the finger squarely at Zeus, who, he informed them, had awarded Persephone to Hades.

Left: Art historians believe that this Carthaginian terracotta mask was meant to symbolize the goddess Demeter. The mask dates from the third or second century BCE.

Demeter and Triptolemus

Triptolemus was a mortal from Eleusis who was favored by Demeter and taught other mortals how to cultivate crops, particularly corn. In early versions of the Demeter myth, Triptolemus was merely an honored citizen of Eleusis, but later stories have him either as the eldest or youngest son of King Celeus. As the youngest son his story was the same as that of Demophon, the royal infant Demeter tried to make immortal by burning away his mortality. The goddess taught the adult Triptolemus how to cultivate crops, gave him a supply of corn, and instructed him to travel around the world teaching others how to farm. To aid him in his travels Demeter awarded Triptolemus a chariot drawn by two winged dragons.

Triptolemus featured in several myths following his gifts from Demeter, and in two he had to be rescued by the goddess because he was nearly killed by men jealous of his chariot and knowledge. He also founded the city of Antheia, named in honor of a boy who was killed while trying to drive Triptolemus's dragon-powered chariot.

Below: This vase painting depicts the goddess Demeter (right) giving Triptolemus a vessel of corn. Triptolemus sits on his winged chariot.

Demeter in Eleusis

Zeus's involvement overwhelmed Demeter with anger and grief. She left Mount Olympus and disguised herself as an old woman, wandering aimlessly about the earth in despair over her lost daughter. By chance she strayed near the city of Eleusis, in Attica, which at that time was ruled by the wise King Celeus. Demeter stopped to rest at a popular watering hole called the Maiden's Well, which was shaded by a large olive tree. As the despondent goddess sat by the well, the daughters of the king came upon her. They pitied the old woman and invited her to the royal palace.

At the palace none of the girls was able to brighten Demeter's mood or please her in any way. One of the servants, Iambe (from whose name comes the term *iamb* for a metrical foot in poetry and verse), found a stool for Demeter to sit on. The servant woman tried buffoonery, lewd jokes, and even obscene gestures to lighten the goddess's spirits, but nothing worked. Eventually Iambe gave the sad visitor a special drink, called *kykeon*, made of water, barley, and mint. The drink cheered Demeter, and for the first time since Hades had abducted Persephone, the goddess lifted her head and smiled.

Above: *The ancient Greeks believed that winter ended when the goddess Demeter, depicted on the left in this late-19th-century painting by Frederick Leighton (1830–1896), was reunited with her daughter Persephone, shown being carried up from the underworld by Hermes.*

Metaneira, the wife of Celeus, believed, like the rest of Eleusis, that Demeter was merely a lonely old woman. Hearing that the visitor's mood had improved, Metaneira offered the goddess employment as nurse to her infant son, Demophon (or Triptolemus; see box, page 67).

Demeter's temple

Demeter appreciated the kindness she had been shown and decided to make Demophon immortal by performing a secret ritual. Every night, when all the people of the palace were asleep, the goddess would take the baby, smear him with ambrosia (the food of the gods), breathe on him with her divine breath, then hold him in the fire of the hearth to burn away his mortal parts.

These secret rites went on for several nights until one night the queen crept into the nursery at the very moment the goddess held the infant in the flames. The queen screamed in horror at the sight, waking everyone in the palace. Demeter, angry at the interruption, resumed her divine form and ordered Metaneira and the people of Eleusis to build her a great shrine in the city. When the temple was completed, Demeter moved in and stayed there for a year, refusing to return to Mount Olympus. During this time the goddess neglected to perform her duties, and as a consequence the earth grew barren. Soon mortals everywhere were starving.

Demeter's reunion with Persephone

Because of Demeter's failure to produce crops, Zeus feared for the existence of humankind. He sent the gods one by one to placate Demeter, but the only thing that would appease her was the return of Persephone. Finally Zeus was forced to relent, and he ordered Hades to set Persephone free. Hades agreed, but before he permitted Persephone to leave, he tricked her into eating a few pomegranate seeds. Since she had eaten in the underworld, Persephone was bound to stay there forever and had to remain Hades' wife.

When Zeus found out about Persephone's permanent tie to the underworld, he proposed a compromise between Demeter and Hades. Since Persephone had eaten only four seeds, Zeus decided that she should stay with Hades in the underworld for four months of the year; the remaining eight months she could live with her mother in the land of the living. These comings and goings of the daughter, along with the reactions of the mother, are reflected in seasonal changes. Winter, when the land is barren, symbolized the four months when Persephone lived with Hades, and the rest of the year, when the crops were cultivated and the seeds grew, she was with Demeter.

Eleusinian Mysteries and Thesmophoria

The story of Demeter and Persephone represented the annual process of birth, growth, death, and rebirth inherent within nature. To commemorate the story and to honor the goddess for bestowing on mortals the wisdom of agriculture, the Greeks practiced the Eleusinian Mysteries. It is thought that the ritual was performed annually for nearly two thousand years, ending in 395 CE when the temple at Eleusis was destroyed. Anyone who spoke Greek and had not committed murder could become an initiate into the sacred mysteries, with the stipulation that he or she never reveal the secrets learned during the ceremony.

These mysteries, historians believe, included the sacrifice of pigs, a procession from Athens to Demeter's temple at Eleusis marked by "iambic" obscenities and verbal abuse, and a ritual within the temple viewed only by initiates. The psychological effect of the celebration was enhanced, it seems, by the drinking of the sacred drink *kykeon*, which may have had other ingredients besides water, barley, and mint, that induced intoxication, hallucinations, and other psychedelic effects. The ritual also appears to have included a dramatic reenactment of the story of the abduction and surrender of Persephone. Chroniclers recorded that initiates emerged from the ceremony filled with joy and hope for a better life after death.

In the Peloponnese the celebration was performed differently. There the Greeks tended to emphasize a darker side to Demeter's character. They believed that Demeter was angry that she had to surrender herself constantly to the fertilizing power of Poseidon, the god of water, and as a result she had to be convinced to set aside her anger. How she was convinced is not known.

Another ceremony, although not secret, was open to women only. The Thesmophoria festival was a five-day agricultural celebration, during which women danced, feasted, and made sacrifices to Demeter. The women believed that they were securing the goddess's blessings, ensuring both their own fertility and that of the community's fields.

KIRK SUMMERS

Bibliography
Agha-Jaffar, Tamara. *Demeter and Persephone: Lessons from a Myth.* Jefferson, NC: McFarland and Company, 2002.
Foley, Helene P. *The Homeric Hymn to Demeter.* Princeton, NJ: Princeton University Press, 1994.
Kerenyi, Karl, and Ralph Manheim, trans. *Eleusis.* Princeton, NJ: Princeton University Press, 1991.

SEE ALSO: Hades; Persephone; Zeus.

DIANA

Diana was originally an ancient Italian goddess of the hunt, but the Romans later attributed to her many of the myths and characteristics of the Greek goddess Artemis. A cult dedicated to Diana was centered on a grove at Aricia, near Lake Nemi, between Rome and Naples.

Many Indo-European cultures had a goddess of the hunt. The Greek version was Artemis, and her main characteristics and the greatest of her powers were taken up by the Romans and ascribed to their own deity, Diana. However, Diana also had some unique traits of her own.

The name Diana probably means "bright one." The first syllable (di-) may come from an Indo-European word meaning "to shine."

Diana was closely identified with the moon, which she personified in all its phases—waxing, full, and waning. Because the human female cycle of ovulation, like the phases of the moon, occupies a 28-day period, Diana also became the goddess of women in pregnancy and childbirth. She was responsible for young maidens' success in marriage, but not for love and sex, which were ruled by Venus.

Diana was, in addition, the protectress of wild animals—this did not conflict with her responsibilities for the hunt, because she looked after young and pregnant creatures, neither of which are hunted as game.

Divine trinity
Diana is described both as a wife and as a daughter of Jupiter (Zeus). She became closely associated with two other deities, and together they formed a trinity. One was the water nymph Egeria, who became Diana's servant and assistant midwife after the death of Egeria's lover, Numa Pompilius, the second king of Rome. According to legend, Egeria cried so much at his loss that Diana turned her into an eternal spring of water.

The other member of the trio was Virbius, a shadowy figure in the Roman pantheon, who was either Diana's servant or her husband. He is thought to have been a reincarnation—his name means "twice a man"—of Hippolytus, the son of Theseus and Antiope. Hippolytus was wrongly accused of rape and cursed by his father. The sea god Poseidon responded to the curse by causing Hippolytus to fall from his chariot. He became entangled in the reins and was dragged to his death by his horses. Because of the way Hippolytus (Virbius) died, most scholars believe that horses were banned from the temple of Diana, although some have suggested that they were

Right: This sculpture of Diana shows the goddess within both her temple (above her head) and an oak tree (below her waist).

Above: In this 17th-century painting by Luca Giordano (1632–1705), Diana falls in love with the sleeping shepherd Endymion.

used as sacrifices. With the exception of Virbius, men were denied entry to Diana's hallowed ground: the goddess had no interest in them, and they might have had a bad influence on women.

How Diana reached Italy

Most temples to Diana were built in groves of oak trees, which were particularly sacred to the goddess. The most famous, and possibly the first, shrine to her was at Aricia (modern Ariccia, Italy) in a grove on the shores of a lake known then as Speculum Dianae ("Diana's Mirror"), and now as Lake Nemi.

The exact date of the temple's foundation is unknown, but it was said to have been built in the aftermath of the Trojan War in the 12th or 13th century BCE. At the start of the conflict between Greece and Troy, Iphigeneia, the eldest daughter of Agamemnon, King of Troy, and his queen, Clytemnestra, had been offered as a sacrifice to the goddess Artemis. At the last minute, however, Artemis substituted a deer for Iphigeneia on the altar, and

transported the maiden to the land of the Taurians in the Cimmerian Chersonese (part of the Crimea, in modern Ukraine). There Iphigeneia served Artemis as a priestess, in which role she was required to sacrifice anyone who landed on the shores of the island. She carried out her duties until one day she recognized a newly arrived traveler as her long-lost brother, Orestes. Joyfully reunited, the pair plotted their escape. They killed King Thoas of the Chersonese and fled to Italy, where Orestes built a shrine at Aricia in thanksgiving for their deliverance. In time, the goddess who had inspired the shrine became known as Diana Nemorenis (Diana of the Woods) instead of Artemis.

This myth is important because it connects Diana with the earlier Greek deity, and it also indicates that human sacrifices were made to her. Although there is no firm evidence of such sacrifices, and although the Iphigeneia story could mean that Artemis/Diana was opposed to such practices, persistent rumors that sacrifices might have taken place both maintain Diana's mystique and cast a shadow over her reputation. Like Virbius, Diana is an ambivalent deity: fundamentally good, but with a hint of menace.

Another tradition that developed at Aricia was that of Rex Nemorensis or "King of the Grove." Historians believe that the figure may well have been a version of the Green Man, or forest spirit, a common figure in European mythology. Rex Nemorensis, who was supposedly a runaway slave or a fugitive, was the goddess's priest and guardian of the grove. He was obliged to reassert his right to his position annually by a ritual fight to the death with an opponent, who would challenge him by plucking a golden bough from the sacred oak. It is on this legendary ritual that Scottish anthropologist James Frazer based the title of his monumental book on comparative mythology *The Golden Bough* (1890–1915).

The golden bough was reputed to open the passageway to the underworld, and, as such, was sought by Aeneas for his descent in Book Six of the *Aeneid*, the epic poem by Virgil (70–19 BCE). The bough in question was mistletoe, a plant that grows on the oak, and was sacred to the druids, the priests of the ancient Celts.

The oak figures in Celtic lore as the Cosmic Tree, which marks the shaman's gateway to his trance. The Greek word for oak (*drys*) is related to the word for "door." (In Old Irish, both are called *dair*.) It is also related to the word for "tree." (The oak was believed to be the first tree.)

Diana in literature and art
In most works of art, Diana is depicted indulging in one of two main activities: consorting with a sisterhood of nymphs around pools and springs, or racing with them through the forest in pursuit of wild game. She often wears a short tunic that seductively exposes her legs or shoulders, and she carries a quiver of arrows on her back. She is usually accompanied by a hound or an antlered stag, her traditional familiars.

Such images are derived from several earlier legends of Artemis. In Asia Minor, for example, Artemis had been known as Lady of the Beasts, and was depicted giving birth to various wild animals. Animals play a large role in myths related to Artemis. When the hunter Actaeon surprised Diana and her nymphs while they were bathing, Artemis was so angered by his intrusion that she turned him into a stag, although his mind remained human. He fled into

the forest, pursued by his wolflike hunting hounds, which eventually caught him and tore him to pieces.

The symbolism of this myth is complex, and obscure. Petroglyphs, carvings or inscriptions on rocks, dating from as early as the third millennium BCE document the hunter as animal-man, identified with and empowered by the spirits of particular animals. It is through these animal "friends" that the hunter attained the wild nature needed to guide him in the hunt. To kill the animal, the hunter needed to become totally familiar with its habits and to identify with its spirit. Ritual ceremonies ensured that the hunter would make a good kill, helped protect him from the potential anger of Nature, and sought the renewal and fertility of the

Right: This painting (1867) by Pierre-Auguste Renoir (1841–1919) depicts Diana the huntress with Actaeon in the form of a dead stag.

Above: This watercolor painting, Lake Nemi *(1818), is by English artist J. M. W. Turner (1775–1851).*

Other Temples to Diana

In addition to the shrine at Aricia, there were numerous other temples to Diana throughout the ancient Roman world. One of the most famous was built on Mount Tifata (modern Monte Maddaloni, north of the Italian town of Capua). The mountain's ancient name indicates that a grove of holm oaks once grew on it. This has led some commentators to conclude that, long before the mountain was taken over by followers of the goddess, it had been a cult sanctuary of the druids, whose name is derived from *drys*, the Greek word for their sacred oak tree.

According to legend, Mount Tifata was originally dedicated to Diana by the Roman dictator Egerius Baebius (or Laevius) of Tusculum, during the time of the Latin League, a confederation of various peoples of central Italy from the sixth to fourth century BCE. Partly in an effort to control this politico-religious movement, Servius Tullius, the sixth king of Rome (578–534 BCE), relocated the cult to Rome, where he established its new headquarters and decreed the construction of the specially designed Temple of Diana on Aventine Hill. In this poor area of the capital city, the main worshipers would have been the lower classes and female slaves. Female slaves were one of Diana's responsibilities: Diana was their patroness, and they could claim asylum in her temples. The festival of Diana was held every year on the Ides of August (August 13).

animal species. The hunter "begged permission" of the animal's spirit to be allowed to hunt it. Rituals such as these have been practiced by many hunting peoples through the ages, including Native Americans and Aborigines. Animals that served as guides, such as the horse, the wolf, and the bear (all of which have been associated with Diana), were not usually hunted, or if they were, they were objects of sacrificial offerings, as on occasion was the hunter.

Later, Diana figured in various occult practices. In alchemy she represented the conjunction of Luna and Sol, the moon and the sun. As goddess of the moon she was linked to Hecate, the patroness of black magic and witchcraft. According to Gnostic, or occult, Christian heresy, her "shining" persona as Lucina was divided from its opposite, darkness, to produce Lucifer, the devil.

CARL RUCK

Bibliography

Bulfinch, Thomas. *Bulfinch's Mythology.* New York: Barnes & Noble, 2006.

Hamilton, Edith. *Mythology: Timeless Tales of Gods and Heroes.* New York: Grand Central, 2011.

SEE ALSO: Apollo; Artemis; Jupiter; Pan.

DIONYSUS

Dionysus was the Greek god of wine, and, among other things, vegetation and human emotion. Worshiped throughout the Hellenic world, he was particularly honored with a major festival in Athens. He was believed to be the resident god at Delphi during the winter months when Apollo was away.

Dionysus was the son of Zeus and Semele, a mortal daughter of Cadmus, King of Thebes. When Hera, the wife of Zeus, found out that Semele was pregnant with her husband's child, she was consumed with jealousy and devised a plot to destroy the girl. Disguising herself as an old nursemaid, she persuaded Semele to ask her lover to show himself to her in all his divine glory. When Zeus promised Semele he would grant all her wishes, she asked to see him as he appeared on Mount Olympus. Knowing in advance the frightful consequences of complying with this request, Zeus tried to deny Semele her wish, but she insisted. Zeus drew himself up to his full height, thunder echoed around him, and lightning flashed from his body. Semele was at once destroyed by the divine fire.

Born from his father's thigh
Zeus did not want his child to die with its mother, so he snatched the unborn baby from the ashes of Semele's body and sewed the child into his own thigh. In time, Zeus gave birth to his twice-born son. Dionysus was therefore known as the god of double birth, because he had been reborn from the body of Zeus. Although half mortal, Dionysus was made wholly divine from the time of his birth, because the mortality of his mother had been burned away in the flash of Zeus's lightning.

Hera's spite did not end there, however. She then ordered the Titans to eat the infant Dionysus. The Titans were an older generation of gods who had been defeated in battle and replaced by Zeus and the Olympians. They tore Dionysus limb from limb and had just started to cook him when Rhea, a Titan and fertility goddess, intervened and hid him, disguised as a girl, at the court of Athamas, king of Orchomenus in Greece. Hera then drove Athamas mad, so Dionysus had to find refuge elsewhere. He was eventually raised by mountain nymphs in Phrygia, a remote area of Asia Minor (part of modern Turkey), and later moved to eastern Thrace, another isolated region that bounds the Hellespont (the modern Dardanelles, the straits between the Aegean and the Black Sea).

This distance from civilization is crucial to the cult of Dionysus—he represented, more than anything, submission to the urge to "let oneself go," and to behave in a way that would be embarrassing if anyone else were watching. That explains his association with wine, an alcoholic drink that reduces inhibitions.

Once Dionysus had established his rites in this farflung corner of the Hellenic world, he brought them to the heart of Greece. Yet his cult always remained to some extent furtive, and he was generally worshiped in wild fields, mountains, and other remote places, away from the cities.

Dionysus and Art

Dionysus is a shadowy, ambivalent god whose followers flirt with drunkenness, insanity, and death. Because of the association between creativity and the abandonment of self-control, Dionysus has been attractive to artists through the ages. He is usually depicted as a bearded youth, wearing a crown of vines with grapes. Often he holds the *thyrsos*, a wand that is a fertility symbol, and a cup of wine. He is often accompanied by maenads (female acolytes) and goatlike deities—usually satyrs, but sometimes Silenus or the pipe-playing Pan.

Images of Dionysus are common on classical Greek vases. In Renaissance European art, Dionysus became more or less interchangeable with Bacchus, his Roman equivalent. Among the best-known depictions of Dionysus or Bacchus are by Michelangelo (1475–1564), Titian (c. 1489–1576), Caravaggio (1573–1610), Peter Paul Rubens (1577–1640), Nicolas Poussin (1594–1665), and Diego Velázquez (1599–1660).

Below: Bacchus and Ariadne *was painted from 1523 to 1524 by Titian, an artist of the Italian Venetian school.*

Women in particular followed him and his rituals, for thus they could escape from their domestic duties and live at one with nature. In time men too joined in these rites.

Honoring Dionysus

The followers of Dionysus were said to have many extraordinary powers. They could make fountains of water, milk, and wine spring from the earth. They could not be harmed by fire, which they carried in their hands or on their heads. The priest and other prominent worshipers would also carry a *thyrsos*, an ivy-twined wooden rod or staff tipped with a pinecone.

Celebrations in honor of Dionysus varied from time to time, but they would often involve hunting. Any wild animal that was caught would be torn apart with bare hands (a deed called *sparagmos*). Its blood would then be drunk, and its flesh eaten raw (a ritual known as *omophagia*). Through these rites it was thought the participants could become one with nature and take the god within them.

As a god of nature, Dionysus looked after the earth while Apollo (the sun god) was away for the winter;

Dionysus was responsible for bringing the crops back to life each spring. He represented such natural forces as the sap which rises in the trees and brings out their leaves; he caused the flowers to bloom and the fruits to come from them. Dionysus also inspired animals to mate and bring forth their young. When plants died off in the fall, people prayed to Dionysus that he would return nature to its bloom in the spring, and when the plants reappeared they thanked him for restoring nature.

God of wine

One of the plants Dionysus especially cared for was the grapevine, the source of wine. We are told that he taught the art of winemaking to an Athenian farmer named Icarius. When Icarius shared his new drink with his fellow farmers, they thought he had poisoned them and killed him. His daughter Erigone looked for him everywhere in vain until her dog Maera led her to her father's grave. In

Below: The image on the inside of this bowl from the fourth century BCE depicts Dionysus and one of his attendant maenads.

despair she hanged herself, while Maera jumped into a well and drowned. Dionysus was so angry at these events that he drove all Athenian girls mad, causing them to hang themselves as well. Finally, an annual festival for Dionysus was established at the time of the wine harvest. As part of the ceremonies young girls would swing on suspended ropes with platforms—according to legend, this was the invention of the swing.

Dionysus was also the god of human emotion. While Apollo represented thought and rational action, Dionysus cared for the opposite elements of the human soul—instinct and self-indulgence. Excitement and any feeling of freedom are inspired by this god.

Adventures of Dionysus

There are many legends associated with Dionysus. One story reports how he was once kidnapped by pirates. As they sailed over the seas, Dionysus suddenly revealed his true identity, causing a grapevine to grow from the ship's mast and a bear to appear suddenly on deck. He then turned himself into a lion. The terrified pirates jumped into the sea, but they did not drown: Dionysus changed them into dolphins. That is why dolphins are always friendly to humans, because they were once human themselves.

Another story of Dionysus is that he cared for Ariadne, a mortal princess who helped Theseus after he had slain the Minotaur in Crete. The thoughtless hero then abandoned her on the island of Naxos. Dionysus saw the frightened maiden on the shore and swept down to rescue her. He took her up to Mount Olympus and married her. He later changed her wedding crown into the constellation Corona Borealis.

The fate of those who denied Dionysus

Because Dionysus touched the mind in a special way, when he was angered by those who ignored him, he drove them mad. When he was honored, Dionysus was a most gentle god, but when dishonored, he was one of the most terrible divinities in the pantheon. To the Greeks, therefore, the crucial fact about Dionysus was that those who submitted to him—in other words, acknowledged the wild side of their own nature—would be rewarded with joy, while those who denied his power would be punished. Many stories show the god's vengefulness and extreme brutality to the impious. The most famous of these legends is set in Thebes. When Dionysus returned to the city in which he had been conceived, King Pentheus refused to honor him and tried to imprison him. Dionysus took swift revenge on the king and his city. First, he drove all the Theban women mad, sending them to the mountains as maenads, and made Agave, Pentheus's mother, their leader. Then Dionysus slowly maddened Pentheus as well. Persuading him to dress as a woman, he led the king to the mountains. There the women saw him spying on them from a pine tree and rushed to destroy him. Agave herself pulled down the tree and tore him apart with her bare hands. All the women joined in the violence. Thus Pentheus died for denying Dionysus. The god then restored Agave to sanity and made her realize what she had done. Agave had to go into exile forever, knowing that she had killed her own son.

Dionysus is also central to the myth of Hephaestus, god of fire and metalwork, who, having been thrown off Mount Olympus, landed on the island of Lemnos. There he stayed, unforgiven by his parents, Zeus and Hera. In time, however, the king and queen of the gods realized that they needed Hephaestus. So Dionysus descended to Lemnos, made the fire god drunk with wine, and led him back up to Olympus, where he was reconciled with his parents. Hephaestus then married Aphrodite, the goddess of love, and built for her a beautiful home with robots to do all the housework.

The Dionysia

A five-day festival known as the City Dionysia was held in Athens between the first quarter and the full moon of March (usually March 24–28). The festival marked the end of winter (the Dionysian part of the year) and the start of spring, the resurgence of Indestructible Life (Zöe).

The Dionysia began when a wooden image of Dionysus was taken from his principal temple in the city and replaced on the *eskhara* (hearth) of the temple near the Academy. There would be a ceremony comprising hymns and the sacrifice of a male goat to Dionysus. Following that ritual, there was a banquet and wine from the god. Then every morning for the next three days, three tragedies would be performed. These plays were based on myths known to every Greek, but each playwright told the familiar story in a different way. After the main event, a short and rowdy entertainment, called a satyr play, was staged. This cartoon-like retelling of another famous myth was intended to bring the audience out of the fear aroused by the tragedies, and prepare them for the comedy that evening. On the last day of the festival, judges awarded first, second, and third prizes to the playwrights whose tragedies had been performed.

Right: This vase, with an engraved image of Dionysus reclining on a couch during the grape harvest, was excavated at Pompeii, Italy.

Above: The theater of Dionysus on the hillside below the Acropolis in central Athens, Greece. Some of the most important plays in history were first performed in the amphitheater.

The rituals practiced by the Greeks for Dionysus were known as *orgia,* meaning "holy ceremonies." The followers of the god, the maenads, who as a group were called a *thiasos,* went to the mountains wearing unbelted robes and wearing crowns of ivy (some vase paintings also show crowns of snakes). They carried the *thyrsos,* and tamborines and drums to make music. They would dance wildly, then rush upon an animal to sacrifice it to the god. There was no priest or priestess to kill the victim, but the maenads themselves would tear the animal apart, drink its warm blood, and eat its raw flesh. By these rites they would become one with Dionysus.

Although many of the celebrations of Dionysus took place in remote locations, the most famous annual celebration of the god was held on the south slope of the Acropolis, in the center of Athens. This was the City Dionysia, a drama festival that was put on each spring. During this five-day event both tragedies and comedies were performed in a theater dedicated especially to the god. It was here that the plays of famous Greek dramatists, such as Sophocles, Aeschylus, Euripides, and Aristophanes

were first acted out—three tragedies in the morning, and a comedy in the evening. Although few of the plays were about Dionysus himself, they were all put on in his honor.

Dionysus in art

It was believed that when he set foot on earth, Dionysus was usually accompanied by small bands of satyrs. These creatures—half man, half goat—enjoyed drinking, chasing nymphs, and generally leading a wild, dissolute life. Many vase paintings from ancient Greece show the god with his crown of ivy, holding his *thyrsos,* and surrounded by attendant dancing satyrs.

Dionysus is the god most frequently shown in ancient art. Perhaps this is because he represents so many aspects of our world, including the plants that arise from the earth each spring, and the emotions of joy and excitement we all feel.

KARELISA HARTIGAN

Bibliography

Bulfinch, Thomas. *Myths of Greece and Rome.* New York: Penguin, 1998.

Howatson, M. C. *The Oxford Companion to Classical Literature.* New York: Oxford University Press, 2005.

SEE ALSO: Aphrodite; Hephaestus; Hera; Titans; Zeus.

DIS

Although there are few myths about Dis, and little evidence that he was widely worshiped, he remains one of the most important gods in the Roman pantheon because of his dual role as the god of death and the lord of the underworld.

The Romans identified Dis with the Greek god Pluton (Latin: Pluto), which is an alternative name for Hades. Hades was both the god of the underworld and the underworld itself. Dis was also equated with the pagan Italian god Orcus, and was at times identified with Soranus, a god of the Sabines, an ancient people who lived to the northeast of Rome. The name Dis is originally a contracted form of *dives*, the Latin for "riches," just as the name Pluton (or Plouton) is derived from the Greek word for "rich": *ploutos*. The element of "riches" in the names Dis and Pluto could suggest that Dis was originally a god of the fields, responsible for the wealth of the crops, which were sent up from underneath the earth. Alternatively, it might indicate that Dis is to be understood as a collector (rather than a giver) of wealth, since everyone who dies goes to Hades, often taking various valuables with them in their graves.

Dis as Hades

Although there are no known myths of Dis himself, Hades is so closely associated with him that the same stories are equally applicable to both deities. Hades, Zeus, and Poseidon were the sons of Cronus and Rhea. When Zeus ousted his

Below: The Last Judgment *(1541), by Italian painter Michelangelo (1475–1564), depicts the arrival of damned souls in the underworld.*

The Last Judgment

The idea of someone being judged after death on the life they have led on earth is an old one, predating Christianity. Romans believed in such a judgment, as murals painted in the tomb of a Sabine priest, Vincentius, and his wife, Vibia, demonstrate. Three murals, with explanatory inscriptions, depict the anticipated afterlife adventures of Vibia.

The first mural depicts Pluto carrying Vibia to the underworld in his four-horse chariot. In the second mural, Vibia appears in the company of Alcestis. In the same mural Mercury leads the two women toward the middle of the scene, where the lord of the underworld, Dispater ("Dis the father"), sits on a raised platform with Aeracura. Dispater stretches out his right hand toward a group of three goddesses, the Divine Fates. (In mythology, the Fates determine the length of human lives.)

This second mural has the solemn character of a judgment scene. Alcestis appears to be present as a character witness for Vibia, to testify that Vibia was as virtuous as she herself had been.

In the third mural, a "good angel" (*angelus bonus*) leads Vibia to a celestial banquet, where she sits with the other guests. She no longer wears her cloak over her head as in the previous scenes, but instead wears a wreath. In the foreground, two young men appear to be playing some game, emphasizing the carelessness of the scene, and to the far right a large amphora (wine jar) reminds us that there is wine to drink in the afterlife. The party that Vibia has joined is identified by an inscription as "those who have been chosen by the judgment of the good."

father, the three children divided the realms: Hades received the underworld, Zeus the sky, and Poseidon the sea.

In some works of art, Hades is envisaged as the judge in the Last Judgment (see box). The most famous myth associated with Hades, however, is the story of his niece, Persephone, whom he abducted to the underworld to be his wife. Persephone's mother, Demeter, was overcome with grief at her loss, and searched the world for her until Zeus, who had originally authorized the kidnapping, took pity on her and sent his messenger, Hermes, down to the underworld to fetch Persephone back. Persephone, however, had eaten in the underworld and therefore could never leave it. Although she was allowed partial freedom, she had to return below the earth for four or six months of every year. Her return to earth each year coincided with the start of spring. Thus Hades represents the attempt to thwart annual renewal.

Worship

Unusual for a Roman deity, Dis is associated with very few cults. It was believed by the Romans that the only way that it was possible to communicate with Dis was through oaths and curses, which were generally frowned on and discouraged. People sacrificed black animals to him, and they were always careful to look away while performing the sacrifice. The most common shrines for Dis or Pluto were the so-called Plutonia, which were said to mark entrances to the underworld.

According to legend, the servants of a Sabine named Valesius miraculously discovered a marble altar inscribed to both Dis and Proserpina (Persephone) at the edge of the Campus Martius (Field of Mars) near the Roman capital city. They found it at a depth of 20 feet (6 m) while they were digging to lay the foundations for an altar, following instructions given in dreams to the children of Valesius. In historic times, this altar was used for sacrifices during the Ludi Saeculares (Secular Games), an event held every century to avert the plague. An altar found in Rome in 1886–1887 underneath the Palazzo Cesarini was for a long time wrongly identified as the legendary altar of Dis and Proserpina. The real location of the altar must have been near the Vittorio Emanuele II bridge over the Tiber River, where fragmentary records of the Ludi Saeculares were unearthed in the 20th century.

Art

In the art from ancient Greece, the god Hades, or Pluton, is represented as a bearded figure with a strong familiar resemblance to his brother Zeus. He is usually depicted holding a scepter or a cornucopia (horn of plenty). Pluton should not be confused with the boy Plutus (or Ploutos), son of Demeter and Iasion, who played a role in the myth of the Eleusinian Mysteries, and is also frequently shown holding a cornucopia. Dis is represented only rarely in Roman art. When he does appear, he is usually shown in the company of his consort Aeracura, who is a Persephone-like figure. Dis does not appear in later art, while Pluto appears only in scenes of the abduction of Persephone.

FEYO SCHUDDEBOOM

Bibliography
Bulfinch, Thomas. *Myths of Greece and Rome.* New York: Penguin, 1998.
Howatson, M. C. *The Oxford Companion to Classical Literature.* New York: Oxford University Press, 2005.

SEE ALSO: Demeter; Fates; Hades; Persephone; Zeus.

EOS

Eos was the ancient Greek goddess of dawn. She took many mortal lovers, who usually suffered as a result of her attentions. The most famous was Tithonus, who was cursed to grow old while his divine lover remained young.

Eos was the daughter of Hyperion, who was associated with the sun, and Thea, both of whom were Titans, children of the sky god Uranus and the earth goddess Gaia. Eos's siblings included a brother, Helios, another solar deity, and a sister, Selene, goddess of the moon, which, like the sun, casts light on Earth.

In art, Eos has traditionally been depicted as a beautiful young woman with wings; like Helios and Selene, she is often shown driving a flying chariot. Her youth is probably a metaphor for the start of the day, and her ability to fly is probably a reference to the fact that dawn appears to start in the sky. She is commonly referred to as "rosy-fingered" in poetic descriptions of pink-tinted dawn.

Eternal lust

Eos was by nature sexually voracious, and her obsession was intensified after she had an affair with the god Ares. Another of Ares' lovers, the goddess Aphrodite, became jealous and cursed Eos with perpetual lust. Thereafter, Eos became insatiable and started to take men as well as gods as lovers. Mortals were usually not strong enough to rival gods, and thus tended to be the victims in any relationship between them. In one version of the story of Orion, Eos carried off the mortal hunter against his will; Artemis became jealous but was powerless to take revenge on her fellow goddess, so she killed Orion instead.

Eos also abducted Cephalus, whose wife, Procris, also became jealous. Procris hid in a bush to keep an eye on him while he was hunting. Cephalus heard rustling in the undergrowth, thought it had been made by an animal, and hurled a spear, killing her.

Among the many other mortal lovers of Eos was Kleitos, one of a family of soothsayers. Although he died, he did better than most out of his association with Eos, because he was granted the consolation of immortality. Not surprisingly, in view of the attendant dangers, mortal characters in myth were usually disinclined to mate with gods, but often they had no choice.

Above: The painting on this Roman vase (c.440–420 BCE) depicts Eos riding her chariot out of the sea.

As a result of her numerous affairs, Eos gave birth to many children. These included Phaethon, her son by Cephalus; he in turn was destined to be carried off by a goddess, in this case Aphrodite. Eos was also the mother of three wind gods, Zephyrus, Boreas, and Notus; their father was Astraeus, another child of the Titans.

Eos and Tithonus

The most famous story of Eos concerns her attraction to Tithonus. This man and his family suffered from an excess of good looks, for their beauty attracted the gods. One of

Above: Eos fell in love with Cephalus and carried him off to Olympus. This painting (1811) is by Pierre-Narcisse Guérin (1774–1833).

his brothers, Ganymede, was taken to Mount Olympus by Zeus; while Paris, the son of another brother, Priam, king of Troy, was seduced by the nymph Oenone. Most of the gods were perfect in their beauty, so when they seized mortals they naturally went only for specimens in the prime of life, and either immortalized them, as happened to Ganymede, or discarded them once they grew old.

Eos abducted Tithonus, and, pleased by her catch, not long afterward appealed to Zeus to grant him eternal life. Her wish was granted, to the letter, but unfortunately she had forgotten to request eternal youth for him as well. As a consequence, Tithonus could not die; but when he began to age, Eos refused to be with him any longer, and shut him away in a room, where he babbled endlessly to himself. Eventually he changed into a cicada whose chirps preserve the remnants of his once beautiful voice.

Tainted heredity

The son of Eos and Tithonus, Memnon, also met a tragic end. He became king of the Ethiopians and led them to defend his ancestral home of Troy against the Greek invaders during the Trojan War. In battle, Memnon killed Antilochus, a friend of Achilles, who then killed Memnon in revenge. Eos was grief-stricken and petitioned Zeus to immortalize her son. This time she phrased the request carefully to avoid the mistake she had made with his father.

The stories of Memnon and Achilles are very similar. Both have divine mothers and mortal fathers; both die at Troy; and Achilles is also immortalized at his mother's request. These heroes are likely to have derived from a common myth pattern, in which a mortal hero and a goddess sire a glorious son who dies young on behalf of his community, which then worships him as a god.

Indo-European roots

Many cultures conceive of natural phenomena—sunshine, rain, thunder, and so on—as gods or the manifestation of gods. In ancient India, the dawn goddess was called Usas; like Eos, she drove a flying chariot and was sexually aggressive. Usas was often described as having "reddish breath," a description that recalls "rosy-fingered," the epithet most commonly applied to Eos. These parallels are not coincidental, for the peoples of ancient Greece and ancient India seem to have descended in part from common Indo-European ancestors, and it is likely that the names Eos and Usas both derive from the same Indo-European root word meaning "dawn." The ancient Romans were also of Indo-European descent, and the Latin word *aurora* which, like the Greek *eos*, is used for

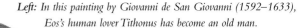

Left: In this painting by Giovanni de San Giovanni (1592–1633), Eos's human lover Tithonus has become an old man.

Roman religion. Roman poet Ovid (43 BCE–17 CE) seems to confirm this in *Metamorphoses*, in which he has Aurora remark: "I am lesser than all whom golden heaven holds, for my temples are very rare in all the world."

Yet, although Eos may never have been among the first rank of Greek deities, her very human frailties—particularly her indiscriminate lust for men and her devotion to her children—have made her an abiding favorite subject for writers and artists since antiquity. Greek painters and sculptors represented Eos both as a seductress and as a bereaved mother. These facets of her character are also revealed in Ovid's description of Aurora, who is jealous and spiteful in her dealings with Cephalus but tender and vulnerable when later confronted with the death of their son, Memnon.

The character of the Greek Eos and the Roman Aurora continued to inspire European artists from the Renaissance onward. One of the most famous paintings on this theme is *Cephalus and Aurora* by French master Nicolas Poussin (1594–1665), which recaptures the contrast between mortal revulsion and divine desire that animated Greek vases two thousand years earlier. Another famous painting, *Aurora*, is by Italian baroque classicist Guido Reni (1575–1642). The theme remained popular in the 18th century; one of the greatest works of that epoch is *Aurora* by French rococo painter Jean-Honoré Fragonard (1732–1806).

JIM MARKS

both the dawn and the goddess associated with it, seems also to be derived from the same Indo-European source.

The idea of a dawn goddess was not, however, uniquely Indo-European. In ancient West Asian myths, for example, the goddess Ishtar (or Inanna)—who was the daughter of either the sky god or the moon god—was associated with the morning star (the planet Venus), and, like Eos and Usas, preyed on mortal men. The Greeks came into contact with long-established West Asian cultures when they separated from Indo-European culture and settled in southeast Europe, probably sometime in the late third millennium BCE. Thus Eos is likely to have been a synthesis of Indo-European, West Asian, and indigenous Greek themes.

Rites of dawn

Unlike many of her relatives, lovers, and children, Eos has no known links to any specific religious rite. That does not necessarily mean that she was never worshiped formally—modern evidence for ancient Greek religion in general is sketchy at best—but it does suggest that she was at most a minor figure in the pantheon. The same seems to have been true of Aurora, the equivalent goddess of the dawn in

Bibliography
Bulfinch, Thomas. *Myths of Greece and Rome.* New York: Penguin, 1998.
Ovid, and A. D. Melville, trans. *Metamorphoses.* New York: Oxford University Press, 2008.

SEE ALSO: Ares; Helios; Selene; Titans.

EROS

According to one source, Eros, the Greek god of sexual love, was one of the earliest deities, created out of the primeval chaos. He was the catalyst for many famous romances and tragedies.

Several different versions exist of the origin and personality of Eros. He is either one of the first deities to have come into existence or a divine child of the goddess of love. He is portrayed either as a handsome young man or a mischievous cherub armed with a bow and arrows of love. The earliest version of the god's origins comes from the Greek poet Hesiod (fl. 800 BCE), whose epic *Theogony* told how Eros, Tartarus, and Gaia were born at the beginning of time out of the primeval chaos. Whereas Tartarus, the darkest and most horrible part of the underworld, and Gaia, the earth, represented places, Eros embodied an emotion—sexual love. According to Hesiod, after Uranus (sky) emerged from Gaia, Eros brought about the union of these two, who became the parents of the first generation of gods. Eros also presided over the subsequent marriages of their offspring and eventually of

Right: The painting on this fifth-century-BCE vase depicts Eros as a young, handsome archer, the common presentation of the god of love in the early years of classical Greece.

humans. Therefore, Hesiod's Eros has an all-important place as the instigator of divine love and passion.

Other versions have it that Eros was the son of Aphrodite, goddess of love, and either Hermes, messenger of the Olympians; Ares, god of war; or Zeus, ruler of the gods. Perhaps because of his Olympian parentage, Eros was depicted in early ancient Greece as being strong, handsome, and athletic. He was also regarded as the protector of homosexual love among men and adolescent boys. In Athens the metics, resident noncitizens of Greek city-states whose status lay between that of slaves and citizens, erected a statue on the Acropolis dedicated to the memory of two young men, Meles, a citizen, and Timagoras, a metic. According to the legend, Timagoras loved Meles, but Meles rejected Timagoras's affections and commanded the metic to leap to his death from the Acropolis. As soon as Timagoras did so, Meles was so overcome by remorse that he followed Timagoras and also jumped to his death. At the statue the metics built an altar to Anteros, who was sometimes seen as the mutual-love aspect of Eros or as Eros's brother and deity of mutual love.

The depiction of Eros as a child with wings began to appear later in ancient Greece and was developed further by the Romans, who called him Cupid or Amor. The cherub Eros tended to have a quiver full of two kinds of arrows: sharp and gold-tipped, and blunt and lead-tipped. The gold-tipped arrows kindled love, while the lead-tipped ones inspired loathing.

Eros in myths

Although Eros did not feature as a central figure in many myths, he was portrayed as the catalyst for several famous stories. One

Left: Eros is depicted as a winged child on this gold medallion, made between the late fourth and early third century BCE. It was discovered in Syria.

of the earliest stories concerning Eros tells how a group of powerful giants, under the leadership of Porphyrion, attacked Mount Olympus. Eros shot one of his arrows at the chief giant's liver, changing Porphyrion's anger and aggression to lustful love for Hera, wife of Zeus. Porphyrion then tried to rape Hera, but this enraged Zeus so much that he struck the giant dead with one of his mighty thunderbolts.

Another example was when Eros made the witch Medea fall in love with Jason when he was on his quest for the Golden Fleece. Hera and Athena, goddess of war, were wanting to aid Jason in his quest, and they asked Aphrodite for help. They convinced the goddess of love to order her winged son to shoot an arrow into Medea's heart. As soon as Eros's arrow found its mark, Medea (whose father, King Aeetes of Colchis, possessed the Golden Fleece) helped Jason and his Argonauts steal the fleece and flee Colchis.

A more tragic example of the god's powers involves the god Apollo and Daphne, a nymph. One day Apollo, who boasted of his expertise with the bow and arrow, ridiculed Eros's archery. In revenge, Eros secretly shot one of his gold-tipped arrows into Apollo, forcing him to fall in love with Daphne. At the same time, Eros shot a lead-tipped arrow into Daphne, causing her to reject Apollo's love. As the nymph fled from Apollo, she was transformed by her father, a river god, into a tree to escape his lustful clutches.

Eros and Helen of Troy

Perhaps the most famous example of Eros's intervention was when one of his arrows caused the Greek queen Helen to fall in love with Paris. After Paris, a Trojan prince, had chosen Aphrodite as the most beautiful goddess over Hera and Athena, the goddess of love promised Paris that he would have Helen as his mistress. Paris then visited Sparta, where Helen lived. Menelaus, king of Sparta and husband of Helen, entertained the Trojan prince but had to leave to bury his grandfather on Crete. While Menelaus was away, Eros shot his gold-tipped arrow into Helen's heart, forcing her to fall in love with Paris, and the couple fled to Troy. When Menelaus returned and learned what had happened, he gathered all the kings of Greece and set sail for Troy to retrieve his wife, thus starting the Trojan War.

Eros and Psyche

The most famous myth in which Eros appears as the central character is the romance between him and Psyche. The story comes from *Metamorphoses*, by Roman writer

Below: In this 16th-century painting, by Niccolò dell' Abbate (c. 1512–1571), Eros is depicted as a young man with his lover, Psyche.

Lucius Apuleius (c. 124–c. 170 CE). Psyche was so uncommonly beautiful that the populace ceased to worship Aphrodite (Venus) and turned their adoration to the beautiful mortal. However, Psyche longed not for divine adoration but for marriage. Nevertheless, Aphrodite could not bear the competition and ordered her son to make Psyche fall in love with the most odious creature he could find. Yet when Eros saw Psyche for himself, he too fell in love with her; he could not obey his mother's command. Instead he asked Apollo to give Psyche's father an oracle that she must be married to an evil spirit atop a certain mountain. The king obeyed, and Psyche was whisked off

Right: This Roman fresco, referred to as Punishment of Eros, *was uncovered from the ruins of a villa in Pompeii. It shows Eros (Cupid) as the winged child on the right, perhaps with his mother Aphrodite (Venus).*

Right: This Roman fresco, referred to as Punishment of Eros, *was uncovered from the ruins of a villa in Pompeii. It shows Eros (Cupid) as the winged child on the right, perhaps with his mother Aphrodite (Venus).*

to a beautiful palace. Inside the palace she was waited on by invisible hands and a gentle voice that told her she had nothing to fear. When night came, she went to bed, where she was joined by Eros in human form. He told her that he was her husband, and that she would enjoy the most blessed of lives if only she would refrain from finding out who he was or attempting to see him.

Although she loved both her mysterious husband and living in the palace, after a few days Psyche felt lonely. To cheer her up, Eros allowed her to be visited by her sisters. The sisters were jealous of Psyche's life and lied to her that they thought her shadowy husband was really an evil serpent. Believing her sisters, Psyche went to bed that night concealing a lantern and a dagger. After Eros had fallen asleep, she lit the lamp and held it up to his face, raising the dagger to murder him. As soon as she saw the beautiful features of her husband, she was so entranced that she let a drop of the lamp's hot oil fall down upon his shoulder, waking him. Realizing that Psyche now knew his true identity, Eros flew away.

Psyche's tasks

Psyche wandered everywhere in search of Eros, eventually ending up at Aphrodite's palace. The goddess admitted Psyche into the palace, but only on condition that the girl become her slave; Aphrodite then gave Psyche various near-impossible tasks to perform.

First she was made to organize a roomful of assorted grains before nightfall. A colony of ants that felt sorry for Psyche came to assist her by dividing the grains into piles. Afterward, Venus told Psyche to retrieve a tuft of wool from a flock of flesh-eating sheep. This time, a reed told her how to safely obtain the wool while the sheep were asleep. Next, Psyche had to fill a vessel with water from the Styx, the mythical river that separated the land of the dead from the land of the living. An eagle, which owed Eros a favor, arrived just in time and retrieved the water for her.

Psyche's final task was to obtain a jar from Persephone containing beauty. This meant that Psyche must die, because Persephone was the queen of the underworld. Psyche climbed a high tower, determined to leap to her death. The tower, however, spoke to her and gave her specific directions of how to fulfill her task without having to die. She entered the underworld by way of Taenarum in the southern tip of the Peloponnese. When she finally

arrived at Persephone's throne, the goddess gave her a tightly sealed jar in response to Aphrodite's request. Meanwhile Eros, who longed for Psyche, pleaded with Zeus for help, insisting that Psyche had been punished sufficiently. Zeus agreed.

Psyche had nearly reached the land of the living when her curiosity got the better of her. She opened the jar and was instantly overcome by a deathly sleep. Soon after, Eros found Psyche and brought her back to life. He then carried her to Mount Olympus, where the couple were given a marriage suitable for deities. Aphrodite put aside her anger, and Zeus made Psyche immortal. Shortly after, Psyche bore Eros a daughter, Voluptas, whose name means "pleasure."

BLAISE STAPLES

Bibliography

Apuleius, and Joel C. Relihan, ed. *The Tale of Cupid and Psyche.* Indianapolis, IN: Hackett, 2009.

Bulfinch, Thomas. *Bulfinch's Mythology.* New York: Barnes & Noble, 2006.

SEE ALSO: Aphrodite; Ares; Cupid; Hera; Hermes; Zeus.

FATES

The Fates (Moirai in Greek, and Parcae, or Fata, in Latin) were spirits whom the Greeks believed determined the course of each human life. They also influenced the destinies of other divine beings and helped the Olympian gods seize power from the Titans.

There are several accounts of the origins of the Fates, but all versions agree that they were early and venerable beings, with great authority. Eighth-century-BCE Greek poet Hesiod, in his history of the gods known as *Theogony*, offers two explanations of how the Fates came into existence. The first account tells how the Fates came into being at almost the very beginning of creation. From the primal void (Chaos) came four beings: Gaia (Earth), Erebus (Darkness, or the underworld), Eros (Love), and Nyx (Night). Nyx and Erebus mated to produce the Fates and the very similar Keres (Destinies), as well as Nemesis (Retribution), Pain, Blame, Sleep, Dreams, Aether (Brightness), and Day. The offspring of Nyx and Erebus were cousins of the Titans, who were the children of Gaia

and Uranus (the sky). This account was a way for the Greeks to explain and personify many of the abstract forces that governed their lives.

Other sources describe the Fates as the children of Cronus, the ruler of the Titans, or even of the primal void (Chaos) itself. However, in a later passage of *Theogony*, Hesiod offers yet another explanation—that the Fates are the offspring of Zeus, the ruler of the Olympian gods, and Themis, a Titan who later became recognized as the goddess of natural law. In this account, Themis gave birth to the Horae (Seasons): Eunomia (the Rule of Law), Dike (Justice), and Eirene (Peace), as well as to the Fates. Arguably, Hesiod's alternative explanation of the Fates' origin is less a contradiction of his previous version and more a way of bolstering the authority of the Olympian gods. The gods gained supremacy by defeating the Titans, who in turn had defeated the earliest beings. Therefore, for Zeus to be the father of the Fates suggests that the ascendancy of the Olympian gods was "fated"; in other words, part of the natural scheme of things rather than arbitrary.

Names, meanings, and roles

The Greeks thought of the Fates as three females, just as they did for other groupings of beings, such as the Graces, the Seasons, and the Gorgons. The first of the Fates was Clotho (the Spinner), the second was Lachesis (the Apportioner), and the third was Atropos (the Inevitable). These names reflect the Fates' roles in determining the course of events in human lives. Clotho spun the thread that made up an

Left: A statuette of Atropos, the third of the Fates, by Italian sculptor Pier Jacopo Alari Bonacolsi (1460–1528). The statuette's scissors, with which she cut the thread of destiny, have been lost.

Above: A medieval tapestry depicting the three Fates standing over a woman's soul. Clotho (right) spins the thread that represents the woman's life, Lachesis (middle) measures it, while Atropos (left) prepares to cut it.

individual's life; Lachesis measured the thread's length, determining the individual's lifespan; and Atropos cut the thread, representing both birth and death. The Greek name *Moirai* means "portion" or "allotment," indicating the

amount and nature of the life the Fates gave each person. The Latin *Parcae* means "bringers forth," suggesting the Fates' additional role in predicting an individual's future.

The Fates and the gods

The Greeks believed that the Fates were present at events of great significance for their gods and goddesses. For example, they were present at the births of Aphrodite,

Athena, and Dionysus, as well as at the wedding of Zeus and Themis—an occurrence that admittedly contradicts one of the stories of their origins. The Fates were also present at the abduction of Persephone by Hades. Persephone's disappearance and subsequent marriage to Hades enraged her mother, Demeter; according to one account, Zeus sent the Fates to soothe her anger and grief, and to help her accept her daughter's marriage.

The Fates played a part in the revolution by which the Olympian gods took power. They participated on the side of the gods in the war against the Titans and their half brothers the Giants, and they helped Zeus defeat Typhon, the monstrous dragon created by Gaia in her final attempt to oppose the takeover of the Olympians. The Fates tricked Typhon into eating some fruit, telling him it would provide strength. However, because Typhon had consumed mortal food, he became weakened. Zeus was thus able to destroy the dragon and bury him beneath Mount Etna.

The Fates and humans

The Greeks believed that the Fates had a crucial, if often remote, role in the history of human communities as well as in the lives of individuals. Some accounts tell of their presence at the creation of humankind by the Titan Prometheus, who molded men and women out of clay. The Fates were frequently associated with the "fateful" events of people's lives—their births, marriages, and deaths. They were in attendance at the births of such significant mortals as Heracles and Pelops, and came to the wedding of Peleus and Thetis, whose marriage prompted the sequence of events that led to the Trojan War.

One of the most famous examples of the Fates' role in defining the course of mortal life can be seen in the myth of Meleager, a fighter and hero. When Meleager was seven days old, the Fates appeared to his mother, Althaea, and warned that her son would live only as long as one of the logs burning on the family hearth. Althaea snatched the log from the fire, doused it, and locked it away in a chest. Many years later, Meleager got into a fatal quarrel and killed two of his mother's brothers. In a fit of anger, and encouraged by the Erinyes, or Furies—close relatives of the Fates who avenged interfamilial killing—Althaea took the log from the chest and threw it onto the fire. Meleager died in agony, and Althaea later killed herself because of her guilt.

The myth of Admetus casts the Fates in a more complex light. Admetus, the king of Thessaly, fell ill and was close to death. The god Apollo, who as a punishment for displeasing Zeus had to serve Admetus for one year, got the Fates drunk and persuaded them to spare the king from dying. However, in exchange for his life, the Fates insisted that someone else die on his behalf. No one in the king's household stepped forward to accept this role; in the end, Admetus's beloved wife Alcestis offered herself as the substitute—although she was saved from death by the intervention of Heracles. This myth has been interpreted in a number of ways: the Fates either can be tricked by the gods or can have the capacity for mercy. One thing is clear, however: there is a price to pay for avoiding death.

Below: The Fates *by Spanish painter Francisco Goya (1746–1828). The painting shows the three Fates, as well as an unidentified fourth figure. Atropos and her scissors are visible at right; another Fate, at left, holds a puppet to symbolize control over human destiny.*

Plato and the Fates

Greek philosopher Plato (c. 428–c. 348 BCE) presented a unique account of the Fates in his *Republic*. The account is a description of Judgment Day in which each of the Fates sits on a throne, dressed in white and with a headband. All three are singing—Lachesis of the past, Clotho of the present, and Atropos of the future—and at the same time turning a spindle, a pin used in a spinning wheel for twisting and winding the thread. As the singing and spinning take place, the souls of the dead prepare to transmigrate (pass into new bodies). Each soul receives a number from lots cast at random by Lachesis. The soul then chooses what life-pattern to have—for instance, whether to be an animal or a human. It must also choose the conditions of life, such as wealth or poverty, sickness or health. After each soul has chosen, it is dispatched by Lachesis to Clotho, who confirms each choice with a turn of the spindle, and from there to Atropos, who makes the web of life irreversible.

Even though the souls are encouraged to choose carefully, and warned that acceptable lives are available for everyone, their decisions are often governed by ambition or by previously established patterns of experience and habit, and they later come to regret their choices. Plato's account implies that humans—and not the gods—are responsible for the choices they make and the outcome of those choices. The Fates allot souls a life, and what they get determines almost

everything about them, from their social and economic position to their mental and physical attributes. However, the way individuals lead their lives is up to them.

Worship of the Fates

The Fates were popular figures of cult worship. Evidence suggests that there were sanctuaries to them in such major cities as Corinth, Sparta, and Thebes. People made offerings to the Fates at festival times in Athens, Delphi, Olympia, and Sicyon, among other places. At Sicyon, worshipers offered sacrifices to the Fates that were similar to those

Right: The Three Fates *(c. 1670) by Sebastiano Mazzoni (c. 1611–1678). The myth of the Fates has captured the imagination of many painters and writers.*

Right: A second-century-CE mosaic of Atropos, the third of the Fates. Because of Atropos's role in cutting the thread of human life, she was the most feared—and the most venerated—of all the Fates.

offered to the Erinyes, the female spirits who punished anyone who killed a member of their own family. One reason people may have honored the Fates was for their role in accompanying the major figures in the Greek pantheon, including Zeus, Apollo, Athena, and Demeter.

Parallels with Norse myth

There are strong similarities between the Greek Fates and the Norse Norns. The Norns, which also means "fates," were three sisters: the oldest was Wyrd (Becoming), the middle was Verdandi (Being), and the youngest was Skuld (That-which-is-to-be). As in some accounts of the Fates, the Norns were older than the gods—they originally came from Jotunheim, the land of the giants, and went to Asgard, the home of the gods, where they spun a thread on which hung the lives of deities and men and the destiny of the universe itself. The Norns had perhaps an even greater significance in Norse mythology than the Fates did in the Greek pantheon, but the similarities between the two cultures' stories suggest the universal power of the belief that an unseen force shapes each person's life.

Representations in art

The Fates have often been portrayed in art. They were found on many works of art throughout the Greco-Roman period, particularly on altars and sarcophagi (stone coffins). On a well-known sixth-century-BCE vase, painter Sophilos depicted the Fates walking alongside a chariot carrying Athena and Artemis during a procession to the wedding of Peleus and Thetis. The Fates also appear on the second-century-BCE Altar of Zeus, which stood in the ancient city of Pergamum (in present-day Turkey) and was regarded as one of the Seven Wonders of the World. The altar depicted the Olympian gods battling the Giants, and showed the Fates fighting in the company of the Hesperides—nymphs who were also their sisters—and close to Aphrodite and Eros. From the start of the Renaissance in the 15th century CE to the 19th century, the Fates were a favorite subject for artists—paintings of them were done by artists such as Correggio, Rubens, and Goya. German writer Johann Wolfgang von Goethe (1749–1832) wrote "Song of the Fates" in his play *Iphigeneia*, and the German composer Johannes Brahms (1833–1897) wrote a cantata with the same title in 1882.

Anthony Bulloch

Bibliography

Hesiod, and M. L. West, trans. *Theogony* and *Works and Days.* New York: Oxford University Press, 2008.

Plato, and Robin Waterfield, trans. *Republic.* New York: Oxford University Press, 2008.

See also: Apollo; Gaia; Nyx; Prometheus; Thetis; Titans; Zeus.

FAUNUS

Faunus was originally an ancient Italian deity of wild forests. As the Roman civilization developed, it was heavily influenced by Greek culture, and Faunus acquired many of the characteristics of the Arcadian nature god Pan, including his depiction as half-goat, half-man.

Few stories exist about Faunus. Mythologically his importance is due mainly to his place in the legendary history of ancient Italy and in the way he was worshiped by Romans. The father of Faunus was Picus, a son of Saturn and an ancient king of Latium, the area of central Italy in which Rome eventually became dominant. According to legend, Picus was turned into a woodpecker by Circe, a powerful enchantress. Faunus fathered Latinus, who was king of Latium when, according to Virgil (70–19 BCE), the Trojan hero Aeneas settled there, eventually marrying Latinus's daughter Lavinia. Several generations later, their descendants would include Romulus and Remus, the legendary founders of Rome.

As for Faunus, he was the protector of animal flocks when they were driven from one place of pasture to another. He was also believed to be the source of mysterious sounds and voices that came from the forest. Farmers and peasants imagined that he could appear to them in the fields bordering on the wild. These unexpected visitations from the god could be helpful, but at times Faunus also teased and tormented people. Because his home was in the wild forests, his most important Latin epithet was *Silvicola*, meaning "one who inhabits the woods." Yet perhaps most important, since Faunus spoke to mortals, he was viewed as an oracular god and was consulted to predict the future.

Faunus's association with wild nature, and the fact that he was more often heard than seen, explains why he was rarely depicted by the ancient Romans in any human or animal form. That changed, however, when he, along with other Roman deities, became identified with deities of the Greek

pantheon. Faunus took on the half-goat, half-man appearance of Pan, as well as many of his mischievous characteristics. The Romans also associated Faunus with two female counterparts, Fauna and Fatua, apparently wives or daughters about whom almost no information exists.

For the early Romans, Faunus was largely the abstract personification of the mysterious wildness of nature, in opposition to civilized life and organized society. This characteristic, scholars believe, explains why the god was included among the earliest mythical kings of precivilized Latium. Yet his divine ability to see the future meant that it was fitting that he should be the one royal ancestor to have predicted Rome's founding.

Influence of Pan

Faunus was identified with Pan because the Greek god, like Faunus, was a god of wild nature and was especially associated with the realm of the forest. Pan was a lascivious god, the promoter of fertility and increase among flocks. Through his identification with Pan, Faunus took on many of the same traits, resulting in his epithet *inuus*, which means "he who enters with the power to arouse desire."

Historians believe that Faunus must have had numerous oracular sites, probably in or near the woods, where he foretold the future. In the *Aeneid*, Virgil wrote that King Latinus, father of the Latin people, went to sleep on the skin of a newly sacrificed sheep at an oracular shrine dedicated to his father, Faunus. The god revealed in Latinus's dreams important elements in the destined struggles of Aeneas and his followers that would lead to the eventual founding of Rome. However, there are few inscriptions or other evidence indicating that Faunus was officially worshiped until about 193 BCE. At the time, according to Roman historian Livy (59 BCE–17 CE), the first temple in honor of the god was built on Tiber Island. Little is known about how Faunus was honored at the temple, but there were various other oracular associations on the same island, which was devoted to the curing of the sick. Rituals of incubation, during which worshipers slept overnight in the temple of Aesculapius—the Roman version of the Greek god of healing, Asclepius—hoping to receive a dream of healing, were a regular feature of the island. Also in attendance were the priests of Aesculapius and medical practitioners.

Above: Faunus (Pan), like this statue by Peter Simon Lamine (1738–1817) from the late 18th century, made his home in the dark woods. The half-goat, half-man nature deity was often depicted playing a panpipe or flute.

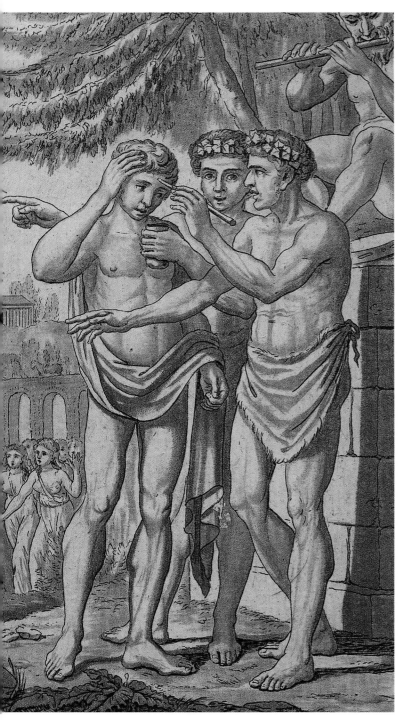

Left: This illustration depicts priests preparing for the Lupercalia festival, held in ancient Rome. They stand beneath a statue of Faunus, top right.

of the Palatine Hill in Rome, the place of Rome's earliest settlers, dressed in goatskins and used goatskin thongs to strike those who stood along the way. The ritual was intended to enhance the fertility of all those, especially the women, touched as the Luperci raced by. At this time of year, the spirits of the dead were thought to be at large, to the detriment of everyone living.

The exact meaning of the Lupercalia is not clearly understood, yet scholars believe that it was celebrated as a purification of the old Palatine settlement, which rid it of all the harmful forces that threatened the life and health of the community. In the archaic Roman religious calendar, the Lupercalia was a preparation for the New Year. It was thought that the Luperci reestablished the essential order in which the wild elements of nature were kept apart from the world of civilized life.

Arcadian origin

Old stories about the Palatine relate that King Evander and a group of Arcadians from Greece inhabited the hill long before the early Romans. The Arcadians celebrated a rite called the Lycaia, a festival name suggestive of wolves. The word *Lupercalia* is based on the Latin noun *lupus*, which also means "wolf." The wolf, a totem animal of Mars, had special significance for Rome. It is perhaps the similarity in festival names, as well as the old traditions associating the Arcadians with the Palatine, that led to the identification of the Roman Faunus with the Arcadian god Pan and made Faunus the god of the Lupercalia. While in origin, Faunus was a divinity of wild nature and the forests, the bringer of terror (much as Pan at times brought panic to the Arcadians), he was also known as a protector of animal flocks. Eventually he became a deity who protected not just animal flocks but his Roman worshipers as well from the threats of wild nature, so that in the Lupercalia, Faunus was the god who purified Rome's human flock.

DANIEL P. HARMON

The Lupercalia

At some point the ancient Romans began to identify Faunus as the god of the Lupercalia. This annual celebration took place in the middle of February, which came just before the month of March, the first month in the pre-Julian calendar of 10 months. It was believed that from February 15 to February 21 spirits representing the world of untamed nature invaded the ordered, everyday universe. Ancient writers describe the Lupercalia as a rite of purification. Priests called Luperci ran around the base

Bibliography

Gardner, Jane F. *Roman Myths.* Austin, TX: University of Texas Press, 1993.

Howatson, M. C. *The Oxford Companion to Classical Literature.* New York: Oxford University Press, 2005.

Virgil, and Robert Fagles, trans. *The Aeneid.* New York: Penguin, 2009.

SEE ALSO: Asclepius; Pan.

FURIES

The Furies were three powerful classical goddesses who exacted retribution on people guilty of serious crimes. Although they were a positive force, maintaining order and justice in the world, they were greatly feared by the ancient Greeks and Romans, who often dared not speak their name.

The three Furies were among the oldest Greek divinities, predating all the Olympian gods and goddesses. The Greeks knew them as the Erinyes, but it is by their Roman name, Furies, that they are best known today. According to the *Theogony* of Hesiod, a poet of the eighth century BCE, they were born when Cronus, at the instigation of his mother, Gaia (earth), cut off the genitals of his father, Uranus (sky). The blood spilled onto Gaia, and from it sprang the Furies, the Titans, and the Nymphs. Because of their close association with the earth, these divinities are described as chthonic, because they are born from *chthon*, a Greek word meaning "earth."

However, that is not the only version of the story. In his play *Eumenides*, Aeschylus (c. 525–456 BCE) calls the Furies "daughters of Night," and says that they produced such powerful offspring as Nemesis (the goddess of retribution), Fate, and Death. Aeschylus's story, although different in detail from Hesiod's, reinforces the idea that the Furies have an ancient, chthonic origin, and that they live under the earth, arising from it only when they are summoned to deal with injustice.

The Furies appear frequently in Greek art and literature. Their role is to uphold the natural order of things. They are responsible for correcting or punishing beings that step outside their conventional roles, especially overreachers who try to climb above their divinely ordained station. Among the most notable incidents in which they participate is the story in Book 19 of Homer's *Iliad*, in which the Furies intervene to stop Achilles' horse Xanthus from talking, because horses are not naturally supposed to speak. Another is

Left: A 14th-century woodcut of the Furies. The Furies were the personification (and thus the avengers) of murder victims.

The Furies and Orestes

The Furies appear frequently in Greek tragedy. They are particularly important in the stories of Agamemnon and his family in the *Oresteia* trilogy by Aeschylus. In these stories, Agamemnon's sacrifice of his daughter Iphigeneia before the Trojan War so angered the mother, Clytemnestra, that, while Agamemnon was in Troy, she took a lover, Aegisthus, with whom she plotted Agamemnon's death. In Aeschylus's *Agamemnon*, the hero returns and is killed by his wife. In *The Libation Bearers*, the second play in the trilogy, and in both Sophocles' and Euripides' versions of *Electra*, Agamemnon's children, Electra and Orestes, meet, plot, and murder Clytemnestra and Aegisthus. At the close of *The Libation Bearers*, the Furies appear and chase Orestes from the stage. The final play of the *Oresteia*, *Eumenides*, has the chorus of Furies, encouraged by the ghost of Clytemnestra, pursue Orestes to Athens, where he stands trial with Athena as judge. At his trial, the Furies defend their punishment of matricide, but Orestes asserts that he acted in just retribution for his father's murder. The jury of Athenians is split equally, but Athena makes her casting vote for Orestes. The Furies take this affront to their authority badly, but Athena placates them by offering them a sacred space in Athens and by changing their name to the Eumenides. However, Euripides' *Iphigeneia in Tauris* changes this ending and has some of the Furies reject this offer, and they continue to pursue Orestes. Euripides' version maintains the Furies as intractable and formidable goddesses.

Right: The painting on this jug from the fourth century BCE shows Orestes and the Furies.

the story of Orestes in Aeschylus's *Eumenides* and *Choephoroe* (also known as *The Libation Bearers*). In these two plays of the *Oresteia* trilogy, the Furies, dressed menacingly in black and with snakes for hair, pursue Orestes to Athens because he has transgressed against the natural order by killing his mother, Clytemnestra (see box).

Ordinary Greeks invoked the Furies to harm those who had done them wrong. For example, in *Amatoriae Narrationes* ("Tales of Love"), a work attributed to Greek historian Plutarch (c. 46–120 CE), two daughters of Skedasos are raped and murdered by a pair of Spartan youths. The grieving father pounds on the ground to summon the Furies from Hades to punish the killers.

Ambivalent figures

The Furies have both positive and negative aspects in Greek literature. They perform an important and powerful role in maintaining order in the universe: they are relentless

in pursuit of justice, and they are avengers of murder. On the other hand, their close association with death and retribution for any sin struck fear into the hearts of all people, regardless of whether they were themselves being hunted. Thus the ancient Greeks venerated and feared the Furies in almost equal measure.

In Greek art, the Furies are usually represented as beautiful winged women wearing simple dresses, and with snakes in their hands or hair. One of the earliest surviving works featuring the Furies is a marble statue from the sanctuary of Hera at the mouth of the Sele River in Italy. It depicts a man defending himself against a single Fury in the form of a snake.

However, it is rare for artists to depict the Furies as fantastic monsters: the mythological creatures are usually given nothing more sinister than a shadowy and angular appearance. Yet their association with snakes, and the fact that they had wings, definitely suggests that they

Left: This painting by Austrian artist Moritz von Schwind (1804–1871) shows Psyche being tortured by the Furies, while Venus watches. She is enraged by Psyche's marriage to her son, Cupid, and seeks to punish her.

were not straightforwardly benign: the Furies existed to avenge evil, but that did not necessarily make them agents of good. There was always a sense of danger emanating from the Furies, and they were thus ambivalent figures. They may have been admired, but they could never be trusted, because, after all, most people have done wrong at some time, and they could not be sure that the Furies would not one day come for them.

Although the Furies were very much in the thoughts of ancient Greeks, they have nearly always been portrayed in fundamentally mythological surroundings. They are most often represented in scenes depicting the house of Atreus, a favorite subject for Greek tragedians.

Linear B script

Classical scholars have long known that the Furies were among the earliest Greek deities, but it was not until the 1950s that archaeologists formed an accurate idea of just how old they were. In Crete, the inscriptions on some ancient stone tablets, dating from the 14th century BCE, had long been indecipherable, but when the key to them was finally discovered in the 1950s, the language in which they were written—now known as Linear B—was found to contain references to a goddess named Erinys, who was described as a recipient of dedications. This archaic divinity may have been a precursor of the goddess Demeter Erinys, who was worshiped in Arcadia in classical times.

The name Eumenides, meaning "the kindly ones," is a euphemistic term for the Furies, and cults to the Eumenides existed in various parts of the Greek world, one of which was at Colonus near Athens. Another name for the Furies was Semnai Theai ("revered goddesses"), whose cave sanctuary near the Areopagus was described by Thucydides, Pausanias, and others as particularly important for suppliants and fugitives. Later, the three Furies were given personal names—Tisiphone, Megaera, and Alecto.

BRIAN SEILSTAD

Bibliography

Aeschylus, and A. Shapiro and P. Burian, eds. *The Oresteia.* New York: Oxford University Press, 2010.
Hesiod, and M. L. West, trans. *Theogony* and *Works and Days.* New York: Oxford University Press, 2008.

SEE ALSO: Cronus; Gaia; Nemesis; Uranus.

GAIA

The Greek earth goddess Gaia (also called Ge) was a primal and elemental figure, the source of almost all life, mortal and immortal. She belonged to the very beginnings of creation and had the largest continuously influential role of all the founders of the universe.

According to the most popular account of the origin of things (preserved in *Theogony* by Hesiod, c. 800 BCE), the universe began with the spontaneous creation of four primal beings: the Void, or "Chaos," which in Greek means a yawning or gaping nothingness; Gaia; Tartarus, or "Deep Dark," the darkest and lowest part of the underworld; and Eros, or "Desire." Each of these beings gave birth to numerous other beings, at first through self-fertilization, but soon, thanks to the creation of Eros, through mating with other beings.

Gaia was the only primal being to produce children who became major divinities, or parents and grandparents of major divinities. Although Chaos, Tartarus, and Eros produced significant offspring, such as Night and Day, Death, and Destiny, Gaia was the mother of several generations of gods who would rule the universe. Gaia also played an active role in the process of succession between generations. At the same time, Gaia was the mother and grandmother of many monstrous creatures and primitive, barbaric, crude beings.

Gaia's offspring

Gaia's first act was to create spontaneously the three other elemental realms of the universe: the sky (Uranus), mountains (Ourea), and ocean (Pontus). Gaia then mated with two of her children—all creation from then on was by procreation between male and female. With Pontus, Gaia produced numerous ocean deities and beings, a number of

which were monstrous. With Uranus, she created her main offspring, the 12 gods who became known as the Titans, followed by the three giant Cyclopes and the three Hecatoncheires (Hundred-Handed Ones).

As night fell, Uranus lay with Gaia, and from their regular union came children. Uranus, however, feared the consequences of creating a new generation of beings, so he refused to let Gaia give birth; instead she had to keep all their children in her womb. In the first of several decisive acts of intervention, Gaia rebelled: she created a sickle from the famously hard metal adamant and then

Right: This relief (600 BCE) depicting Gaia comes from the temple of Artemis, in Corfu, Greece.

Right: This wall painting of Gaia (c. 727) comes from a luxurious palace in Syria built by Caliph Hisham.

sought an ally among her suppressed children.

Cronus volunteered to help. He waited in ambush when Uranus came to lie with Gaia as usual, then castrated his father with the sickle. From the blood that fell on the earth (Gaia) during the act of castration were born the Furies, who avenged murders within families, and the Giants, who later opposed Zeus and the Olympians. With that act of violence, Cronus, prompted and assisted by his mother, took over as sovereign ruler, along with his siblings the Titans.

Cronus married his sister Rhea (daughter of Gaia) and, like his father before him, attempted to suppress his own children. This was because he had learned from Gaia and Uranus that one of his children would eventually replace him. Every time one of his children was born, Cronus swallowed it. Rhea, like her mother before her, found the suppression intolerable, and on the advice of Gaia and Uranus, went to the southern Aegean island of Crete to give birth to Zeus.

Rise of Zeus

Gaia took the baby and concealed him in a cave until he was old enough to return and depose Cronus. She taught her grandson how to trick his father into regurgitating Zeus's brothers and sisters. A battle known as the Titanomachy followed between the generation of Zeus (the Olympians) and their parents, uncles, and aunts (the Titans). Although Gaia generally seems to have sided with the Titans, she also told Zeus that he could win the conflict by releasing the Hundred-Handed Ones from the prison to which Cronus had sent them.

Gaia's advice was critical in enabling the Olympians to defeat the Titans. Then, in a final test for her grandson, she combined with Tartarus to produce one more primitive being to challenge the Olympian, the monster Typhon. He was a terrible creature with a hundred snake heads that alternately hissed, bellowed, and roared. Typhon's ambition, like that of the Titans and the Olympians, was to become supreme ruler of the universe. Zeus, however, defeated him in an awful battle and cast him into deepest region of the underworld. According to some accounts, Typhon had, for a while, disabled Zeus by removing the sinews of his hands and feet. However, Pan and Hermes managed to distract Typhon with a meal of fish, retrieve the sinews and heal Zeus's body.

Continuing in her role as the critical director of events, Gaia now recommended Zeus as the figure to lead the new Olympian regime. After he was established as ruler, she gave him crucial advice that would prevent him from being overthrown. She warned that Metis, his first wife, would have a son who would become ruler of the gods.

As the mother of the Titans and the grandmother of the Olympians, Gaia was thus the parent of all the major beings in the Greek pantheon. She was also the supplier of key

knowledge and advice at each turn of events. She appears to have sided sometimes with the Titans and sometimes with the Olympians, but this was not because she was inconsistent or treacherous. She was the source and creator of all the beings, divine and monstrous, that competed with each other for the supreme rulership of creation. None of the other primal beings occupied quite this role, and Gaia's centrality reflects a characteristically Greek outlook, which elsewhere gives earth-mother figures, such as Demeter and even Hera, particular prominence in both myth and ritual. As such a basic and primal source of power and knowledge, Gaia was sometimes even said to have preceded Apollo at Delphi, the seat of the most famous oracle in Greece.

Gaia in art

Gaia is represented in vase paintings and sculpture of all periods from antiquity, and in several common motifs. One of these motifs was the assault by the giant Tityus, son of Gaia, on Leto, mother of the divine twins Artemis and Apollo. Tityus came to symbolize the outrageous, lawless abductor. He is often depicted in art and literature being punished for his crimes, spread-eagled across many acres while birds of prey feed on his liver, or shot full of arrows by the twins while defending their mother. In these scenes of her son's punishment, Gaia is often present. She appears also in the commonly depicted Battle against the Giants

Below: Part of an altar frieze (c. 180 BCE) from the city of Pergamum depicts Athena fighting the Titans while Gaia pleads for mercy.

Right: This Greek vase painting depicts the birth of Erichthonius. Gaia hands the baby to Athena.

(Gigantomachy), sometimes as a presence rising from the ground, sometimes more specifically among her grandchildren, the Olympians, pleading for the lives of her children, the Giants.

Gaia and Athens

Many of the vase paintings that have survived to the present day came from Athens and the communities with which Athens traded. As a result, their imagery reflects Athenian preoccupations. One of the other common representations of Gaia has significant political symbolism. Numerous paintings from the fifth century BCE depict Gaia emerging from the ground and handing, or having just handed, a baby named Erichthonius to Athena, after Gaia carried him in her womb to full term. Often also present are the three daughters of King Cecrops, and Cecrops himself (another "child of the earth"), who played a major role in the events around this presentation.

Underlying this motif was the claim that the Athenians were an indigenous people, native to Attica: Erichthonius was the "first Athenian," born from the seed of Hephaestus, which Athena wiped from her thigh after the god tried to rape her. The semen fell to the ground and impregnated Gaia. All other Athenians were descended from Erichthonius. The image of Gaia, presenting the baby to Athena and other key members of the community, made a clear and powerful validation of Athenian historical claims. Gaia, in other words, was not just a cosmic element who belonged in the symbolic and philosophical world of abstract myth: she belonged equally to the world of politics and national or ethnic identity.

Gaia today

In the modern world Gaia has come to symbolize ecological concerns and idealistic aspirations about Planet Earth and the universe. In 1979, scientist James Lovelock wrote a book called *Gaia: A New Look at Life on Earth*, which had a huge influence on the way we see our planet. He saw Earth as a self-regulating system that maintains conditions for its survival simply by following its own natural processes. Gaia theory has made people aware of the damage their actions can do to Earth's ecosystem.

Gaia is also the code name for the European Space Agency's 2010 program to carry out an astronomical census of one billion stars. The spacecraft, also called *Gaia*, will be equipped with multiple optical telescopes and other instruments that will make "the largest, most precise map of where we live in space."

ANTHONY BULLOCH

Bibliography

Hesiod, and M. L. West, trans. *Theogony* and *Works and Days.* New York: Oxford University Press, 2008.
Lovelock, James. *Gaia: A New Look at Life on Earth.* New York: Oxford University Press, 2000.

SEE ALSO: Cronus; Eros; Furies; Titans; Typhon; Zeus.

GRACES

The Graces, known in Greek as the Charites and in Latin as the Gratiae, were the goddesses of beauty and graceful behavior. They had minor roles in a number of myths. Their embodiment of kindly manners and charm marks them as representations of the Greek ideal of womanhood.

There is a bewildering variety of information concerning the origins, names, and number of the Graces. Greek poet Hesiod (fl. 800 BCE) recorded that there were three Graces, born to the king of the Olympian gods, Zeus, and Eurynome, one of the Oceanids. The Oceanids were the offspring of the Titans Oceanus and Tethys. According to Hesiod, the Graces' names were Aglaea ("Splendor" or "Shining One"), Euphrosyne ("Joy" or "Gaiety"), and Thalia ("Festivity"). Greek travel writer Pausanias (143–176 CE), however, mentioned another source, which ascribes the goddesses' parentage to the sun god Helios and Aegle, one of the Hesperides, nymphs who guarded a tree bearing golden apples. This account of the Graces' origins would, at least, help explain Aglaea's name.

To confuse matters further, in his epic the *Iliad*, Greek poet Homer (c. 9th–8th cent. BCE) referred to a younger group of Graces, one of whom, Pasithea, he mentions by name. Homer's account suggests that he was aware of a younger and an elder group of Graces, a distinction that is reflected in a number of surviving Greek vase paintings, some of which depict five more Graces—Eudaimonia, Paidia, Pandaisia, Pannykhis, and Antheia. Other writers offer still further information. Greek poet Nonnus (fl. c. 450–470 CE) wrote that Pasithea was the daughter of Dionysus, god of wine, while Pausanias observed that the people of Sparta and Athens worshiped only two Graces. The Spartans called them Cleta ("Sound") and Phaenna ("Light"); the Athenians knew them as Auxo ("Increase") and Hegemone ("Queen").

Roles and relationships

The Graces personified beauty, charm, and grace, as well as acts of kindness or favor. The Greeks honored them in connection with social activities, such as banquets and dancing. In some accounts, the Graces were responsible for bestowing talents on mortals. Their attributes were very similar to those of the Muses, the nine goddesses who inspired artistic creativity, and Greek writers acknowledged this similarity. According to Hesiod, the Graces were the companions of the Muses and lived alongside them, together with Himeros, the personification of desire, on Mount Olympus. According to Hesiod, there were also similarities in the family backgrounds of the two groups of goddesses. Their mothers were both Titanesses or daughters of Titanesses, and their father was Zeus. The Greeks believed that Zeus's children—including the Graces, the Muses, the Fates, and the Seasons—provided humans with all they required to live ordered and moral lives.

The Greeks also associated the Graces with love and linked them with the goddess Aphrodite. References describe the Graces attending on Aphrodite as maidservants, reflecting their status as minor goddesses and Aphrodite's position as a major Olympian deity. During the Trojan War, Aphrodite, who fought on the side of Troy, was wounded in battle by the Greek warrior Diomedes. After this bruising encounter the goddess recovered her strength by putting on clothing made for her by the Graces.

Appearances in myth

A number of Greek myths include references to the Graces, but in general their involvement extended only as far as personifying charm and favor. To an extent, the Graces were similar to the Fates, the divine beings who determined the course of human lives. Both watched over the events of gods and mortals but were remote from them. Like the Fates, the Graces were present at the famous wedding of Peleus, king of Phthia, to the sea nymph Thetis, the first in a series of events that led to the Trojan War.

Right: Italian artist Sandro Botticelli (1445–1510) depicted the Graces, shown here in a detail from his painting Allegory of Spring. *Other deities appear in the complete painting, including Venus (Aphrodite), Cupid (Eros), and Mercury (Hermes), who appears here at left.*

The Graces also helped in the creation of Pandora, the first woman, who, according to Hesiod, unleashed strife on humanity. Hephaestus, god of metalworking, made Pandora out of clay; other deities gave her qualities that would make her attractive to her intended husband, Epimetheus, and the Graces adorned her with necklaces of gold.

Women in Greek Society

The Graces' charming and beautiful natures represented the ideal of femininity in ancient Greek society. In Classical-era Athens (479–338 BCE), for example, girls were educated at home and taught how to be good mothers and housewives. The Greeks believed that a woman's place was in the *kyrios* (home), while a man belonged in the *polis*, the public realms of politics, business, and warfare. The only exception to this rule was religion, where women could become priestesses and perform ceremonial rites at public assemblies. Some scholars argue that when Greek myths portray women as either powerful or aggressive, they represent men's fears about the opposite sex. When they depict women as demure and passive, they reflect men's fantasies about women, and the idealized form of feminine behavior. Mythical characters such as Hera, Athena, and Artemis, as well as the Harpies and the Gorgons, represent the powerful aspect of women; the Graces, the Muses, and the Hesperides are examples of the more passive side.

Greek poet Pindar (c. 522–c. 438 BCE) mentioned the Graces in connection with the myth of Ixion, the first mortal to kill a member of his own family. When Ixion went to Olympus so that Zeus could purify him for his misdeed, he fell in love with the Olympian ruler's wife, Hera. To test Ixion, Zeus made a cloud in the image of Hera. Fooled, Ixion slept with it, causing the cloud to give birth to Centaurus. Centaurus fathered the centaurs, who were part man and part horse. Pindar observed that the Graces did not honor the cloud's pregnancy, which suggests that childbirth was another area in which the goddesses played a role.

The Graces and marriage

The marriages of two of the Graces provide the stories with their greatest involvement in Greek myth. According to Hesiod, Aglaea married Hephaestus—although most other sources maintain that the blacksmith of the gods married the love goddess Aphrodite. In the *Iliad* Homer wrote that Hephaestus was married to one of the Graces. This relationship explains Homer's account of Hephaestus, whose mother Hera threw him out of Olympus when she realized he was lame. The god was rescued by Eurynome, the Graces' mother and, as a result, his mother-in-law. Another myth involves the younger Grace Pasithea, whom Hera offered to Hypnos, the god of sleep, as a bribe to ensure his help in putting Zeus to sleep. Hera wanted to help the Greeks in the Trojan War, but knew she had to do so without her husband's knowledge. Hypnos had sent the Olympian ruler to sleep once before, only for Zeus to find out and become enraged. Nevertheless, despite his fears, the god of sleep accepted Hera's offer because of his deep love for Pasithea.

Worship of the Graces

Pausanias records that the Graces were worshiped in Athens and Sparta, but notes that their most important shrine was in the town of Orchomenus in southern Greece. At the shrine people worshiped the Graces in the form of stones that they believed had fallen from heaven. Today it is widely accepted that these stones were meteorites. Orchomenus was home to a festival for the Graces, the Charitesea. Greek dramatist Aristophanes (c. 450– c. 388 BCE) mentions the Graces in connection with an Athenian festival, the Thesmophoria, in his play *Women at the Thesmophoria*. The festival, attended only by women, was held in honor of the fertility goddess Demeter and involved rituals promoting new life. According to Aristophanes, the participants prayed to the Graces, as well as to other deities, to ensure "that all may happen for the best at this gathering, both for the greatest advantage of Athens and for our own personal happiness."

Below: This sculpture of the Three Graces, by Italian Antonio Canova (1757–1822), is the most famous depiction of the deities from the early 19th century.

The Graces in art and literature

In ancient Greek vase paintings the Graces are often depicted nude and dancing in a circle. One vase, the *François Krater*, which dates from around 570 BCE, shows the Graces as attendants at the wedding of Peleus and Thetis. However, the goddesses inspired painters and sculptors long after the decline of ancient Greek and Roman cultures, most famously in a painting by Italian artist Sandro Botticelli (1445–1510) and as a sculpture by Antonio Canova (1757–1822), also Italian. Writers who have alluded to the Graces in their work include the English poets John Milton (1608–1674) and Edmund Spenser (1552–1599), who wrote about the deities in his long poem *The Faerie Queene*:

> These three on men all gracious gifts bestow
> Which deck the body or adorn the mind,
> To make them lovely or well-favored show;
> As comely carriage, entertainment kind,
> Sweet semblance, friendly offices that bind,
> And all the complements of courtesy.

ANDREW CAMPBELL

Bibliography

Guerber, H. A. *The Myths of Greece and Rome.* New York: Dover Publications, 1993.
Homer, and Robert Fagles, trans. *The Iliad.* New York: Penguin, 2009.

SEE ALSO: Aphrodite; Fates; Helios; Hephaestus; Muses; Oceanus; Titans; Zeus.

HADES

Hades, whose name means "the unseen," was the brother of Zeus, king of the Greek gods. He was the ruler of the underworld, the home of dead spirits, a role that gave him his other name, Polydegmon, "host of many guests." As well as a god, Hades was also the place of the dead, a realm that Greek poet Homer (c. ninth–eighth century BCE) described as being cloaked in mist and cloud.

Hades' early life was marked by abuse and suffering. His father, Cronus, was the son of the sky god Uranus and the earth goddess Gaia. Cronus castrated his father in order to gain supreme power for himself. However, a seer told Cronus that one of his sons would be the death of him. Ignoring the protests of his sister and wife Rhea, Cronus swallowed all their children as they were born. Finally, Rhea deceived her husband when she gave him a stone swaddled in cloth instead of Zeus, her youngest child. The boy was spirited away to a cave in the middle of Crete. When Zeus

Below: A medieval depiction of Hades and Persephone—the king and queen of the underworld—seated inside the mouth of an owl, a symbol of death. At their feet lies the dog Cerberus.

Left: Proserpina (1877) by English painter Dante Gabriel Rossetti (1828–1882). In myth, Hades abducted Proserpina (the Latin name for Persephone) and forced her to become queen of the underworld.

matured, he forced Cronus to vomit up his brothers and sisters: Poseidon, Hades, Hera, Hestia, and Demeter. Working together, the young deities overcame their father and banished him to a distant place.

After deposing Cronus, Hades and his two brothers cast lots for the kingdoms they would rule. Zeus won the heavens and Poseidon won the sea, which left the underworld for Hades. While the gods and goddesses of Olympus frolicked and celebrated, Hades' job was to govern the world of the dead.

The abduction of Persephone

Unlike the other gods, Hades was not known for his many romances. The exception was his love for the beautiful young Persephone, daughter of Demeter, the goddess of fertility and corn. Unknown to Persephone and her mother, Hades had asked Zeus for permission to marry the girl. Zeus agreed, perhaps because he felt guilty about having won a kingdom so much more agreeable than his brother's. Meanwhile, Gaia had planted a narcissus flower in honor of her grandson Hades. She wanted to please the god of death and left him this token of her esteem. Persephone, playing in a meadow with her friends, came upon the flower and was transfixed by it. As she picked it, Hades rose out of the ground in a chariot pulled by black stallions and grabbed the girl. The chariot sped into a dark chasm, which the earth then closed over without a trace.

Demeter sought anxiously for her daughter. She asked all the gods and goddesses if they could tell her where she was, but no one knew. Only the goddess Hecate, who lived in an underworld cave, and the sun god Helios, who served as a lookout for the gods, had heard Persephone's cries. On the 10th day of her search, Demeter learned from Hecate what had happened to her daughter. Hecate led the grieving mother to Helios, who told her that Zeus had given Persephone to Hades, Demeter's own brother.

Demeter was no stranger to the underworld. As a vegetation deity, she went underground during the winter. She was known to the Athenians as the soil in which the dead, called "Demeter's people," were buried. In their own right, and not only through Hades, both she and Persephone were connected with the realm of the dead, and the identities of the three deities mingle in myth. However, Demeter objected furiously to Zeus's agreement that Hades could marry her daughter.

Both mother and daughter pined at their loss of each other and refused to eat. Because Demeter would not help the crops grow, the earth became barren and people starved. For her part, Persephone sulked and ignored Hades, refusing to be queen of the underworld. She wanted to be with her mother and nothing could console her. In a weak moment, she accepted a handful of pomegranate seeds from Hades, unaware that he was tricking her into permanent residence in the realm of the dead. Once any food was tasted there, the one who had eaten could never leave. Finally, Demeter insisted that Zeus arbitrate the dispute. The Olympian ruler agreed, fearful that the people of earth would starve to death.

Demeter accused Zeus of plotting with Hades to abduct her beloved daughter. Hades said that Persephone had eaten the fruit of the underworld and was now his forever. Persephone looked from mother to husband, wringing her hands. She missed Demeter but had come to love the dark, romantic Hades. To begin with, Zeus wanted to allow Persephone to choose where she lived. If she rejected Hades, she could go home to her mother. Although Persephone wanted to be with Demeter, she felt that she now belonged with Hades.

In the end, Zeus had to make the decision himself. He ruled that Persephone should live with her mother in the spring and summer; for the rest of the year, when crops did not grow, she would live with Hades. She therefore became queen of the underworld and lived in the realms of both the living and the dead. Hades proved to be a faithful husband, except for his attempts to seduce the nymphs Leuce and Menthe. Persephone was so angry at Hades' behavior that she turned Leuce into a poplar tree and Menthe into a mint plant. Hades seems to have been abashed by this retaliation, since he did not stray again.

Hades, Theseus, and Peirithous

The myth of Peirithous is closely linked to Hades' marriage to Persephone. Peirithous was a king of a people called the Lapiths, who became the companions of Theseus, the Greek hero and king of Athens. According to the story, both men vowed to marry daughters of Zeus. Theseus chose Helen of Sparta—who was later rescued by her brothers—while Peirithous chose Persephone. The pair traveled down to the underworld and informed Hades of their aim. The god calmly invited both of them to sit

down, which they did, not realizing until it was too late that they had sat on chairs of forgetfulness, from which they could not get up. Some time later, the hero Heracles came to the underworld to fetch the dog Cerberus as the last of his 12 Labors. Heracles was able to rescue Theseus from his seat, but not Peirithous—when he tried to move him, the ground trembled. As a result, Peirithous remained forever a prisoner in the underworld.

Right: The Rape of Proserpina *(1621–1622), by Italian sculptor Gian Lorenzo Bernini (1598–1680), depicts Hades abducting his future bride.*

The Journey to the Underworld

When a Greek or Roman died, a coin was put over each eye of the body or in its mouth. People performed this custom in the belief that the dead souls had to pay Charon, the surly ferryman who carried the dead across the Styx River. Roman poet Virgil (70–19 BCE) described Charon as "frightful and foul, his chin covered with unkempt hoary hair, his fierce eyes lit with fire, and a filthy cloak hanging from a knot on his shoulder." If the dead had no money, they were doomed to remain forever on the shore of the black, subterranean river.

When those who did have coins reached the other side of the river, the god Hermes—known to the Romans as Mercury—guided the souls to their new home. The three-headed watchdog Cerberus (see box, page 113) allowed the dead to enter the gates of the underworld, but he refused to let them pass back out again. Several places in ancient Greece were believed to be entrances to Hades, including the Alcyonian Lake in the northern Peleponnese and Taenarum in the southern Peleponnese.

Right: A Roman relief sculpture of Charon ferrying the dead across the Styx River. The relief, carved on a sarcophagus, represents the journey that awaited the soul of the body inside.

Greek views of Hades

Hades' character was harder to define than that of other gods, although there are parallels between him and several different deities. Like Hermes, the divine messenger, Hades possessed a helmet of invisibility. The personalities of both gods involved elements of trickery and concealment. Hades had a stern, unemotional manner, which made him seem lacking in personality. However, he could be moved to compassion: after the musician Orpheus played his lyre in the underworld, Hades agreed that his dead wife, the nymph Eurydice, could return with him to the world of the living. However, Orpheus could not meet the condition that he could not look at his wife until they had returned home, and he lost Eurydice forever.

Hades also had a passionate side and was sometimes regarded as an aspect of Dionysus, the god of wine. This parallel suggests that Hades, or the underworld, was more than the realm of the dead; it was also a place visited by the living, whether in sexual ecstasy, drunkenness, or mystical bliss. The Greeks also believed that they could journey to Hades during their dreams, or when they suffered from depression. Awareness of both Hades, who ruled the world of shadows, and Zeus, who ruled the world of light, provided people with a deeper sense of the meaning of life.

Unlike gods of the underworld in many other cultures, Hades was not considered evil. However, the Greeks did generally fear and shun him. It was customary for Greeks to avert their eyes when his name was mentioned and to identify him with Plutus, the god of wealth, in order to stay on his good side. Sometimes the Greeks saw Hades as the alter ego of Zeus and called him Zeus-Chthonios, a title that reinforced Hades' earthy qualities since chthonian deities were associated with both the dead and the fertility of the earth. The linking of Hades to more benign deities may have represented an attempt by the Greeks to harmonize dying with living. However, most Greeks did not make sacrifices to Hades because it did no good to plead with death. No hymns were sung to him, and few images of the god exist in Greek art. Hades was a hidden deity, perhaps because people feared that acknowledging his presence would draw them into the void with him.

Other inhabitants of Hades

Other beings also lived in the underworld, including the Furies, or Erinyes, who pursued those who sinned against members of their own family, and Hecate, a deity who bridged the world between living and dead, who had her own cave. The Furies sprang up from drops of blood shed when Cronus castrated his father, Uranus. These fearsome spirits carried serpents in their hands and were hideously ugly. The Athenians, who called them the Eumenides ("kindly ones"), worked hard to appease them lest they destroy Athens in retribution for the crime of Orestes, who had murdered his mother, Clytemnestra. Hades himself did not torture the guilty dead: he left the task to the Furies.

The judges of the dead were Minos, Rhadamanthys, and Aeacus, the gatekeeper. Hades remained hidden from the process of pronouncing judgment on the dead, although it is not clear what effect this judgment had, since those who were punished in the underworld had already been condemned by the gods. There were five rivers in the underworld: the Styx, the river of hate; the Acheron, the river of sorrow; the Lethe, the river of forgetting; the Cocytus, the river of cries; and the Phlegethon, the river of fire. Each river represented an aspect of the death process, such as anger, grief, or surrender. The sections of Hades, therefore, were not just geographical locations, but states of mind or soul.

Changing beliefs about the underworld

Across Europe during the Stone Age, people had seen the underworld as the home of the Great Mother and, as a result, a place of rebirth. Prehistoric sites like the Hypogeum in Malta allowed living worshipers to mingle with their dead. In Çatalhüyük, in central Turkey, where a peaceful civilization flourished in the fifth millennium BCE, dead family members were often buried under the beds of their living kin, indicating that death was not to be dreaded.

However, by the time of the Sumerian empire in Mesopotamia (c. 3000–c. 1900 BCE), the underworld had become a much more negative place. The Sumerians believed it was situated beneath Apsu, a deity and also

Left: Engraving of a sculpture of Hades by English artist Charles Grignion (1717–1810). Hades holds his two-pronged staff, which the Greeks believed he used to drive spirits into the underworld.

the primal ocean, and was ruled by Ereshkigal, the Lady of the Great Place. Like Hades, the Sumerian realm of the dead was dark and dreary. Even Ereshkigal herself dined on dirt and muddy water. Her sexual appetites were insatiable, linking her in a negative way to the Great Mother.

Homer's underworld

Even more than the Mesopotamian peoples, the Greeks saw death as a dreadful event, and the realm of the dead as a place of sorrow. According to Homer, in the endless night of Hades, the sun never shone and the spirits were mere shadows. A few inhabitants, however, had special privileges. The blind seer Tiresias was granted the use of his mind by Persephone, the queen of the underworld, and could speak to questioners once he had been given some sacrificial blood to drink. Elpenor, the friend of the Greek hero Odysseus, died after he drunkenly fell off a roof. He, too, was allowed to speak because his body had not yet been cremated, but other spirits were sad, silent shadows that flitted across the murky landscape. The souls of the dead lived in a vague, dreamlike state, which was so dreary that the warrior Achilles said he would rather be a slave in the upper world than a king in Hades. Occasionally, residents of the underworld were visited by heroes who found hidden

Cerberus, the Hound of Hades

Cerberus, a terrifying three-headed dog with a snake's tail, guarded the entrance to Hades and prevented anyone from returning to the land of the living. He was the offspring of Typhon, a monster with a hundred snake heads, and Echidna, who was half woman and half snake. Other monstrous offspring of Typhon and Echidna included the many-headed Hydra and the Chimaera, who had the head of a lion, the body of a goat, and the tail of a snake.

For the last of his 12 Labors, the Greek hero Heracles had to bring Cerberus to the world of the living. Hades granted his permission, provided Heracles use no weapons. The hero subdued the animal using strength alone. According to Roman poet Ovid (43 BCE–17 CE), Cerberus foamed with rage when he was carried into the bright sunshine, and as his spittle touched the ground it turned into the poisonous aconite plant. In contrast, Orpheus's music calmed the dog, allowing the musician and his wife Eurydice to escape Hades— although for Eurydice the respite was all too brief.

Below: Cerberus *by English artist William Blake (1757–1827). Blake's painting is an interpretation of* The Divine Comedy *by Italian poet Dante (1265–1321), in which Cerberus guards the third circle of Hell—where gluttons are punished.*

entrances to Hades, usually in caves, gorges, or geothermal outlets that emitted steam and heat.

Homer described swarms of dead souls shrieking in terror, some of them enduring eternal torment for crimes they had committed while alive. As a punishment for killing his own son and serving him to the gods as a test of their wisdom, Tantalus spent eternity reaching hungrily for fruit on laden branches that swung away from his grasp. Another dead soul, Sisyphus, strained to push a giant rock up a hill, only to have it roll down again just as he succeeded in moving it to the top. This torment was due to Sisyphus's tattling to the river god Asopus that Zeus had abducted his daughter. Other mortals punished in Hades included Ixion, Peirithous, Tityus, and Ocnus. While extraordinary sinners suffered extraordinary pain, most souls remained in a lackluster, boring state, drifting over a boundless meadow filled with asphodel, the plant of Hades. They were possessed by the same passions and fears that drove the living, but the gods gave them neither punishment nor reward.

Later beliefs about the underworld

In his work the *Republic*, Greek philosopher Plato (c. 428–c. 348 BCE) told the myth of Er, who had a near-death experience and described the underworld. In this account, some of the dead entered through holes in the earth and others through holes in the sky. The first group described life after death as unhappy, while the second group rejoiced amid beauty and happiness. Those who had dishonored the gods or their parents could expect horrible retribution. They might be flayed and dragged to death, then hurled down to Tartarus, the deepest part of Hades. Doers of good deeds, on the other hand, were rewarded in equal proportion to their actions.

According to the Roman poet Virgil (70–19 BCE) in his epic the *Aeneid*, the fortunate souls were admitted to the elysian fields or Elysium. In some myths, paradise was located in the Isles of the Blessed, and inhabitants were able to enjoy the delights of wrestling on the grass and wandering in forest glades, whereas the wicked were suspended in fire or forever blown in howling winds. After a thousand years, the Blessed were called by the gods to the Lethe, where they were made to drink some of its water. In this way they forgot their past and took up another life on earth. These visions of the afterlife as a place of retribution and even reincarnation were far removed from the Hades that Homer described, which was egalitarian—since everyone went there—but depressingly dull.

The underworld in other cultures

Underworld visions from a variety of cultures indicate that human beings have expected to be held accountable for the choices they made during their earthly lives. Their societies generally held out the promise of reward for good behavior and punishment for evil. According to ancient beliefs in India, depending on their virtue or lack of it, dead souls were sent to paradise, a place of torment, or back to earth for another attempt at living a decent life. Yama, the god of death in Hindu mythology, bears close parallels to Hades. He was a son of Vivasvat, the sun. His sister, Yami, was his constant companion and ruled the females in the underworld. According to the sacred scriptures called the Vedas, Yama was the first man to die. Because of his cruel deeds as a warrior, molten copper was poured into his mouth three times a day, until he had done penance for his sins. He was said to inflict feeble old age on humans so that they would be less inclined to behave badly. In later times, Yama became a harsh, punishing figure, who carried a noose and had green-eyed dogs for companions, echoing Cerberus, the three-headed canine guardian of Hades. Dead souls crossed the Vaitarami River—just as the Greek dead crossed the Styx River—and entered the judgment hall. This concept of death reflected the three-fold hierarchical social order of Indo-European warrior tribes, in which a ruler exerted his power over the ruled.

The ancient Egyptian god of the underworld was Osiris. Like Hades, he had a beloved consort, Isis, and similarly did not punish the guilty himself, but had a flock of lesser deities to do this distasteful work. Following a mortal's death, Anubis, the jackal-headed god, weighed the heart, the memory, and thought. If Maat, goddess of truth, said the balance was equal, Thoth, the ibis-headed god, determined that the soul could go on to the realm of the dead. Those who failed the test were eaten by Am-mut, who had the head of a crocodile and a lion's mane. Just as Cerberus guarded Hades, so a similarly frightening animal guarded the entrance to the Egyptian underworld.

BARBARA GARDNER

Bibliography
Bulfinch, Thomas. *Bulfinch's Mythology.* New York: Barnes & Noble, 2006.
Graves, Robert. *The Greek Myths.* New York: Penguin, 1993.
Homer, and Robert Fagles, trans. *The Iliad.* New York: Penguin, 2009.

SEE ALSO: Cronus; Demeter; Dionysus; Furies; Gaia; Hecate; Persephone; Zeus.

HEBE

Hebe, meaning "bloom of youth," was worshiped by the Greeks as the goddess of youth. She was the daughter of Hera and Zeus, although one account suggests Hera became pregnant with Hebe after touching a lettuce.

After Hebe's birth, the gods competed to honor her with their gifts. Both Athena and Poseidon gave her intricate toys, while Apollo tried to surpass them by soothing Hebe with his music. Hebe grew into the form of a beautiful youth—Greek poet Pindar (c. 522–c. 438 BCE) described her as "fairest of all goddesses," and coins discovered near the Greek city of Argos depict her as a young woman in a sleeveless dress.

Cupbearer and wife

As a minor deity, Hebe performed tasks for the other gods. In his epic poem the *Iliad*, Greek writer Homer (ninth–eighth century BCE) describes how she prepared her mother Hera's chariot for battle, harnessing the horses and helping Hera into the chariot. Homer also relates how she looked after her brother, the war god Ares, when he was wounded during the Trojan War by Greek hero Diomedes. According to Homer, Hebe "washed him clean and put delicate clothing on him." Her most famous role, however, was as the gods' cupbearer, providing them with their favorite drink, nectar. She did not retain this role for long. According to one myth, Zeus gave her cupbearing duties to the handsome mortal Ganymede, with whom Zeus had fallen in love. He abducted the youth, installed him on Mount Olympus, and then made him immortal.

Another myth relates that Hebe stopped acting as cupbearer when she married Heracles, who achieved immortality after his death. Hera, who had previously hated Heracles, reconciled herself with the new god by adopting him and arranging his marriage to her daughter. Hebe bore Heracles two sons, Alexiares and Anicetus. It is possible

Right: The graceful figure of Hebe *(1796) was so popular that Italian sculptor Antonio Canova (1757–1822) carved four replicas of his original statue.*

Above: This fresco in the Corsini Villa, south of Florence, Italy, is by Giovanni de San Giovanni (1592–1633). It depicts Jupiter driving Hebe away in order to give her cupbearing duties to Ganymede.

that Hebe's change of status reflected the changing nature of ancient Greek society, which became increasingly patriarchal, or male dominated. An early name for Hebe was Ganymeda, which suggests that the concept of this deity split into two entities: the male, Ganymede, who took over the active role of cupbearer, and the female, Hebe, who adopted the more passive duties of a wife.

A different Hebe

Classical scholar Robert Graves (1895–1985) suggested that the deity who married Heracles might have been an entirely different Hebe from the Greek goddess of youth. He cited evidence from a collection of Greek songs addressed to the hero Orpheus, the Orphic Hymns, which were produced between the third century BCE and the fourth century CE. Two songs in this collection state that Heracles married a goddess called Hipta, whose many alternative names included Hebe. Hipta was worshiped as Mother Earth by the people of Mitanni, an empire in northern Mesopotamia (present-day Iraq) that flourished from approximately 1500 to 1360 BCE. This version of Hebe, known throughout the Middle East, might reflect Heracles' association with Anatolia (part of present-day Turkey), where, according to myth, he carried out 3 of his 12 famous labors.

Youth-giving qualities

As the personification of youth, the Greeks identified Hebe with qualities such as vigor, bravery, and generosity, as well as recklessness, arrogance, and inconsistency. In myths she had the power to restore people to their youth. The sorceress Medea made an altar to Hebe when turning the hero Jason's father, Aeson, into a young man again. Iolaus, Hercules' nephew and assistant on earth, prayed to be restored to his youth in order to kill Eurystheus, the king who had set Heracles his 12 tasks and mistreated both Iolus and his family. As Heracles' wife, Hebe readily granted Iolaus his request.

Hebe's two main centers of worship in ancient Greece were at Phlios and Sicyon, both cities on the Peloponnese peninsula that held allegiance to the region's chief city, Sparta. The Greek traveler and geographer Pausanias, who lived in the second century CE, wrote that one of the main things people requested from the goddess was forgiveness for wrongdoing. Released prisoners in Phlios honored Hebe by leaving their prison-chains on trees in a sacred grove.

Andrew Campbell

Bibliography

Bulfinch, Thomas. *Bulfinch's Mythology.* New York: Barnes & Noble, 2006.
Graves, Robert. *The Greek Myths.* New York: Penguin, 1993.

SEE ALSO: Ares; Hera; Zeus.

HECATE

The goddess Hecate, whose name means "she who works her will," occupies an ambiguous place in Greek mythology. In early accounts she is an all-powerful deity associated with brightness, yet later writers connected her with darkness and the underworld.

Above: A 16th-century Italian woodcut of the goddess Hecate from the book Mythologiae *by Natalis Comitis. Hecate is depicted with three animal heads, a variation on her more usual form of three bodies.*

According to eighth-century-BCE Greek poet Hesiod's epic account of the origins of the gods, *Theogony*, Hecate was a goddess who had strong links to the Titans, the divine race that flourished before the Olympian gods. Her mother was Asteria, the daughter of Titans Coeus and Phoebe; her father was Perses, the son of Titans Crius and Eurybia. In Hesiod's version, Hecate had a special status among the Titans and controlled the three earthly realms: the land, the sea, and the sky. Other divine beings sacrificed and prayed to her because she had the power to bestow wealth and blessing.

A new world order, however, commenced when Zeus vanquished his father, the Titan Cronus, in a ten-year-long battle that put an end to the reign of the Titans and ushered in the rule of the Olympians. Unlike the Titans, whom Zeus imprisoned in Tartarus, a terrible place far below the earth, Hecate was allowed to keep her honors and privileges. In addition, Zeus made her the benefactor of rulers, farmers, horse riders, and sailors, with the power to grant victory in battle and in athletic contests. He also named her the nurse of all the babies who survived to see their second day of life. Hecate reciprocated by fighting on the side of the gods in their epic battle against the Giants, during which she slayed the Giant Clytius with torches—objects with which she was often associated.

Downgrading a deity

In *Theogony*, Hecate's great powers and authority placed her above the Olympian goddesses who oversaw such areas of life as marriage, love, sex, and domestic affairs. However, in later centuries, Greek writers such as fifth-century-BCE dramatist Euripides and third-century-BCE poet Apollonius of Rhodes downgraded Hecate's imposing powers to put her on a par with other goddesses. They described Hecate as a goddess of sorcery and poisoning, whose presence preceded doom and destruction. One reason for this change may have been that, by the time of Greece's classical era (479–338 BCE), an all-powerful female deity did not suit the requirements of its patriarchal, society. The Greek pantheon reflected this male-centered society—the gods ruled the universe and the goddesses played subsidiary roles.

Hecate's treatment in mythology resembles that of another old and powerful female god, Gaia, the primordial goddess of the earth, who mated with Uranus to give birth

Left: A fifth-century-BCE sculpture of Hecate and Persephone, from the ancient Greek city of Eleusis. Hecate is on the right, holding two torches, while Persephone sits on her underworld throne.

goddess of corn, does not know where her daughter has gone and despairs of finding the culprit. She is counseled by Hecate, whose "shining headband" and torch symbolize the light of understanding. Hecate tells Demeter that she has heard the voice of the abductor but has not seen his identity. She suggests that they seek out the sun god Helios, whose lofty position makes him privy to many secrets. Helios reveals that Hades is the perpetrator. After mother and daughter have been reunited, Hecate lovingly tends Persephone. Because Persephone is forced to spend part of every year with Hades, Hecate becomes her attendant in the underworld.

Two aspects of the poem may have influenced Hecate's later, sinister reputation. The first is that Hecate lives in a cave, a part of the earth that links what is above the ground to what is underneath it. Caves are also associated with monsters—in Homer's epic the *Odyssey*, the giant one-eyed Cyclopes live in caves. The second aspect is Hecate's role as Persephone's servant in the underworld. This role foreshadowed the deity's connections with death and dark forces. In his epic the *Aeneid*, Roman writer Virgil (70–19 BCE) describes Hecate as "queen of the sky and the dark domain below the earth," which emphasizes her estrangement from the world of mortals, who could not journey to either of these realms. Many Roman writers also identified her as one aspect of the triple moon-goddess, called Luna in heaven, Diana on earth, and Hecate below the ground.

Hecate's mythological transformation, from Hesiod's account to that of later writers, contains a series of reversals. Initially she was a goddess of light, but later her torches signified not their own light but the darkness that they dispelled. Hecate had also been a goddess of blessing, who was honored for making crops grow. According to later writers, however, her role was quite different: Hecate governed the harmful and destructive weeds that sprouted into the earth from the underworld.

Hecate's ambiguous role

In classical Greece and later, people believed that Hecate inhabited the space between the world of the dead and the world of the living. This position made her a frightening goddess, but also suggests an ambiguity—she may have been both bad and good. The idea that Hecate could cross normally unbridgeable boundaries shows up in the myths

to the Titans. As happened with Hecate, Gaia's authority was subsumed by the Olympian gods, but she retained some prestige as a result of her earlier power. Both goddesses may represent the attempt to assimilate pre-Greek deities into the Greek pantheon. Gaia's origins can be traced back to the Pelasgians, Stone Age Greeks who strongly believed in a mother goddess. Some scholars think that Hecate may first have been worshiped by the Carians, an ancient people of western Asia.

Changing reputation

As well as downgrading Hecate's status from that described in *Theogony*, later writers further broke with Hesiod's account by associating the deity with darkness and destruction. One possible source for this change may be the "Homeric Hymn to Demeter," an anonymous poem—once thought to have been the work of the ninth- or eighth-century-BCE Greek poet Homer—written in or around the seventh century BCE. The poem tells the story of the abduction of Persephone by Hades, king of the underworld. Demeter, Persephone's mother and the

Left: A third-century-BCE marble herm of Hecate. The deity's three bodies may relate to her link with crossroads—they would allow Hecate to look in all directions.

that developed her darker side. She was the goddess of highways and especially of crossroads, where, according to Virgil, she could be invoked at night by cries of alarm. Travel in the ancient world was notoriously dangerous, and bandits often ambushed people at crossroads at nighttime. For some people, Hecate may have personified the evil forces operating at night and, in order to appease her, they left food offerings called "Hecate's supper" at crossroads. Other people, however, may have looked to the goddess to keep away evil spirits—pillars known as Hecateae were erected at crossroads and doorways for this purpose.

Magic, gods, and monsters

Hecate appears in many myths as a deity with magical powers, and one from whom mortals could learn dark secrets. In Virgil's *Aeneid*, the Sibyl, or prophetess, of Cumae orders Aeneas to sacrifice to Hecate upon entering the underworld. Then she guides Aeneas safely through this realm, because she has learned all about it from Hecate. In his account of Jason and the Argonauts, Apollonius of Rhodes tells how Hecate taught the witch Medea to use magic herbs. Roman poet Ovid (43 BCE–17 CE) elaborated that Hecate's followers picked their poisonous herbs in the dark of the moon. Worshipers used honey as a libation for the goddess, one of many traditional offerings to the dead.

Hecate was connected with many divinities and monsters. According to several sources, she mated with the sea god Phorcys and gave birth to Scylla, a beautiful nymph who, when she grew up, rejected all her suitors. The witch Circe grew jealous of Scylla's charms and poisoned the pool in which she swam, causing six terrible dogs to sprout from her body. Greek historian and geographer Pausanias (143–176 CE) mentions Hecate in his account of the Trojan War. When a lack of wind prevents the Greek forces from sailing to Troy, the seer Calchas declares that Agamemnon, king of Mycenae and commander of the Greek army, must sacrifice his daughter Iphigeneia to appease the goddess Artemis. In Pausanias's retelling, Iphigeneia does not die at her father's hand but, by the will of Artemis, becomes Hecate. This curious mythological variant can be explained by the association of Iphigeneia with Artemis, and of Artemis with Hecate. Many scholars consider Iphigeneia to have been a form of Artemis, while Hecate represented the dark side of Artemis. In her role as

Above: Hecate *by English artist and poet William Blake (1757–1827). The painting shows Hecate's three bodies and depicts the goddess surrounded by real and imaginary creatures in a nightmarish scene.*

the goddess of highways and meeting points, Hecate was sometimes known as Artemis of the Crossroads. Roman writers' identification of Hecate as one aspect of the moon, with Diana—the Roman name for Artemis—as another aspect, further strengthens the connection between the two deities.

Representations of Hecate

A number of surviving descriptions and representations of Hecate reveal her as having three complete bodies joined together. This form makes her slightly different from the mythical character Geryon, whose herds of cattle the hero Heracles stole as his 10th labor and who had three torsos joined at the waist. One explanation for Hecate's three bodies is her association with crossroads—three bodies would allow the goddess to look in all directions at once. Virgil called Hecate the triple-shaped Diana and the three-faced virgin—the latter description indicates that he did not credit her as the mother of Scylla. Pausanias, however, observed that in Hecate's temple on the Greek island of

Aegina the statue of the goddess had only one head and body. He believed that it was the fifth-century-BCE sculptor Alcamenes who originated her triple-bodied form in a statue that the Athenians called Epipurgidia, meaning "on the tower." Apollonius of Rhodes wrote that Hecate wore on her head a wreath of serpents entwined with oak leaves, a description that links her to the three female monsters known as the Gorgons. Hecate appears in the frieze on the Great Altar of Zeus (c. 180 BCE), which archaeologists discovered on the site of the ancient Greek city of Pergamum. The frieze depicts the battle between the Olympian gods and the Giants, in which Hecate fought on the side of the gods.

KATHRYN CHEW

Bibliography

Apollonius Rhodius, and R. Hunter, trans. *Jason and the Golden Fleece.* New York: Oxford University Press, 2009.

Hamilton, Edith. *Mythology.* New York: Grand Central, 2011.

Hesiod, and M. L. West, trans. *Theogony* and *Works and Days.* New York: Oxford University Press, 2008.

SEE ALSO: Artemis; Demeter; Diana; Gaia; Hades; Helios; Persephone; Titans; Zeus.

HELIOS

Helios, called Sol Invictus by the Romans, was the Greek god of the sun, but he was not one of the most important deities in the Greek pantheon. He was responsible for bringing light to the heavens and earth, usually by hitching the sun to his chariot and dragging it across the sky. As the sun god he could observe everything that occurred in the world during his daily journey from east to west. However, unlike most of the other Olympians, Helios had little interaction with mortals.

Helios, the sun god, was the cousin of Zeus, king of the Olympian deities. In Greek mythology they were both sons of Titans. The Titans were among the first offspring of the creation deities, Uranus (sky) and Gaia (earth). According to the *Theogony*, an epic poem of Greek mythology attributed to the poet Hesiod (fl. c. 800), two Titans, Theia and Hyperion, were the parents of Helios. Their other children were Selene (moon) and Eos (dawn). Two other Titans, Cronus and Rhea, parented most of the other Olympians, including Zeus.

In Greek and Roman art and literature, Helios is usually depicted as a youthful male deity with rays of light beaming from his head. He also usually drives a four-horse chariot. In some versions the sunlight emanates either from Helios's chariot or from Helios himself; in others the sun is attached to Helios's chariot and hauled across the sky.

Below: Helios in His Sun Wagon, *by Fabrizio Chiari (c. 1615–1695), is a fresco of the Greek sun god making his daily journey east to west across the sky, bringing light to to the world.*

Occasionally he is shown riding on horseback or having wings. The rays of light distinguish Helios from his sister Selene, whose head is often marked by a crescent moon. Helios, like Uranus, Oceanus (ocean), and Selene—all of whom embodied or were responsible for overseeing elements of nature—played a minor role in the stories concerning mortals and in the religious life of the ancient Greeks. In other ancient cultures, such as Egypt, the sun god had a much more prominent position; however, for the Greeks, Apollo, the god of light, emulated many of the characteristics of earlier sun gods (see box, page 123).

References to and children of Helios

It was generally believed that Helios rode his four-horse chariot across the sky from east to west each day, bringing light to the world. Each night he would sail in the celestial waters that surrounded the earth back to his home in the east in time to start his daily journey. Although there are few stories that feature Helios, he was said to have fathered several famous characters, such as Pasiphae, the mother of

Right: This Roman bronze head, from around the second century CE, is believed to depict Helios.

the Minotaur, and Aeetes, king of Colchis, father of Medea, and possessor of the Golden Fleece.

Another of Helios's sons was Phaethon, who pleaded with his father to allow him to drive the chariot for one day. Reluctantly Helios agreed, but the steeds proved too powerful for Phaethon to control, and the chariot scorched the earth. It would have destroyed all the mortals if Zeus had not intervened. The king of gods hurled one of his thunderbolts at Phaethon, killing him instantly. The youth's lifeless body fell from the chariot and landed in a river.

A few other stories either have references to Helios or include him in a minor role. For example, in the *Odyssey* Homer writes that Odysseus's companions slaughtered and ate some cattle that belonged to Helios. When the sun god learned of this, he traveled to Olympus and demanded that Zeus punish Odysseus's men. Zeus agreed and destroyed Odysseus's ship with a thunderbolt, drowning Odysseus's crew. Only Odysseus, who had not taken part in eating Helios's cattle, survived.

In another story, it is explained that Helios used a giant golden cup, forged for him by the god Hephaestus, in which the sun god and his horses rested as they floated around the earth each night, always reaching their starting point in the east in time to raise the sun again. Helios loaned the cup to Heracles when the hero was searching for the cattle of Geryon. The mythographer Apollodorus, who lived during the second century BCE, claimed that Heracles used his bow and arrow to force Helios to give up the goblet, which the hero used to sail far westward. On his return journey, Heracles again rode in Helios's golden cup and had room in the vessel for the cattle of Geryon.

Helios's Cult in Rhodes

The Greek island of Rhodes was the site of the main worship of Helios. It was believed that when Zeus originally divided the world among the gods, Helios was away in his chariot. Some time later, when Rhodes appeared, Helios claimed the island. In recognition of their patron, the people of Rhodes held an annual festival, the Halieia, where four horses were thrown into the sea to relieve Helios's tired ones. Also the Rhodians built the Colossus of Rhodes, a huge statue of Helios and one of the so-called Seven Wonders of the World. It stood at the entrance to the main harbor and served as a kind of lighthouse. According to legend, a nymph of the island gave birth to seven of Helios's sons, and three of his grandsons were the namesakes of three Rhodian cities: Cameiros, Ialysos, and Lindos.

Helios and Apollo

The ancient Greeks sometimes called Helios Phoebus, meaning "shining." Beginning around the fifth century BCE, Apollo, the Olympian god of prophecy and divination, was also called Phoebus. From then on Helios and Apollo were often identified with each other. Greek dramatist Euripides (c. 486–c. 406 BCE) wrote a short play *Phaethon* that made the connection between Apollo and Helios explicit for the first time in Greek literature. Scholars believe that Apollo, whom the Greeks believed was a son of Zeus and Leto, may have originated as a divinity in Asia and was adopted by the

Greeks early on. Unlike Helios, Apollo intervened in the lives of mortals and featured in several myths. In Greek art Apollo was often depicted in a manner similar to Helios: as a youthful figure with rays of light shining from him. He was also adopted by the Romans and highly revered by Emperor Augustus (63 BCE–14 CE).

Below: This Greek bowl depicts Helios in his horse-drawn chariot with rays of light emanating from his head. The god Apollo, who was also linked to the sun but held a more prominent position in the pantheon than Helios, was often depicted similarly in Greek art.

Another story involves Helios and Hephaestus. Because Helios traveled so high in the sky, he was able to witness everything that went on. One day he saw the goddess of love, Aphrodite, making love to Ares, the god of war. Aphrodite was married to Hephaestus, and Helios felt obliged to tell the god of metalworking what he had observed. After hearing of his wife's adultery, Hephaestus fashioned an invisible metal net and captured the lovers in

Aphrodite's bed. Hephaestus hauled the lovers before the other Olympians, who howled with laughter.

In a subsequent story Aphrodite took her revenge on Helios. She made him fall in love with a girl named Leucothoe. The girl died either because as a mortal she could not bear Helios's power when they had sex, or because her father buried her alive when he found out that she had made love to a god.

Although Helios did not appear frequently in Greek myth or have much direct religious significance in Greek culture, he did play an important role in watching over oaths. Because he saw everything that went on during the day, Helios was sometimes called on to be a witness to oaths. His omniscience also made him privy to whether oaths were being kept or not.

Sun gods in other cultures

In other ancient polytheistic cultures the sun god usually held a prominent or chief position in the pantheon. For example, in Egyptian religion the sun god, Re, was the

Right: In this statue, Helios is given the face and hairstyle of Roman emperor Caracalla (188–217 CE). Helios was the favorite god of Caracalla's hero, Alexander the Great.

Sol Invictus

The Roman god Sol Invictus, whose name in Latin means "the invincible sun god," was based on the Greek sun god Helios and the god of prophecy, Apollo, who was linked to the sun. Generally, the older Roman pantheon that included Jupiter, Mars, Venus, and so on maintained prominence in Roman religion, but Sol Invictus became increasingly important in Roman religious and imperial life from the first century CE onward. There was even a temple dedicated to the deity in Circus Maximus, an important site in the city of Rome. From the first to the third century, the importance of sun worship grew until Sol became the chief object of imperial worship. Even the father of Constantine I, the first Christian emperor of Rome who ruled the empire from 306 until his death in 337, dutifully worshiped Sol Invictus.

creator and master of the world. Re's rising and setting symbolized the cycles of death and renewal prevalent in life. His center of worship was the city of Iunu, which the Greeks called Heliopolis or "city of the sun." Other sun gods included the Syrian sun god, El-Gabal, whose supreme position was alluded to in depictions of the deity standing alongside an eagle, the sign of celestial authority; and the Hindu god Surya, who has temples dedicated to him throughout India.

The Romans

As the Roman armies and their culture spread throughout the Mediterranean from the second century BCE, the Roman belief system began to incorporate other religions traditions. The worship of the sun was no exception, and the god Sol Invictus (Helios) became increasingly important (see box). Christianity displaced the worship of Sol Invictus in the fourth century CE, although the imagery of the sun with its blinding light and fire remains an important motif in Christian theology and art. The sun god maintained considerable influence in the Greco-Roman mind through Helios to Sol Invictus and beyond.

BRIAN SEILSTAD

Bibliography

Bulfinch, Thomas. *Bulfinch's Mythology.* New York: Barnes & Noble, 2006.

Howatson, M. C. *The Oxford Companion to Classical Literature.* New York: Oxford University Press, 2005.

SEE ALSO: Apollo; Eos; Hephaestus; Selene; Titans.

HEPHAESTUS

Hephaestus was the Greek god of fire and metalworking. He was one of the 12 major Olympian gods, but the only one to be lame. The other gods constantly ridiculed Hephaestus for his disability—as a result his actions were frequently motivated by his desire to punish those who mocked and abused him.

There are two versions of Hephaestus's birth and lameness. According to the Greek poet Homer (c. ninth–eighth century BCE), Hephaestus was born to Zeus and Hera. When he took his mother's side in an argument, Zeus knocked him off Mount Olympus. After falling through the air for a day, Hephaestus landed on the island of Lemnos, permanently injuring his leg. One of the peoples on the island, a mysterious group called the Sintians, nursed the fallen god back to health.

This version possibly reflects the ancient Greek view that Hephaestus's attachment to his mother was excessive and deserved to be punished. In elite society in Greece, boys were raised by their mothers until they were of school age, at which time they would leave behind the women's quarters and join the company of men. Hephaestus's punishment from Zeus may have been because he preferred the company of women to men. The suggestion that Hephaestus was insufficiently masculine is enhanced by his subsequent physical frailty and the teasing he received from his healthier siblings.

The other account of Hephaestus's origins comes from the Greek poet Hesiod (fl. 800 BCE). According to this source, Hera created Hephaestus on her own in retaliation for Zeus's creation of Athena, the goddess of war and handicrafts who emerged from the king of the gods' head, but when Hephaestus turned out to be lame, Hera rejected her son and threw him out of heaven. He fell into Oceanus (the sea) and was rescued by the sea nymphs Thetis and

Right:
A classical bronze statuette of Hephaestus, depicting him trailing his left leg. Hephaestus's disability led to his humiliation by other deities—itself a reflection of Greek attitudes toward physical handicap.

HEPHAESTUS

The Greeks and Disability

The reactions of Hera and her fellow deities toward Hephaestus's physical handicap reflected the ancient Greek attitude toward infirmity. They saw it as a sign of inferiority—mental as well as physical. In Homer's world, physical beauty always accompanied mental agility, while people with physical problems were regarded as slow-witted. Ironically, Hephaestus did not fit this model at all—as his skillful creations demonstrate—but he was treated as though he did. The fact that Hera's sole attempt to create life apart from her husband resulted in a flawed offspring suggests that the Greeks believed that the female creative potential was insufficient on its own to produce viable beings. Hephaestus always remained a second-class citizen on Mount Olympus. He was the only major deity who worked for a living—this perhaps represents the encroachment of a lower artisan class upon the ruling leisured class in Greek society.

Eurynome, who instructed him in the art of metalworking. To punish Hera for her ill treatment, Hephaestus designed for her an exquisite throne of gold. When she sat in it, the throne entrapped her in a fine mesh of chains. None of the other Olympians could free her or persuade Hephaestus to release his mother. Finally Dionysus, the god of wine, succeeded in getting Hephaestus drunk. Under the influence of alcohol, he agreed to return to Olympus and release his mother. Vase paintings show Dionysus either supporting a drunken Hephaestus on the walk up to Olympus or leading Hephaestus, who sat on a donkey. Hephaestus's return to Olympus remained a popular artistic topic, although this story did not survive in literature.

Special powers
Hera's casting of Hephaestus into the primal waters of Oceanus and his subsequent rescue symbolize a second birth. Like other mythical characters who passed through the portals of birth or death more than once—such as Orpheus, Heracles, Asclepius, Hippolytus, and Dionysus—Hephaestus emerged with a special power. In his case, it was the power to control and give life to metals, including gold, bronze, and silver.

There were three different accounts of where Hephaestus had his smithy, or workshop: on Mount Olympus itself, in the active volcano of Mount Etna on the Italian island of Sicily, or on Lemnos. According to Homer, Hephaestus made two golden robots to assist him. Roman poet Virgil (70–19 BCE) related that Hephaestus had his

cavernous smithy in Mount Etna. In Virgil's account, Hephaestus was in charge of the one-eyed giants the Cyclopes, who forged Zeus's thunderbolts.

Helping gods and mortals
Hephaestus assisted various deities and mortals with his artistry and metalworking skills. During the Gigantomachy, the war between the Olympian gods and the Giants, he killed the giant Mimas with red-hot pellets of metal. He then designed and built palaces for all the Olympians, as well as for the mortals Aeetes and Oenopion. According to the second-century-BCE mythographer Apollodorus, Hephaestus constructed a mechanical bronze dog that Zeus gave to King Minos of Crete; a gold wedding necklace for Harmonia, the daughter of the war god Ares and the love goddess Aphrodite; and the bronze rattles that Heracles used to put the Stymphalian birds to flight during one of his 12 labors. He also purified Pelops, son of the king of Lydia, after his treacherous murder of the charioteer Myrtilus, who had helped Pelops win his bride.

Hephaestus's work did not end there. According to some myths, he assisted in Athena's birth by splitting open Zeus's head with his ax and releasing the fully grown goddess. When the Titan Prometheus challenged Zeus's supremacy by giving fire to mortals, Hephaestus riveted him to a cliff—said to be Mount Kazbek in the Caucasus—where he was tortured. Hephaestus also helped create the first woman, Pandora, whom Zeus offered as a gift to Prometheus's gullible brother, Epimetheus. Hephaestus designed and composed her body from clay, and the other gods endowed her with personal qualities. When Epimetheus accepted Pandora, he condemned humans to a life of suffering because she released sorrow and disease from the jar she brought with her.

Love and revenge
According to Hesiod, Hephaestus married Aglaea, the youngest of the goddesses known as the Graces. Other sources, however, name Aphrodite as his wife, but Aphrodite preferred Hephaestus's strong, virile brother Ares, and continued her love affair with the war god after her marriage to Hephaestus.

The sun god Helios, who saw all things and often played the role of informant in various myths, revealed to Hephaestus that his wife had been secretly sleeping with

Right: Vulcan Forging the Arms of Achilles *by Italian artist Giulio Romano (c. 1499–1546). Vulcan was the Roman god of elemental fire, later identified with Hephaestus. Both gods were patrons of metalworkers.*

Ares. As he had done with his mother, Hephaestus exacted his revenge by indirect methods rather than direct confrontation. He may also have realized that he would be no match for Ares if an aggressive approach ended in a brawl. Instead, Hephaestus fashioned a chain that was inescapably strong, but so fine that it was invisible to the eye. He made the chain into a net, fastened it over and around the marital bed, and loudly announced that he intended to visit Lemnos on business. As soon as they thought he had departed, Aphrodite and Ares climbed into bed, but found themselves caught fast in the invisible net. At this point Hephaestus returned, accompanied by the rest of the Olympian gods. His shame at having been cuckolded was tempered by the comedy in the couple's naked and public embarrassment. This story demonstrated to the ancient Greeks what happens when a weak male marries a strong female: the husband is disgraced by his wife's bad behavior. It also showed that brains could sometimes overcome beauty and physical strength.

Below: Venus Receives Mars *by Italian painter Giovanni Battista Tiepolo (1696–1770). Venus and Mars were the Roman names for Aphrodite and Ares, whom Hephaestus punished for their affair.*

The Island of Lemnos

In Greek mythology, the Aegean island of Lemnos was associated with horrible smells. When the women of the island failed to honor Aphrodite, the love goddess cursed them with a foul bodily stench, which drove their husbands to seek alternative wives among the Thracians. The Lemnian women then murdered their husbands, and remained without men until the Argonauts stopped at the island. Either the Argonauts did not mind the women's smell, or, by the time they arrived, Aphrodite had shown forgiveness.

Another myth relates how a snake bit the archer Philoctetes, causing a wound that festered and began to smell badly. The odor, combined with Philoctetes' constant moaning, drove his comrades to maroon him on Lemnos, where he lived until he was rescued.

Hephaestus's smithy on Lemnos would have produced foul smells because of the chemicals used in metalworking. Today, doctors know that the toxicity of the materials used by blacksmiths (metalworkers) can cause a degenerative neurological disease that can lead to lameness. Hephaestus's physical condition may have reflected the fact that blacksmiths tended to become crippled after a number of years in their profession.

Above: The Temple of Hephaestus, Athens. The temple, which is older than the Parthenon (447–432 BCE), was dedicated to both Hephaestus and Athena as the patron and patroness of arts and crafts.

This was not the only occasion when Hephaestus was humiliated by the object of his desires. When Athena visited his smithy to ask for the god's assistance, Hephaestus chased after her. The virgin warrior goddess had no trouble fighting off the crippled blacksmith, but not before Hephaestus had ejaculated on her thigh. Athena wiped off the god's seed with a piece of wool and cast it on the earth, which was immediately impregnated, giving birth to the snake-footed Erichthonius. Two of Hephaestus's other children also inherited his lameness: the Argonaut Palaemonius and the club-wielding bandit Periphetes, whom the hero Theseus killed.

Cult of Hephaestus

It is likely that Hephaestus was originally a non-Greek deity. Herodotus named him as the father of a group of Phrygian gods called the Cabeiri, whose cult was practiced on the islands of the north Aegean. One reason that Lemnos became Hephaestus's main cult center could have been its once-active volcano—the island's inhabitants may have interpreted volcanic eruptions as the workings of Hephaestus in his smithy. Little is known about how Hephaestus was worshiped. However, it is known that metalworking artisans observed the yearly festival of the Chalcheia, and every five years Athenians celebrated the Hephaestia in the god's honor, a festival that featured a torch race and rich sacrifices. The most complete and beautiful surviving temple in Athens belongs to Hephaestus. It stands on a hilltop overlooking the agora, or marketplace, which is fitting, for according to one account, Hephaestus taught humans his crafts and opened the way to commerce.

Hephaestus was not a favorite subject among artists. Besides vase paintings, the best known picture of him is by Dutch painter Maerten van Heemskerck (1498–1574), who in 1536 painted Aphrodite and Ares caught in the god's snare. In the picture, Hephaestus stands nearby holding a cane as the other Olympians look on.

KATHRYN CHEW

Bibliography

Graves, Robert. *The Greek Myths.* New York: Penguin, 1993.

Homer, and Robert Fagles, trans. *The Odyssey.* New York: Penguin, 2009.

SEE ALSO: Aphrodite; Ares; Athena; Dionysus; Graces; Helios; Hera; Prometheus; Zeus.

HERA

Hera, the daughter of Cronus and Rhea, was queen of the Olympian gods. Her marriage to Zeus was troubled by his numerous infidelities, and many of the most celebrated Greek myths concern Hera's acts of vengeance against her husband, his mistresses, and their offspring.

Hera was queen of the Greek gods, and both sister and wife to Zeus. The goddess of women and marriage, she was one of the so-called 12 great Olympians; the others were Zeus, Aphrodite, Apollo, Ares, Artemis, Athena, Demeter, Dionysus, Hephaestus, Hermes, and Poseidon. The Romans later identified Hera with Juno.

As a mythical figure Hera is thought to have evolved from a prehistoric "great goddess" who was associated with the calendar year and with fertility. When the Pelasgians (early ancestors of the modern Greeks) first settled along the shores of the Mediterranean, their supreme male sky god, Zeus, merged forces with the local great goddess, who eventually became Hera.

Hera, the child of the Titans Cronus and Rhea, was born under a willow tree on the island of Samos. Cronus swallowed all his children at birth because he feared a prophecy that one of them would overthrow him. However, Rhea tricked him after the birth of their youngest child, Zeus, by replacing the baby with a wrapped stone and hiding him on the island of Crete. When Zeus grew to manhood he forced his father to disgorge the other children: Hestia, Hera, Demeter, Hades, and Poseidon. With their help, Zeus then defeated Cronus and became king of the gods.

Marriage

Zeus loved Hera and wanted to marry her, even though she was his sister. He courted her for a long time, but Hera showed little interest in him. Zeus then disguised himself as a bedraggled cuckoo on the summit of Mount Thornax. When Hera held the bird to her breast to warm it, Zeus resumed his real form and raped her. Because of this myth, the mountain was renamed Mount Kokkux, "Mount Cuckoo." Pregnant and ashamed, Hera agreed to marry Zeus. Their wedding took place on Crete. Annual celebrations were held at Hera's sanctuary in Argos to commemorate the event. The newlyweds spent a 300-year honeymoon on Samos. Hera

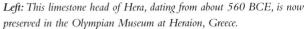

Left: This limestone head of Hera, dating from about 560 BCE, is now preserved in the Olympian Museum at Heraion, Greece.

never fully resigned herself to married life, however. To renew her virginity, she bathed yearly in the translucent, purifying waters of the Canathus Spring.

Described as "chief among the gods in beauty," "golden-shod," and "golden-throned," Hera was definitively regal. She was often depicted with a crown, a lotus-tipped scepter, and a pomegranate, which is a symbol of marriage. Her plant was the willow, and her sacred birds were the cuckoo, the hawk, the crow, and the peacock. Peacocks, symbols of pride, pulled her wagon. Hera's sacred animal was the cow; she was sometimes known as Bopis Hera ("cow-eyed Hera," later translated as "Hera with big eyes"). Hera's character represented womanhood in all its aspects. Temenus of Arcadia (a great-great grandson of Heracles) was said to have given Hera three names: Pais (girl or maiden); Teleia (grown-up or married); and Khera (widow).

Hera and Zeus had three children: Ares, Hebe, and Eileithyia. Ares, a terrifying, murderous god of war, was bloodstained, maniacal, and ever ready for battle. Hebe, the

cupbearer of the gods, personified youth. She helped Hera to prepare her chariot, and washed Ares' wounds after he had been fighting. Eileithyia, the goddess of childbirth, was often identified with Fate and was sometimes said to be even older than her grandfather, Cronus.

When Zeus gave birth to the goddess Athena on his own, Hera was angry. She wanted to prove that she could do anything Zeus could do, so she alone produced Hephaestus and Typhon, although some sources claim Typhon was the son of Gaia. Hephaestus, a blacksmith who was the god of fire and the patron of craftsmen, was always represented as lame. There are two different accounts of his lameness. In one, Zeus quarreled with Hera and flung Hephaestus down from Olympus to the island of Lemnos for siding with her in the quarrel. In the other, Hephaestus

Hera's Battles with Other Gods

Hera quarreled with Poseidon over ownership of Argos, a city-state in the Peloponnese. The chief river, Inachus, declared that the land belonged to Hera, so Poseidon caused all rivers and springs to go dry. According to another version of the myth, the rivers chose Hera as their patron deity, so Poseidon made them disappear. These stories explained why the riverbeds in Argos remained dry except after rainfall.

In the Indian Wars of Dionysus, Hera sided against Artemis, so Artemis tried to shoot her. Hera wrapped herself in one of Zeus's clouds. Artemis shot arrow after arrow into the cloud until her quiver was empty, but caused Hera no injury. Hera then threw a frozen, jagged mass of hail, which broke Artemis's bow, defeating her.

Right: This Roman copy of an ancient Greek statue of Hera is displayed in the Pio-Clementine Museum in the Vatican City.

was born lame, and Hera, disgusted by his disability, flung him from Olympus. When Hephaestus became a man, he avenged himself on Hera by sending her a golden chair that trapped her when she sat in it. Hephaestus then refused to release her. According to some sources, Dionysus, the god of wine, got Hephaestus drunk to convince him to release Hera; other stories state that Hephaestus refused to set Hera free until she swore by the Styx River that she alone had created him.

Like Hephaestus, the monster Typhon had no father: Hera gave birth to him by invoking the powers of Heaven and Earth. Typhon's eyes dripped venom; his hundred horrible heads touched the stars, and red-hot lava poured from his gaping mouths. He tore up Mount Etna to throw it at the gods, but Zeus struck the mountain with a hundred thunderbolts and it fell back on to Typhon, trapping him inside. There he remained for eternity, belching fire, lava, and smoke—an explanation for the mountain's volcanic nature.

Love-hate relationship

Hera and Zeus had a stormy, complicated, and contradictory relationship. They did not trust each other. In one myth, Hera left Zeus after they argued. Zeus consulted Cithaeron, king of Plataea, who advised him to fake a new marriage: Zeus should dress a wooden female image and place it in a processional wagon. Zeus took his advice. In a rage, Hera approached the wagon, tore the dress from her rival, and found the image. Pleased at Zeus's effort to gain her attention, Hera was reconciled with him. The Daidala (meaning "wooden image") festival commemorated their reunion.

Zeus was jealous of Hera, too. When she complained that the centaur Ixion had tried to seduce her, he created a cloud in Hera's image and placed it on Ixion's bed. When Ixion raped the cloud, Zeus punished the centaur by tying him to a fiery, winged wheel to roll ceaselessly through the sky. On another occasion, Zeus made the giant Porphyrion fall in love with Hera, but as soon as Porphyrion approached her, Zeus struck him with a thunderbolt.

Contradictory behavior was a constant in the two Olympians' relationship. They argued about everything, including the question of whether men or women enjoyed sex more. Hera said that men did; Zeus maintained that it was women. Unable to agree, they consulted Tiresias, who had been a woman for seven years before being turned back into a man. He told them that women enjoyed sex nine times more than men. Hera was so annoyed by his

Above: The painting on this Greek ornamental jar (c. 580 BCE) shows Zeus and Hera on their way to be married.

answer that she struck Tiresias blind. Zeus then gave him the power of prophecy.

Despite their differences, Hera was proud of her relationship with Zeus. When Polytechnos, a Lydian carpenter, and Aedon, a daughter of Pandareus, boasted that their love for each other was greater than that between Hera and Zeus, Hera provoked them into a contest to see which of them could finish their work faster. The loser would give the winner a female slave. Aedon won because Hera had secretly helped her with her task. Polytechnos was infuriated. He raped Aedon's sister, Celidon, and then disguised her as the slave. The sisters discovered each other's identities, and in revenge they murdered Polytechnos's son, Itylus, and fed the boy to his father.

Zeus's love affairs

When Zeus had an affair with the gentle Leto, Hera relentlessly harassed the pregnant woman, partly because she knew that Leto would bear a son whom Zeus would love more than their own child, Ares. Leto gave birth to Artemis, who then delivered her own brother Apollo.

Io was another unfortunate mistress of Zeus. When Hera suspected their relationship, Zeus changed Io into a beautiful white heifer and denied the affair. Hera demanded the cow for herself as proof that he did not care for it. Zeus could not refuse, but later sent Hermes to steal the creature back. Meanwhile, however, Hera had set the hundred-eyed giant Argos to guard Io. Hermes killed Argos, but at that point Hera intervened: she placed Argos's eyes in the tail feathers of a peacock and sent a gadfly to pester Io for eternity. Io was finally able to resume her human shape in Egypt, where she gave birth to Epaphus. Hera tried to have the boy kidnapped, but Zeus saved him.

In another myth Zeus raped the nymph Callisto, a servant of the goddess Artemis, in whose honor she had promised to remain a virgin. According to one version of the story, Zeus changed Callisto into a bear to avoid detection by Hera. In another account, Hera changed Callisto into a bear in revenge. Hera then persuaded Artemis to shoot the pregnant Callisto. The arrow pierced Callisto's heart but Zeus managed to seize their baby, Arcas, from the dying body of his mistress. Zeus eventually installed both Callisto and Arcas in the heavens. Callisto

became the Great Bear constellation (Ursa Major or Big Dipper) and Arcas became the brilliant star Arcturus ("Bear guardian" or Little Dipper).

Hera's wrath could last for years. Zeus had an affair with Aegina, who then gave birth to a son, Aeacus. Hera waited until Aeacus was grown up before sending a serpent to poison the water of his native region. Many men died, drastically reducing the size of Aeacus's army. When Aeacus begged Zeus for help, he changed some nearby ants into men, thus foiling Hera's revenge.

Zeus's affair with Semele provoked a gruesome response from Hera. Zeus had sworn to give Semele anything she wanted, so Hera tricked Semele into asking Zeus to appear before her in his full glory. Zeus knew that no mortal could survive the experience, but he was unable to refuse her request. He appeared in his chariot, flashing lightning and thunder. Semele burst into flames. Zeus took their unborn child from her fire-scarred body and sewed it into his own thigh, from which he subsequently gave birth to Dionysus. Hermes took the boy to be raised by a mortal couple, Ino and Athamas. Determined to kill Dionysus, Hera drove the adoptive parents mad, causing them to kill their own children. Dionysus escaped only because Zeus changed him into a baby goat. Still Hera would not give up: she later drove Dionysus mad and forced him to wander Egypt and Syria.

Hera and Heracles

When Zeus fell for Alcmene, the beautiful wife of Amphitryon, the god disguised himself as her husband and ordered Helios to prolong the night to three times its usual length. During that night both Zeus and Amphitryon spent time with Alcmene, who became pregnant with twins. Zeus had foolishly boasted that the next child born in the line of Perseus would rule over Argos; Hera responded by making Eileithyia delay the birth of Heracles so that his cousin, Eurystheus, could be born first. Eurystheus duly became king of Mycenae.

However, Hera was still bent on revenge. When Heracles was eight months old she sent two huge serpents to kill him in his crib. The baby had superhuman strength, however, and squeezed them to death. When Heracles became an adult, Hera sent a fit of madness on him and he killed his wife and children. The Oracle at Delphi told Heracles that he could atone for his crime only by working for Eurystheus. The Mycenaean king ordered him to carry

Left: This painting by Italian artist Correggio (1494–1534) shows the seduction of Io by Zeus.

Familial Battlefield

According to Homer in Book Five of his epic poem the *Iliad*, written around the eighth century BCE, Hera and Athena joined forces against Ares because he had promised them that he would fight for the Greeks, but instead sided with their enemies the Trojans. Hera and Athena rode in Hera's chariot to Mount Olympus, where they asked Zeus for permission to rid the battlefield of Ares.

Zeus agreed to their request, and the two goddesses rode back down to the battlefield. There Athena assured the great Greek warrior Diomedes that he could strike Ares without fear, because she would be by his side. Diomedes wounded Ares as the invisible Athena guided his spear, and Ares retreated to Olympus. Ares complained to Zeus, but he received short shrift from his father, who called him "the most hateful to me of all Olympians," and blamed his fractious nature on his heredity:

"This beastly, incorrigible truculence of yours," Zeus told Ares, "comes from your mother, Hera, whom I keep but barely in my power, no matter what I say to her."

Right: This Roman statue depicts the infant Heracles preparing to deal with one of the snakes sent by Hera to kill him.

out 12 great labors. Even while Heracles was trying to perform these tasks, Hera continued to oppose him. One of the labors involved fetching the belt of Hippolyte, the Amazon queen. Hippolyte volunteered to give her belt to Heracles, but Hera, disguised as a woman in the crowd, shouted that Heracles intended to kidnap the monarch, so the Amazons armed themselves. Seeing that, Heracles jumped to the conclusion that Hippolyte had tricked him, so he killed her. Another labor required Heracles to round up the cattle of Geryon. Again Hera interfered, sending a gadfly to disperse the beasts into the mountains. Heracles caught some of them and brought them back to Eurystheus as a sacrifice intended to appease Hera.

Hera was not placated, however. As Heracles returned to Greece from Troy, Hera sent storms that forced his ship aground on the island of Kos, where he was almost killed. Later Heracles restored Tyndareos as king of Sparta by battling Hippocoon the Usurper and his 13 sons. During this adventure, the hero found that, for almost the first time in his life, Hera had not opposed him. In gratitude, he founded a sanctuary in Sparta for her and sacrificed goats in her honor. When Zeus made Heracles immortal, Hera relented and allowed Heracles to marry her daughter Hebe.

Most of the myths about Zeus and Hera have the same basic plot: he pursues a mortal female, mates with her, and then attempts to hide the relationship from his wife. A child is born, and Hera causes grief to mother and baby. There are two exceptions to this rule. Zeus's affair with Aphrodite was unique because she was the only other Olympian with whom he ever consorted. In his encounter with the witch Iynx, Zeus was the quarry not the hunter: he was seduced while under her spell. True to form, Hera responded violently to both infidelities. She tried to disfigure Priapus, Zeus's son by Aphrodite, while he was still in his mother's womb, and she turned Iynx to stone.

Injured pride

Many myths show that Hera's pride was easily wounded, and she punished women who believed that their beauty rivaled hers. She caused the three daughters of the giant Proitos to roam throughout Argos because they had not worshiped her image in the required manner. She threw Orion's first

wife, Side, into Hades because she claimed to be as beautiful as the goddess herself. When a flawlessly beautiful Pygmaioi girl named Oinoe showed no reverence for Hera, the goddess turned her into a crane. After the transformation, Oinoe still yearned to see her child Mopsos, so she kept flying over the Pygmaioi with her long neck outstretched. The Pygmaioi tried to chase away the irritating crane, a response that led to a perpetual state of war between the Pygmaioi and the birds.

Hera and Jason

When Pelias, king of Iolcus in Thessaly, murdered his stepmother in Hera's shrine, the goddess was offended and determined to destroy him. Pelias was a usurper. As the rightful heir, his nephew Jason, was on his way to claim the throne, Hera, disguised as an old woman, asked him to carry her over the Anaurus River. During the crossing Jason lost a sandal. When he reached Iolcus, Pelias, who had never previously met the boy, knew who he was because an oracle had told him that he would be dethroned by a "one-sandaled man." In an attempt to avert his fate, and inspired by Hera, who put the idea into his head, Pelias told Jason that he would willingly surrender the kingdom if Jason

Below: German artist Franz von Stuck (1863–1928) created this painting, The Three Goddesses: Athena, Hera, and Aphrodite *(1922).*

Above: Worship of Hera was not confined to Greece. This temple to the goddess is at Paestum, near Naples, Italy.

would steal the Golden Fleece from Colchis, a land on the east coast of the Black Sea (part of modern Georgia). That was generally acknowledged to be an impossible task, but Hera helped Jason and his 50 companions throughout their adventure, at one point guiding their ship, *Argo,* through the impassable Clashing Rocks, huge cliffs that constantly crashed together. When Jason returned to Iolcus in triumph with the Fleece, he was accompanied by the witch Medea, who—as Hera knew—was fated to destroy Pelias.

Hera and the Judgment of Paris

When Peleus, king of Phthia married the sea goddess Thetis, all the Olympian deities were invited to the wedding except Eris, the goddess of discord. In revenge, she appeared for an instant and threw down among the guests a golden apple, on which was inscribed "To the Fairest." Hera, Athena, and Aphrodite all vied for the fruit. When there was no outright winner, they appealed to Zeus, but he did not want to choose between them himself, so he sent them to Paris, the son of King Priam of Troy, who at the time was living as a shepherd, unaware of his royal birth. Each of the goddesses tried to bribe him: Athena promised him victory in war, Hera promised to make him king of all men, and Aphrodite promised him the most beautiful woman in the world. Paris chose Aphrodite, only to find that his prize, Helen, was already married to Menelaus, king of Sparta. Paris then abducted Helen and took her back with him to Troy. Menelaus assembled a

great army to retrieve his wife, and the Trojan War began. Hera aligned herself against Paris and the Trojans. She schemed and battled throughout the war on behalf of the Greeks, and even tricked Aphrodite into seducing Zeus in order to distract him from supporting the Trojans.

Popular goddess

Revered in every home, Hera was immensely popular in ancient Greece. Her temples, known as Heraion, were built throughout the country; the most important were at Argos, Samos, and Olympia. Her games at Olympia, called the Heraia, were foot races for unmarried women, staggered according to age groups, with the youngest setting off first. In many ways the Heraia were similar to the Olympic Games: every event-winner received a crown of olive branches and a portion of a sacrificed cow. Women ran with their hair down, their right shoulders bare, and wearing short tunics cut above their knees.

ALYS CAVINESS

Bibliography
Bulfinch, Thomas. *Bulfinch's Mythology.* New York: Barnes & Noble, 2006.

Hesiod, and M. L. West, trans. *Theogony* and *Works and Days.* New York: Oxford University Press, 2008.

Homer, and Robert Fagles, trans. *The Iliad.* New York: Penguin, 2009.

Howatson, M. C. *The Oxford Companion to Classical Literature.* New York: Oxford University Press, 2005.

SEE ALSO: Aphrodite; Ares; Athena; Cronus; Dionysus; Hebe; Hephaestus; Juno; Typhon; Zeus.

HERMAPHRODITUS

In Greek myth, Hermaphroditus was the child of Hermes, the messenger of the gods, and the love goddess Aphrodite. His story—which reflects Greek ideas about gender and marriage—relates how he took on both male and female sexual characteristics.

Hermaphroditus was the only child of Hermes and Aphrodite, born after Zeus took pity on the messenger of the gods' unrequited love for the goddess. Zeus sent an eagle to steal one of Aphrodite's sandals and give it to Hermes. When Aphrodite came to recover it, he won her love and she bore him a beautiful son, whose name combined both of theirs.

The first full account of Hermaphroditus's story occurs in the epic poem *Metamorphoses* by Roman poet Ovid (43 BCE–c. 17 CE). Ovid relates that Hermaphroditus grew up in the caves of Mount Ida, southeast of Troy, in the care of nymphs. When he was 15 years old he set out to travel the world. On his journey he came to a pool where he met another nymph, Salmacis. She instantly fell in love with Hermaphroditus, but he rejected her. Then, as he began to swim in the pool, Salmacis threw herself upon him and embraced him so forcefully that boy and nymph melted together into one body, which was therefore androgynous—both male and female. After the change, Hermaphroditus prayed to his parents that the pool— located near Halicarnassus, one of the ancient cities where Hermes and Aphrodite were both worshiped together— should cause any other man who swam in it to become similarly androgynous.

Worship of Hermaphroditus

Evidence that people worshiped Hermaphroditus as a god comes from a fourth-century-BCE inscription, which records a woman named Phano making a dedication to him "in prayer." A later source refers to a sanctuary of Hermaphroditus in the countryside near Athens: it mentions that a woman brought to it an offering of woven flowers. From the third century BCE onward, figurines of Hermaphroditus were fairly numerous in the Greek world. They were installed as decorations in gymnasia, baths, and theaters, and were also placed in graves and left in sanctuaries as dedications.

Right: This second-century-BCE statue depicts Hermaphroditus sleeping. The mattress and pillow were added in the 17th century.

The earliest written reference to Hermaphroditus occurs in Greek philosopher Theophrastus's (c. 372–c. 287 BCE) *Characters*, in which he portrays various types of eccentric people. According to Theophrastus, on the fourth day of the month, the "superstitious man crowns the hermaphroditus" in his house. It is possible that the use of the word *hermaphroditus* refers to a sculpture of Aphrodite in the form of a herm, a square pillar with a deity's head at the top. However, scholars believe that Theophrastus was referring to the mythical character, who was invoked in a sacred ritual.

Hermaphroditus and marriage

Theophrastus's account also suggests a link between Hermaphroditus and the institution of marriage. The reference to the "fourth day of the month" is telling: this was the luckiest day to hold a wedding. Hermaphroditus's association with marriage seems to have been that, by embodying both masculine and feminine qualities, he or she symbolized the coming together of men and women in sacred union. Various marriage rituals involving switching genders emphasized this fusion of the sexes. On the island of Kos, for instance, the bridegroom wore women's clothes, while in Sparta it was the brides who dressed like men. In Argos the marriage ritual was even more pronounced— brides wore false beards. The thinking behind these customs appears to have been that the bride and groom could switch roles since, in the union of their marriage, one became indistinguishable from the other.

Another factor linking Hermaphroditus to weddings was his or her parents' role in protecting and blessing brides. Hermes and Aphrodite were worshiped together in a number of Greek sanctuaries, and they were sometimes represented as a pair, most notably in the early fifth-century-BCE terra-cotta statuettes from the sanctuary of Persephone in Epizephyrian Locri in southern Italy. These statuettes were almost certainly dedicated by women on the occasion of their marriage, in the expectation of the deities' joint blessing. Aphrodite's importance to brides stemmed from her role as the deity of love and mature sexuality, and as the patroness of the mutual attraction of marriage partners. In Greek weddings a woman known as the *nympheutria* impersonated Aphrodite during the ceremony, accompanying the bride and helping her to assume her new sexual role and social position. Roman weddings followed a similar custom, with the part of the Roman love goddess, Venus, played by a woman called a *pronuba*.

Hermes was significant for brides for quite different reasons. Besides his role as the messenger of the gods, he was the deity of boundary crossings and rituals that marked the transfer from one condition to another, particularly at funerals and weddings. The Greeks believed that Hermes

patronized the social aspect of marriage, symbolized by the transfer of the bride from her father's house to her husband's. In classical depictions of wedding scenes, Hermes is portrayed leading the wedding procession.

Greek views about gender

The myth of Hermaphroditus touches on the sexual differences between men and women—a notion that, for the Greeks, was both highly important and ambiguous. Early Greek sources suggest a fundamental distinction between the genders. In *Theogony*, for example, the eighth-century BCE-Greek poet Hesiod's account of the origins of the gods, the first union was between the male Uranus (sky) and the female Gaia (earth). Writings produced by followers of the Orphic mystery religion, based on the teaching and songs of the Greek hero Orpheus, similarly describe a union between a male and female deity at the creation of the world. According to an Orphic account by the fifth-century-BCE Greek writer Pherecydes of Syros, the world began with the marriage of Zas, the high god and maker of order, to Chthonie, the goddess of earth. As a wedding gift, Zas gave Chthonie a robe on which was embroidered the entire universe.

For the Greeks, gender differences prefigured social differences. People believed that men reached their perfect condition as philosopher-king while women achieved this state through marriage. Furthermore, men were in charge of government while women asserted their powers in the home and through the performance of certain rituals. Any variance from these rules—for instance, a cowardly man or a woman in authority—challenged the social and cosmic order. A creature belonging to both sexes was, therefore, profoundly threatening to this way of thinking. Yet one aspect of the Hermaphroditus myth directly reflected real life—the birth of dimorphic children, with male and female sexual characteristics. Today, dimorphic humans, plants, and animals are called hermaphrodites for the Greek myth. Roman sources report that, during the third, second, and first centuries BCE, there were large numbers of such births. People perceived dimorphic children to be dangerous monsters and evil omens.

Androgyny in Greek society

To say that the Greeks were afraid of anyone who merged the characteristics of male and female does not explain why people worshiped Hermaphroditus and represented him or her in their works of art. One reason for honoring Hermaphroditus was that he or she represented in extreme form what people could aspire to only moderately. In other words, the fusing together of Hermaphroditus and Salmacis dramatically symbolized the act of sexual union. The extreme aspect of Hermaphroditus also suggests why people worshiped him or her alongside Pan, the god of the wild countryside, and the river god Achelous—fertile, erratic, and sometimes dangerous figures that evoked the powers of nature. Similarly, in classical art, Hermaphroditus is depicted in the company of the wild, part-human, part-animal satyrs and fauns.

Another explanation for Hermaphroditus's popularity was the role androgyny played in Greek society. Besides wedding ceremonies, a number of other rituals involved people of one sex taking on the dress and behavior of

Left: Salmacis and Hermaphroditus *(c. 1581), by Flemish artist Bartholomeus Spranger (1546–1611), depicts the nymph spying on the bathing god.*

Above: This first-century-CE wall painting from the Roman city of Pompeii depicts the notoriously lustful Pan fleeing from the beckoning Hermaphrodite.

members of the opposite sex. In the Athenian ritual honoring the voyage of Theseus and his companions to Crete, where the hero slew the Minotaur, young men acted the parts of girls who had accompanied Theseus. At Argos, during the annual festival called the Hybristika, the "festival of outrage," all the participants dressed as the other sex. The events in both Athens and Argos were ceremonies of disorder—similar to carnivals such as Mardi Gras and to Halloween—where order was broken only to be strengthened by its restoration. Transvestism (dressing and acting like the opposite sex) was also frequent in rituals celebrating Dionysus, the god of wine, intoxication, and the theater. Athens held several dramatic festivals each year in which an image of the god had the seat of honor among the audience. Generally women were not permitted to take part in Greek drama, so in performances during these festivals all the women's parts were played by men.

Androgyny also appears in an acceptable light in a variety of Greek myths. For example, the heroes Achilles and Heracles both spent time in women's clothing—Achilles in the female quarters of the palace of Lycomedes, king of Scyros; Heracles in the company of Queen Omphale of Lydia. The myth of Tiresias, the seer from Thebes, relates how he became a woman after hitting two snakes. Seven years later he struck the same snakes again and returned to being a man. He thus had an understanding of the inner thoughts of both men and women. This led Zeus and Hera to consult him in an argument over which gender gained the most pleasure from sex. Caenis was a beautiful woman who was raped by the sea-god Poseidon. He then granted her wish that she might never be raped again by turning her into a man. After this transformation Caenis took the name Caeneus.

JAMES M. REDFIELD

Bibliography

Hesiod, and M. L. West, trans. *Theogony* and *Works and Days.* New York: Oxford University Press, 2008.
Ovid, and A. D. Melville, trans. *Metamorphoses.* New York: Oxford University Press, 2008.

SEE ALSO: Aphrodite; Dionysus; Hermes.

HERMES

Hermes was the messenger of the Greek gods, and he was often sent on errands by his father, Zeus. At times he was mischievous and thieved, but he was also a divine guide who led other gods and mortals from harm to safety. One of his most important roles was as god of boundaries. A herm, named for Hermes, was a stone square pillar the Greeks would erect to mark the boundary between properties. Hermes was known as Mercury by the Romans.

Above: This Roman sculpture of Hermes, whom the Romans called Mercury, was made in the second century BCE and is a copy of a fifth-century-BCE Greek original. It depicts Hermes with a beard, but most later depictions have him without one and appearing younger than he does here.

Although Hermes is described in many myths as having been one of the youngest of the gods, historically he was not a latecomer to the Greek pantheon. His name appears in early inscriptions from the time of the Mycenaean Greeks, who first inhabited mainland Greece around 1500–1100 BCE. Specifically, Hermes is listed on tablets in Linear B, the ancient Mycenaean writing system, as one of the gods to whom tribute was owed.

Despite being one of the youngest deities in Greek mythology—of the main Olympian deities only Dionysus was younger—Hermes was usually depicted in pre-fifth-century-BCE art as a mature male with a full-grown beard. In sculptures and paintings after the fifth century BCE, he was most commonly shown as a beardless youth, wearing a winged cap and sandals, symbols of his speed. He is also often shown carrying a herald's staff—called a *kerykeion* by the Greeks and a *caduceus* by the Romans—decorated with intertwined snakes, which were symbols of immortality. Asclepius, the god of healing, carried a similar staff with intertwined snakes. The staff is now commonly used as a symbol of healing by the modern medical profession in North America and many other parts of the world.

The god of boundaries

It has been argued that Hermes' role as the god of boundaries (see box, page 143) relates in some ways to most of his other responsibilities and characteristics. For example, he was the god of shepherds because they try to keep herds within the bounds of a pasture, and he was the god of heralds and messengers because they travel across boundaries to deliver messages. Occasionally Hermes also led the souls of the dead across the boundary separating the land of the living from the underworld, to hand them to Charon, the ferryman of Hades. In this guise he was called Hermes Psychopompos ("soul-leader"), and he was the only god, besides Persephone and Hades, who could cross into the land of the dead and out again.

Another of Hermes' responsibilities was to watch over the safe passage of a bride from her father's house to her new husband's on her wedding day. According to Hesiod, a

Hermes and Herms

In recognition of Hermes' role as god of boundaries, the ancient Greeks built herms, named in honor of the god. Herms were stone square pillars placed at the boundary between properties or at crossroads. Many herms were crowned with a bust of the god or other mythological characters, and some had an erect phallus on the pillar. In addition to their practical purpose of demarcating the boundary, herms were thought to bring good luck.

One legend has it that herms were formerly people who had angered Hermes and as punishment had been transformed into the stone pillars. Cursed to stand at a boundary forever, the victim would be forced to observe everyone who passed, but would be unable to prevent their passing or to tell anyone later who had gone by.

Herms had great religious significance and were common in classical times. When most of the herms in Athens were mutilated one night shortly before a major military expedition against Sicily, it was thought that war protesters were casting bad omens. The men who were held responsible for the crime, including Alcibiades (c. 450–404 BCE), the leader of the expedition, were put on trial or forced into exile.

Above: This ancient Greek herm was built at the boundary of a theater in what is now Libya. The bust of a satyr, perhaps in recognition of Hermes' son Pan, is mounted on top.

Greek poet who lived around 800 BCE, Hermes would give the bride the soft words with which she could win her new husband's love.

Similar deities in other cultures

Several of Hermes' characteristics have parallels in West Asian and Indo-European myth. Hittite gods and their messengers, for instance, were described as "wearing the winds as shoes" when they set out on their journeys. Hermes wore winged sandals, which, according to Homer, enabled him to travel "as swiftly as the blowing winds." The intertwined snakes on Hermes' staff also appear in the traditions of ancient West Asian cultures. Hermes' equivalent in Indo-European tradition is the Indic god Pushan, who appears in the Rig Veda, the earliest of the Sanskrit sacred texts, written around 1500 BCE. Like Hermes, Pushan was a god of herds, a messenger, and a traveler. Pushan was also involved in marriage as the god who prepared a new bride for her husband.

Hermes tricks Apollo

The longest myth told about Hermes is found in "Hymn to Hermes," a poem composed by an anonymous Greek oral poet, probably at the end of the sixth century BCE, although some scholars attribute its authorship to Homer. This myth tells the story of the first two days of Hermes' life. "Born at dawn," it tells us, "at midday he played the lyre, and in the evening he stole the cattle of the far-shooting Apollo." The hymn goes on to describe Hermes as a "wily child, a thief, a cattle driver, a dream bringer, and a night watcher." The myth shows Hermes' nature as a trickster, a figure common in many mythologies who can be both helpful and destructive, trustworthy and deceitful.

According to the hymn, Hermes was born in a cave on Mount Cyllene, where his mother, Maia, lived. Maia was either a nymph or one of the seven Pleiades, daughters of the Titan Atlas. Shortly after his birth, Hermes climbed out of his cradle and left the cave to steal the cattle of his older brother, Apollo. Just outside the door, he caught sight of a tortoise, which he killed. He took the tortoiseshell and strung it with catgut to make a lyre. He then set out for the meadows where Apollo pastured his cattle, in Pieria, more than 150 miles (240 km) away, and arrived at sunset.

Hermes stole 50 cows and drove them backward to confuse their route. According to Hesiod, he tied brushwood to the cows' tails to brush away their footprints

Left: French artist Claude Lorrain (1600–1682) based this painting on the "Hymn to Hermes." In the painting Apollo, at left, guards a herd of cattle, but while his back is turned Hermes steals the cows.

as they walked; another legend has it that he put sandals on the cattle to deceive Apollo. He also wore sandals to obscure his own footprints. He drove the cattle into a cave near his home, where he butchered two of the cattle, roasted the meat, and divided it into 12 equal portions as a symbolic sacrifice for each of the Olympian gods, including himself. Afterward he crept home, slid into his mother's cave on Mount Cyllene, and lay back down in his cradle.

When the angry Apollo arrived at the cave to demand his cattle back, Hermes said that he was only a baby and did not know what cows were. His exasperated elder brother took him to Olympus to face the judgment of Zeus. Zeus was amused at Hermes' exploits, but commanded him to guide Apollo to his cattle. Once Hermes had shown Apollo where the cattle were hidden, he soothed Apollo by playing a tune on the tortoiseshell lyre. He also sang a song about the origins of the gods.

Apollo, the god of music, offered to take the lyre as recompense for the theft of the cows. Hermes agreed, and then as a replacement for the lyre he invented the panpipes.

Protector of children

In several myths Hermes was entrusted with the protection of children, carrying them away from danger. According to Apollodorus, a Greek writer who collected and recorded myths in the second century BCE, Hermes took Dionysus from Zeus after his birth and brought him to his nursemaid, Ino, and later to the nymphs who raised him. Dionysus's mother was Semele, and Zeus did not want his wife, Hera, who was often jealous of Zeus's affairs, to find the newborn infant, so Hermes did all of this in secret.

In another episode Hermes rescued Asclepius, who became the god of medicine, from his mother's womb on the funeral pyre and brought him to Apollo to raise. In other examples, Hermes did not carry the children but instead provided them with modes of transport. For instance, he sent a flying golden ram to rescue the children Phrixus and Helle, who were about to be killed by their stepmother.

In his role as guide, Hermes was said to have led the three goddesses Hera, Athena, and Aphrodite to the competition where they were judged by Paris for the prize of being the most beautiful, the event that instigated the Trojan War. Hermes also led the goddess Persephone back from Hades. According to Apollodorus, Hermes guided the hero Perseus to the Phorcides, old women who could tell him where to find the Gorgon Medusa, whom he had been sent to kill.

Children of Hermes

Hermes had several children, and his most famous included Hermaphroditus, his son by the goddess Aphrodite. Hermaphroditus was extremely beautiful, and a nymph named Salmacis fell in love with him. One day she clasped him tightly to her body and prayed to the gods

Right: The most famous surviving statue by the greatest of all Greek sculptors, Praxiteles, is of Hermes holding the baby Dionysus. It was carved during the mid-fourth century BCE.

Hermes the Thief

Hermes was not only useful to the gods as a messenger, he was also a wily thief who both helped and hindered them. His best-known exploit was the theft of Io. Zeus fell in love with the mortal Io and disguised her as a cow to hide her from his jealous wife, Hera, but Hera promptly asked for the beautiful heifer as a gift, which Zeus could not deny her without arousing suspicion. Hera then put Io under the guard of the hundred-eyed giant Argus; only half of those eyes slept at one time. Zeus ordered Hermes to steal Io away, and Hermes put all of Argus's eyes to sleep by playing the panpipes. He then killed Argus, for which he was given the often-used title Argeiphontes, which means "Argus killer."

Hermes' skill as a thief was useful to the gods at other times as well. According to Apollodorus, when the sinews of Zeus's legs were stolen by the giant monster Typhon, who was trying to take control of Mount Olympus, Hermes helped to retrieve them. Another example, told by Homer, came when the god Ares was imprisoned by the twin giants Otus and Ephialtes in a brass pot. Hermes used his skill and cunning at thieving to rescue Ares.

that they never be separated. The gods heard her prayer and joined their two bodies together so that they became one person, part male and part female. It is from this myth that the word *hermaphrodite* comes.

Some ancient sources say that Hermes was the father of the god Pan by the mortal Penelope, wife of the Greek hero Odysseus, as well as of Autolycus, Odysseus's

Right: This ancient Greek pottery painting depicts a bearded Hermes with a dog disguised as a pig. The story from which the scene comes has been lost, but, as with most Hermes myths, it probably refers to an incident when he was either guiding the canine to safety or stealing it.

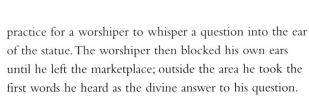

grandfather. Another offspring, according to the writer Pausanias (143–176 CE), was Cephalus, by the Athenian princess Herse. When he grew up, Cephalus was brought by Eos, goddess of the dawn, to Mount Olympus, where he became her lover. Hermes was also said to be the father of Eleusis, for whom the Greek city was named.

For many centuries Hermes has been a favorite subject of great artists. One of the first was Praxiteles, a great Greek sculptor of the fourth century BCE, whose statue of Hermes holding the baby Dionysus is a masterpiece of antiquity. Some famous painters who used Hermes—or Mercury—as a subject include Peter Paul Rubens (1577–1640) and Diego Velázquez (1599–1660), both of whom painted versions of Argus and Mercury (see box, page 145).

Worship of Hermes

Little is known about the worship of Hermes. Herodotus, a Greek historian who lived during the fifth century BCE, believed that the practice of carving images of Hermes with an erect phallus began with the early Greeks known as Pelasgians. He based this on a sacred story told to initiates in the mystery religion of Samothrace. There is, however, no archaeological evidence to support this claim.

Hermes was frequently invoked on curse tablets. These were tablets asking a god or gods to curse someone, which would be hidden in the grave of a recently deceased person so that the spirit of the dead could carry the curse with them to the underworld. Because Hermes was the god who led the souls of the dead to the underworld, he was an appropriate god to invoke in a curse.

Hermes was occasionally associated with oracles. In the marketplace of the Greek town of Pharae there was a statue of Hermes where, historians believe, it was common practice for a worshiper to whisper a question into the ear of the statue. The worshiper then blocked his own ears until he left the marketplace; outside the area he took the first words he heard as the divine answer to his question.

Because Hermes was the god of boundary-crossing, he was also seen as the god of exchanges of goods and of commerce. Statues to Hermes were frequently found in marketplaces, and today an image of Mercury (Hermes) is the central figure in the pediment above the doors of the New York Stock Exchange.

LAUREL BOWMAN

Bibliography
Calame, Claude, and Daniel W. Berman, trans. *Myth and History in Ancient Greece.* Princeton, NJ: Princeton University Press, 2003.
Graves, Robert. *The Greek Myths.* New York: Penguin, 1993.
West, Martin L., ed. *Homeric Hymns, Homeric Apocrypha, Lives of Homer.* Cambridge, MA: Loeb Classical Library, 2003.

SEE ALSO: Aphrodite; Apollo; Dionysus; Eos; Hera; Mercury; Pan; Persephone; Zeus.

HESTIA

Hestia, meaning "essence" or "true nature," was the goddess of the hearth in ancient Greece. She was the eldest child of the Titans Cronus and Rhea and, according to some accounts, was one of the 12 great Olympians. Like Artemis and Athena, she was a virgin goddess with no interest in suitors. She was usually represented either as a living flame or as glowing charcoal under a pile of white ashes. She was known to the Romans as Vesta.

Although Hestia played a minimal role in Greek mythology—she is rarely personified in art and scarcely mentioned in literature—she was of great significance to ordinary Greeks as a symbol of fire, life, hope, warmth, nourishment, and domesticity. While other Olympian deities were frequently away at war or indulging in romantic dalliances, Hestia stabilized and held together the homes of humans on earth as well as the home of the gods on Mount Olympus. Constantly present in the fire of the hearth, Hestia was important but easy to overlook.

Often dismissed by contemporary scholars, some of whom refer to her as "the forgotten goddess," Hestia was nevertheless in many ways the bedrock of ancient Greek society. Most of her worshipers were ordinary people who

Below: To the ancient Greeks, the hearth was more than the seat of the flames for warmth and cooking—it was a shrine to the goddess Hestia.

worked all day and came together as a family at night around the fireside in their homes. There they cooked and ate their food, offered sacrifices to Hestia and the house-spirits, talked, and told stories. Women especially venerated Hestia because they believed that the goddess attended to their daily needs.

First and last

The few recorded details of Hestia's early life are as follows. As soon as she was born, she was swallowed by her father, Cronus, who was fearful of a prophecy that he would one day be overthrown by his children. She fell deep into the hot center of his belly—to its "hearth," in a sense. There, motherless and alone, but unintentionally warmed by her father's body, she spent her early infancy.

Four siblings joined her in their father's stomach. First there were two sisters: Demeter, the goddess of grain, and Hera, the goddess of marriage and heaven. Next came two brothers: Hades, the god of the underworld, and Poseidon, the god of the sea. A third brother, Zeus, the sixth and youngest child, escaped being swallowed when their mother, Rhea, successfully substituted him for a stone

wrapped in a blanket. Zeus spent his childhood in hiding on the island of Crete. When he grew up, he and his mother conspired to make Cronus vomit up the first five siblings by lacing his favorite honey drink with mustard and salt. The children came out of his mouth in reverse order: Poseidon, Hades, Hera, Demeter, and finally Hestia. Together the six defeated their father and founded the Olympian dynasty.

Hestia was thus both the oldest and the youngest child of Cronus—the first to be born, but the last to reemerge from his body. Consequently she was often called "Hestia, first and last." As the goddess of domestic fire, without which no civilization could flourish, Hestia's special honor was to be the recipient of the first and last libations poured at every mealtime and feast, just as she herself had been the first and last of her parents' offspring. Insofar as she was characterized at all, Hestia was always depicted as calm and maternal in a general way—she had no children of her own, and no favorites among humankind: she was evenhandedly beneficent to everyone who worshiped her.

Virgin goddess

Unlike her brothers and sisters, Hestia had no interest in wars and steadfastly avoided taking sides in any conflict, domestic or international, mortal or divine. She also had no desire for sexual gratification—in that respect she was like two of her nieces, Zeus's daughters Artemis and Athena. Hestia demonstrated her resolve to remain celibate when her younger brother, Poseidon, and her nephew, Apollo, wooed her simultaneously. She refused to choose one rival over the other, and swore to remain a maiden forever. When

Public and Private Hearths

In the days before matches and lighters, making a fire was a difficult and time-consuming activity that involved rubbing flints or wooden sticks together to produce a spark. A domestic fire might go out at any time—usually by accident, but sometimes as part of an act of mourning—so the Greeks kept a constant fire in a public hearth, or *prytaneion*, in the city hall, which individuals could use to reignite their domestic fires.

When the ancient Greeks built houses, it was usually the hearth that they constructed first: the home was centered on the fireplace. The easiest way of heating a room was to assemble mounds of red-hot charcoal and cover them with white ash to keep the fire alive. The heap of charcoal radiated warmth and security without the inconvenience of smoke or crackling flames. Such a heap often represented Hestia herself; in the rare instances when she is portrayed as a goddess, her veil may be a symbol of the white ashes covering her internal heat.

When a bride departed from her family, she took fire from her mother's hearth and used it ceremonially to start the fire in her new abode. Until this was done, her house was not her home. The tradition survives today: some newly married couples light a candle together from the flames of two candelabra to symbolize the creation of a new family from two old families.

Right: Hestia, Deione, and Amphitrite. These headless statues are part of the Elgin marbles, classical Greek sculptures from the fifth century BCE that decorated the Parthenon in Athens.

Hestia and Priapus

According to Roman poet Ovid (43 BCE–17 CE), Hestia once attended a boisterous rustic festival with all the other deities, including the drunken and lecherous Priapus. After the guests had eaten and drunk their fill, they nearly all sank into a deep sleep. Only Priapus remained woozily awake. As he stumbled among the sleeping deities, his eyes fell on the fair Hestia. Clumsily, he started to climb on top of her. At that moment a nearby ass brayed loudly, and Hestia awoke. Seeing the huge, ungainly Priapus on top of her, she screamed, sending him into shock as he fell backward. Still shaken, he lurched to his feet and lumbered off. According to British novelist and poet Robert Graves (1895–1985), this was a moral tale, which warned against any attempt to violate female guests at a hearth, for they were to be considered as inviolable as Hestia herself.

she took this oath she touched Zeus's head—the same head from which the chaste Athena had been born. Hestia must have known Zeus's reputation as a philanderer, yet in swearing by his head she honored his intelligence and discernment. As the supreme god, Zeus could have forced Hestia into marriage, but he was relieved to have a deity on whose behalf he would not have to adjudicate in disputes between suitors. So he honored Hestia by giving her a place in Mount Olympus, where she was henceforth a sort of divine estate manager, and the hearth was her sacred domain. Hestia also became the goddess of architecture, and one of her precepts was that a "good" house should be built from the center out (see box, page 148).

Some scholars have suggested that Hestia's steadfast chastity might have been a consequence of the fact that, as an infant, she had been deeper in her father's belly than her siblings. Certainly, some modern psychologists have noted that female children who have been unusually close to their

fathers may have difficulty in forming sexual relationships in later life because they doubt the ability of other men to live up to their own male parent. It is possible that the story of Hestia—like so many of the other most enduring Greek myths—was a metaphor for an observable pattern of human behavior.

Hestia and Hermes

In view of the inviolability of Hestia's maidenhood, it may seem paradoxical that the goddess was often associated with Hermes, a mischievous and restless god who had many amorous adventures, as a result of which he became the father of Pan, the thief Autolycus, and possibly Eros. Yet in "Hymn to Hestia," one of the 33 so-called Homeric

Below: This painting of Hestia appears on the side of a Greek cup dating from the fifth century BCE.

Hymns composed between the eighth and the sixth century BCE, the two deities are linked. Scholars have debated the meaning of this reference: it seems likely that the poet intended to draw attention to the complementary natures of the adventurous, outgoing Hermes—the god of travel and communication—and Hestia, the goddess of domestic bliss. In mythology the two were friends but made no attempt to marry or cohabit.

Goddess of hearth and home

In ancient Greece, Hestia's domain, the hearth, was a sacrificial altar as well as a place for cooking. Thus it was the focus of both the spiritual and the practical life of the household. Later, *focus* became the Latin word for "hearth," and the origin of the French word for fire, *feu*; in English, the word has been adopted in its original form and is also the source of the word *fuel*.

Before the start of any meal, small offerings of the food that was about to be eaten would be thrown onto the fire to gain the favor of Hestia. In addition, a portion of all the first fruits brought into the house at harvest time would be offered to the goddess in the same way. At the end of the meal, leftover food and the dregs of the wine would also be put on the fire.

To reflect the fact that a town was basically a family on a larger scale, every city had its own *prytaneion*, a public hearth sacred to Hestia, where the fire was never allowed to go out. Situated in the town hall, it was more than a mere symbol: it had a practical significance as a public utility. If a domestic fire went out, householders could renew it from the central resource. When the Greeks conquered a foreign land, the first fire they lit there would be taken from the *prytaneion* of their native city, a tradition that was carried on by the Romans. This ancient practice has a famous echo today in the Olympic flame, which is carried by runners from one venue to the next.

During domestic naming ceremonies, a parent or one of the guests would traditionally carry the infant child around the hearth to introduce him or her to Hestia and to welcome the new addition into the family home.

KATHLEEN JENKS

Bibliography

Bulfinch, Thomas. *Bulfinch's Mythology.* New York: Barnes & Noble, 2006.

Howatson, M. C. *The Oxford Companion to Classical Literature.* New York: Oxford University Press, 2005.

SEE ALSO: Apollo; Artemis; Athena; Cronus; Hermes; Poseidon; Priapus; Zeus.

HYPNOS

Hypnos was the ancient Greek god of sleep, the son of the goddess Nyx (night) and Erebus (darkness), and the twin of Thanatos (death). He was usually depicted as a winged and bearded man, often in the company of his brother. He could also take the form of a mortal, or of an owl, as befitted a god who worked by night.

Above: This bronze Roman copy (first–second century BCE) of an ancient Greek statue of Hypnos depicts him with winged temples.

Nyx and her children belonged to the ancient group of deities who came before the Olympian gods over whom Zeus ruled. These ancient gods were grouped into families of related abstractions. According to some myths, Hypnos's siblings included the Oneiroi (dreams), Moros (fate), Oizus (pain), and his twin, Thanatos (death). In other versions, the Oneiroi were his sons. Each represented different aspects of dreams, and the most important of the four was Morpheus. According to some accounts, Hypnos dwelled in the underworld with his mother. In others his home was the island of Lemnos.

For the ancient Greeks, sleep and death were particularly closely related concepts, and Hypnos and Thanatos often appeared together. For example, Zeus sent both twins to bring the body of the hero Sarpedon back to Lycia. Sarpedon, the leader of the Lycians, was the mortal son of Zeus and an ally of the Trojans during the Trojan War.

The gods often asked Hypnos to help them carry out their plans by distracting other gods or humans. He did this by "pouring" sleep on the selected target, sometimes by dripping onto their temples water from the rivers of the underworld, which were said to cause forgetfulness. In an interesting parallel, West Asian myths also speak of sleep being "poured" over people.

Zeus fell in love with a mortal named Alcmene. In order to visit her and conceive a child, he wanted a long night. Zeus instructed Hypnos to make people so drowsy that they would not notice that Helios, the sun god, did not rise for three days, or that Selene, the moon goddess, moved slowly. Zeus then assumed the form of Amphitryon, Alcmene's husband, and slept with Alcmene. When the real Amphitryon arrived, he also enjoyed a night with his wife. Alcmene became pregnant with twins—Heracles, the son of Zeus, and Iphicles, the child of Amphitryon.

Zeus himself was put to sleep by Hypnos on a number of occasions. When Hera became angry with the hero Heracles and wished to torment him, she persuaded Hypnos to put Zeus to sleep. Hera enlisted Hypnos's help

Left: The Realm of Hypnos *(late 1660s), by Giulio Carpioni (1613–1679) depicts a gloomy realm of suffering souls.*

the one hand, sleep was seen as a respite from daily cares, which is perhaps why it was often described as "sweet." On the other hand, sleep was thought to be dangerous. In Homer's *Odyssey*, for example, Odysseus repeatedly loses control of his crew while asleep, and the tyrant Peisistratos reportedly took control of Athens while the citizens were sleeping. This ambivalence extended to dreams, which could be either good and true or destructive and false.

Hypnos also occupied an ambiguous position in the Greek pantheon. He was a servant of the ruling Olympian gods, but he was also to some extent beyond their control. Zeus, for example, was unable to punish Hypnos for his role in Hera's attack on Heracles.

Hypnos was not only a figure of literature and art: the citizens of Troezen dedicated an altar to him and the Muses, and statues of him were located in or near the sanctuaries of other gods in Sparta and Sicyon.

Somnus

The Roman god Somnus, whose name means "sleep" in Latin, just as *hypnos* does in Greek, shared a number of characteristics with Hypnos. He too practiced the art of deception. According to Virgil's *Aenead*, Somnus tricked Aeneas's helmsman Palinurus into giving up his post. When Palinurus fell asleep, the god pushed him overboard. According to Roman poet Ovid (43 BCE–c. 17 CE), Somnus lived under a hollow mountain in silence broken only by the gentle lapping of the rivers of the underworld. His home was protected neither by a watchdog, lest it bark, nor by doors, lest their hinges creak, but by poppies and other narcotic plants. The god lounged on an elaborately draped couch, his eyelids heavy and his limbs drooping, scarcely able to raise his head from his chest. He was attended by his thousand sons; among them were Phobetor, Phantasos, and above all Morpheus. All his sons were skilled in crafting lifelike shapes with which to deceive dreamers.

JIM MARKS

again during the Trojan War, when she wanted to subvert Zeus's plan for the war by helping the Achaeans, who were enemies of the Trojans. Hypnos agreed, provided that she gave him Pasithea, one of the three Charites, or Graces, to be his wife. While Zeus was asleep the Achaeans won their battle with the Trojans. Like many characters in Greek myth, Hypnos's affections were not always restricted to the opposite sex. He became enamored of the handsome young man Endymion and put him to sleep for eternity with his eyes open, so that the god could always look into them.

Attitudes toward sleep

The ambivalent attitude that ancient Greeks had toward sleep helps explain why Hypnos is a more complex figure than most of the other gods who represent abstractions. On

Bibliography

Bulfinch, Thomas. *Bulfinch's Mythology.* New York: Barnes & Noble, 2006.
Homer, and Robert Fagles, trans. *The Odyssey.* New York: Penguin, 2009.
Virgil, and Robert Fagles, trans. *The Aeneid.* New York: Penguin, 2009.

SEE ALSO: Hera; Morpheus; Nyx.

JANUS

Janus was an important Roman god who protected doorways and gateways. He had two faces, one looking forward, the other backward, just as a door faces two ways. He was also the god of beginnings and endings: January, the first month of the modern calendar year, was named for him.

Janus was one of the oldest of the ancient Italian gods. He was the guardian of all entrances, thresholds, beginnings, and endings. For most Romans, Janus's crucial role was to keep evil from crossing the threshold of the home. As the divine gatekeeper, he was depicted holding a porter's staff in one hand and a set of keys in the other. According to Roman poet Ovid (43 BCE–17 CE), these were the keys to the gates of heaven, which Janus opened whenever Jupiter wanted to pass through them himself or allow others to do so. It was also Janus's responsibility to close them afterward. The first hour of every day belonged to Janus, as did the first day of every month, and the first month of every year. Without Janus's blessing, new undertakings were doomed—thus, when Romans prayed, Janus was usually invoked first, even before Jupiter, the ruler of the gods.

Guardian of the threshold

However, Janus's month was not the first month of the year until the Julian calendar was introduced in 45 BCE, and the start of the Roman year was moved from March to January. After this, Janus's role was extended to protect the threshold of the New Year. In his honor, people celebrated the first of January with gift-giving—coins with the faces of Janus were especially popular. For many centuries Janus had been portrayed with two faces as a sign of his watchfulness over a house's doorway. Now, with the calendar change, his two faces took on a new significance: one face looked back at the year just ended, the other

looked forward to the year ahead. No other Roman deity had a double aspect of this nature.

Some early statues of Janus from the second century BCE depict him with four faces, but later representations show him with just two, one bearded and the other clean-shaven, possibly symbolizing age and youth. Later still, he is most often shown with two bearded faces. In Book Seven of the *Aeneid*, the poet Virgil (70–19 BCE) describes a statue of Janus Bifrons ("with two faces") in the palace hall of Latinus, a mythical king of Latium.

Mortal beginnings

According to one legend, Janus was born a mortal in Thessaly (part of modern Greece, northwest of Athens), the son of the god Apollo. Exiled from his native country, he fled to Latium, a region of central Italy extending from the Apennines to the Tyrrhenian Sea, and the capital of which was Rome. There he was welcomed by the ruler, Camesus, who shared the kingdom with him. Another version of the story names the ruler of Latium as a woman, Camese, whom Janus married, becoming coruler. Janus had several children with Camese, including a son, Tiberinus, who drowned in the river that flows through Rome, which was subsequently named the Tiber in his memory. After the death of Camesus, or Camese, Janus ruled Latium alone. One legend says that he built a city on the highest hill in Rome and named it Janiculum after himself. Other myths claim that he received the exiled Saturn into his kingdom.

Saturn was the Roman god of agriculture and the father of Jupiter, Juno, Ceres, Pluto, and Neptune. He later became identified with the Greek Titan Cronus, whom some accounts linked to plentiful harvests. When Saturn was banished from Mount Olympus, the home of the gods, by his son Jupiter, he took refuge in Latium, where the hospitable Janus shared his throne with him. Saturn established the village of Saturnia on the Capitoline Hill, across the Tiber from Janus's settlement, and introduced agriculture and wine making to the district. Together Janus and Saturn created a Golden Age, ruling over a race of blissful humans who never showed signs of aging.

Saturn gave Rome one of its major festivals—the midwinter Saturnalia, a time of abundant food, wine, and boisterous behavior. In this manifestation, Saturn was a god

Above: Janus and Juno *was painted around 1553 by Giambattista Zelotti (1526–1578).*

The Two-Faced Dog of Greek Mythology

The two-faced Roman god Janus had no true equivalent in Greek mythology. The closest likeness to him was Orthus or Orthrus, the two-headed hound that guarded the beautiful red cattle belonging to Geryon, the mighty three-bodied, three-headed, six-handed grandson of Medusa. For many years, Geryon lived peacefully on the remote island of Erytheia with his watchdog, his herds, and a herdsman. Then, Heracles came to steal the cattle as one of his labors. Orthus tried to stop the hero, rushing toward him and barking fiercely, but Heracles killed him with a single blow of his club. After slaying the herdsman and then Geryon, Heracles rounded up the cattle and took them in tribute to his cousin Eurystheus, king of Argos. As Geryon's

blood spilled out, a tree sprang up that would later bear red, cherry-like fruits when the constellation of the Pleiades rose in the night sky.

Orthus was the brother of two of Heracles' other adversaries—Cerberus, the canine guardian of the underworld, and the many-headed serpent the Hydra—and he was the father of a third, the Nemean lion. Some sources say the dog's other offspring was the Theban Sphinx, a monster with a woman's head, a lion's body, and the wings of a bird. The Sphinx waylaid travelers and asked them a famous riddle—"What has four legs in the morning, two legs in the afternoon, and three legs in the evening?" She killed those who failed to answer it correctly. The riddle was finally solved by Oedipus, who gave the answer, "Man." Like his master, Orthus also became connected with the heavens—with Sirius, the Dog Star. The first rising of Sirius occurs in July, after it has been obscured by the sun. The event marked the start of the New Year in Athens. Like Janus, Orthus was depicted with one head looking backward at the old year and one looking ahead to the new year. However, Orthus and the summer New Year never had the same significance in Greece as Janus had in Rome.

of joy and plenty. He had another, less pleasant, aspect, however: the Saturn of astrology was the grim ruler of the sign of Capricorn, which begins at the winter solstice and runs through the first half of Janus's month of January. This Saturn was a dour lord of time and a stern, inflexible taskmaster.

Savior of Rome

Janus is credited with having intervened personally to save Rome from its enemies. After Romulus—the legendary eighth-century-BCE founder of Rome—kidnapped the women of the Sabine tribe to the north of the city, the Sabine men gained entry to the Capitol with the aid of an insider and were poised to attack the Romans. Suddenly Janus caused hot springs to erupt in mighty torrents, scalding the Sabines and scattering them in all directions. From then on, the

Above: This Roman effigy of Janus was carved from marble and measures about 10 inches (25 cm) in height.

Right: This ancient Roman silver coin bears the double face of Janus. It dates from 235 BCE.

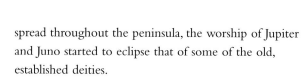

door of Janus's shrine was always kept open in wartime so that he could personally help defend the Romans.

Some sources name Janus's wife as Juturna (or Diuturna in earlier versions). She was a healer goddess of springs— her own sacred well was near Janus's shrine in the Roman Forum, the city's religious and commercial center. Janus and Juturna had a son, Fontus or Fons, who was a god of springs like his mother.

According to Ovid, Janus also fathered the beautiful nymph Canens, whose singing voice was so lovely that it could soothe savage beasts and move rocks and trees. She married the handsome Picus, a son of Saturn. While hunting one day in the forest, Picus was seen by the enchantress Circe, who fell in love with him. When Picus spurned her attentions, she turned him into a purple woodpecker. After searching in vain for Picus for six days and nights, Canens lay down beside the Tiber River, where she wasted away and died of grief.

In another Ovid story, Janus pursued and outwitted Carna, a capricious nymph who delighted in teasing her suitors by directing them to wait for her in a shady cave, where she promised to join them shortly. She would then go and hide in the forest, leaving them in the lurch. However, Janus saw Carna taking refuge behind a rock with the eyes in his backward-looking face. He caught her, and in recognition of his victory over her she slept with him. In gratitude, Janus made Carna the protectress of door hinges, giving her the power to keep out evil spirits.

Origins of Janus's name

Some legends state that Janus's wife was Jana—her name is a variant form of Diana (or Dione), just as Janus may be a corruption of Dianus. Janus and Jana, or Dianus and Diana, may have been the sun and moon deities of central Italy's earliest inhabitants. When Rome came to dominate all of Italy, and the customs of its Latin-speaking people

spread throughout the peninsula, the worship of Jupiter and Juno started to eclipse that of some of the old, established deities.

Opinion varies about the origins of Janus's name. The Latin word *ianua* means "door," but modern scholars are divided about whether Janus took his name from "door" or *ianua* took its name from the god. According to American mythologist Joseph Campbell (1904–1987), the Romans believed that a divine presence (*numen*, plural *numina*) existed everywhere, with its most important manifestations being those connected to the home. So, for example, the divine presence of fire was personified as the goddess of the hearth Vesta and that of the door was personified as Janus. From this perspective, Janus would have taken his name from the door. The opposite view was expressed by Scottish anthropologist James Frazer (1854–1941), the author of *The Golden Bough*, who pointed out that the same root for door appears in many Indo-European languages—for example, *dur* (Sanskrit), *thura* (Greek), *Tür* (German), *door* (English), *dorus* (Old Irish), and *foris* (Latin). But *ianua* is unique, with no similarities

Left: Dating from the 12th century CE, this sculpture of Janus stands above the entrance to Ferrara Cathedral in Italy. Janus's two-headed aspect remained familiar in the Christian Middle Ages.

either end. A bronze statue of Janus stood in the middle of the temple, which had no roof. In wealthy private households daily offerings were made to the god. These normally consisted of wine and a sacred cake, known as the *strues*. Prayers were offered for the safety of the household and family, and from time to time a young pig would be sacrificed.

From the earliest times an annual festival known as the Agonium was held on January 9 in Rome in honor of Janus. The ceremonies were conducted by the god's high priest, who was known as the *rex sacrorum* ("king of rites"); the votaries (attendants) wore new robes for the occasion. After aromatic plants and incense had been ritually burned on the altar, a young ram would be sacrificed to the deity.

The public faces of Janus

Janus had a crucial part to play in Roman civic matters. He protected bridges, shipping, and trade; he was credited with the introduction of agriculture, civil law, and worship. He was also strongly linked to currency— Rome's oldest bronze coins bore an image of Janus on one side and a ship's prow on the other. In the Forum, the massive gates of the Janus Geminus were oriented on an east–west axis, the path of the sun across the sky. Through these gates the Roman legions marched off to battle. In times of peace, the doors would be closed to safeguard the power of the shrine. In times of war, they would be opened in a state ritual that marked the outward flow of military power. Some sources have suggested that returning victorious Roman armies also marched through the gates of the Janus Geminus, and that this gave rise to the idea of a triumphal arch. Certainly Janus's influence extended to all gateways and arches, and his likeness appeared on many archways throughout Rome.

KATHLEEN JENKS

elsewhere in the Indo-European world. From this observation, Frazer concluded that *ianua* must be a derivation from the name of Janus.

Worship of Janus

Romans worshiped Janus in temples and in the home, and during an annual festival. The god's main center of worship was the temple of Janus Geminus, situated on the north side of the Forum. It was a small rectangular building of bronze, with two side walls and two great double gates at

Bibliography

Gardner, Jane F. *Roman Myths.* Austin, TX: University of Texas Press, 1993.

Virgil, and Robert Fagles, trans. *The Aeneid.* New York: Penguin, 2009.

SEE ALSO: Apollo; Cronus; Diana; Juno; Jupiter; Prometheus; Saturn.

JUNO

Juno was one of the three most important Roman deities—the others were her husband, Jupiter, and Minerva. Juno was the goddess of marriage and childbirth, and the mother of Mars, the god of war.

Juno's origins are obscure, but it is generally agreed that she was a Romanized version of Uni, the Etruscan goddess who embodied the lunar cycle. Later Juno became merged with the Greek goddess Hera, although the pair had little in common except that they were both celestial queens who became consorts for divine kings—Jupiter in Juno's case, Zeus in Hera's. Juno, Jupiter, and Minerva (the goddess of warriors and artisans) were Rome's major state deities: collectively they were known as the Capitoline Triad. Juno was also closely associated with Janus, the guardian of the thresholds, another very old pre-Roman deity. *Juno* is a variant of *Jana*, the feminine form of *Janus*.

Most Roman gods did not have distinct personalities of their own. What little biographical information there is about them was often simply taken from earlier Greek myths and reapplied, often fairly randomly, to members of the Roman pantheon. In some cases this worked well, but in others the characters of the deities did not seem appropriate for their supposed exploits. For example, despite the assimilation of the Greek Artemis into Diana, there were differences between the goddesses: Diana was more closely associated with the moon than Artemis, and she formed a trinity of deities in the Roman pantheon with the water nymph Egeria and the god Virbius. One way the Romans reconciled the difference between Artemis and Diana was by investing Juno with Artemis's responsibilities as protector of women and childbirth.

Poetic license in Virgil and Ovid
The identification of Juno with Hera is similarly problematic. In the *Aeneid*, the epic poet Virgil (70–19 BCE) took the characters of Juno and Jupiter and turned them back from, respectively, the goddess of marriage and a well-behaved, jovial ruler into their old Greek equivalents: Jupiter the philanderer and Juno the jealous wife. Virgil's Juno was bitterly opposed to the Trojan hero Aeneas, a descendant of Jupiter, who set sail for Italy at the end of the Trojan War. She did everything in her power to destroy him—she summoned violent storms, tricked him with

Left: This sculpture of Juno is a Roman copy, carved in the first century CE, of a Greek original dating from the fourth century BCE.

Above: In this painting by Pieter Lastman (1583–1633), Jupiter turns Io into a heifer in order to prevent Juno from catching him with his mistress. This myth is not originally Roman, but a Romanized version of one of the Greek legends of Zeus and Hera.

love-plots in Carthage, and even personally flung open the gates of war in the temple of Janus. She finally sought help in the underworld itself, crying: "If I cannot bend Heaven, I can raise Hell." The Juno of the *Aeneid* is a vengeful goddess who is ultimately thwarted when the hero achieves his proper destiny.

The other famous story about Juno—related by the poet Ovid (43 BCE–17 CE) in the *Metamorphoses*—is also derived from Greek mythology, this time the legend of Hera's conception of Mars without the involvement of her husband, Zeus, or any other male. Ovid told how Juno was angry that Athena had been born without a mother, and decided to produce a child without a father. She became pregnant by using a magic herb or possibly a lily obtained from the goddess Flora. The son she gave birth to was Mars.

Although Juno was in many respects a Romanized Hera, she did develop a few characteristics and functions of her own. One of her most important civic roles was as the goddess of the calends (the first day of the month, when there was a new moon), or the mother of time. This area of responsibility, which again links her with Janus, probably originated in an archaic age when the moon was the only dependable method of figuring out the calendar.

Juno was known by a wide variety of names that acknowledged her numerous functions. They include Juno Fortuna (goddess of destiny), Juno Regina (queen of the Romans), Juno Curiitis (mother of all the clans), Juno Populonia (mother of the people), Juno Martialis (mother of Mars), Juno Moneta (goddess who warns and advises), Juno Caprotina (goddess of erotic love), Juno Pronuba (arranger of marriages), Juno Domiduca (leader of brides), Juno Nuxia (perfumer of the bridal chamber), Juno Cinxia (bridal dresser), Juno Sospita (goddess who rescues endangered women and preserves and protects them in labor), Juno Lucina (goddess of celestial light), Juno Rumina (giver of mother's milk), and Juno Ossipago (strengthener of bones).

As many of these names indicate, Juno was, above all, the patroness of marriage and the family. She oversaw the marriage ceremony, guided the bride across the threshold of the perfumed bridal chamber, presided over

Left: Juno Showering Gifts on Venice *was painted by Italian artist Paolo Veronese (1528–1588).*

her undressing, inspired the love-making, and extended her care to the birth and growth of healthy children.

In her aspect as Juno Moneta, the goddess had a temple in Rome where sacred geese were kept. In 390 BCE invading Gauls planned a night attack on Rome's Capitoline Hill; as they stealthily climbed up the hill below Juno's temple, her loudly cackling geese sounded an alarm that saved Rome.

In 275 BCE, during a war against King Pyrrhus of Epirus, the Romans became afraid of running out of money. The leaders consulted Juno Moneta, who told them that they would never go short as long as they fought their wars justly. In gratitude for her guidance, the coinage was placed under her care. The fact that coins were minted in Juno's temple provides a further link between the goddess and Janus, for he is said to have invented coinage.

Festivals and symbols

The many-eyed, all-seeing peacock was Juno's special bird—Romans carried shimmering *flabella* (peacock-feather fans) during rituals honoring her. Lilies, roses, and cowrie shells were among her symbols. As early as 735 BCE, the Matronalia, a festival for married women, was celebrated in Juno's honor on the calends of March in the temple to Juno Lucina on Rome's Esquiline Hill; women demanded money from their husbands on this day and then offered it to Juno. Juno's other major festival was the Nonae Caprotinae, which was held every year on July 7. This event was a rowdy celebration in which young women engaged in mock fights connected with the artificial fertilization of fig trees.

In ancient Roman art, Juno is depicted in several different guises that reflect her varied functions. However, the Roman statue of Juno that stands in the National Archaeological Museum, Naples, is typical of many representations—it depicts the goddess as a severe but dignified matron.

Kathleen Jenks

Bibliography

Ovid, and A. D. Melville, trans. *Metamorphoses.* New York: Oxford University Press, 2008.
Virgil, and Robert Fagles, trans. *The Aeneid.* New York: Penguin, 2009.

See also: Artemis; Hephaestus; Hera; Janus; Jupiter; Minerva; Zeus.

JUPITER

Jupiter, or Jove, was the supreme deity in the Roman pantheon. Based closely on the Greek god Zeus, Jupiter was originally an ancient Italian sky god associated with storms, thunder, and lightning. As the Romans expanded their territory, Jupiter also took on qualities of sky gods from vanquished cultures in the empire.

Many of the myths attached to the Roman god Jupiter were originally told about the deity's Greek counterpart, Zeus, and were simply borrowed from the earlier culture by the Romans. The story of his origins is no exception. Jupiter was the youngest son of the Titans Saturn and Rhea. When Rhea started having children, her husband swallowed them whole, fearing that his offspring would one day overthrow him as king of the universe. The first child born to and eaten by Saturn was Vesta, who would become the Roman goddess of the hearth. According to most versions of the story, Saturn consumed his next four newborn children until Jupiter, his sixth child, was born.

Right: Jupiter, depicted here in a bust from ancient Rome, was often shown as a bearded, muscular, and older man exuding wisdom and strength.

Conquering Saturn

In order to protect the baby from his father, Rhea hid him on an island, where he was raised by nymphs. Immediately afterward, Rhea gave Saturn a stone wrapped in swaddling clothes. Thinking it was the newborn baby, he swallowed it. When Jupiter grew up, he and Rhea devised a plan for rescuing his siblings. Together they made Saturn's favorite honey drink but secretly added to it mustard and salt. When the Titan gulped it down, the sickening mixture made him vomit. He heaved up the stone he had thought was his last child; then he vomited up the other five children, who by now were fully grown.

Saturn's offspring—the Olympians—immediately declared war on the Titans. The war raged for a decade before Saturn was finally deposed and banished with his Titan allies. Roman historian Plutarch (c. 46–120 CE) wrote that Saturn was banished to the Isle of the Blessed far to the west, near Britain. Other accounts state that Jupiter made Saturn ruler of Elysium, the fabled place where the souls of dead heroes live forever.

Jupiter and his children

Once enthroned as king of the universe, Jupiter married his sister Juno. Together the couple ruled the other gods

and all creation. They also had four children, including Mars, god of war, and Vulcan, god of metalworking. However, as several myths make clear, Jupiter and Juno's marriage was not always a happy one. Jupiter was often unfaithful, and many of the myths concerning Jupiter pertain to his extramarital adventures with lesser goddesses and mortal women.

In wooing these women, Jupiter took on many different shapes. For instance, he pursued Antiope in the shape of a satyr, visited Danae as a light shower of golden rain, and fooled Callisto by taking on the form of Artemis, the goddess of the hunt whom Callisto served. Jupiter also transformed himself into animals; for example, a bull in the story of Europa, a swan in the story of Leda, and an eagle in the story of Ganymede, the beautiful young male from Troy whom Jupiter desired and later immortalized.

As with other deities who changed their shape, such as Proteus or Vertumnus, the many metamorphoses that Jupiter underwent in his love affairs were, argue some scholars, symbolic of the unbridled forces of nature. They would, therefore, seem to agree more closely with the deity's original function as a god of nature, in his case storms, rather than with his other function as father and ruler of the Olympian gods.

As a consequence of Jupiter's many extramarital affairs, he fathered a younger generation of gods and goddess—including Apollo, Diana, Mercury, Minerva, and Venus—and had several semidivine children with mortal women. Juno rarely overlooked her husband's affairs and often targeted her jealous anger at Jupiter's lovers or offspring, especially the semidivine ones. The most famous of Jupiter's children to suffer Juno's wrath was Hercules, the name by which the Romans knew the Greek hero Heracles. Juno's first act of spite against Hercules occurred when he was an infant. Juno put snakes into his crib, but the baby Hercules strangled the snakes. After that she raised deadly creatures, such as the Hydra of Lerna, to try to kill Hercules. Yet all her attempts at defeating the boy failed until one day she succeeded in driving the hero insane, causing him to murder his own wife and children. Eventually, Jupiter grew so tired of Juno's relentless persecution of Hercules that he banished her from the home of the gods. It was not until Hercules died and was transformed into a god that Juno finally made her peace with him.

Left: This large ceiling fresco, painted between 1526 and 1535 by Italian artist Pippi de' Gianuzzi, is titled Olympus. *It tells the story of the Olympian gods defeating the Titans and depicts in detail here Jupiter and his queen, Juno, throwing thunderbolts at the Titans.*

Jupiter Columns

In northeastern Gaul (modern Belgium) and the Rhineland, about 150 stone columns have been found with inscriptions that dedicate them to Jupiter. These monuments are known as Jupiter columns. Their precise origin and function are unknown, yet they are regarded as evidence of the existence of a local syncretism (combination of different forms of belief) between the Roman Jupiter and the Celtic sky god, Taranis.

Jupiter columns stood up to 50 feet (15 m) in height. The base of a typical column consisted of a four-sided plinth with sculpted figures of deities, often related to the sun, moon, and planets. Also on the base were inscriptions to Jupiter and Juno. On top of the base stood the column itself, often with carved decorations symbolizing a tree (both Jupiter and Zeus were associated with oaks). At the top of the column there usually stood a carved group of figures, generally a horseman slaying a monster with snake limbs. However, Jupiter is not normally portrayed on horseback, and the horseman figure usually has all the symbols of the Celtic sky god rather than those of the Roman Jupiter. It has been argued, therefore, that the horseman is the figure of Jupiter portrayed as the Celtic sky god.

Interaction with mortals

Despite all the hardship and perils Juno caused Hercules, Jupiter never aided his son. In fact, it was rare for Jupiter to intercede on behalf of any of his semidivine children. In this regard he was a rather distant god who usually allowed fate to run its course. One example of Jupiter actually interfering with mortals came when Aeneas was avoiding his destiny, which was to settle in Italy and found the Roman race. Aeneas was the hero of the *Aeneid*, an epic poem written by Roman poet Virgil (70–19 BCE).

The poem depicts Aeneas as a minor prince of Troy who, along with his family, fled the city after its destruction by the Greeks. While he was escaping, the gods gave Aeneas a premonition of his destiny: he was to travel to Italy and lay the foundations of a new kingdom. On his journey, however, he had many adventures before stopping at Carthage, where he fell in love with Dido, queen of the city. Aeneas grew so content with Dido that he forgot his fate, until Jupiter sent Mercury to remind him of his duty. Saddened at having to leave his love, he set sail once more in search of Italy. While his ship sailed out of the harbor, he saw smoke rising from a funeral pyre. The queen, grief-stricken at the loss of Aeneas, had taken her own life.

Another, nonsexual instance of Jupiter interacting with mortals is found in the myth of Philemon and Baucis.

Jupiter and Mercury, disguised as mortals, were traveling in the hills of Phrygia looking for a place to rest. Only one house took them in. It was a humble home and belonged to two elderly people, Philemon and Baucis, who shared what little they had with the two guests. In gratitude, Jupiter saved Philemon and Baucis from the fate of the rest of the country, which he turned into marshland. He also granted them their wish that death would carry them both off in the same instant.

Worship of Jupiter

In ancient Italy Jupiter was originally worshiped on the summits of hills. The Romans continued this practice and built temples to the supreme god on certain hilltops believed to be sacred. One of the oldest temples to Jupiter was on the Alban Hill, south of Rome. In the city of Rome, Jupiter's oldest temple was built on the Capitoline Hill, in the center of the city. According to legend, the small temple, built in the eighth century BCE, was founded by Romulus, the first king of Rome. Augustus (63 BCE–14 CE), the first emperor of Rome, is said to have restored the temple.

Jupiter also had another, larger place of worship on the Capitoline Hill. It dated from the period of the Roman Republic, which began in 509 BCE and ended when Augustus was crowned emperor in 27 BCE. It was regarded as the most important sanctuary in all of Rome. Dedicated to Jupiter Optimus Maximus, meaning "the best and greatest of all the Jupiters," it also had places of worship for Juno and Minerva. It is believed it was one of the first temples in Italy to have accommodated more than one deity, a practice that was common in ancient Greece. For centuries, the Sibylline books, an important collection of

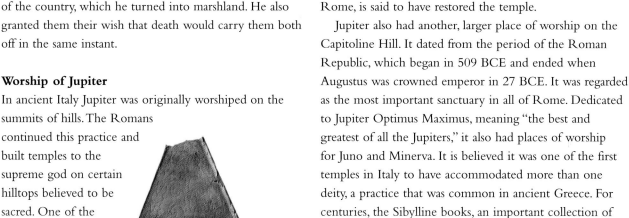

Jupiter Dolichenus

Jupiter Dolichenus was the amalgamation of Jupiter and Dolichenus, the chief god from an older culture conquered by the Romans. Dolichenus was the local name for the Phoenician god Baal. Originally worshiped in Doliche, a small town in what is now Turkey, Dolichenus was a sky and weather god whom the Romans equated with Jupiter and made their own. The cult of Jupiter Dolichenus spread westward throughout the empire with Roman soldiers and merchants. At times the deity was also identified with Jupiter Heliopolitanus, another version of Baal from Baalbek–Heliopolis, an ancient city northeast of modern Beirut, in Lebanon. Jupiter Dolichenus was usually depicted standing on the back of a bull, wearing a Roman military uniform, and holding a thunderbolt in one hand and a double-headed ax in the other. He was one of the most prominent of the west Asian deities adopted and worshiped by the Roman army. There were even shrines dedicated to Jupiter Dolichenus on the Aventine and Esquiline hills in Rome. The main sanctuary of the cult in Doliche was sacked by the Persians in the middle of the third century CE, after which the cult declined rapidly.

Left: A votive slab dedicated to Jupiter Dolichenus (center) found in Rome. Originally from western Asia, the deity was popular in the imperial capital.

Above: A temple dedicated to Jupiter Heliopolitanus, built during the mid-first century CE, in Baalbek, near modern Beirut, Lebanon. Jupiter Heliopolitanus was a deity who combined aspects of both Jupiter and the Phoenician god Baal.

sacred prophecies, were stored underground in the temple. Moreover, the temple was the traditional center of the Roman state: it was where the Senate met for war councils, international treaties were concluded, where victorious Roman generals dedicated part of their spoils to Jupiter, and where consuls, one of usually two annually elected officials who governed Rome along with the Senate, made sacrifices of white oxen when they entered office.

In addition to the temples, places that had been struck by lightning were thought to be sacred to Jupiter and so were protected by circular walls. Certain festivals were also observed as honoring Jupiter. Two of the most important of these festivals were the Ludi Romani and Feriae Latinae.

The Ludi Romani, meaning "Roman games," were made up of sporting events and were held in September on the Capitoline Hill. The Feriae Latinae ("Latin Festival") honored Jupiter as the patron deity of the ancient Latin League, which was the oldest federation of cities in Latium, the region around Rome. This festival originated in the days when Alba Longa, not Rome, was the chief city of central Italy, and was therefore celebrated on the Alban Hill. The festival continued to be performed for more than a thousand years until the Roman Empire went into decline at the end of the fourth century CE.

The many names of Jupiter

As with all the gods, the Romans gave Jupiter several different names or second names that depicted aspects of his personality or particular roles. For example, Jupiter Caelestis meant "Jupiter of the sky," Jupiter Fulgur stood for "Jupiter of lightning," and Jupiter Lucetius was "Jupiter of

Above: Danae, *painted around 1530 by Italian artist Correggio, depicts the moment when Jupiter, disguised as a cloud, showers golden rain onto Danae, impregnating her. Their union produced the hero Perseus.*

light." The oldest known cult of Jupiter involved worship of Jupiter Feretrius. The meaning of this name is unclear, but worship of this aspect of the god took place in the ancient temple on the Capitoline Hill accredited to Romulus.

As the Roman Empire expanded, several foreign gods were identified with Jupiter, such as the Phoenician god Baal (see box, page 164) and the Egyptian gods Amun and Serapis. In certain places there was also a fusion of local and Roman cult practices. In northeastern Gaul (modern Belgium) and the Rhineland, for instance, Jupiter was identified with the Celtic sky god on stone pillars known as Jupiter columns (see box, page 163). The Germanic thunder god Thor was also equated with Jupiter, an association that explains how the Roman weekday *dies Jovis* (Jove's day) became Thursday (Thor's day) in English.

Jupiter in art

In art, Jupiter, like Zeus, is either depicted as the mightiest of the deities or disguised during one of his many sexual exploits. As the king of gods he usually sits on a cloud above Olympus wielding a thunderbolt. As a lover he is transformed into, for example, golden rain as in the myth of Danae, a swan with Leda, a bull with Europa, an eagle in the story of Ganymede, or Artemis with Callisto.

FEYO SCHUDDEBOOM

Bibliography

Bulfinch, Thomas. *Bulfinch's Mythology.* New York: Barnes & Noble, 2006.

Matyszak, Philip. *Chronicle of the Roman Republic.* New York: Thames and Hudson, 2003.

Virgil, and Robert Fagles, trans. *The Aeneid.* New York: Penguin, 2009.

SEE ALSO: Apollo; Janus; Juno; Mars; Mercury; Minerva; Saturn; Venus; Zeus.

LARES

The Roman Lares were among the most important household gods, alongside the Genii and the Penates. The Lares, who were usually depicted in pairs or larger groups, offered protection in a number of different locations, from the home to the sea.

Roman poet Ovid (43 BCE–17 CE) provided a mythological account of the origins of the Lares in his work the *Fasti* (*Calendar*). Ovid described the over-talkative nymph Lara, who could not hide the truth of the chief god Jupiter's passion for another nymph, Juturna. Jupiter punished Lara for her indiscretion by tearing out her tongue; on her subsequent journey down to the underworld she was raped by Mercury, the messenger of the gods, and bore him twin sons, the Lares.

The special concern of the Lares was the protection of their worshipers in specific locations, such as in the family home, in fields, or at crossroads. Often, an adjective or epithet identified different Lares' particular sphere of concern. The *Lares domestici* cared for the house (*domus*), the *Lares viales* safeguarded those who travel the road (*via*), the *Lares semitales* watched over path and lane (*semita*), while the *Lares permarini* protected those at sea (*mare*).

Guardians of the home

The most widespread of all the Lares was the *Lar familiaris*, the "family Lar," who was worshiped in the home. Unlike the other, related deities, the *Lar familiaris* was a single entity, although according to some Roman writers there were several household guardians. In the prologue to his comedy *Aulularia*, Roman playwright Plautus (c. 254– 184 BCE) had the *Lar familiaris* directly address the audience: "I am the *Lar familiaris* of the family from whose house you just saw me walk. I have owned this house for a long time and have preserved it for the father who now lives here and for his father before him." The passage shows that the Lar was thought to inhabit the house from generation to

Above: A Roman bronze figurine of one of the Lares, dancing and holding a drinking horn. Representations of the Lares suggest similarities between them and nature spirits, such as nymphs and satyrs.

generation, and that he was revered as a protective divinity who looked after the family's interests. In the *Fasti*, Ovid called the Lares "watchful," and compared their protection of a house to that of a family dog. Roman poet Tibullus (c. 55–c. 19 BCE) reflected a similar conception of the household gods, which he defined as *patrii Lares*, the "ancestral Lares." He recorded how, as a child, he used to play at the feet of the Lares' wooden statuettes, which were venerated in a humble family shrine. Tibullus, who at the time of writing about the Lares was on military duty far from home, beseeched the family gods to protect him.

Gestures of appreciation to the Lares were made at various important stages in a person's life: in childhood, during celebrations that marked a boy's passage to manhood, in marriage, and even in death. When young men assumed the *toga virilis*, the garment worn by freeborn adults and the symbol of manhood, they dedicated the *bulla*, the child's amulet for magic protection, to the Lares. On first entering the home of her new husband, every bride offered coins to the Lares. Romans also offered the deities wreaths of flowers and incense at the time of a marriage. After a death, the bereaved family would make a sacrifice to the Lares at the end of the period of mourning. The favorite gift to the *Lar familiaris*, suitable on any occasion, was a garland of flowers.

Honoring the Lares

The most important place of worship for the Lares, outside the house itself, was at crossroads (*compita*), where the boundaries of farmlands or households met. The *Lares compitales*, or Lares of the crossroads, had their most important festival, the Compitalia, around the time of the winter solstice in late December. The exact date was determined annually. At this time of the year the institution of the family itself was celebrated in various ways, most dramatically at the festival of Saturnalia, when people exchanged gifts and the master of the house waited on his slaves at table. The reversal of roles at the Saturnalia recognized the fact that slaves counted as members of the family. The same emphasis marked the Compitalia, which venerated the *Lar familiaris* as the protector of the entire family, including the slaves. The most striking feature of the festival was the suspension of small woolen dolls, one representing each free man, woman, and child, at the shrine of the *Lares compitales*. Participants also hung woolen balls, one for each slave, alongside the dolls. The Compitalia ended with a sacrifice of purification to prepare the family and its land for the approaching new year. The emphasis on

Right: The remains of a crossroads in the Roman city of Jerash in Jordan. The Lares were the guardian deities of crossroads, as well as of homes, farmland, roads, and lanes.

property boundaries of neighboring families, along with the symbolic representation of family members by the woolen dolls and balls, fits the nature of the Lares, who watched over well-defined plots of land and those living on them. All members of the family—both free and slave— were meant to share in the benefits of these yearly rites. While ordinarily the *paterfamilias*, the male head of the family, conducted a family's religious ceremonies, by contrast a steward (*vilicus*), who might be either a free man or a slave, could take charge of the Compitalia ritual.

The worship of the Lares, however, was not confined to the Compitalia. The deities were regularly invoked for their protection in prayer and ritual, especially on the key dates of each month: the calends (the first day of the month), the nones (the ninth day of the month), and the ides (the middle of the month). The typical Roman home had a special shrine devoted to the family gods. The shrines were often simple niches in the wall of the atrium, the central room in a Roman house, but they could also be quite

elaborate, taking the form of a miniature temple front known as an *aedicula*, with columns and a triangular pediment, or gable. Statuettes of the Lares—in early Roman history made from wood, but later bronze—usually rested on the floor of the shrine, along with representations of other divinities favored within the household. People offered the Lares such everyday foodstuffs as grapes, grain, honey cakes, and, on occasion, wine.

Representations of the Lares

The Lares were characteristically depicted as happy, mirthful youths, dancing on tiptoe and carrying a *rhyton*, a Greek-style drinking horn, in one hand, and a *situla*, a small pail for carrying wine, in the other. Occasionally, they carried a *patera*, a wine saucer, instead of a pail. They usually wore high-laced shoes, a tunic, and a draped shawl over their arms. The Lares' fondness for dancing, their clothing, and their attributes, in particular drinking horns, are reminiscent of nymphs and satyrs, the nature spirits in the

retinue of the Greek god of wine, Dionysus, whom the Romans worshiped as Bacchus. Like water and woodland nymphs and other nature spirits who were imagined to dance in harmony with nature itself, the Lares did not have individual personalities and were often venerated in pairs or groups. While some writers referred to the singular *Lar familiaris*, the plural form *Lares* was almost always used and indicated that these minor divinities were thought to occur in pairs, or indistinct groups. Ovid, for example, called the Lares that guarded the crossroads *geminos* (twins).

The cheerful, playful nature of the Lares may be reflected in the origin of their name. It is possible that the word *lares* was derived from the root *las*, meaning "longing" or "spirited," which formed the basis of a number of ancient words, including the Latin *lascivius*

Below: A Roman family shrine in the form of a miniature temple (first century CE). Roman families often honored the Lares in shrines like this, which contains a fresco of the goddess Minerva.

Right: A Roman citizen honors the Lares in this artwork by German illustrator Hermann Vogel (1854–1921). The Romans offered food and wine to their household gods.

(playful). An older form of the name, *Lases*, was preserved in an archaic Latin prayer. *Lases* became *Lares* by a regular process that occurred in the development of Latin, in which an *s* between two vowels became an *r*. Since family cults, characterized by worship of the Lares, honored departed ancestors, the word *Lar* was sometimes used to refer to departed family members, whom death had made heroic. However, the somber busts and masks of Roman ancestor worship stand in contrast to the statuettes of the dancing Lares. The use of *Lar* as a Latin translation of the Greek *heros* ("hero") was clearly a secondary development.

Role in Roman religion

The Lares took on an increasingly important role in Roman state religion. They had a temple at the height of the Sacra Via in Rome, the sacred processional way from the Palatine Hill through the Roman Forum, probably near the Arch of Titus. There was a festival in their honor on the first of May, when they were worshiped under the title *Lares praestites*, the "protective Lares," because of their watchfulness over the state of Rome and its territory. Greek scholar Plutarch (c. 46–c. 120 CE) observed that the *Lares praestites*, in sharp contrast to all their other representations, wore dogskins—evidently to suggest their watchful nature. On a denarius (a small silver coin) dated to 90 BCE, *Lares praestites* appear as seminaked spear-carrying youths accompanied by a dog.

When Roman emperor Augustus (63 BCE–14 CE) became pontifex maximus, the high priest of Rome, he remodeled the old Compitalia rites so that his own family Lares came to be identified with those traditionally worshiped at the festival. Each of Rome's 265 *vici* (wards), which Augustus had established in his reorganization of the capital, had its own *vicomagistri*, officials usually drawn from the humbler classes. These local leaders were responsible for offering prayers and sacrifice to the *Lares Augusti*, the "Lares of Augustus." In traditional family worship, the Lares and a person's Genius—an individual's birth spirit, similar to a guardian angel—were venerated together at the household shrine. The *vicomagistri* under Augustus and his successors promoted worship of the emperor's Genius along with the Lares on the appointed festival days. As a result, old family customs were endowed with a new dynastic meaning that emphasized the emperor's role as the father of the entire Roman state.

DANIEL P. HARMON

Bibliography

Scheid, John, and Janet Lloyd, trans. *An Introduction to Roman Religion*. Bloomington, IN: Indiana University Press, 2003.

Turcan, Robert, and Antonia Nevill, trans. *The Gods of Ancient Rome*. New York: Routledge, 2001.

SEE ALSO: Dionysus; Jupiter; Mercury.

LETO

Leto was the daughter of the Titans Coeus and Phoebe. The Titans were among the earliest Greek gods, born to Uranus and Gaia. Leto was one of the first loves of Zeus, the king of the Olympian gods. Their union resulted in the birth of two great deities, Apollo and Artemis, and Leto was revered for her devotion to them.

According to Greek writer Hesiod (fl. 800 BCE), Leto was mild, gentle, and kind. When she became pregnant as a result of her love affair with Zeus, she feared the jealous wrath of his wife, Hera. Leto began searching for a quiet place to give birth but found that no land would accept her because they all feared Hera's anger. Leto wandered the earth until she arrived at the floating island of Delos, in the Cyclades. The island felt sorry for Leto and said, "You have roamed the earth as I have

Below: The Fountain of Latona (the Roman name for Leto) by sculptor Jean-Baptiste Tuby (1635–1700) at the palace of Versailles, France. Latona, at the top, holds her two children, Apollo and Diana (Artemis).

Left: Latona and the Lycian Peasants *was painted by Dutch artist Cornelis van Poelenburg (1586–1667).*

roamed the sea. Therefore I will give you a place to deliver your babies." Zeus chained the island securely to the bottom of the sea so that Leto could give birth in peace. Leto positioned herself between a palm tree and an olive tree and gave birth to twins—Apollo and Artemis.

According to some versions of the myth, Leto was in labor for nine days and nine nights because Hera refused to let Eileithyia, goddess of childbirth, attend her. Eventually, the other goddesses bribed Eileithyia to come, offering her a necklace strung with gold threads. As soon as she arrived, Artemis was born. In one version of the myth, Artemis then helped in the birth of her brother, Apollo. In another version, Apollo was born first.

Leto and the Lycian peasants

Hera's wrath was increased by the birth of the twins, and Leto was forced to flee the island. She finally arrived in Lycia, a region in what is now Turkey. The sun was high in the sky, scorching the earth, and Leto was parched with thirst. Her children had drunk the last drops of milk from her breasts and were crying for more. To her great relief, she spotted a little lake, far down in the valley. Beside the lake, peasants were gathering reeds and willow twigs.

Leto scrambled down the hillside and rushed toward the lake. She knelt at the waterside to drink from the cool water, but the peasants prevented her from drinking. Leto pleaded with them, saying that water, like the sun and the air, belonged to everyone. She did not want to dirty the water by bathing in it; all she wanted was to quench her thirst. The peasants remained unmoved, however. They scolded Leto and stirred up the water of the lake with their hands and feet, making it muddy.

In her rage, Coeus's daughter forgot her thirst. She raised her arms to the sky and cursed the peasants: "Then live in this lake forever!" The peasants' voices, still angry, became harsher, and their necks puffed and swelled. Their mouths became wider, their backs turned green, and their bellies turned white. They were changed into frogs, destined to live in the lake forever.

Devoted children

Leto's children were fiercely supportive of their mother. When Hera sent a monstrous python to pursue Leto, Apollo killed it. When the giant Tityus tried to abduct and rape Leto, the twins shot him with their arrows. He was then chained to a rock for eternity, while two eagles

Above: This marble relief (c. 27 BCE–14 CE) from a temple on the Palatine Hill in Rome, Italy, depicts (from right) Nike (virgin goddess of victory), Apollo, Artemis, and Leto.

pecked at his liver. The tissue always regrew, so there was no end to his torment. According to another version of the myth, Zeus killed the giant with his thunderbolt. Apollo and Artemis also shot down the children of Niobe, wife of the king of Thebes, to punish her for bragging that she was better than Leto because she had more children. Apollo shot all her sons and Artemis shot all her daughters. In her grief, Niobe returned to her father's land, where she was turned into a rock with water flowing down its face.

Worship

Leto was not generally worshiped on her own account but in conjunction with her children. Her chief center of worship was on Delos, where she was represented in her temple by a shapeless wooden image. Because Delos was the birthplace of Apollo and Artemis, it became one of the most important Greek sanctuaries, with many temples and other sacred buildings. In western Asia, however, Leto had her own individual cult at Letoon, a Lycian city near

Xanthus. There were three temples to the goddess in the city. They attracted many pilgrims who walked the Sacred Way between Letoon and Xanthus.

Leto in art

Leto was a common subject for Greek vase paintings. She was not distinguished by any special attribute, but was usually accompanied by her children. Leto's abduction by Tityus and her rescue by Apollo and Artemis was a particularly popular subject. In later art, Leto appears almost exclusively in the story of the metamorphosis of the Lycian peasants into frogs. Among the best known are paintings by Flemish artist Jan Brueghel the Elder (1568–1625), Dutch artist Moses Van Uyttenbroeck (1626), and Italian artist Marcantonio Franceschini (1648–1729).

FEYO SCHUDDEBOOM

Bibliography
Bulfinch, Thomas. *Bulfinch's Mythology.* New York: Barnes & Noble, 2006.
Hesiod, and M. L. West, trans. *Theogony* and *Works and Days.* New York: Oxford University Press, 2008.

SEE ALSO: Apollo; Artemis; Hera; Zeus.

MARS

Mars, the god of war, was the most important Roman deity after Jupiter. He became equated with the Greek Ares and therefore came to be regarded as the son of Juno, who was herself the Roman equivalent of Hera. He was believed either to be the son of Jupiter, or to have been conceived when Juno was touched by a magic flower.

Originally known as Mavors, it is thought Mars began as the Roman god of fertility and vegetation and protector of cattle, and only later became associated with war, although reasons for the change are unknown. As the god of spring, the season in which his major festivals were held, he presided over agriculture in general. In his warlike aspect, Mars was offered sacrifices before combat and was said to appear on the battlefield accompanied by Bellona, a warrior goddess variously identified as his wife, sister, or daughter.

In classical Roman art, Mars was most often depicted as a warrior. The Latin people as a whole—of which the Romans formed only one part—worshiped him as their most important protective divinity, particularly along the borders of their territories. There they performed the god's special rite, which began with a boar, a ram, and a bull being led around the boundaries and culminated in the sacrifice of the three animals at a ceremony known as the Suovetaurilia. Mars was the god of combat against all types of hostile force, whether visible or unseen. His priest was the flamen of Mars (*flamen martialis*).

Right: This statue of Mars dates from about the second century BCE. It is now displayed in the Capitoline Museum, Rome, Italy.

Mars and the founding of Rome

Although Jupiter was the chief god of the Latin people, Mars—often known as Mars Pater ("Father Mars")—enjoyed a special place of honor in the pantheon because the Romans traced their origins to him. The story of how this came about began when Amulius of Alba Longa, a settlement in the mountains outside Rome, deposed his older brother Numitor as king. He then forced Numitor's daughter, Rhea Silvia (also called Ilia), to become a vestal virgin because he wanted to ensure that the princess would not produce offspring who might avenge their deposed grandfather. Despite Amulius's precautions, one day while Rhea was fetching pure spring water from the sacred grove of Mars, the god himself appeared to her and fathered the twins Romulus and Remus. Amulius, alarmed at this turn of events, had the infant boys abandoned on the Tiber River, but the vessel in which they were set adrift was washed up on a bank downstream. There the twins were nursed by a she-wolf, the sacred animal of Mars. In some versions, they were fed morsels of food by a woodpecker, the bird of Mars. The infants were later discovered by the shepherd Faustulus, who gave them to his wife, Acca Larentia, to look after. When the twins grew up, they built Rome around the place where they had come ashore.

There are many different versions of the myth of Rome's origins—especially in regard to the ultimate fate of Remus, who is most often said to have been killed by his brother on the Palatine Hill—but the twins are central to nearly every account. Rome was the city of Mars, and it was founded by his son, Romulus. Martius or March ("belonging to Mars") was the name given to the first month of the old Roman calendar, which was used until 43 BCE.

Mars and the Ver Sacrum ritual

Romulus and Remus appear in several legends as the leaders of bands of young herdsmen and warriors. These bands are reminiscent of the companies of youths, who were ritually devoted to and trained for the task of founding new Roman colonies when they grew up. The rite was known as the Ver Sacrum ("Sacred Spring"), and the groups of youths were under the patronage and protection of Mars. In the usual tradition, a sacred animal of Mars led the youthful colonists to their new home. For example, a wolf would conduct the Hirpini (from *hirpus*, a

Below: This photograph shows the modern remains of the temple of Mars Ultor (Mars the Avenger) in Rome, Italy. Construction was completed in 2 BCE.

Latin word for "wolf") to their destined place of settlement; a woodpecker (*picus*) led the way to new homes for those who afterward called themselves the Picentes. Other similar groups, such as the Mamertines and the Marsi, took their names from adjectival forms of *Mars*. The story of Romulus and Remus—suckled by the she-wolf that was sacred to Mars and fed by the god's woodpecker—thus acquired a special place in the collective consciousness of the Roman people.

Despite the importance of Mars, his role in Roman society during the Republic (509–31 BCE) was strictly limited: he was responsible only for protective combat. That was because the Romans always drew a sharp distinction between the dangerous activities of war and the settled life of peace, which they cherished, of course, as the optimal condition for agriculture. The point is well illustrated by the semilegendary story of Lucius Quinctius

Below: In Mars and Venus, *by Sandro Botticelli (1445–1510), the god of war is asleep and unarmed, while the goddess of love is awake and alert. The meaning of the picture is that love outlasts war.*

Cincinnatus, the peaceloving farmer who answered his city's appeal for help in time of war and became dictator in the fifth century BCE. Sixteen days after taking power, having won the campaign, he resigned from public office and went back to his farm. The moral is clear: war was sometimes a necessary evil, but peace was the only desirable state of being.

Rituals held at the temple of Janus in the Roman Forum also reflected the perennial yearning for peace. The temple was a small, boxlike shrine with two arched openings parallel to one another and fitted with bronze doors. Roman soldiers, before setting out for battle in the company of Mars, went through these double arches in a rite of passage that marked the transition from peace to war. For as long as the hostilities continued, the doors would remain open in anticipation of the return of the warriors. When the soldiers did come back from battle, they once again passed through the arches in another rite of passage, this one intended to rid them of battle frenzy (*furor*) so that they could be reintegrated into civilian life. Only when the war was over and the surviving soldiers had

all returned to their homes would the doors of the temple of Janus be closed again.

Blind Mars

Throughout recorded history, the Roman army depended largely on discipline, cooperation, and collective effort for its success. The character and symbolism of Mars, however, had been formed long before, in a prehistoric era when most battles were fought as single combat between two adversaries. Mars therefore belongs very much to the heroic age, during which the warrior was driven to fight by emotions of intense hostility. The god was often called Mars Caecus ("blind Mars") because of the irrational frenzy that he personified. Some stories of Romulus and Remus, the sons of Mars, include dramatic accounts of such rage, a state that was also manifested by old heroic Roman warriors such as Horatius, but which had no place in civilized society. As a result, Mars was worshiped in Republican Rome with great pomp and ceremony; nevertheless, he was largely kept apart from daily life in times of peace.

The boundaries of early Latin cities were ritually marked out by a plow, an implement from the peaceful world of agriculture. The furrow thus created marked a mystical barrier that was regarded as sacred and protected by the gods. The dividing line was known as the *pomerium*, a word probably derived from the preposition *post* ("after") and the noun *murus* ("wall").

Throughout the republic, Mars was almost invariably worshiped outside the *pomerium:* the people venerated the god, but they wanted to keep him at arm's length because of his associations with war. It was not until the reign of the first emperor, Augustus (27 BCE–14 CE), that Mars had any significant temple within the boundaries of Rome.

There was a temple of Mars on the edge of the city, just outside a city gate in the Servian walls that led to the Via Appia. The god's most important shrine, however, was an outdoor altar that stood in an uncertain location somewhere on the Campus Martius (Field of Mars). This expanse of land in a large bend of the Tiber River remained outside the *pomerium* throughout the Republic. It was there that the Roman army assembled and prepared for combat.

However, some activities concerned with preparations for war did take place within the *pomerium*. These included declarations of war by priests known as fetiales. However, such ceremonies, in which the fetiales cast a spear into a plot of land defined for ritual purposes as enemy territory, were concerned with justice and legality. As such they were not strictly matters for Mars but for Jupiter.

During the period when Rome was ruled by kings (traditionally 753–509 BCE), the Regia had been the royal palace. It stood in the Forum, inside the consecrated city. After the last king, Tarquinius Superbus (Tarquin the Proud), had been banished and Rome became a republic, the Regia became first the home and then the office of the pontifex maximus (the high priest of the Roman religion), and a sacrarium, or repository, where the spears and shields of Mars were stored. According to tradition, Jupiter had dropped one shield, of which the rest were later copies, from the sky as a sacred pledge of his divine favor. The shields were used in rituals that marked the beginning of the fighting season in spring and its end in fall.

Mars and the calendar

The Roman religious calendar emphasized the clear demarcation between times appropriate for war and times reserved for peace. The festivals of Mars were clustered in two parts of the year. The ceremonies that marked the opening of the military season were performed in the early spring during March (Martius). Rituals that signaled the close of the military season were held in October. On March 1 (New Year's Day in the archaic Roman calendar) priests known as Salii performed war dances that continued at intervals throughout the month.

Each of these holy men wore ancient military dress consisting of a tall, cone-shaped helmet (*apex*), a painted tunic (*tunica picta*) with a bronze belt, a breastplate, and a short cloak (*trabea*) bordered in purple. The dancing priests formed into two companies of 12 and carried Bronze Age octagonal shields (*ancilia*) taken from the sacrarium of the Regia. Their dances were meant to arouse war madness (*furor*) for the campaign season. As they passed through the city, the Salii halted at various points to perform their dance step (*tripudium*) and recite the "Carmen Saliare," an archaic hymn that was symbolically potent but written in a form of Latin so ancient that it was scarcely comprehensible to most of the audience. The Salii repeated their dance in the assembly (*comitium*) of the Roman Forum during the festival of the Quinquatrus on March 19. The celebrations continued until the festival of the Tubilustrium, "the cleansing of the trumpets," on March 23, when arms, shields, and trumpets were ritually polished.

Right: *This gold coin, minted in Rome in the third century BCE, shows the head of Mars.*

Above: Carved in about 100 BCE, this marble relief shows a bull and a ram about to be sacrificed to Mars, the Roman god of war.

The campaign season closed in October. The festival of the Armilustrium, "the cleansing of arms," on October 19 recalled the purification rites of March. This festival took place outside the *pomerium*: it was held on the Aventine Hill near the temple of Minerva, the goddess who blessed and guarded all craftspeople, including the metalworkers who made Roman weapons. Arms and shields were again ritually polished before being put away until the following year.

The October horse sacrifice

The most remarkable rite connected to Mars was performed on the Ides of October (October 15), when Mars received in sacrifice the right-hand horse of the victorious team in a chariot race held earlier in the day on the Campus Martius. The October Horse (*Equus October*) was killed by the thrust of a spear and offered to Mars. The priests quickly severed the horse's head from the body and decorated it with loaves of bread made from the freshly harvested grain. Two teams of men, one from the Via Sacra in the Roman Forum and the other from the Suburra, an adjoining residential area, then competed for possession of the head. If the former won, they suspended their prize on the walls of the Regia; the latter, when victorious, displayed it on an unidentified building (probably in Suburra) known as the Mamilia Tower. While the contest was in progress, a runner took the horse's tail to the Regia, where he sprinkled an altar with the still liquid blood. All of this was done *ob frugum eventum* ("because of the successful outcome of the crops").

In archaic Rome, the king had been both the head of the armed forces and the priestly regulator of the calendar. That may explain why the annual round of Mars's festivals opened and closed with ceremonies in his former palace, the Regia. Mars, the god of warriors, served the Roman people as a whole, and the farmers in particular, by keeping watch over the crops. He not only protected the harvest by averting enemy raids but also, as is clear from old prayers and hymns such as the "Carmen Arvale," by warding off blight, plague, storm, and other forms of natural and preternatural attack.

During the reign of Augustus, Mars became fully integrated into the life of the city. His new sanctuary in the Forum of Augustus acknowledged the god's place, as father of Romulus and Remus, in the history, and indeed the genealogy, of the Roman people.

The Romans also used the word *martialis* to refer to anything having to do with or belonging to Mars. In English the word became *martial*, meaning of, relating to, or suited for war. Another modern reference to Mars is as the name of the fourth planet in our solar system. The planet is called Mars because of its red surface. Astronomically Earth lies between Mars and the planet Venus, thus keeping the mythological lovers apart.

DANIEL P. HARMON

Bibliography

Goldsworthy, Adrian. *The Complete Roman Army*. New York: Thames and Hudson, 2003.

Scheid, John, and Janet Lloyd, trans. *An Introduction to Roman Religion*. Bloomington IN: Indiana University Press, 2003.

Turcan, Robert, and Antonia Nevill, trans. *The Gods of Ancient Rome*. New York: Routledge, 2001.

SEE ALSO: Ares; Hera; Janus; Juno; Jupiter; Zeus.

MERCURY

Mercury, the Roman god of travelers and merchants, was renowned for his trickery and quick wits. He was the Roman equivalent of the Greek deity Hermes, the messenger of the gods, and in many cases stories of Hermes were retold in Latin, substituting his name with Mercury's.

Mercury was the son of Jupiter, the chief Roman god, and Maia, one of the seven daughters of Atlas and Pleione known as the Pleiades. He was the god of commerce, wrestling and gymnastics, storytelling, thieves, travelers, liars, vagabonds, and everything that required skill and dexterity. Classical astronomers named the planet closest to the sun Mercury or Hermes, because its path in the sky is swift and erratic, like that of the god.

Like Hermes, Mercury wore a winged cap and winged shoes and carried a rod entwined with two serpents, called a caduceus, and a purse or bag full of money. He was often accompanied by a ram and a rooster. Another similarity with Hermes was Mercury's association with the phallus. Some ancient images depict him with phalluses sprouting from all over his body; in other images he is represented by a single, phallus-shaped stone marker commonly called a herm, which was named for Hermes. This phallic symbolism was connected with Mercury's role as a god of business—the Greeks and Romans regarded wealth as an outcome of fertility.

Mercury in myth

Mercury figured prominently in Roman retellings of Greek myths. He served as an assistant to his father, Jupiter, helping the king of the gods carry out many sexual liaisons behind the back of his wife, Juno. In the poem *Metamorphoses*, Roman poet Ovid (43 BCE–17 CE) related the story of Jupiter's passion for Io, a beautiful girl, whom he changed into a white cow to disguise his adultery from Juno. Juno was suspicious, however: she demanded the cow as a gift from her husband and set the 100-eyed monster Argus to guard over it. Jupiter took pity on Io and sent Mercury to kill the monster. Mercury told Argus stories until 50 of its eyes fell asleep; he then played his pipes until the other 50 also dozed off. Then he cut off the monster's head and set Io free.

Other retellings of Greek stories included Mercury's theft of the sun god Apollo's cattle within hours of his own birth. To avoid detection, the infant Mercury cleverly disguised his footprints and returned to exactly the same

Above: A Roman silver coin, dated to 84 BCE, depicting the head of Mercury. The coin shows the god wearing his familiar winged hat, and also features his caduceus—a rod entwined with two serpents.

Trickster Deities

Mercury's associations with life and death, as well as his use of cunning in myths such as the killing of Argus and the theft of Apollo's cattle, mark him as a trickster god. Such beings were among the most widespread of mythological characters. Besides Mercury and Hermes, other examples include the Norse deity Loki, the spirits Wakdjungkaga, Hare, and Coyote in Native American mythology, and even Bugs Bunny, Bart Simpson, and Spike the vampire in modern popular culture. Tricksters transcended boundaries and categories—they may, for instance, have been both creative and destructive. Similarly, a trickster may have been simultaneously young and old or perpetually young or perpetually aged; male and female; or animal and human. They could also form a connection between this world and the afterlife, a role that allowed them a privileged freedom from some of the demands of normal behavior. Tricksters created trouble, for themselves and others. However, they embodied the type of destruction that was necessary for new growth to occur and new ideas to arise.

position in his bed as his mother had left him asleep. In another myth, Mercury freed Ulysses (the Greek Odysseus) from the nymph Calypso and brought him the herb he needed to counteract her spells. Mercury also fetched Paris to judge the beauty contest between Juno, Venus, and Minerva that sowed the seeds of the Trojan War.

Two myths involving Mercury had Roman origins. In his epic *Aeneid*, the poet Virgil (70–19 BCE) explained how Rome was founded by Aeneas, a refugee from Troy. In Virgil's account, Mercury appears to remind Aeneas that Jupiter has ordered him to found a city—Rome—in Italy, and that he therefore must break off his affair with Dido, the queen of Carthage. In his work *Fasti* (Calendar), Ovid told the story of the overtalkative nymph Lara, who could not keep secret Jupiter's love for another nymph, Juturna. Lara told Juturna and even Juno about Jupiter's passion; in response, Jupiter tore out Lara's tongue and arranged for Mercury to take her down to the underworld. On the journey Mercury raped Lara, who later gave birth to twin sons, the Lares, worshiped by Romans as guardian spirits of the household, the fields, crossroads, and the sea.

Worship of Mercury

The name *Mercury* derives from the Latin root *mer*, which referred to various aspects of commerce and from which come words such as *mercantile*, *merchant*, and *market*. This Latin root, however, may in turn have derived from an unknown Etruscan root, in which case the god Mercury may have a pre-Roman source. However, the fact that Mercury did not have a flamen, a priest who served the most ancient Roman deities, suggests that his worship in Rome did not stretch back to the oldest times.

According to Roman tradition, worship of Mercury began shortly after the end of the Roman monarchy and the beginning of the Republic, in 509 BCE. Legend has it that the god's cult was initiated in accordance with the instructions of the Sibylline Books, a collection of oracles that the Sibyl, or prophetess, of Cumae in southern Italy sold to the Roman king Tarquinius Superbus. Mercury's main temple in Rome was located near the Circus Maximus on the Aventine Hill. His chief festival was the Mercuralia, celebrated on May 15, during which merchants sprinkled both their heads and their merchandise with water from Mercury's well near the Porta Capena, one of the city's entrance gates.

As the Roman empire expanded between about 30 BCE and 200 CE and Romans came in contact with alien cultures, they tried to understand foreign gods by comparing them to Roman deities, a practice known as the *interpretatio Romana*. Mercury played an important role in this process. The Romans identified the Anglo-Saxon god Woden—himself an equivalent of the Norse god Odin—with Mercury. This comparison explains the origins of the English word *Wednesday* (Woden's Day), which was influenced by the Roman word for the same day of the week, Mercurii (Mercury's Day). When the Roman leader Julius Caesar (c. 100–44 BCE) encountered the Celtic people in Gaul (modern France), he described them as worshiping Mercury as their chief god. Clearly, Caesar meant that one of the more than 300 Celtic deities corresponded to Mercury; what is less clear is precisely which one he had in mind. The most commonly accepted theory is that the Celtic Mercury was the god Lugh. Like Mercury and Hermes, Lugh was a young god, a shapeshifter, and a traveler who appeared to have associations with commerce, dexterity, and magic shoes.

Mercury and the afterlife

The association of shoes with Mercury, Hermes, and Lugh appears to be related to their role as guide of the dead, someone who accompanied souls on their way to the afterlife. Remains found in Celtic graves, dating from the time after the Roman conquest of Britain in the first century CE, show that people were buried with new shoes, revealed by finds of unworn hobnails (nails put in the

181

Above: The Purification of Mercury, *an engraving in the* Tripus Aureus *(1618), a book on alchemy. In the Middle Ages, alchemists believed that they could change low-grade metals into gold. According to tradition, Mercury passed alchemical knowledge to humans.*

soles). It is possible that people perceived the road to the otherworld as being long and arduous, and they believed that sturdy shoes would help the soul on its journey. The practice of hobnailing was introduced into Britain by the Romans, so it is unclear whether the Celts adopted the custom from the invaders or had been burying people with new shoes all along—since the rest of the material in the shoes was perishable, there are no remains predating Roman Britain.

The afterlife was situated underground in Roman and Greek mythology, and while this location was the home of the dead, it was also the place where seeds germinated and new life began. Mercury, too, was connected with life and death. He led souls down to the underworld, but he also governed the world of commerce, which was linked to wealth and fertility. Without life, there is no death, and without death, there is no life. Mercury's association with both was a reflection of his function as a trickster god, a type of deity who often acted as a link between the worlds of the living and the dead (see box, page 181).

Representations in art

Mercury is depicted in a large number of works of art dating from the classical period to the present. One of the most famous is a statue of Mercury completed by Italian sculptor Giovanni Bologna (1529–1608) in 1580. The image shows the god poised on one foot, holding the caduceus in his left hand while his right hand points to the sky. Peter Paul Rubens (1577–1640) was one of many painters to depict Mercury and Argus; another was Diego Velázquez (1599–1660). Another popular subject for artists was Mercury's delivery of the infant Bacchus (Greek: Dionysus) to the nymphs who raised him—both François Boucher (1703–1770) and Nicolas Poussin (1594–1665) portrayed this scene. Today, Mercury appears as the logo of the flower delivery service FTD, swiftly delivering the floral messages of mortals rather than those of the gods.

LESLIE ELLEN JONES

Bibliography

Ovid, and A. D. Melville, trans. *Metamorphoses.* New York: Oxford University Press, 2008.

Virgil, and Robert Fagles, trans. *The Aeneid.* New York: Penguin, 2009.

SEE ALSO: Apollo; Bacchus; Hermes; Juno; Jupiter; Lares.

MINERVA

Originally an Etruscan deity of the dawn, in Roman mythology Minerva became the goddess of wisdom, arts and crafts, and war. When Minerva was later invested with many of the characteristics of the Greek goddess Athena, she was said to have sprung fully armed from the head of Jupiter.

Minerva was originally described as the daughter of Pallas, a giant whom she killed when he tried to rape her. The Romans soon identified Minerva with the Greek goddess Athena Promachos ("battle leader" or "champion"), and through that association she acquired her responsibility for the conduct of war. Minerva thus became an armed goddess, like Athena. Both deities carried a goatskin aegis bearing an image of the monstrous Gorgon head, the sight of which paralyzed enemy warriors with fear.

The Roman Minerva was also concerned with women's lives, especially domestic work such as spinning and weaving. In this capacity she was like Athena Ergane ("the worker"). Both goddesses also came to be associated with wisdom.

Below: This photograph shows the ruins of the three adjacent Roman temples of (left to right) Juno, Jupiter, and Minerva in Sbeïtla, Tunisia.

Left: This statue of Minerva forms part of the collection of ancient art treasures in the Capitoline Museum, Rome, Italy.

The origins of the Roman Minerva are elusive. According to Roman epic poet and dramatist Quintus Ennius (239–169 BCE), Minerva was one of the 12 great gods, which implied that she was Roman in origin. However, she did not appear in the earliest Roman religious calendars, a fact that has been taken as a clear indication that she was a goddess of exotic origin. In *De Lingua Latina* (*The Latin Language*), scholar Marcus Terentius Varro (116–27 BCE) claimed that Minerva came from Sabine territory, to the northeast of Rome. It is more likely, however, that the goddess came from Falerii (modern Civita Castellana), a city in southern Etruria (part of modern Umbria, in Italy). When Falerii fell to the Romans in 241 BCE, its cult of Minerva was transferred to Rome, where the goddess became known as Minerva Capta ("the captured"). A temple, the Minervium, was dedicated to her on the Caelian Hill in the city.

A goddess of importance

Regardless of whether she came to Rome from Etruria or was adopted by both civilizations from an independent source, Minerva was certainly one of the most important goddesses in the Etruscan pantheon. In Etruria her name was originally written as Menerva. Later it became Menrva, which is the form that appears on ancient vase paintings, sculptured reliefs, statues, and engraved bronzes.

Although her legend was almost certainly influenced by that of Athena, the Etruscan Menrva also shows traits that are not Greek in origin. Servius, a Latin grammarian of the fourth century CE, noted that Minerva could hurl lightning bolts, and the Etruscan Menrva was sometimes depicted carrying such weapons in her hand. Athena had no such power.

As Menrva, the goddess was worshiped at the Portonaccio sanctuary, which dates from the sixth century BCE, in the Etruscan city of Veii, about 12 miles (20 km) northwest of Rome. She was also worshiped in Santa Marinella, the ancient Punicum, a harbor of the Etruscan city Caere, which dates from about 540 BCE.

Beneath the altars of both these sanctuaries were channels that ran into the soil below, suggesting that the worship of Menrva was oriented to the earth. There seems also to have been a healing and probably an oracular aspect to her cult, which is indicated by the discovery of one of the lots that were used to predict the future. Small models of bodily organs and limbs offered to the goddess indicate that she was also seen as a healing divinity. Images of babies in swaddling clothes further suggest that one of the goddess's concerns was the welfare of children.

In her role as a warrior goddess, Minerva was often associated with Mars, the Roman god of war. Among the important archaeological relics unearthed at Praeneste—a town founded before the eighth century BCE in the Apennine Mountains north of Rome—is an engraved bronze container. Strongly influenced by Etruscan art, it bears an image of Minerva, who has put aside her shield and helmet and is tending the infant Mars. The child is naked except for his helmet, and he carries a shield. He is kneeling on the rim of a *pithos*, a large ceramic storage jar, in which depictions of what seem to be flames or moving water can be seen. Directly above Mars and the *pithos* is an image of Cerberus, the three-headed dog that guarded the entrance to the underworld. These symbols indicate that the *pithos* holds the water of the Styx River, which bordered the underworld and burned with fire. Minerva is carefully touching the lips of the little Mars with a styluslike instrument, anointing him with ambrosia, the divine food that gave the gods immortality.

The Etruscan Menrva frequently appears elsewhere in contexts that suggest the role of a children's nurse. Unlike the Greek Athena, Menrva is almost invariably a motherly figure, and there is little or no evidence that the Etruscans regarded her as the deity of handicraft and the arts, both of which roles she fulfilled in Athens and Rome.

Roman evidence of Minerva

From the mid-sixth century BCE, Minerva played an increasingly important role in the emerging Roman civilization. In Rome she shared with Juno a monumental presence on the Capitoline Hill in the great temple of Jupiter Optimus Maximus, which is traditionally dated to 509 BCE. The significance of Minerva's presence with Juno and Jupiter has never been entirely clear, although it may have been because all three deities were involved in the fall of Troy, from which the Romans believed that their ancestors had escaped.

Elsewhere in Rome substantial remains dating from about 530 BCE have been found at the Forum Boarium, a cattle market near the Tiber River. One of the artifacts unearthed there is a terra-cotta sculpture group depicting the helmeted Minerva standing beside the hero Heracles. It was originally

Right: This terra-cotta statue of the fourth century BCE comes from Lavinium and represents a female worshiper of Minerva.

positioned on the roof of a temple that was almost certainly dedicated by King Servius Tullius (578–534 BCE) to the goddess Fortuna (the Roman goddess of fate, chance, and luck). The work probably represents the deification of Heracles. In this version he was introduced to the society of gods on Mount Olympus by Minerva. The inspiration for this scene came from Greek myths, which were probably brought to Rome by merchants from the east who frequented the markets near the port.

Other early images of Minerva have been found in ancient Lavinium (modern Pratica di Mare). Excavations there have brought to light a sanctuary of Minerva that dates to the second half of the sixth century BCE. Remarkable terra-cotta statues and two nearly life-size cult statues of Minerva from about 400 BCE confirm the

importance of the goddess during this period. They show Minerva with a helmet, a round shield, and an aegis with the Gorgon head. Beside her body, which is entwined by a three-headed snake, is the small sea god Triton. This association with Triton occurs again in the epic poem the *Aeneid*, in which Roman poet Virgil (70–19 BCE) calls Minerva *Tritonia virgo* (Tritonian maid).

The sanctuary of Lavinium was for centuries a place of pilgrimage for Romans and other peoples of Latium. For them, Minerva was a goddess concerned with young men and, especially, young women at the time of their passage from adolescence to adulthood. The sumptuous gifts offered by her youthful worshipers at Lavinium underscore this aspect of her cult.

The Quinquatrus

The extent of Minerva's appeal to ordinary Romans is well illustrated by the expansion of her major festival. Originally a one-day annual event held on March 19, the Quinquatrus was gradually extended to five days of revelry. The date was originally also sacred to Mars, and although the rituals of Mars continued to be observed at the Quinquatrus, Minerva became the primary focus of the event.

March 19 was the dedication day of her temple (which archaeologists have never found) on the Aventine Hill in Rome, and a notation on an ancient calendar notes that it was the *artificum dies* ("day of the artisans"). According to Roman poet Ovid (43 BCE–17 CE), March 19 was Minerva's birthday, and on this date every year she was worshiped by all sorts of artists and craftspeople, but especially by boys and girls and their teachers, who enjoyed a five-day recess from school.

Minerva was a favorite of Emperor Domitian (ruled 81–96 CE). In his Forum Transitorium at Rome (also known as the Forum of Nerva), the goddess is pictured on a relief panel of the colonnade, surrounded by scenes of spinning and weaving. Minerva herself is shown in long, flowing robes, suggestive of the garments worn by musicians and performers—she was also the patroness of actors.

Whenever she first arrived in Rome, and wherever she came from, there can be little doubt that Minerva found her way into the hearts of all classes of Roman people.

DANIEL P. HARMON

Bibliography

Scheid, John, and Janet Lloyd, trans. *An Introduction to Roman Religion*. Bloomington IN: Indiana University Press, 2003.

Turcan, Robert, and Antonia Nevill, trans. *The Gods of Ancient Rome: Religion in Everyday Life from Archaic to Imperial Times*. New York: Routledge, 2001.

SEE ALSO: Athena; Juno; Jupiter; Mars; Triton.

MNEMOSYNE

In Greek myth, Mnemosyne was the personification of memory. She played a personal role in only one story, that of her affair with Zeus, king of the gods, which produced nine offspring—the Muses, the goddesses of the arts. However, Mnemosyne's symbolic significance ensured that she was an important member of the Greek pantheon, since people recognized that storytelling and recorded history were impossible without memory.

Mnemosyne was one of the Titans, the 12 divine beings born from the union between Gaia (earth) and Uranus (sky). Some of the Titans personified aspects of the natural world—Oceanus (the world river), Hyperion (the sun), and Phoebe (the moon). Others represented abstract ideas. Mnemosyne belonged

to the latter category, as did her sister Themis (justice), and—possibly, since the sources are not entirely clear—Coeus (intelligence) and Theia (sight).

Birth of the Muses

Unlike monotheists, who believe that creation was the action of a single god, ancient Greeks believed that the world was generated by a series of divine matings. Zeus, who became king of the gods after the Olympian deities defeated the Titans, fathered numerous divine beings through his affairs with a succession of female Titans, goddesses, and nymphs. He also sired many legendary heroes and demigods through a string of liaisons with mortal women. According to one story, after the Olympians defeated the Titans, they asked Zeus to create deities who would help them to celebrate their victory. In response to their request, Zeus went from Mount Olympus to nearby Pieria, where he disguised himself as a shepherd and seduced Mnemosyne. The couple slept together for nine consecutive nights. The result of their union was the birth of nine female children. These were the Muses, each of whom held sway over one particular artistic

Below: The exterior of this sarcophagus, dated about 150 CE, is decorated with bas-reliefs of the Muses, the nine daughters of Mnemosyne.

Memory, Writing, and Forgetfulness

Are books essential for culture and learning? We are brought up to believe that they are, but Greek philosopher Plato questioned this assumption. In his book *Phaedrus* he acknowledged the importance of memory for speech and intellect, but doubted the benefit of writing to memory. *Phaedrus* contains an imaginary conversation between two Egyptian deities, Thamus, the chief god, and Theuth, a god of inventions. In the book, Theuth invents writing and shows it to Thamus, suggesting that the skill should be taught to all Egyptians. Thamus, however, doubts Theuth's assertion that writing will make people wiser and improve their memories. The chief god fears that writing will encourage forgetfulness, since people would no longer use their memory to recall names, events, and ideas, but would instead look things up in books. "You offer your pupils the appearance of wisdom, not true wisdom," Thamus says, "for they will read many things without instruction … when for the most part they are ignorant."

form: Calliope (epic poetry), Clio (history), Euterpe (flute playing), Erato (lyric poetry), Melpomene (tragedy), Thalia (comedy), Terpsichore (dancing), Polymnia (music), and Urania (astronomy).

Greek geographer Pausanias (143–176 CE) gives a different account of the origins of the Muses. According to him, the people of Sicyon in the northern Peloponnese believed that there were only three Muses, each of whom had responsibility for a different aspect of art in performance: Melete was the goddess of practice, Mneme of memory, and Aeode of song. Pausanias further related that it was a man named Pierus, from Macedonia, to the north of Greece, who established belief in nine such goddesses. Pausanias is the only source of this alternative version, and it is likely that for most Greeks the Muses were always nine in number.

Abstract concept

Except for the story of the birth of the Muses, the character of Mnemosyne does not really figure in Greek mythology. This is perhaps unsurprising, since she was the personification of an abstract quality. Nevertheless, ancient writers occasionally described Mnemosyne's physical appearance. One Greek poet, Hesiod (fl. 800 BCE), wrote that she had "beautiful hair"; another, Pindar (c. 522–c. 438 BCE), described her as "golden-robed." A surviving fragment of poetry by Alcman, a Spartan of the

seventh century BCE, refers to Mnemosyne's big eyes, and this has been taken as a reference to the fact that memory allows people to "see" their past.

Although Mnemosyne had no other role than mother of the Muses, ancient Greeks still afforded the female Titan much significance. They believed that she was present in the recollection of every story told, since all narrators need memory to tell their tales. This was particularly true in oral cultures. By the ninth and eighth centuries BCE, writers such as Homer had begun to record stories by writing them down, but many people could still neither read nor write, so they relied on the tradition of oral storytelling to learn about gods and heroes.

Many sources reflect the symbolic importance of Mnemosyne, who not only personified memory, but also represented everything that memory made possible. An orphic hymn—from an undated collection of ancient Greek poems used by cult followers of the mythical musician Orpheus—describes how Mnemosyne freed the human mind from oblivion and, as a result, represented the joining of the soul with the intellect. In *Critias*—the title of which refers to one of the characters who take part in a series of dialogues—Greek philosopher Plato (c. 428–c. 348 BCE) discusses Mnemosyne's role in human intelligence. Critias explains that it is only because of his capacity to remember information and past events that he can participate in rational argument.

Language and history

Elsewhere in the work of Plato, Critias goes even further, suggesting that Mnemosyne played a major part in the development of human speech. This role was elaborated by Greek historian Diodorus Siculus (90–21 BCE), according to whom Mnemosyne gave humans the capacity to name and remember everything they saw and felt, which therefore allowed them to hold conversations with each other. Diodorus did, however, acknowledge that not everyone assigned such a role to Mnemosyne. He suggested that some people believed the power of language was a gift to humans from Hermes, divine messenger and god of eloquence. Another source, the undated "Homeric Hymn to Hermes," establishes a connection between the two deities. The hymn relates that Hermes honored Mnemosyne and was one of her followers.

The importance of Mnemosyne reflects that of the mental capacity she represents. Memory is widely regarded

Right: This painting of Mnemosyne is by English artist Frederick Leighton (1830–1896).

Left: This illustration depicts the oracle of Trophonius, which was associated with rites venerating Mnemosyne. Traditionally bees were reared there.

to history with the lines: "Holy Memory, reveal/the glories of yore:/how Spartans and Athenians/won the Persian war." This is a reference to the series of wars between the Greek states and Persia between 492 and 449 BCE.

Ancient Greeks believed that the Muses inspired the writing and performance of songs that honored famous events and noble deeds. Pindar wrote that, if people were successful, they would hope that the Muses would see to it that their success was recorded in song. Like their mother, the Muses—whose name in Greek means "remembrances"—were regarded as patronesses of memory.

Honoring Mnemosyne

Pausanias, in his travels around Greece in the second century CE, observed images of Mnemosyne and the Muses on the altar of Athena, goddess of arts and war, at Tegea in Arcadia, a mountainous region in the central Peloponnese. This was not the only example of Greeks honoring the female Titan: in his biography of the first-century CE philosopher Apollonius of Tyana, Philostratus (c. 170–c. 245 CE) recounted how Apollonius would chant a hymn to Mnemosyne. The hymn declared that, while everything is worn away by time, time itself does not age because of memory.

Pausanias also told of a ritual in honor of Mnemosyne that was held at the oracle of Trophonius in Lebadea, a town of Boeotia in east-central Greece. Anyone who wished to consult the oracle was taken by priests to two water fountains. Petitioners drank from the first fountain, which contained the waters of Lethe (Forgetfulness); thereafter they drank from the second, which contained the waters of Mnemosyne. They then consulted the oracle itself, and when they had finished they sat on a seat known as the chair of Mnemosyne, where the priests asked them to tell all that they had seen or learned.

KARELISA HARTIGAN

as the foundation of everything that distinguishes humans from animals. It enables people to know who and what they are, and to retain that information. It is important at all times and in all cultures, but it was of particular significance in the ancient world, before scribes began to create and reproduce manuscripts. Memory remained crucial to the transmission of knowledge until the invention of the printing press in the 15th century CE. Henceforth, authors needed to remember information only until they had written it down.

Although memory is no longer so important to the survival and transmission of knowledge, it remains vital to human life. One of the ways in which people commit information to memory is with the aid of mnemonics—systems designed to assist or improve memory. Such aids—still important to modern people—were indispensable to ancient Greeks. Oral poetry was common in ancient Greek life; wandering bards and storytellers were able to entertain the Greek public using mnemonics to string together long recitals of tales they had learned or history they had experienced. In *Lysistrata*, Greek dramatist Aristophanes (c. 450–c. 388 BCE) invoked Mnemosyne's importance

Bibliography

Bulfinch, Thomas. *Bulfinch's Mythology*. New York: Barnes & Noble, 2006.

Pausanias, and Peter Levi, trans. *Guide to Greece*. New York: Viking Press, 1984.

Plato, and Robin Waterfield, trans. *Phaedrus*. New York: Oxford University Press, 2009.

SEE ALSO: Athena; Gaia; Hermes; Muses; Titans; Uranus; Zeus.

MOMOS

In Greek mythology Momos was the personification of blame, and was associated with similar phenomena such as criticism, scorn, mockery, and ridicule. Momos was one of the earliest beings created. His sole parent was Nyx (or Night), herself a child of Chaos, the earliest entity in the creation of the cosmos.

Momos had several brothers and sisters; they included a number of unpleasant and grim figures such as Moros (Dissolution), Apate (Deceit), Nemesis (Retribution), Thanatos (Death), Oizus (Pain), Eris (Discord), and the Keres (Doom). Night created these offspring herself, without the help of any male consort. Momos was thus a primal entity

that came into being very early in the history of creation, at the same time as the Titans, the Cyclopes, and the Hecatoncheires (Hundred-Handed Ones). The idea that a quality as negative as unrelenting sarcastic criticism is a fundamental component of reality reflects a characteristically Greek view of the world.

Momos and the Trojan War

In his poem the *Cypria*, Greek poet Stasinos (seventh century BCE) wrote that Momos played a key role in the early history of human affairs. Earth (Gaia) was weighed down by the overpopulation of the human race. To make matters worse, men and women were also insolent and disrespectful in their behavior toward the gods. Gaia complained to Zeus about her burden. The king of the gods considered using natural phenomena (such as thunderbolts, floods, or earthquakes) to relieve Gaia. However, Momos advised that the best way to bring about a reduction in population would be to use human beings' natural proclivity to fight one another. To prompt a great

Below: This illustration from a sixth-century-BCE drinking cup shows a scene from the Trojan War, a conflict that was partially instigated by Momos.

war Zeus would have to do two things: marry the sea nymph Thetis to a mortal, and father a daughter, Helen. Zeus accepted Momos's advice. At the wedding of Peleus and Thetis, Momos's sister Eris, who had not been invited, threw a golden apple into the midst of the guests, so setting into motion the chain of events that would lead to the Trojan War.

Below: This Greek statue from the first century BCE depicts Aphrodite (left, holding the squeaking sandal) with Cupid (center) and Pan. Although Aphrodite embodied physical perfection, Momos was still able to find fault with her.

The niggling, griping character of Momos is well illustrated in a traditional fable attributed to legendary Greek writer Aesop. Momos, who mixed with the gods on Olympus, was once called upon to judge the creations of three of them: Zeus, Prometheus, and Athena. Zeus had created the bull, Prometheus man, and Athena the house. Momos spitefully criticized their work. He argued that the bull should have its eyes above its horns, so that it could see where it was striking; man should have his heart hanging outside his body, so that his intentions would be apparent to everyone and the wicked would not be able to get away with things; and the house should be on wheels, so that people could easily move away if they had a bad neighbor. The incident annoyed Zeus so much that he expelled Momos from Olympus.

Momos became an emblem of continuous, insistent dissatisfaction, no matter what the circumstances. For example, he was so unable to resist being critical that he even found fault with Aphrodite, who was seen as a paragon of physical perfection. Momos agreed that although he could see nothing else wrong with the goddess, he did find it very irritating that her sandal squeaked.

Momos was often linked to the idea of Phthonas (Envy), especially when it was contrasted with reasonable appreciation or praise. For this reason Momos entered the language of literary debate. When their work was attacked, ancient Greek writers would often describe their critics as "children of Momos." In later writings, the term *momos* came to mean a defect or an immoral and reprehensible act of behavior that could invite reproach.

Momos experienced something of a revival in the mid-15th century when Italian mathematician, writer, and painter Leon Battista Alberti (1404–1472) wrote the fictional work *Momus* (an alternative spelling of *Momos*). It resurrected the mythical figure to satirize numerous aspects of contemporary society. In the late 16th century, poet Thomas Lodge the Younger (1558–1625) wrote the collection of poems *A Fig for Momus*.

ANTHONY BULLOCH

Bibliography

Alberti, Leon Battista, and Virginia Brown, ed. *Momus*. Cambridge, MA: Harvard University Press, 2003.

Hesiod, and M. L. West, trans. *Theogony* and *Works and Days*. New York: Oxford University Press, 2008.

SEE ALSO: Aphrodite; Prometheus; Zeus.

MORPHEUS

In Greek and Roman mythology, Morpheus was originally the guardian of dreams. A son of Hypnos (Sleep) and Pasithea, the oldest of the Graces, he was generally depicted as a rotund, sleeping child with wings. It was only much later that poets began to identify him as the god of sleep.

The name *Morpheus* is derived from the Greek word *morphe*, meaning "shape." Morpheus and his brothers were said to have been the originators of the shapes and figures that appear in dreams. Morpheus could take on the form and behavior of any human; one of his brothers, Phobetor, could assume that of

any other creature; and another, Phantasos, that of any object. They lived in dark, cavernous places near the entrance to the underworld, the land of their uncle Thanatos (Death), the brother of Hypnos.

The earliest existing reference to Morpheus occurs in *Metamorphoses* by Ovid (43 BCE–17 CE). The poet tells the story of how Ceyx and Halcyone, the king and queen of Trachis (an ancient city in Thessaly, central Greece), were so happy that they referred to themselves as Zeus and Hera, the supreme king and queen of the gods. For this act of pride they were punished terribly. Ceyx was washed away in a storm at sea, and Hera ordered Hypnos to convey the bad news to Halcyone. The god of sleep sent his son, Morpheus, into the queen's dreams, where he assumed the

Below: Halcyone Discovering Ceyx, *a marble carving by English sculptor Thomas Banks (1735–1805). In Greek legend, Morpheus tells Halcyone of Ceyx's death by appearing to her in a dream in the form of her drowned husband.*

Left: Morpheus and Iris *by Pierre-Narcisse Guérin (1774–1833).* In this painting, the colors of dreams are symbolized by a union between the god of sleep and the goddess of the rainbow.

needed to set out on his final journey home. By contrast, in the same author's *Iliad*, Zeus sends a deceptive dream to Agamemnon, leader of the Greek army besieging Troy, to mislead him into taking the wrong course of action.

Dreams also featured prominently in certain ancient Greek religious practices. There were numerous oracles whose responses to questions were transmitted through dreams, and at many healing centers patients seeking cures slept out in the holiest areas of the sanctuaries in the hope of dreaming about their treatment and recovery.

Interpreting dreams has been practiced for millennia. Ancient Egyptians and Babylonians, who recorded dreams and their interpretations, believed dreaming was a method of communication with the gods; prophetic dreams are alluded to in many west Asian texts, notably the Bible. Most ancient Greeks believed that dreams served a predictive function, but Greek philosopher Aristotle (384–322 BCE) perceived dreams to be more expressive of the dreamer's senses and emotions than future events.

form of the drowned Ceyx and announced his own death. Halcyone, overcome with grief, committed suicide by jumping off a cliff into the sea. Finally the gods took pity and turned Ceyx and Halcyone into kingfishers, or halcyons, and calmed the winds during their breeding season. This is the origin of the phrase *halcyon days*, meaning a period of peace and tranquillity.

The memory of dreams

Although Morpheus himself does not appear until the work of Ovid, the idea that dreams contained important messages from the gods was a common feature in Greek literature from centuries earlier. There, deities might appear in the form of individual humans in order to warn, threaten, or impart information to the dreamer. The information thus conveyed may have been literally true or it may have been cryptically deceptive. Either way, the mind of the dreamer was being infiltrated by a god who meant to influence the course of events in the world of mortals. Thus in the *Odyssey* by Homer, Greek epic poet of the ninth or eighth century BCE, the goddess Athena appears to Phaeacian princess Nausicaa in a dream in the guise of one of Nausicaa's friends. Athena's intention was to stir the princess to action so that she would meet the shipwrecked Odysseus in an apparently chance encounter and give him the help he

Morpheus in art

Morpheus rarely appeared in the art of antiquity and the Middle Ages. However, the god became more prominent in western Europe after the Renaissance. He is alluded to in the poem "Il Penseroso" by English author John Milton (1608–1674) and in various songs by English composers Henry Purcell (c. 1659–1695) and Georg Friedrich Handel (1685–1759). Morpheus became even more popular with the Romantic movement of the 19th century, and his name was often invoked as a figure representing the whole world of sleep and unconsciousness as well as dreams. Association of the name Morpheus with an entity that exercises powerful control over the human mind, especially in a narcotic state, led Friedrich W. A. Sertürner (1783–1841), the German pharmacist who first extracted the juice of the poppy seed in 1805, to name his pain-relieving product "morphine."

ANTHONY BULLOCH

Bibliography

Homer, and Robert Fagles, trans. *The Iliad* and *The Odyssey*. New York: Penguin, 2009.
Ovid, and A. D. Melville, trans. *Metamorphoses*. New York: Oxford University Press, 2008.

SEE ALSO: Athena; Hypnos; Zeus.

MUSES

In Greek and Roman mythology, the Muses were the nine goddesses of all artistic, intellectual, and scientific pursuits. They were the daughters of Zeus (Jupiter) and Mnemosyne, goddess of memory. Their names were Calliope, Clio, Erato, Euterpe, Melpomene, Polymnia, Terpsichore, Thalia, and Urania.

The nine Muses had separate identities and special areas of responsibility. Each was commonly depicted with something evocative of her particular expertise. Calliope was in charge of epic and heroic poetry; she held a writing tablet and a stylus. Clio, the Muse of history, clasped a half-opened roll of parchment. Erato inspired lyric and erotic poetry; she played a small lyre. Euterpe was responsible for music, especially wind instruments, or lyric poetry; she played a double flute. Melpomene, the Muse of tragic poetry, held a tragic mask. Polymnia looked after sacred poetry, hymns, and mime; she was normally portrayed looking modest and pensive, with one finger raised to her lips. Terpsichore was the goddess of dance and choral poetry and song; she was usually seen dancing and holding a large lyre. Thalia, the Muse of comedy and bucolic, or rustic, poetry, held a comic mask and carried a shepherd's crook. Urania was the Muse of astronomy; she pointed at or held a globe and sometimes also carried scientific instruments.

Overlapping roles

The ancients, however, did not adhere tightly to this neat arrangement of one job for each goddess—they usually invoked the Muse of their choice, regardless of her traditional role. For example, Homer, a Greek epic poet of the ninth or eighth century BCE, described the Muses as

Below: This painting, entitled Dance of Apollo and the Muses, *is by Italian artist Baldassare Peruzzi (1481–1536).*

singers in a choir performing at a banquet of the gods; in this he was followed by many later writers. Roman poet Horace (65–8 BCE) called on Melpomene rather than Erato to help him write his "Aeolian" (lyric) verse.

Springs of inspiration

From time to time the Muses inhabited numerous locations, but one of their perennial favorite haunts was Mount Helicon, a large mountain in Boeotia (a region in central Greece). It was there that Greek poet Hesiod

Below: This mosaic from the third century CE depicts Virgil, flanked by the Muses Clio and Melpomene, writing the Aeneid.

(fl. 800 BCE) claimed to have been inspired by drinking the waters of the Hippocrene, a sacred spring that was said to have been created by the winged horse Pegasus with a kick of his hooves.

According to legend, the Muses danced around the Hippocrene, singing songs about the Olympian gods, the adventures of heroes, and the creation of the world. Mortal artists, musicians, and poets could not hope to tackle these or any other subjects without first beseeching the Muses to imbue them with their divine power. "Tell me, Muse, of the man of many turns," prayed Homer as he began his epic poem the *Odyssey*. "Help me, O Muse, to recall the reasons why," asked Virgil (70–19 BCE) at the start of the *Aeneid*.

The Muses were often at pains to stress the distinction between what they had to offer—inspiration—and what humans may, in their limited way, have been looking for in art—the truth. The nine goddesses answered the prayers of Hesiod thus: "Listen, you country bumpkins, you swag-bellied yahoos, we know how to tell many lies that pass for truth, and we know, when we wish, how to tell the truth itself." Yet although they are not always strictly truthful, the Muses playfully tease out an artistic truth that may be deeper than mere fact. They are, after all, trying to communicate with humans, who can never fully comprehend the workings of the gods. Therefore they must impart to mortals knowledge that has been manipulated and elevated by art. Thus it is only after the nine sisters have plucked a branch from a laurel tree in full bloom and given it to Hesiod for a staff, while breathing into him their divine song, that he can find the appropriate words to describe the birth of the deathless gods. "Happy the one whom the Muses love," says the "Homeric Hymn to the Muses," "for from his lips the speech flows sweetly."

Another spring, the Aganippe, in an area known as the Vale of the Muses at the foot of Mount Helicon near Thespiae, was also sacred to the nine deities. It was there that the Thespians—the local people whose name has since become a synonym for *actors*—honored the goddesses every five years with a series of competitions in a wide range of disciplines, including poetry composition, playing the Kithara (a lyrelike musical instrument), and devising tragedy and comedy. Excavations in the Vale of the Muses have uncovered the theater in which these contests were held, a temple with an attached stoa (a covered walkway with a colonnade) for votive offerings, and the bases of nine statues inscribed with epigrams of the poet Onestos. Roman poet Catullus (c. 84–c. 54 BCE) summoned the Muses to come from Aganippe to lend their song to the wedding of a certain Junia Aurunculeia. In the *Eclogues*, Virgil complained of their absence from Aganippe while Gallus pined away for his beloved Lycoris nearby.

Pierian springs

Among the water sources that were sacred to the Muses were the Pierian springs in the foothills of Mount Olympus in Thrace, part of what later became Macedonia. This was the native land of Orpheus, the mythical musician and poet who, according to some accounts, was a son of Calliope. A ceramic tile of the region dating from about 440 BCE depicts six Muses holding instruments and watching as Orpheus's severed head is retrieved from the water. The composition of the scene suggests that

Choosing between a God and a Satyr

In a well-known classical story, the Muses were called to judge a musical contest between the god Apollo and Marsyas, a satyr from Phrygia (part of modern Turkey). When the goddess Athena abandoned the double flute because playing it distorted her face, Marsyas took it up and became famous for his beautiful music. He challenged Apollo to a musical contest: the winner could do whatever he liked with the loser. At first the players matched each other, note for note, but Apollo then challenged Marsyas to play his instrument upside down. Apollo could do this without difficulty on his instrument, the lyre, but on the flute the task was impossible. The Muses therefore awarded the contest to Apollo, who suspended Marsyas from a pine tree and flayed him alive. The Marsyas River is said to have formed either from the blood of the satyr or from the tears of his friends. In another version of the story, the contest was judged by Midas, who declared Marsyas the winner; Apollo punished Midas by giving him the ears of an ass. Marsyas became a popular subject in Roman art, and a statue of him stood in the Forum in Rome.

Orpheus's head will continue to sing songs and give oracles under the inspiration of the Muses. Orpheus's student (or, according to some accounts, teacher) Musaeus, who was supposed to have spread the Orphic cult, obviously takes his name from the goddesses.

According to Roman poet Ovid (43 BCE–17 CE), the nine daughters of king Pierus of Pella impiously assumed the names of the Muses and challenged the supremacy of the genuine Helicon goddesses. They even dared to wager that their own Pierian springs were a greater source of inspiration than those of the Hippocrene and Aganippe. The Helicon Muses soundly defeated the princesses in a song contest, and then turned the mortal upstarts into magpies. In other accounts, notably that of Diodorus Siculus (90–21 BCE), Archelaus, king of Macedonia in the fifth century BCE, organized dramatic and athletic festivals at Dion (near Mount Olympus) lasting nine days, one day for each of the Muses. King Philip II of Macedonia (382–336 BCE) used to make grand sacrifices at Dion to Zeus and the nine Muses to celebrate his military victories, and his son Alexander the Great (356–323 BCE) feasted there in their honor before setting off on his conquest of Asia. In the same way, Spartans traditionally sacrificed to the Muses before doing battle; they marched forth from their city not to the sound of trumpets, but to flute and lyre accompaniment.

Below: This statue of Polymnia, muse of divine poetry, is housed in the Vatican Museum, Rome, Italy.

The Music of the Spheres

In the minds of historians there is no doubt that the ancient Greeks comprehended the workings of the universe in terms of musical harmonies. We still speak of the "music of the spheres," for example, a notion that is derived from the Pythagoreans and Plato. This belief in the musicality of the universe is reflected in the Muses themselves. They were born from the supreme god Zeus, or perhaps even from the Titan Uranus, and serve as the only source of information humans have about the heavens. The Pythagoreans in fact made the Muses special patrons of their schools and gave special primacy to the cult of the nine goddesses. Memory is the basis of artistic performance, which the Muses personified, and it figures in Pythagorean doctrines about the transmigration of souls. The idea is that the soul retains a memory, put there by the Muses, of its former lives (or for Plato, of the ideal forms with which it came in contact in a prenatal state). The recollection of our past lives helps us eventually to escape the cycle of life and achieve immortal immutability, the blessed state of the gods.

Greek geographer and historian Pausanias (143–176 CE) gave a different version of the legend. According to him, the cult of the Muses had been established by Ephialtes and Otus, sons of Poseidon, at Ascra, the town they had founded at the foot of Mount Helicon. These brothers believed that the Muses were three in number—Melete (Meditation or Practice), Mneme (Memory), and Aoede (Song). When Pierus came to Thespiae he discovered that there were actually nine Muses, and it was he who gave them the names that have come down to us. Pausanias suggests that Pierus, a Macedonian, may have taken the number from the Thracians, who practiced a very old cult of the three Muses, but he also notes the tradition that Pierus himself had nine daughters. Pausanias cites a poem by Mimnermus (c. 630 BCE) that makes a distinction between the three Muses, who were daughters of Uranus, and the younger nine Muses, who were daughters of Zeus.

Other sources of inspiration

Yet another water source that was sacred to the Muses was the Castalian spring on the slopes of Mount Parnassus. There the Pythian Sibyl used to bathe before giving her oracular pronouncements. Likewise those who consulted the oracle had to cleanse themselves in the sacred spring and carry out other rites in order to obtain a response. This spring was close to Delphi, where the Muses came into contact with the god Apollo, who shared their interest in music. In the work of Pindar (c. 522–c. 438 BCE), the god is known as Apollo *Mousagetes* (leader of the Muses) because he strums the lyre while the "violet-tressed" goddesses sing and play along.

A new job for Heracles

Later, in Rome, this *Mousagetes* role was taken by Heracles. Although images of Heracles playing the lyre were not unknown in Greece, the traditional story was that the hero had struggled to learn music under the tutorship of Linus, a child of Urania, and that he had killed his teacher in a fit of rage and frustration. Nevertheless, after a successful campaign against Ambracia (later known as Árta, a city in western Greece) about 187 BCE, Roman general Marcus Fulvius Nobilior erected a temple in Rome in which he placed an image of Heracles playing the lyre along with images of the nine Muses. In the same year he placed a small and very old shrine to the Muses in the temple. Because of this the temple became known as Herculis Musarum Aedes (the Temple of Heracles of the Muses), which also may have led to Heracles being referred to as *Mousagetes*. Although the original temple may have been intended for the worship of the Muses themselves, the

statues within it suggest that there may have developed a cult of Hercules Musarum. This may have been invented by Quintus Pomponius Musa, a moneyer (a manufacturer of coins or a banker). The cult's festival was held annually on June 30 (Julian calendar), but nothing is known of the rituals that were performed on that day. The temple became a famous landmark: Roman statesman and author Cicero (106–43 BCE) described it as an outstanding example of how a man of war had turned to the arts of

Muses and Museums

In ancient Greece the *mouseion* or "museum" was an open space or a building devoted to collecting artwork inspired by the Muses. Ancient museums typically contained statues of the nine Muses, along with an altar or shrine. The first such museum was established at the foot of Mount Helicon in the Vale of the Muses. There, statues of mythical and historical musicians stood on display, along with archives of distinguished works of poetry. In ancient Alexandria, Egypt, the museum appears to have had other functions as well. In particular, it was used as a place for research, education, and literary discussion. Another smaller museum existed at Athens. As storehouses of Greek culture, museums did much to preserve literature and learning for later generations.

Below: Modern museums reflect their origins in collections of works inspired by the Muses.

peace. In the first century BCE, L. Marcius Philippus, the stepfather of Emperor Augustus, rebuilt and enhanced the temple with great splendor and increased its importance.

In Rome the Muses replaced the Camenae, an old set of Italic nymphs whose name they adopted. They inhabited a spring below the Caelian Hill, from where they inspired mortal songs, the best-known surviving examples of which are by Livius Andronicus (c. 284–c. 204 BCE) and Gnaeus Naevius (c. 270–c. 199 BCE). The Camenae continued to make occasional appearances in the work of later Roman writers, but usually only as a fanciful title for the Greek goddesses, while their festival on August 13 gradually faded into insignificance.

Blind with love

The Muses are associated with numerous characters of Greek myth who sing, play instruments, dance, or tell riddles. In one legend the mythical musician Thamyris, whom Linus taught to play the lyre, challenged the goddesses to a contest. If he won, he would make love to all nine of them in succession; if he lost, they would take from him whatever they wished. The Muses won, naturally, and then deprived Thamyris of his eyesight and his musical skills. However, the loss of sight was not always a punishment from the Muses. According to Homer, the bard Demodocus was especially beloved by the Nine. As a mark of their affection, they blinded him, while at the same time blessing him with the gift of song and an unfailing memory (Homer himself may also have been blind).

Link with the Sphinx

When the Sirens challenged the supremacy of the Muses, they, too, were defeated and forced to submit to having their feathers plucked. The Muses also taught the nymph Echo her musical skills. After she had incurred the jealousy of Pan and been torn to shreds, they gave her dismembered parts the ability to make music all over the earth. The Sphinx that tormented Thebes is said to have learned her riddle from the Muses. According to Hesiod, when the Muses went to Mount Olympus to attend the banquets of the gods and provide the entertainment, they sat alongside the Graces (Charities), the goddesses of charm and attraction, and Himerous, the god of desire. Pausanias reported that at Troezen (an ancient Greek city on the northeast tip of the Peloponnese) there was an altar on which worshipers sacrificed to the Muses and to Hypnos, the god of sleep. The Muse Clio was often credited with the introduction of the alphabet into Greece, although in *Prometheus Bound*, a play by Aeschylus (525–456 BCE), the hero claims that he introduced it himself, and that the Muses took it up as one of their creative tools.

KIRK SUMMERS

Right:
This vase, dating from the fifth century BCE, depicts Thamyris being blinded by the Muses.

Bibliography

Hesiod, and M. L. West, trans. *Theogony* and *Works and Days*. New York: Oxford University Press, 2008.
Homer, and Robert Fagles, trans. *The Odyssey*. New York: Penguin, 2009.
Ovid, and A. D. Melville, trans. *Metamorphoses*. New York: Oxford University Press, 2008.

SEE ALSO: Apollo; Graces; Mnemosyne; Titans; Uranus; Zeus.

NEMESIS

In Greek and Roman mythology, Nemesis was the goddess of retribution. Her mother was Nyx (Night), and Erebus (Darkness) was usually said to be her father, although in some accounts he is Oceanus (Ocean).

Above: This painting, entitled Nemesis' Triumph over Sin, *is by Italian artist Paolo Veronese (1528–1588).*

Nemesis usually appears in myths as the personification of justice. Her role was to show that wrongdoing deserves, and will receive, punishment. In one legend she is the true mother, by Zeus, of Helen of Troy; Helen's abduction to Troy by Paris started the Trojan War. As a goddess, Nemesis was worshiped in dedicated temples at Rhamnous in Attica (near Athens, Greece) and in the city of Smyrna (modern Izmir, Turkey).

In art, Nemesis is usually portrayed as a virgin deity. She is often associated with various instruments of punishment and torture, such as bridles, cudgels, swords, and whips. However, there are few representations of her in art and literature, which possibly allowed her meaning to change more than that of most other Greek divinities. Nemesis was first identified with other personifications of moral ideas, such as Adrasteia, who personified the inescapability of fate, and Themis, whose province was order and justice. Later, Nemesis took on aspects of an underworld divinity.

Nemesis in literature

Nemesis as a divinity appears in neither the *Iliad* nor the *Odyssey*, Greek poet Homer's epic poems of the ninth or eighth century BCE, but both epics reveal familiarity with nemesis as a concept. Characters express awareness of the negative sentiments that others will feel toward them if they behave badly or attempt to take more than their fair share of any reward. The fear of retribution for such misdeeds is known as "nemesis," but it is not personified and it does not have divine force. In the *Iliad* it is the Erinyes (Furies) who sometimes intervene to prevent violations of the accepted order.

According to the *Theogony* of Greek poet Hesiod (fl. 800 BCE), Nemesis belonged to one of the older generations of gods. A sister of Aidos (who represented shame and modesty), she was the child of Night. In *Works and Days* Hesiod predicted a time when mortal behavior would become so disgraceful that Nemesis and Aidos would withdraw from the earth in disgust.

The root of retribution

For the ancient Greeks, nemesis was always just. The word itself is derived from the root *nem/nom*, which has to do with distribution or apportionment. The verb *nemein* means "to apportion, distribute, or graze." Related words are *nomós*, meaning "pasture," and *nómos*, meaning "law, established custom." Pasture is an area of communal land allotted to an individual for the purpose of grazing livestock; laws and customs are allotted to the community as a whole. The verb *nemesan* means "to begrudge," and, by

Attributes of Nemesis

Artists and sculptors such as the master sculptor Phidias and his pupil Agoracritus set out to represent classical gods and goddesses thousands of years ago, in the fifth century BCE. However, little evidence of how Nemesis was portrayed has been discovered intact. The most celebrated statue of the goddess was found in a temple at Rhamnous in Attica, a peninsular state in southern Greece that juts out into the Aegean Sea. This statue was sculpted by Phidias. Parts of the sculpture are exhibited in the British Museum in London, and in Athens.

In representations of her, Nemesis's attributes change according to the characteristic that is being emphasized. Agoracritus's statue of Nemesis presents a regal woman wearing a diadem, holding an apple branch in her left hand and a phial in her right hand. The objects Nemesis carries and the crown she wears help to reveal the goddess's character. Her diadem is decorated with winged figures called victories that symbolize the many times Nemesis has had her retribution, and they show her aspect as an avenging goddess. Deer also adorn the diadem. Some historians argue that the deer are an indication that Nemesis belonged to an earthbound group of deities. Called underground gods—as opposed to the Olympian gods, such as Zeus—they were often charged with the delivery of punishment or retribution. The apple branch, a symbol of the earth, further supports this idea of Nemesis's origins and also symbolizes health and long life or immortality. The phial, which is a ritual vessel, represents Nemesis's righteousness. This particular phial is reported to be decorated with Ethiopians. In the classical period, Ethiopia was considered to be a great distance from Greece, and this design symbolizes the far-reaching power of Nemesis.

In classical art, the position in which a statue was sculpted often reflected the attitude of the represented figure. The pose of this statue of Nemesis suggests that an exchange is in progress. Nemesis offers righteousness with her right hand and keeps retribution by her side in her left hand. This attitude implies that any decline of righteousness will be met with retribution.

In his description of this statue, Greek travel writer Pausanias says that, although early artistic representations of Nemesis are similar, later ones adorn her with different tools of retribution. In some cases she is even changed physically. Like Eros, the god of love, Nemesis has been represented with wings, since some artists believed her acts were a consequence of love.

extension, to be indignant at another's undeserved good fortune. In other words nemesis is the feeling provoked by seeing someone get more than his or her fair share, or feeling oneself to have received less than a fair share. While the original meaning of nemesis was "allotment" or "apportioning," in time it came to mean the feeling provoked by a violation of the rules that governed the division of benefits.

According to the ancient Greeks, the road to ruin ran along the following route. A successful mortal achieved *olbos* (prosperity), which could lead to *koros* (excess), which caused hubris (pride, outrage, or insolence, even violence). This brought nemesis (indignation or retribution), which brought on *ate* (madness, ruin, destruction). This classic process of degeneration is described by the chorus in the play *Agamemnon* by Greek playwright Aeschylus (525–456 BCE), although Aeschylus does not use the word *nemesis*.

Nemesis and Helen of Troy

As for how Nemesis came to be associated with the myth of Helen, we must turn to the so-called cyclic epics, which never achieved the same status as the Homeric epics. One of these epics, the *Cypria*, concerns the beginning of the Trojan War. It recounts how Zeus and Themis decided to bring about the conflict in order to relieve the suffering of

Right: This Roman bas-relief was carved in Syria in the second or third century CE. It depicts Nemesis holding the scales of justice.

the earth, which groaned under the weight of too large a population. The ensuing 10 years of fighting lightened the earth's load by killing many men. According to another fragment of the *Cypria*, Zeus desired Nemesis, and although she changed into many forms in an effort to escape him, he ultimately fathered Helen by her by disguising himself as a swan.

Perhaps humankind seemed to the gods to have taken over more than its fair share of the earth, and the disaster set in motion by Helen's birth was a means of redressing the balance. If Helen was the daughter of Nemesis, she was therefore an agent of divine retribution.

Worshiping the goddess

The temple to Nemesis at Rhamnous in Attica was built about 430 BCE. According to Greek travel writer Pausanias (143–176 CE) in his *Description of Greece*, the cult statue of the goddess in the temple was carved by famous Greek sculptor Phidias (fifth century BCE) from a block of marble brought by the overconfident Persians. They had intended to use it to sculpt a trophy at nearby Marathon. Their unexpected defeat at the hands of the Greeks in 490 BCE is just the sort of punishment for hubris (pride) that Nemesis would be expected to inflict, so it is most fitting that she should be honored in this way.

It seems, however, that Nemesis's association with the town of Rhamnous went back earlier than the Battle of Marathon. Remains of an earlier temple have been found, dedicated to both Nemesis and Themis, that may date from the sixth century BCE. The pairing of Nemesis with a goddess who stands for justice and order is evidence that Nemesis had moral significance long before the classical era.

Above: This photograph shows the modern remains of the fifth-century-BCE sanctuary of Nemesis at Rhamnous in Attica, Greece.

Ancient people of Smyrna, again according to Pausanias, worshiped two Nemeses. They believed them to be the daughters of Nyx (at Rhamnous the father of Nemesis was believed to be Oceanus). Pausanias provided some details of the temple decoration, but no archaeological evidence survives. The double Nemeses may refer to the two daughters of Nyx in Hesiod—Nemesis herself and Aidos. It has also been suggested that the two aspects of Nemesis here correspond to two divine representations of fate—the fearsome Adrasteia, "she who cannot be escaped," and the more benign Tyche, who represents "chance" or "destiny."

In the Hellenistic period (323–30 BCE), Nemesis became associated with the afterlife. She was frequently mentioned on epitaphs, some of which even suggested that the dead would have their personal Nemesis in the underworld.

The term *nemesis* is still used in English today, but with a subtle change in meaning. One person may now be described as another's nemesis, whereas in strict, classical, mythological terms a mortal could only be an agent of Nemesis. The modern Nemesis has thus returned to her Homeric roots.

DEBORAH LYONS

Bibliography

Hesiod, and M. L. West, trans. *Theogony* and *Works and Days*. New York: Oxford University Press, 2008.

Pausanias, and Peter Levi, trans. *Guide to Greece*. New York: Viking Press, 1984.

SEE ALSO: Dionysus; Furies; Poseidon; Zeus.

NEPTUNE

In Roman mythology, Neptune was the god of the sea. He was the son of Saturn and Ops; his brother was Jupiter. He was the husband of Amphitrite, and the father of Triton.

The Roman god Neptune became, through identification with the Greek Poseidon, the divine lord of the sea. This equivalence was established as early as the fourth century BCE, when Neptune first appeared on coins holding a trident (a long, three-pronged, pitchfork-shaped fish harpoon), which had been the main symbol of the Greek god. Neptune, like Poseidon, was conventionally represented as a naked, bearded figure in the prime of his maturity, very much like his divine brother Jupiter. He lived in a golden house deep beneath the sea. His chariot glided across the waters so quickly that the axles of its wheels never got wet.

In Greek mythology, Poseidon's wife was the beautiful nymph Amphitrite, and in Rome Neptune was celebrated as being betrothed to the same goddess. Neptune, like Poseidon, was one of the few gods to whom bulls were sacrificed, and the Roman god also adopted his Greek predecessor's special affinity for horses. One major characteristic of Poseidon was his role as the Earth Shaker,

Below: This painting by Peter Paul Rubens (1577–1640) of Neptune calming the storm is based on an episode from Virgil's Aeneid.

who caused seismic tremors. This attribute did not become part of Neptune's usual functions. Indeed, while the Greek Poseidon was in many respects the embodiment of the elemental, irrational forces of nature, Neptune was usually depicted by the Romans as a friendly and helpful god. At one point in the *Aeneid* by Virgil (70–19 BCE), a prophecy made by the oracle of Apollo on Delos teaches the Trojan hero Aeneas that he must seek out a place to settle. Aeneas's perilous journey to Italy to found Lavinium is eased by Neptune's intervention. Fearful of a new Troy being founded in Italy, the Roman goddess Juno—who took the side of the Greeks in the war against the Trojans—orders a storm to disrupt Aeneas's journey. Neptune stills the storm and calms the sea to ensure the safe passage of Aeneas, the ancestor of the Roman people.

Although by the dawn of the Common Era Neptune had taken on nearly all the characteristics and responsibilities of Poseidon, the Roman god's true origins were almost certainly not Greek. His Latin name has a possible counterpart in the Etruscan divinity Nethuns. This god might be the forerunner of Neptune, but there are problems with such an interpretation. While Neptune was one of the most ancient Roman gods—a note of his festival, the Neptunalia, celebrated on July 23, appears in the oldest pre-Julian calendar—the name of Nethuns did not feature in any pre-Roman Etruscan religious (liturgical) documents. It is thus generally assumed that the Etruscans at some point adopted the Roman Neptune into their pantheon, rather than vice versa.

Although there is no firm evidence, there are strong indications that the Romans derived the god Neptune from their Indo-European heritage (the Etruscan language was not Indo-European in origin). In Old Irish, which is an Indo-European language, there was a water divinity known as Nechtan, a name that can be traced to a common root with the Latin Neptunus. Old Welsh (which is closely related to Irish) has a rare counterpart Neithon, and this too may be related to

Neptunus. Irish lore tells of Nechtan's Hill (located in modern County Kildare, Ireland), which had a sacred and secret well. The light of knowledge was said to reside in this well, to which a formidable taboo was attached: only the water god Nechtan and his three cupbearers were permitted to approach its source of water. However, Nechtan's wife, Boand, broke the ban. Either to purify herself of guilt or perhaps out of defiance and daring, Boand approached her husband's well. When she did, the waters burst forth violently and pursued her as she fled in terror toward the sea, creating a great river, the Boyne

Right: This statue of Neptune adorns the Trevi Fountain in Rome, Italy, celebrating the god's association with fresh water.

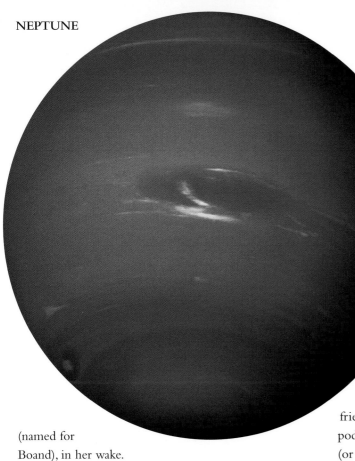

Left: The planet Neptune was named for its blue, watery appearance.

Rome near the banks of the Tiber River. It was probably nearby that the celebrations took place. Historian Dio Cassius (c. 150–c. 235 CE) adds the information that Agrippa, an associate and friend of Emperor Augustus, completed a building named the Basilica of Neptune, also on the Campus Martius. It therefore seems likely that Neptune enjoyed a special place with the god Mars in the religious ideology of the Campus Martius, which was in many ways the most popular quarter of ancient Rome. Neptune and Mars both appear on a large marble frieze of the early first century BCE that was unearthed on the Campus Martius, probably on the site of Neptune's temple. The frieze, which likely adorned the base of a large statue podium, shows the wedding of Neptune and Amphitrite (or Salacia) accompanied by a cortege of water nymphs and sea creatures. Pliny, in the passage mentioned above, seems to describe this very monument. At a slightly later date a separate relief was added to the monument depicting a ritual sacrifice to Mars, who is shown by his altar at the conclusion of a census. The pairing of Mars, the god of war, and Neptune, who by Augustan times was envisioned as the god of the sea, was almost certainly prompted by Roman land and naval victories. Yet Neptune's old Roman

(named for Boand), in her wake.

It is significant that Nechtan, while a god of waters, was not a god of the sea. He has special associations with a particular sacred well. Linguists usually relate the Latin Neptunus and its cognates in Old Irish to a root meaning "wetness, dampness, moisture." The Roman Neptune was almost certainly not, in origin, a sea deity but a god of freshwater sources who protected wells and rivers. While in the most common Roman version of Greek myth, Neptune's wife was, like Poseidon's, Amphitrite, Latin authors also recalled that Neptune had a cult partner, later interpreted as his wife, named Salacia. Her name has usually been related to a root meaning "spring," both in the sense of "water" and in the sense of "jump." Salacia, then, seems to personify the springing forth of waters, an activity that lay within Neptune's area of responsibility.

The festival of Neptune

Neptune's great festival, the Neptunalia, makes evident the god's role in bringing forth water. The feast was held annually on July 23, a time of year when scorching heat and the danger of drought made the need for water critical. Neptune's presence was felt to be embodied in the water of the river, and the people must have invoked the god for continuing help at such a crucial time. According to Pliny the Elder (23–79 CE) in *Natural History*, Neptune had a shrine (later a temple) in the Circus Flaminius, the large open space on the Campus Martius (the Field of Mars) in

Neptune in Art

Neptune is one of the Roman deities most frequently depicted in art. Among the most famous paintings of the sea god are two works of the 17th century. One is *The Triumph of Neptune and Amphitrite*, painted about 1610 by French artist Nicolas Poussin (1594–1665). The other, based on Virgil's description in the *Aeneid*, is *Neptune Calming the Tempest* (1635) by Flemish artist Peter Paul Rubens (1577–1640) (see page 204). The former is housed in the Philadelphia Museum of Art; the latter belongs to Harvard University.

Of the countless statues of Neptune himself, either alone or with his horses and attendant minor sea deities, perhaps the most celebrated is the work by Michelangelo's apprentice Bartolommeo Ammannati (1511–1592), which stands in the Piazza della Signoria in the heart of Florence, Italy.

Above: Built around 460 BCE, the Temple of Neptune is one of the great surviving classical buildings in Paestum, Italy.

festival, the Neptunalia, originally had nothing to do with war or with military victory: it was a celebration and an invocation of springwater.

Few details have survived about what went on at the festival. We do know that leafy arbors or booths (*tabernaculum*) were constructed from the boughs of trees to shade the worshipers from the summer sun. The ordinary folk seem to have camped out along the banks of the Tiber. There was surely a holiday atmosphere in the celebration of the Neptunalia, much as there was in the New Year's feast of Anna Perenna on March 15, when the Romans also set up rude huts of branches and boughs on the same Campus Martius. On that day they drank wine and sang and danced in happy fellowship, wishing each other well for the year ahead. Such a spirit of camaraderie also marked the Neptunalia. The poet Horace (65–8 BCE) seemed to recall this holiday mood in his *Odes*, where he pondered how best to celebrate Neptune's festival day. He writes that he will open a jar of choice wine reserved for a special occasion and will sing into the night, exchanging alternate verses with his beloved Lyde, praising Neptune and his sea goddesses.

The festivities were later enhanced in Roman imperial times by the addition of games (Ludi Neptunales), which included chariot and boat races and other naval spectacles. The appeal to ordinary folk of a midsummer celebration is clear from the fact that the Neptunalia are mentioned in "rustic calendars," the ancient lists of festivals observed by country dwellers. Roman poet Ausonius (c. 310–c. 395 CE) gave a vivid account of the Neptunalia in the fourth century, attesting to the enduring popularity of the festival, which enjoyed a much longer life than most other pre-Christian Roman holidays. Over time, as Roman influence spread, Neptune was identified with a host of water divinities. In Rome, however, the character of the old Neptune persisted, especially in the celebration of his summer festival, into the late imperial epoch, c. 310 CE.

DANIEL P. HARMON

Bibliography
Horace, and David West, trans. *The Complete Odes and Epodes.* New York: Oxford University Press, 2008.
Virgil, and Robert Fagles, trans. *The Aeneid.* New York: Penguin, 2009.

SEE ALSO: Apollo; Juno; Mars; Poseidon; Saturn; Triton; Zeus.

NEREUS

Nereus, whose name in Greek means "wet one," was a sea god associated with the Mediterranean Sea in general and the Aegean Sea in particular. He was regarded as a wise old man who had the ability to see the future as well as to change into a variety of different shapes at will.

advice on how to steal the golden apples from the Garden of the Hesperides. Nereus, reluctant to answer Heracles, changed into many different shapes in an effort to escape from him. However, Heracles eventually grabbed hold of the sea god and refused to let go of him until he got his prophecy. This story has strong parallels with myths involving Proteus, another sea god, prophet, and shape-changer. Greek king Menelaus grappled with Proteus—who tried to evade capture by changing himself into, among other things, a lion, a snake, a tree, and running water—in order to learn how he could get home to Greece after the Trojan War. The similarities between the

Nereus was the son of Gaia, the earth goddess, and Pontus, the personification of the sea. His family tree demonstrated the inbreeding that was common in the Greek pantheon. His mother was also his grandmother, having given birth to Pontus through a union with the sky god Aether. Further, Doris, wife of Nereus, was another of Gaia's children, although her father was Oceanus, the personification of the river that the Greeks believed encircled the earth. In his epic poem *Theogony*, Greek author Hesiod (fl. 800 BCE) praised Nereus for his manner, calling him: "Trustworthy and gentle, and never forgetful of what is right." These qualities made the deity an ideal tutor for Aphrodite, the goddess of love.

Shapeshifter
The prophetic and shapeshifting abilities of Nereus were clearly demonstrated in the 11th of Heracles' 12 labors. Heracles went to ask the god's

Right: This ancient Roman sculpture portrays a Nereid—one of the 50 daughters of Nereus—riding a sea serpent.

The Nereids

Nereus and Doris were the parents of 50 daughters, known collectively as the Nereids. Although they were goddesses, descriptions of the Nereids are similar to those of mermaids, mortal marine creatures from many different folklore traditions. Both species were sea dwellers with the upper bodies of beautiful women and the tails of fish. Only a few individual Nereids played significant roles in Greek myths. One Nereid, Amphitrite, married the chief sea god, Poseidon, and became queen of the sea. Another, Galatea, fell in love with the shepherd Acis but was in turn loved by Polyphemus, a Cyclops or one-eyed giant. In his jealousy, Polyphemus killed Acis with an enormous rock from a mountain, leaving Galatea to transform her lover into a river. Probably the most famous Nereid is Thetis, mother of Greek hero Achilles.

Other myths involved the Nereids as a group. In one story, Cassiopeia, queen of Ethiopia, declared that both she and her daughter, Andromeda, were more beautiful than all the daughters of Nereus. The Nereids reported this insult to Poseidon, who sent a sea monster to attack the coast of Ethiopia. Cassiopeia and her husband tried to regain Poseidon's favor by offering to sacrifice Andromeda to the monster, but the beast was killed in the nick of time by the hero Perseus. In another famous legend, the Nereids helped Jason and the Argonauts steer their ship clear of both the sea monster Scylla and the nearby Charybdis, a whirlpool now believed to have been situated in the Straits of Messina between Sicily and southern Italy.

Left: This 1840 painting by Théodore Chassériau (1819–1856) is entitled Andromeda Chained to the Rock by the Nereids.

two legends are so great that some scholars have even suggested that Nereus and Proteus were one and the same—both are described by Homer, the famous Greek poet of the ninth or eighth century BCE, as "the old man of the sea." According to other sources, however, Proteus, unlike Nereus, was the son of either Poseidon or Oceanus.

Nereus and Poseidon

In the Greek pantheon, Nereus, although an ally of Poseidon, was a minor deity compared to the mighty king of the sea. *Dionysiaca*, a Greek epic poem by Nonnus (fl. c. 450–470 CE), contains an account of how Nereus helped Poseidon in a battle against Dionysus, the god of wine, after the latter had claimed the island of Naxos for himself. Historians believe that Nereus was worshiped before the arrival of Greek-speaking peoples in Greece around 2100 BCE. Nereus was their preeminent sea god, but he was later overshadowed by a new culture and its new gods, such as Poseidon and Zeus. One piece of evidence in support of this view is that the name of Nereus's daughter, Amphitrite, is not Greek in origin. Some academics think that the *trit* part of the name represents a pre-Greek Indo-European word for "sea."

ANDREW CAMPBELL

Bibliography

Hesiod, and M. L. West, trans. *Theogony* and *Works and Days.* New York: Oxford University Press, 2008.

Homer, and Robert Fagles, trans. *The Iliad* and *The Odyssey.* New York: Penguin, 2009.

SEE ALSO: Aphrodite; Dionysus; Gaia; Oceanus; Poseidon; Proteus; Thetis.

NIKE

Nike was the Greek goddess of victory. She was more a personification of victory than an actual character and consequently did not appear in stories. However, her symbolic importance to the Greeks in connection with battles, athletic contests, and even weddings was considerable. Many surviving representations in stone and pottery depict her dancing, running, or flying.

While one source suggested that Nike was the daughter of Polemos, the personification of war, and another related that she was the child of Zeus, king of the gods, the best-known account of her origins was provided by Greek poet Hesiod (fl. 800 BCE). He wrote in *Theogony* that Nike's mother was the underworld Styx River and that her father was the Titan Pallas. Nike's siblings, in this account, were Zelus (Aspiration), Bia (Force), and Cratos (Power). Hesiod recounted that Styx and her children were the first to join Zeus in the war against the Titans that established the sovereignty of the Olympian gods. Zelus appeared solely in connection with this myth; Cratos and Bia, however, played roles in other stories carrying out the will of Zeus. They appear, for example, in the tragedy *Prometheus Bound* by Greek dramatist Aeschylus (525–456 BCE).

Link with Athena

Nike was associated with Zeus and with his daughter Athena, goddess of arts and war. Indeed, the two female deities were sometimes combined into a single figure: Athena Nike. Phidias (fl. c. 490–430 BCE) erected a great statue of Athena inside her chief temple, the Parthenon, built on the Acropolis in Athens between 447 and 432 BCE. The sculptor included a little winged Nike fluttering in the palm of Athena's hand. Several decades after the completion of the Parthenon, the Athenians constructed a small temple of Athena Nike on a bastion above the entrance to the Acropolis. Around the temple ran a balustrade decorated with little Nikai (the plural of *Nike*) engaged in preparations for a sacrifice. Athena appears several times among them.

Below: This relief sculpture of Nike has been reconstructed from an ancient tablet unearthed at Ephesus, Turkey.

Nike and Weddings

Nike's symbolic importance extended to weddings. Her role in such ceremonies is suggested in *The Birds* by Greek comic dramatist Aristophanes. In this play, the chorus sings to the bridegroom "Hail to the victor." In addition, in ancient Greek art Nike appears in representations of the wedding cortege, flying over the cart transporting the happy couple. The linking of Nike with marriage explains the goddess's association with Eros, the god of love. In other artistic representations, Nike and Eros appear as a pair of small winged figures.

However, while Nike played a role in Greek weddings, it is not clear exactly whose victory the ceremonies were supposed to represent. While Aristophanes implies that the groom is triumphant over the bride, Nike was a familiar figure on Greek women's possessions, such as jewelry and ornamental seals, which represented power. Marriage was an indirect means for Greek women to achieve power, so it is possible that, in that sense, the bride was the victor. However, perhaps the most convincing answer is that the wedding was the joint victory of the couple. Victory, for the Greeks, was a moment when humans achieved perfection. Athletic victory was one such moment; so too was marriage, the joyous and triumphant union of two people, whether for love or personal advancement.

Nike and military victory

For the Greeks, Nike was a symbol of military victory. They prayed to the goddess for success in battles—if victory was forthcoming, they regarded it as indication of her favor. On the temple of Athena Nike, some of the Nikai are depicted building trophies of the kind Greek armies customarily left on the battlefield as tokens of their victory. These were cairns, or mounds, constructed of broken weapons and armor gathered from the fallen enemy. Such ritual objects were the concrete embodiments of Nike's favor for the

Below: The Temple of Athena Nike forms part of the Acropolis that overlooks Athens, Greece.

winning side. No victorious Greek army would have left the battlefield without building such a trophy. They were also put up on nearby shores after sea battles.

The ancient Greeks' greatest military triumph was the naval victory over the Persians at the Battle of Salamis in 480 BCE. Writing about the battle, Greek historian Herodotus (c. 484–425 BCE) related how the Greeks remembered an oracle which promised them that "the day of freedom" would be granted by "Zeus and Lady Nike." To give thanks for the victory, the Greeks dedicated a statue to Nike at Delphi.

Besides wars and battles, Nike was important on other occasions when people sought victory, including lawsuits

and athletic and musical competitions. Several works by Greek dramatist Euripides (c. 486–c. 406 BCE) end with a prayer by the chorus for Nike to attend to them through life and continue to crown them—in other words, to ensure their success.

Understanding personification

Like other figures in the Greek pantheon, such as Mnemosyne (Memory), Thanatos (Death), and Polemos (War), Nike was a personification of an abstract force and not a developed personality in the manner of deities such as Zeus and Athena. However, the distinction between person and personification was not always clear. For example, at certain moments Polemos seemed to be a minor divinity in his own right and appeared as a character in a play by Aristophanes (c. 450–c. 388 BCE).

Right: The Winged Victory of Samothrace *was created in the early second century BCE. It is now housed in the Louvre in Paris, France.*

Personifications tended to develop into personalities as stories were told about them, whereupon they became objects of cult worship and were represented in art. Nike did not appear in any stories and was not the object of cult worship—the Greeks prayed for victory and offered battlefield trophies to her if they were successful, but these were tributes to a symbol rather than a person.

Yet Nike did become something of a personality through artistic representation. Greek artists frequently represented her in paintings on pottery, in small bronze figures, in stone sculptures and terra-cottas, and on jewelry, coins, and seal rings. The goddess was nearly always shown with wings, dressed in flowing garments, and in motion.

On early pottery paintings she is depicted running; in later representations she is often swooping down to touch the earth. One of the greatest sculptures of the deity, Nike of Paionios (c. 420 BCE), stood high on a pillar at the sanctuary of Olympia on the Peloponnese peninsula, supported by her bare toes which just grazed the base. In other representations, such as those on Sicilian coins that commemorated racing victories at the Olympic Games, Nike flies over chariots with her wings outspread. Another portrayal of the goddess is the eight-foot- (2.4-meter-) high *Winged Victory of Samothrace* (c. 190 BCE), which shows Nike touching down on the prow of a ship. The statue, which now stands in the Louvre, in Paris, France, commemorated victory in a sea battle. Nike's Roman counterpart, the goddess Victoria, was also frequently represented by artists and sculptors. Roman Emperor Augustus (63 BCE–14 CE) placed Victoria's most important altar in the Senate House in Rome in 29 BCE.

In the world of commerce, in 1972 the name Nike was adopted by a U.S. company that has since become one of the world's leading manufacturers of sportswear and sports equipment.

JAMES M. REDFIELD

Bibliography

Bulfinch, Thomas. *Bulfinch's Mythology.* New York: Barnes & Noble, 2006.

Hesiod, and M. L. West, trans. *Theogony* and *Works and Days.* New York: Oxford University Press, 2008.

SEE ALSO: Athena; Eros; Mnemosyne; Titans; Zeus.

NYX

Nyx (also spelled Nux) was the ancient Greek goddess of night. Born from Chaos, the primordial darkness, Nyx herself gave birth to a host of deities. She also shared with her daughter Hemera (Day) a home in the underworld, but the two goddesses were never there at the same time. Each day, while Hemera passed over the earth, Nyx rested until it was her time to bring darkness to the world.

Nyx had many children, most of whom personified negative aspects of the human condition. They included the Keres (Doom), Thanatos (Death), Hypnos (Sleep), Oneiroi (Dreams), Nemesis (Retribution), Geras (Old Age), Eris (Discord), Apate (Deceit), and Philotes (Desire). She also gave birth to the three Fates—Clotho, Lachesis, and Atropos—who measured out each person's lifespan; and to the Hesperides—Aegle, Erytheia, Hesperia, and Arethusa—whose golden apples were stolen by Heracles. Nyx's other children—Aether (Brightness) and Hemera (Day)—were by her brother, Erebus (Darkness).

Below: Nyx appears in this scene from a Greek bas-relief of the second century BCE depicting the battle between Olympians and Titans.

Above: This painting by Edward Burne-Jones (1833–1898) shows the garden of the Hesperides. The Hesperides were daughters of Nyx who guarded a tree that bore golden apples. Here they are depicted dancing around it.

Nyx lived in Tartarus, the deepest part of the underworld, where she shared with Hemera a house with a threshold of bronze. Other inhabitants of Tartarus included Nyx's children Hypnos and Thanatos.

Most ancient Greeks probably became acquainted with the details of this version of Nyx's story through hearing performances of an ancient Greek epic called *Theogony*; the title means "birth of the gods" in Greek. The poem, attributed to Greek poet Hesiod (fl. 800 BCE), is one of the earliest surviving examples of Greek literature. *Theogony* offered a view of the gods that brought together many local traditions about the origins and nature of the gods. Most Greeks recognized Hesiod's version of Greek mythology as being authoritative.

Orphic versions of Nyx's story

There were other versions of Nyx's origins besides Hesiod's, however. For example, adherents to Orphism, an obscure religious sect, made Nyx the daughter of a creator god named Phanes. According to this version, Nyx and Phanes had an incestuous relationship that produced Uranus, who in the mainstream account of Greek mythology was the son of Gaia (Earth). Nyx served first as Uranus's adviser, then as adviser to Uranus's son, Cronus, and finally to Cronus's son, Zeus, when he became ruler of the Olympian gods.

In another version of the Orphic story, Nyx laid an egg, from which hatched Phanes and other deities. Some scholars suggest that Nyx may have been the supreme deity in an earlier phase of Orphic belief, and there is evidence that some Greeks considered her the original creator deity.

Most Greek deities that personified the natural world and aspects of existence remained relatively minor figures in Greek mythology, and this is largely true of Nyx. Although she features in the Orphic liturgy, there is little evidence that Nyx was worshiped with temples and sacrifices, as were major Olympian deities such as Zeus and Athena. On the other hand, Greek travel writer Pausanias (143–176 CE) mentions an oracle of Nyx in Megara, a Greek city west of Athens.

Witches in Greek myths sometimes prayed to Nyx, suggesting that ancient magicians may have invoked her in curses and spells. As for the arts, no play or hymn is known to have been devoted to Nyx, and there are few depictions of her in Greek painting or sculpture.

As a symbol of darkness and night, Nyx was believed to have enormous power. In the epic poem the *Iliad* by Greek poet Homer (c. ninth–eighth century BCE), a story told by Nyx's son Hypnos is evidence of this power. Hera, Zeus's

wife and queen of the Olympian gods, hated the hero Heracles because he was Zeus's son by a mortal woman. One day she decided to wreck Heracles' ships. In order to distract Zeus from her deed, Hera persuaded Hypnos to make Zeus fall asleep. Hera then sent a storm against Heracles' fleet. When Zeus awoke, he flew into a rage because he knew he had been sent to sleep by Hypnos, and he began searching for him. Zeus was intent on hurling the god of sleep from Mount Olympus, but Hypnos fled to his mother, Nyx, for protection. When Zeus learned that Hypnos was with Nyx, he abandoned his pursuit because he was unwilling to do anything that would displease Nyx.

Personification in myths

Ancient Greek myths contain numerous references to deities who are also personifications of things or concepts. Thus, *nyx* as a common noun is the ancient Greek word for "night," and *hypnos* is the Greek word for "sleep."

Many of these personifications belong, like Nyx and her offspring, to a family that is older in the chronological timeline of Greek mythology than the Olympian family ruled by Zeus. The most fundamental elements of the universe appear earliest in this timeline. So it is that the first generation of gods brings forth Chaos, the dark void; Gaia, the earth from which all else springs forth to fill the void; and Eros, the impulse to procreate. Nyx is among the second generation of gods, the offspring of Chaos, who represents the all-engulfing darkness of the heavens. Nyx personifies the specific darkness experienced on earth at night.

In mythology these pre-Olympian gods tend to be grouped into subfamilies of related ideas and concepts. Ideas that are connected by the circumstances in which they tend to occur—such as night, sleep, and dreams—are represented as close kin. Thus Nyx's offspring include the personification of sleep (Hypnos) and dreams (Oneiroi).

Family relationships can also represent more general connections among abstract ideas. Since night is a time when people tend to feel more vulnerable, or helpless, the goddess Nyx is viewed as the matriarch of a family of concepts that impose limits on human power, such as death, old age, and fate. Nyx was also the mother of concepts such as strife, deception, and sexual desire—ideas that often come to mind during dreams and that reflect a darker side of human nature.

A similar way of thinking can be seen in the way people used the names of major gods to refer to broad concepts. Ancient Greek poets, for example, used the name of the

war god Ares to mean "war." Likewise, a common way to say "it's raining" in ancient Greece was *Zeus huei*, meaning "Zeus is making water."

Coming to terms with abstract concepts

In cosmological myths (those relating to the nature of the universe) and cosmogonic myths (those relating to the origins and development of the universe), personification was a useful way for the ancients to think about abstract concepts. In turn, the system of relationships among human families was as a useful way to organize these concepts.

Ancient Greek philosophers also used personification to rationalize ideas in poetry that seemed strange or irreligious to them. The battles among the gods during the Trojan War, for example, were interpreted as an allegory that described the relationships among the constituent elements of the universe as the Greeks saw them. The clash between the fire god Hephaestus and a river god in the *Iliad*, for example, represented the opposing natures of fire and water.

Personification in ancient myths reveals a complex and systematic way of understanding the world. The religious systems and myths of cultures the world over feature sun gods, moon gods, and so on, and relate them to one another as members of the same mythological family.

The personified concept of night has a place in the religions of a number of other cultures, too. The pre-Hindu Vedic texts of ancient India, for example, recognized a night goddess. She, like Nyx, was associated with phenomena of the heavens, being the sister of the dawn and daughter of the sky. The Roman name for the goddess of the night was Nox. Most of the evidence we have for Nox shows the influence of the Greek Nyx.

JIM MARKS

Bibliography

Apollodorus, and Robin Hard, trans. *The Library of Greek Mythology*. New York: Oxford University Press, 2008.

Graves, Robert. *The Greek Myths*. New York: Penguin, 1993.

Hesiod, and M. L. West, trans. *Theogony* and *Works and Days*. New York: Oxford University Press, 2008.

Howatson, M. C. *The Oxford Companion to Classical Literature*. New York: Oxford University Press, 2005.

Ovid, and A. D. Melville, trans. *Metamorphoses*. New York: Oxford University Press, 2008.

SEE ALSO: Cronus; Fates; Gaia; Hera; Hypnos; Nemesis; Uranus; Zeus.

OCEANUS

In Greek mythology Oceanus was one of the earliest beings to exist in the cosmos. Despite his name, Oceanus was not a personification of the world's oceans. Instead he symbolized the great river that the ancient Greeks believed encircled the earth. He was also the father of an enormous brood of children, 6,000 in all, who comprised some of the basic natural features of the earth's landscape.

Oceanus was the first of the children born to Gaia and Uranus, the personifications of the earth and the sky respectively. Oceanus was thus the eldest of the 12 Titans. However, although he appeared at an early stage of the story of the creation, Oceanus was not the first figure to be associated with water. The ancient Greek account of the creation of the universe, as told by the poet Hesiod (fl. 800 BCE) in his *Theogony*, differentiated between two elemental beings associated with the oceans: Pontus and Oceanus. Of these, Pontus was the elder.

The story of creation

According to the Greek story of the creation of the universe, the first thing to come into being was Chaos, a vast, yawning void. It was followed by Gaia (the earth), Tartarus (a region that lay thousands of miles below the earth's surface), and Eros (sexual attraction). Gaia's first act was to create three fundamental realms in addition to herself. They were Uranus (the sky), Ourea (the mountains) and Pontus (the ocean). The creation of Pontus and his siblings neatly divided the world into four basic realms—earth, sea, sky, and mountains—a division that reflected the geographical nature of Greece itself.

Gaia mated with each of her three offspring in turn. Pontus's coupling with Gaia produced a number of creatures who dwelled in the depths of the ocean. One of the most famous was the sea god Nereus, often known as the Old Man of the Sea, who fathered thousands of sea nymphs, the Nereids.

Oceanus, on the other hand, was one of the next generation of beings to come into existence after the creation of Uranus, Ourea, and Pontus. He was the first of the 12 Titans whom Gaia created by mating with Uranus. Oceanus was not a clumsy duplicate of Pontus. Nor was he a simple embodiment of freshwater, as opposed to the salt water of Pontus. Instead Oceanus represented water as a source of life and vitality. This aspect of the god is reflected in the nature of his many offspring. Unlike the children of Pontus, Oceanus's offspring were not just creatures of the deep. They were beings of great vitality and beauty. Oceanus had 3,000 daughters and 3,000 sons (see box, page 219). The daughters, known as Oceanids, were nymphs who dwelled in springs and wells, while his sons were rivers that ran through land, providing drinking water and acting as sources of irrigation.

In Greek myth Oceanus is seen less as an embodiment of the sea and more as a world river, encircling the earth. In the *Iliad*, the account of the last year of the Trojan War by Greek poet Homer (c. ninth–eighth century BCE), Hephaestus, blacksmith of the gods, forges new armor for the great Greek warrior Achilles. He decorates Achilles' shield with a representation of the whole world, including the sun, moon, and heavens. Around the rim, encircling all, is the river of Oceanus.

Although Oceanus was one of the Titans, he did not take their side in the battle they fought with the Olympian gods for the control of the universe. Even after the Olympians proved victorious, Oceanus retained his role as the great world river. The Olympian Poseidon took over the sea as his realm, and to some extent replaced Pontus, but he never really encroached on Oceanus. Like another great pre-Olympian figure, his grandson Prometheus, Oceanus was seen as a benefactor of humankind. In some myths he and his mother Gaia were said to be the parents of Triptolemus, who brought

217

Above: *A Roman mosaic depicting Oceanus. In Greek art Oceanus was usually portrayed as a creature that was half human and either half fish or half serpent. However, the Romans usually depicted him simply as a bearded man.*

Oceanus's Family

Oceanus and his wife Tethys had 6,000 children—3,000 sons and 3,000 daughters—many of whom played important roles in Greek mythology. Oceanus's daughters, known as Oceanids, were nymphs who inhabited wells and streams. Often the gentle daughters of Oceanus married the more tempestuous sons of Pontus, god of the ocean, and produced famous offspring. One was Doris, who mated with Nereus, the Old Man of the Sea, to produce 50 sea nymphs known as Nereids, all renowned for their beauty. Among the best-known Nereids were Amphitrite, who became the wife of the Olympian sea god Poseidon, and Thetis, the mother of the hero Achilles. Another celebrated Nereid was Metis, the goddess of wisdom and the first wife of Zeus. According to one story, it was Metis who helped Zeus overthrow his father, Cronus. However, when Zeus learned that Metis was destined to bear a son who would become king of the gods, he swallowed her.

Other Oceanids married other sons of Pontus. Electra, for example, mated with Pontus's son Thaumas to produce both Iris, the goddess of the rainbow, and the Harpies, winged female monsters who tormented the blind king Phineus. Another Oceanid who produced a famous son was Clymene, who was the mother of the Titan Prometheus. Like Oceanus, Prometheus was a great benefactor of humankind, introducing fire to the world. A more malevolent descendant of Oceanus was the notorious murderer and sorceress Medea, wife of Jason. Medea was daughter of the Oceanid Eidyia.

While the daughters of Oceanus were usually nymphs, the sons of Oceanus were almost always identified with rivers. They included Scamander, god of the chief river of Troy; Istros, god of the river today known as the Danube; and Neilos of the Nile River in Egypt. Oceanus was also the father of Achelous, identified with the river of the same name that runs through northwestern Greece. The god Achelous is famous for his wrestling match with the Greek hero Heracles. One daughter of Oceanus who was identified with a river was Styx, who personified the chief river of the underworld.

Below: This painting by Joachim de Patinir (c. 1485–1524) depicts Charon the ferryman crossing the Styx River.

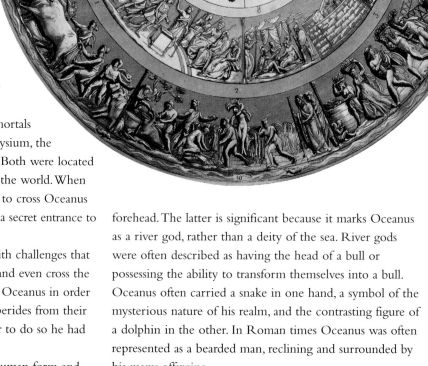

Right: A re-creation of the shield of Achilles by Antoine Chrysôthome Quatremère de Quincy (1755–1849). The river Oceanus is depicted around the rim of the shield, encircling the earth.

Demeter's gift of agriculture to the world. It is not difficult to see how the idea arose that agriculture came about as the result of a union between earth and water.

The ends of the world

As an all-encompassing world river, Oceanus was also thought of as an outer limit, a boundary beyond which lay only the unattainable and the mysterious. The ancient Greeks believed that the sun god Helios rode across the sky every day in a chariot, beginning his journey in the east, in Ethiopia. During the night, he was thought to travel back through the waters of Oceanus in either a cup or a golden bowl.

Oceanus also separated the realm of mortals from Hades, the land of the dead, and Elysium, the paradise reserved for the greatest heroes. Both were located on the banks of Oceanus, at the edge of the world. When the hero Odysseus visited Hades, he had to cross Oceanus to reach the grove of Persephone, where a secret entrance to the underworld was hidden.

Greek heroes were often presented with challenges that involved their having to reach Oceanus and even cross the river. For example, Heracles had to cross Oceanus in order to retrieve the golden apples of the Hesperides from their garden at the edge of the world. In order to do so he had to borrow Helios's golden bowl.

Oceanus was rarely seen as having a human form and personality in the way that Olympian deities such as Zeus and Poseidon were. However, he did appear in this guise in *Prometheus Bound*, a play by Aeschylus (525–456 BCE). In the play he advises his grandson not to do anything to aggravate Zeus, king of the gods.

Oceanus in art

In ancient art Oceanus was sometimes depicted as a creature that was half human and half animal. The lower half of his body was that of either a serpent or a fish. Although the upper half was basically humanlike in appearance, a bull's horn projected from the center of his forehead. The latter is significant because it marks Oceanus as a river god, rather than a deity of the sea. River gods were often described as having the head of a bull or possessing the ability to transform themselves into a bull. Oceanus often carried a snake in one hand, a symbol of the mysterious nature of his realm, and the contrasting figure of a dolphin in the other. In Roman times Oceanus was often represented as a bearded man, reclining and surrounded by his many offspring.

There were few cults dedicated to the worship of Oceanus. However, Alexander the Great (356–323 BCE) is said to have set up altars to him and Oceanus's wife Tethys at the delta of the Indus River. Also, the rivers and springs that were his offspring were the objects of worship in local cults throughout the Greek world.

ANTHONY BULLOCH

Bibliography

Hesiod, and M. L. West, trans. *Theogony* and *Works and Days.* New York: Oxford University Press, 2008.

SEE ALSO: Gaia; Helios; Prometheus.

PAEON

Paeon was an early god of healing sometimes called "the physician of the gods," to whom he ministered on Mount Olympus. However, there are relatively few references to Paeon in classical literature, and very little is known of what were thought to be his character and attributes.

There are passing allusions to Paeon in the *Argonautica* of Alexandrian poet Apollonius of Rhodes (third century BCE), where the name is used as a byword for skill in healing. He is also mentioned in the *Odes*, by another Greek poet, Pindar (c. 522–c. 438 BCE), and the *Dionysiaca* by Nonnus (fl. c. 450–470 CE), an account of a journey by the god Dionysus to India. However, Paeon is written about at greatest length by Homer (c. ninth–eighth century BCE) in the *Iliad*, an account of the 10-year war between the Greeks and the Trojans. According to Homer, after Hades, the god of the underworld, was shot by one of Heracles' arrows, he fled to Mount Olympus to seek the help of Zeus. He was healed by Paeon, who treated the wound with soothing herbs.

Later, when the god Ares entered the war on the side of the Trojans, he was wounded in battle by Greek hero Diomedes. Aided by the goddess Athena, Diomedes thrust a spear into Ares' stomach. Like Hades before him, Ares retreated to Mount Olympus. Zeus then told Paeon to treat the war god's wound. Homer tells us that Ares' wound was healed the moment that Paeon's herbs touched it.

Some classicists believe that Paeon can be identified with Asclepius, the son of Apollo, who became the major god of medicine in the world of antiquity. The name Paeon itself is of obscure origin, although some scholars believe it derives from the name of the Cretan god Paiawon, who was mentioned in inscriptions at the palace of Knossos. Paiawon, however, was a god of war, not of healing, and any link between the two figures remains unexplained.

Other Paeons

In addition to the god of healing, there were several other figures in classical mythology named Paeon. One was a Trojan mentioned in Homer's enumeration of the forces of Troy. He was the husband of Cleomede and father of Agastrophus and Laophoon. Another Paeon was the king of Messenia, son of Antilochus and grandson of Nestor. A third Paeon was the son of Endymion. He lost a footrace at Olympia against his brother Epeius and went into exile in the region of Macedonia known as Paeonia.

PETER CONNOR

Right: This marble statuette from around 400–200 BCE depicts the Greek god of medicine Asclepius, with whom Paeon was often identified.

Bibliography

Bulfinch, Thomas. *Bulfinch's Mythology.* New York: Barnes & Noble, 2006.

Homer, and Robert Fagles, trans. *The Iliad.* New York: Penguin, 2009.

SEE ALSO: Ares; Asclepius; Dionysus; Zeus.

PAN

Pan, the shepherd god usually depicted playing upon his pipes, is one of the most instantly recognizable of the Greek gods. As well as his musical abilities, he was also famous for the fear (or "panic") that he was able to inspire in people.

Pan's familiarity in the modern world is reflected in the fact that he was both the inspiration for James M. Barrie's Peter Pan and a model for the depictions of Satan in medieval art. At that time in European history, the lusty earthiness and supposed brutishness of the Arcadian shepherd deity stood in sharp contrast to the Christian notion of what "a good shepherd" should be. The goat-man's very appearance suggested "lower forces" like sexual instincts and raw emotions. With his hairy nudity, horns, pointed ears, and hooves, Pan became a figure of satanic evil. The ancient Greeks saw Pan quite differently—neither eternally boyish nor a devil.

Family background

According to the Homeric "Hymn to Pan," the author of which is unknown, the god was the son of Hermes, messenger of the Greek gods, and an unnamed daughter of the nymph Dryope. Like Hermes, Pan was known for his cunning and fleet-footedness. Both Hermes and Pan

were associated with Arcadia, a region in the central Peloponnese known for its forests and wild, mountainous terrain. Pan was part man and part goat. Although his exact composition varied, he was usually depicted as having the legs and cloven hooves of a goat and the upper body of a man. However, a pair of horns protruded from his human head. Pan's association with the goat was connected to the terrain of his homeland—much of Arcadia was too mountainous for sheep and cattle, and only goats could survive there.

Other sources give different accounts of Pan's parentage. According to one, Pan was the result of a liaison between Zeus, the king of the gods, and Penelope, the wife of the Greek hero Odysseus. A rarer legend makes him the magical offspring of a shepherd named Crathis and a she-goat.

The Homeric "Hymn to Pan" says that Pan was given his name because he brought joy to the hearts of all the Greek gods—*pan* is the Greek word for "all." Because of this connection, some scholars have suggested that Pan was in some way a cosmic god who could be identified with the whole universe. However, most scholars believe that it is more likely that Pan's name is derived from the same root as the Latin word *pasco*, meaning "feeder" or "shepherd."

A creature of the night

Although artists have often depicted Pan playing his pipes and dancing with nymphs in sunny meadows, most classical sources say that he lived a nocturnal existence. Greek poet Theocritus (c. 310–250 BCE) tells us he became touchy and cranky in the midday sun. Because the hot, draining sun depressed Pan, he escaped by sleeping in shady groves. He favored those who slept at the same

Left: This statue depicts Pan playing the panpipes or syrinx, the musical instrument that became his most famous attribute.

time, even giving them secret knowledge. Pan healed, too, appearing in the noontime dreams of others to heal a dying child or to impart crucial information. However, when noisy humans accidentally or intentionally interrupted Pan's midday sleep, he flew into a violent rage. Then he would project an overwhelming sense of fear that would afflict anyone within a certain range. This sensation was known to the ancient Greeks as "panic" (see box, page 224).

Many of the myths about Pan revolve around his attempts at seduction, which involved goddesses, nymphs, and mortal women. These attempts were usually unsuccessful. One of the few exceptions was his pursuit of Selene, the goddess of the moon. There are various accounts of Pan's seduction of her. One says that he lured her into the woods by disguising himself in a silky fleece of white wool; another says that he persuaded Selene to engage in a brief affair by giving her a herd of white oxen. The implication of these stories is that Selene found the god too ugly and ungainly to warrant her attentions without being tricked or bribed.

Pitys and Echo

Most of the objects of Pan's attentions were nymphs. One nymph who suffered because of Pan's love for her was Pitys. Like most of those he pursued, Pitys found Pan hideously unattractive and fled from him when he approached her. She was then turned into a pine tree. In a tribute to her memory, Pan often wore a crown of pine sprays or carried a pine branch. Another version of this myth says that Pitys was loved by both Pan and Boreas, the god of the north wind. In a fit of jealously Boreas blew her off the top of a cliff. In pity, the earth goddess Gaia transformed her into a pine tree at the point where she fell.

Another nymph who was unfortunate enough to attract the attention of Pan was Echo. There are various myths associated with her, all of which attempt to explain the phenomenon of echoing. While the most famous involve the goddess Hera and the beautiful mortal Narcissus, a third has Pan as a central character. As in the myth of Pan and Pitys, the central theme is Pan's unrequited love. Echo rejected all of Pan's advances and fled when he pursued her. Infuriated by his failure, Pan used his powers to make a group of shepherds crazed with desire. Unlike the god, they found a way to capture the poor nymph and brutally dismembered her until only her voice remained.

Another version of the myth has a less violent ending. It says that Echo bore Pan a daughter named Iambe. Iambe was associated with a two-syllable poetic phrase or meter called an iamb—a term familiar to all students who study

Horned Gods

Pan's characteristic horns, beard, and love for music and dance link him to nature gods from many other ancient cultures. Scholars such as archaeologist Marija Gimbutas (1921–1994) have linked Pan to images of a prehistoric horned god that date from the Upper Paleolithic period (c. 40,000–10,000 BCE). Cave paintings found in France and Spain show a strange figure, sometimes known as the Master of Animals or God of Wild Nature, wearing bison or stag horns, apparently performing a ritual dance. In classical and later times, related horned figures appeared. They include not only Pan and his Roman equivalents Faunus and Silvanus, but also the Celtic god Cernunnos, the Russian Leshy and Vidassus, the Scandinavian Rå, the Welsh Merlin, the Lithuanian Ganiklis, and many others.

Like Pan, these divine guardians of animals and nature were said to have eerie voices and considerable powers of prophecy. By historical times, these ancient figures had become mysterious shepherd-gods of forests and remote mountainous regions. Their hold on human imagination was so strong that they were never in danger of becoming extinct, however. For example, Pan had more than a hundred cult sites where he was worshiped in ancient Greece, an indication of his importance to ordinary people.

Above: Scholars believe that the Celtic god Cernunnos is related to Pan. This depiction of the horned deity is found on the Gundestrup Cauldron, a silver vessel dating from the second century BCE.

Panic

Pan was known for his ability to inspire sudden and irrational fear in people—the sensation we know today as panic. Most of the stories in which Pan unleashed this power involve military conflicts. The most famous is that of the Battle of Marathon, which was fought between the Athenians and the Persians in 490 BCE. Legend has it that Pan appeared before the Athenian messenger Pheidippides in the mountains and asked him why the people of his city did not worship him. Pan said that he had helped the Athenians in the past and would do so again. True to his word, Pan came to the aid of the Athenian army at Marathon. In gratitude the Athenians dedicated a shrine to him on the slopes of the Acropolis.

The Battle of Marathon was only one instance when Pan was said to have helped Athenian or Greek forces. In many cases the battle in question was said to have taken place close to one of the god's sanctuaries or caves. In 480 BCE, during the second Persian War, the Greeks defeated Xerxes' fleet near Psyttaleia, an island sacred to Pan. In 403 BCE at Piraeus, the army of the Thirty Tyrants was said to have been overtaken by panic when a heavy snowstorm fell out of a clear sky at midday—again, a cave sacred to Pan was nearby.

Below: This illustration from a sarcophagus depicts a scene from the Battle of Marathon. According to legend, the god Pan intervened on behalf of the Athenians, spreading panic in the Persian ranks.

poetry. This daughter of Pan is also famous for her rough wit, which restored laughter to a grieving Demeter and thereby brought fertility back to the earth. Yet another myth has Pan and Echo producing a daughter named Iynx. She became famous for her ability to work love charms. Her best-known spell attracted Zeus to Io, an act that led to Io's being turned into a bird by Zeus's wife Hera. The idea that the unlucky-in-love Pan could father a daughter who could make people fall in love at will is particularly ironic.

Syrinx and the pipes of Pan

Pan's most famous involvement was with the tree spirit Syrinx. Their story is recorded by Roman poet Ovid (43 BCE–17 CE) in his *Metamorphoses*. Pan fell deeply in love with Syrinx, but she fled from him, just as Pitys and Echo had done. Syrinx was frightened that Pan would rape her,

so she ran until she reached the Ladon River, where Pan caught her. At this point she prayed to the river nymphs to save her. Syrinx was immediately transformed into a bunch of reeds. As Pan held the reeds in his arms, the wind blew through them, producing a haunting note. Enchanted by the noise, Pan cut the reeds to different lengths and bound them together, producing what would come to be known as a set of panpipes. The instrument's Greek name, however, is the *syrinx*.

Scholars have put various interpretations on the myths involving Pan's tragic attempts at seduction. Some have suggested that the myths highlight the impossibility of "owning" what belongs to nature. Even a god such as Pan has to respect these boundaries. Pan's lustful nature compels him to attempt to seize the nymphs—personifications of aspects of the natural world—but these efforts simply lead to destruction and grief.

Pan the musician

Pan's set of pipes became his most famous attribute—in art he is almost always depicted with the instrument. In the ancient world he was renowned for his musicianship. In one myth, Pan competed with the god Apollo in a musical contest (although in some variants, the competition was between Apollo and the satyr Marsyas). Pan had earlier boasted that the god's skill was inferior to his own. The judge was the mountain god Tmolus. Apollo played on a lyre inlaid with gems and ivory, an ornate instrument that contrasted sharply with the crude pipes that Pan played upon. Tmolus was entranced by the god's music and declared the sun god the victor. However, Tmolus was not the only person to overhear the contest. Midas, king of Phrygia, was also listening. Midas, famous for his greed and lack of refinement, preferred the simpler, rustic sounds of Pan's music and said so. Apollo was so angry that he changed Midas's ears into asses' ears, a visible sign of his lack of taste.

Not all of the myths attached to Pan show him in a bad light. For example, the myth of Pan and Psyche shows his benevolent side. Psyche was the lover of the god Eros, who visited her in the hours of darkness so that she could not see him. When she discovered his true identity, he left her. Psyche was distraught by this loss and tried to drown herself because of her despair. Pan found her near death among the herbs on a riverbank. Remembering his own agony after losing Syrinx in the reeds of the Ladon River, he comforted Psyche and persuaded her to attempt to win back her lover.

The worship of Pan

Greek historian Herodotus (c. 484–425 BCE) says that the Greeks first worshiped Pan around 800 years before the historian was born—that is to say, in the 13th century BCE. Other classical literary sources suggest that Pan was first worshiped in Arcadia, the mountainous area of the Peloponnese where he was believed to have lived. The Greek travel writer Pausanias (143–176 CE) names several sites in the region sacred to the god. He tells of a bronze statue of the god at Megalopolis, and also mentions a stone image of Pan at the town's temple to Zeus. Pausanias also writes about several other sanctuaries to Pan in the area: one at Mount Lycaeus, another in the Nomia mountains, and one on the road from Tegea to Laconia. Pausanias also says that on Mount Parthenios there were tortoises whose shells were ideal for making lyres. However, the local inhabitants were afraid to kill the tortoises because they believed that they were sacred to Pan.

Pan is widely depicted in both classical and more modern art. Illustrations of ancient Greek drinking cups show Pan plucking grapes and carrying wineskins. The story of Pan's attempt to seduce Syrinx has been a popular subject for later artists. It is captured by Flemish artist Jacob Jordaens (1593–1678) in his 1625 painting *Pan and Syrinx*; by Nicolas Poussin (1594–1665) in *Nymph Syrinx Pursued by Pan*; and by Alessandro Turchi (1578–1649) in *Pan and the Nymph Syrinx*. Pan's attempt to soothe Psyche, meanwhile, is the subject of a painting by Edward Burne-Jones (1833–1898), *Pan and Psyche*.

KATHLEEN JENKS

Below: This Roman statue depicts Pan showing the herdsman Daphnis how to play the pipes. Later, Daphnis was blinded by a jealous nymph and spent the rest of his life singing mournful songs about his tragic fate.

Bibliography

Ovid, and A. D. Melville, trans. *Metamorphoses*. New York: Oxford University Press, 2008.

Pausanias, and Peter Levi, trans. *Guide to Greece*. New York: Viking Press, 1984.

Ruden, Sarah, trans. *The Homeric Hymns*. Indianapolis, IN: Hackett, 2005.

SEE ALSO: Apollo; Eros; Faunus; Hermes; Zeus.

PENATES

The Penates were among the most important household gods of the ancient Romans, along with Vesta, the Lares, and the genii. Romans recognized two types of Penates, domestic and public. They distinguished between the private worship of the Penates in the home and the public worship of the Penates as protective gods of the state. The domestic Penates were not depicted in a recognizable way, but the public Penates, considered indispensable to the very existence of the city, had a clear visual image.

The name Penates itself helps define the nature of these gods. The Latin word *penates* is based on *penus*, a noun that refers both to food and to the place in which provisions were stored. The *penus* was further defined as the innermost recess of the house, where the essentials of life were safeguarded. This notion that the *penus* was at the very heart of the home is reflected in the related verb *penetrare*, meaning "to penetrate, to get to the interior." The second element of Penates is the suffix *–ates*, which indicates that a person or thing belongs to a particular location.

Protectors of the home

The Penates belonged to the *penus*. They were deities of the innermost recesses, the safest area—the heart or core—of the house. In a larger sense the Penates were considered protectors of the home and of everything in the house that was necessary for the family. The word *penates* is virtually always found in the plural and was, in origin, an adjective modifying an unexpressed noun such as gods. Often the word *penates* is used in a general sense.

Latin orator and writer Cicero (106–43 BCE) used the phrase *patrii penatesque di* ("ancestral gods and Penates") to describe all the family gods. The Penates and gods of the ancestors are, in this quite typical usage, synonymous. In fact, it is often assumed that the wide variety of statuettes found in various family shrines of Pompeii and elsewhere indicates that many gods—Venus, Fortune, Bacchus, and Mercury, among others—were worshiped in particular houses and were considered Penates by the families who displayed their images.

The public Penates

The public Penates were revered as the guardians of the state and its most basic needs. They were worshiped as guarantors of Rome's security. In the public sphere the Penates did have a recognizable form. Greek historian Dionysius of Halicarnassus (first century BCE), who lived in Rome, treats this subject at length. In *Roman Antiquities* he describes a small temple of the Penates on the Velia, a hill near the Roman Forum. The images of the gods, he reports, are there on display for all to see, unmistakably

Penates in the House

The household gods, including the Penates, were worshiped in the sacrarium (or *lararium*), a shrine in the wall of the atrium (main room) or the kitchen. This family shrine was sometimes in the form of a niche but was often in the more elaborate shape of a small temple front, with columns and triangular pediment.

On the back wall of the shrine there were frequently paintings of the Lares (guardian spirits of the house) and the genii, along with other divinities venerated in a particular family. Statuettes of the gods were normally placed on the floor of the shrines. Family worship consisted of offerings of wheat, flour, and wine.

Latin poet Horace (65–8 BCE) advised his friend Phidyle that the Penates were satisfied "provided that pure hands touch the altar" with the gift of sacred meal mixed with crackling salt. Roman hero Aeneas, in the epic poem the *Aeneid* by Latin poet Virgil (70–19 BCE), followed the usual Roman custom when he urged his companions to call their Penates and ancestral gods to join them in a dinner.

Above: This picture shows an altar to the Roman Lares, discovered in a house in the Roman town of Pompeii. Lares were domestic gods much like Penates, who protected the home.

identified as the Penates by an inscription. Dionysius writes, "They are two seated youths holding spears," and he relates the images to the twin gods of Samothrace (an island in the Aegean Sea), an identification also made by other ancient scholars. This identification was encouraged by the fact that both the Penates and the Samothracian gods (who were, in turn, sometimes equated with the Greek Castor and Pollux) were called the Great Gods (Magni Dei) and shared some iconographic features.

More important than such ancient speculation is the Roman belief that statuettes of the Penates were carried by the hero Aeneas on his voyage from Troy to Italy after the Trojan War. In his epic poem the *Aeneid*, Roman poet Virgil (70–19 BCE) has Aeneas cry out, soon after reaching Italy, "Hail, O Land given to me by the Fates! Hail, O Penates of Troy! This is our home! This is our country!"

The Trojan Penates, in finding a new home in Italy, assure Aeneas and his companions that Italy is indeed their new land. The Romans saw themselves as descendants of the Trojans and the early Latins, among whom Aeneas and his companions were thought to have settled in Lavinium (present-day Pratica di Mare), a village not far from Rome near the Mediterranean coast. There, special veneration of the Penates continued well into the age of the Roman Empire (31 BCE–476 CE).

There is, however, an indication that the Penates of the Velia had come to Rome not from Lavinium but from the mountain settlement of Alba Longa (see box). Roman lore celebrated this place as the homeland of Romulus and Remus (mythical founders of Rome) before they settled with their companions on the site of the future Rome.

Tradition recalled that the third king of Rome, Tullus Hostilius (c. 672–641 BCE), not only defeated Alba Longa but demolished most of it so that it could not rise again. He did this probably because the old mother city was seen as a threat to the safety or ambitions of early Rome. Ancient writers add that the temple of the Penates on the Velia was near or even on the site of the palace of Tullus Hostilius.

The Penates must have been moved from Alba Longa to the Velia, where Tullus Hostilius lived in Rome. This scenario explains the fact that there was another, and probably earlier, public cult of the Penates at Rome, which belonged to the *Penus Vestae*, the "holy of holies" of the

Below: In this fifth-century-CE picture, Aeneas, founder of Rome, is visited by the Penates of Troy, who appear to him in dream.

hearth goddess Vesta, whose worship was established by the second Roman king, Numa Pompilius (c. 715–673 BCE). Religious custom required that Roman civic officials, the consuls and praetors, accompanied by priests, make a joint sacrifice every year to Vesta and the Penates at Lavinium before entering office.

Alba Longa

The Penates had a special place in the legends of Alba Longa. Ascanius, the son of Aeneas, set out to found a colony of Lavinium at Alba Longa 30 years after the arrival of the Trojans in Italy. The colonists built a temple with an inner sanctuary (the *penus*) for the Penates in their new city, but the images of these gods, which Aeneas had brought from Troy, fled the new Alban sanctuary and returned to their pedestals in the old temple at Lavinium. The colonists brought them back to Alba Longa, but the Penates fled again.

The myth explains why the descendants of Aeneas were compelled to return to Lavinium, as were the Albans (and later the Romans), to worship their ancestral Trojan gods. According to this myth, the Penates venerated at Alba Longa itself must thus have been local Alban, not the old Trojan, gods.

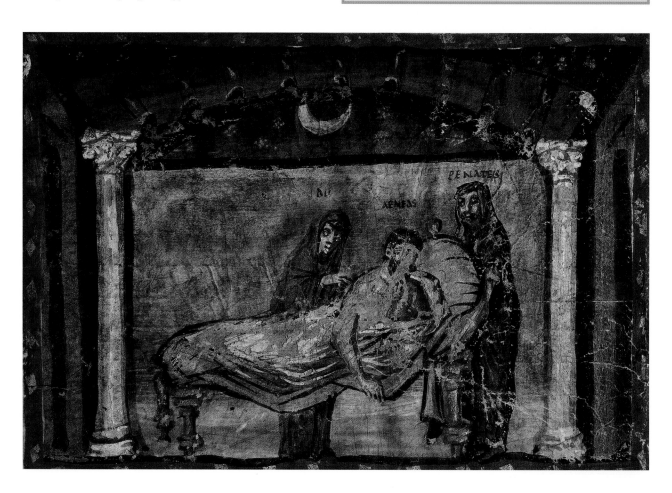

Left: This marble relief is part of the Ara Pacis Augustae, a monument to the Roman emperor Augustus (63 BCE–14 CE). Aeneas is depicted with two children in the sanctuary of the Penates, an area guarded by the spirits.

The importance of the Penates cult is well attested in Lavinium. Greek historian Timaeus (c. 350– 260 BCE) visited the sanctuary and reported that holy objects concerning the Penates were kept there, including iron and bronze heralds' wands and an earthenware vessel from Troy. The wands are reminiscent of the staffs held by the Penates in their Velia temple, and the vessel may well have been an ancient storage jar for food, since it was associated with the Penates.

Archaeological finds

Archaeologists have unearthed a row of 13 archaic altars just below the citadel of Lavinium that date from the sixth to the fourth centuries BCE. They have also found remains of a nearby seventh-century-BCE tomb that was turned into a monument in the fourth century, evidently to serve as the hero shrine of Aeneas.

Not far from the citadel area, near life-size votive statues, along with a fifth-century-BCE statue of the goddess Minerva, have come to light, attesting the presence of a sanctuary for the goddess nearby. The temple of Vesta and of the Penates was probably on the citadel itself.

A relief panel beside the front entry to the Augustan Altar of Peace in Rome depicts Aeneas about to offer a sacrifice. The scene is obviously set in Lavinium. Two youthful figures, surely the Penates, are seated at the front of a little temple and hold staffs. They look down upon Aeneas from the hill above (probably the citadel). The image of these seated figures with their staffs evokes Dionysius's description of the Penates on the Velia in Rome.

By the later fourth century BCE, Lavinium was under the control of the Roman state. Rome maintained religious ties with its Trojan ancestors through annual sacrifices to the Penates of Aeneas's old city, Lavinium. In a similar way, the Romans continued to venerate the Penates of their more immediate mother city, Alba Longa, in the temple on the Velia in Rome. This worship of the Penates was believed essential to assure the continuity and safety of both family and city-state.

DANIEL P. HARMON

Bibliography

Scheid, John, and Janet Lloyd, trans. *An Introduction to Roman Religion*. Bloomington, IN: Indiana University Press, 2003.

Turcan, Robert, and Antonia Nevill, trans. *The Gods of Ancient Rome: Religion in Everyday Life from Archaic to Imperial Times*. New York: Routledge, 2001.

SEE ALSO: Lares; Vesta.

PERSEPHONE

Persephone was the Greek goddess of agriculture and the underworld. She was daughter of Demeter, goddess of grain, and Zeus, king of the gods. Her name took many forms, including Proserpina in Latin and Proserpine in English.

Persephone was abducted by Hades, her uncle and god of the underworld, to be his wife. Angry and distraught at her daughter's disappearance, Demeter first made the earth barren, and then wandered weeping through the world until she discovered Persephone's location and demanded that the girl be returned to her. Zeus persuaded Hades to give up Persephone, but before Hades let her go, he forced her to eat six pomegranate seeds. The fruit was sacred to Hades, and for that reason Persephone was forever obliged to return to her husband for several months of every year, during fall and winter. While Persephone was below ground, nothing grew on earth, but fertility returned when she was reunited with her mother in spring.

Homeric Hymn

The earliest detailed account of the myth of Persephone is found in the Homeric Hymns (works in the style of Homer, but written long after his death). In the "Hymn to Demeter"

(sixth century BCE), Hades swoops down on Persephone and carries her off to his realm below. Hearing her cries, Demeter searches everywhere before hearing of her daughter's fate from Helios, the sun god. On learning that Zeus was behind the abduction, Demeter withdraws from divine society. In her wanderings she arrives at Eleusis—a Greek city on the Saronic Gulf about 13 miles (21 km) northwest of Athens—disguised as an old woman. There the daughters of King Celeus take her home to care for their baby brother Demophon. At first the royal infant thrives, anointed with ambrosia by his divine nurse, but when his mother, Metaneira, sees Demeter holding the baby in a fire in an effort to make him immortal, she screams in fright. The offended goddess drops the baby and announces that now Demophon will be subject to death like all other mortals. Demeter then orders the people of Eleusis to build a temple in her honor, and she promises to teach them mystery rites.

Enraged by her double loss, Demeter withdraws to her temple, and for an entire year no crops grow on earth. Famine looms, and the gods, concerned that the annihilation of mortals will lead to the loss of sacrifices, intervene. Every deity comes in turn to Demeter, but she will not be swayed until Hermes brings Persephone back to her. Mother and daughter are reunited, but their joy is allayed to some extent when Persephone tells Demeter that she has eaten pomegranate seeds. As a result, the year is henceforth divided into a time of barrenness and a time of fertility, which the hymn explicitly connects with the coming of spring.

Right: This Greek statue of Persephone on her throne dates from the sixth century BCE.

Right: In this 19th-century bookplate, Persephone is so hungry that she eats some pomegranate seeds, thus sealing her own fate.

Persephone and the Seasons

The period of Persephone's annual withdrawal to the underworld is usually correlated with winter, and the period of her return with spring. The Homeric Hymn makes this explicit. However, this does not exactly correspond with the climatic realities of Greece, where the heat of the summer makes it the barren time of the year. Nonetheless, it seems that the ancient Greeks interpreted the myth's seasonal chronology much as we do today. This has caused some scholars to suggest that the myth may have originated in a more northern climate and was adopted by the Greeks, although such speculations are difficult to prove.

In its simplest form, the myth of Persephone and Demeter symbolizes the origin of the seasons, but it has several other layers of meaning. In some versions of the legend, Demeter also bestows the secrets of agriculture on mortals as a token of her gratitude for their help in the search for Persephone. The hymn itself assumes that agriculture is already well known at the time of the myth, and that the goddess's grief and anger disrupt it. Because Demeter's contribution to human life is the technique of crop cultivation, scholars have assumed that earlier versions of the myth are the ones that explain the origins of agriculture. The hymn also explains the origins of the Eleusinian Mysteries and has often been used to try to interpret details of those rites.

In psychological readings, the myth represents the struggle of a mother and daughter to come to terms with the separation brought about by the latter's marriage. In some versions of the legend, the power of patriarchy is made explicit: Zeus wants to marry Persephone off to his brother and does not consult her mother before doing so. It is only after Demeter has been reassured that Hades will be a good husband and that her daughter will not lack for honor that she is reconciled to the union. Persephone's awakening

sexuality and the pull of divided loyalties are evident in the hymn's two different versions of the episode of the pomegranate seeds. The first contains nothing about coercion, but in the second Persephone tells her mother that Hades forced her to eat the seeds. Since Homeric style allows for the exact repetition of lengthy passages, this variation is significant. It may suggest the daughter's reluctance to admit to her mother that she is not an entirely unwilling bride. The pomegranate conventionally symbolizes death and eternal life, but here the eating of the seeds also suggests sex and procreation.

A timid young girl in the Homeric Hymn, Persephone is elsewhere a fearsome queen of the underworld. In the *Odyssey* by Homer (c. ninth–eighth century BCE), the hero Odysseus fears that if he lingers in the underworld Persephone will send a Gorgon against him. Persephone also becomes involved in a romantic triangle that is oddly reminiscent of her own situation. The goddess Aphrodite falls in love with the beautiful young Adonis. When he is killed by a boar, Persephone, who has also fallen in love with him, refuses to let him leave the underworld. Eventually a compromise is arranged: Adonis will spend half the year with her and half the year with his other divine lover.

Persephone in art

The myth of Persephone was often depicted in Greek and Roman art. The abduction was also the subject of *The Rape of Proserpina* by Roman poet Claudian (c. 370–c. 404 CE). Although extremely popular in Latin literature, the legend of Persephone did not become widespread in Western

Above: In this painting of hell by the French artist François de Nome (1593–1634), Persephone sits on her underworld throne next to her husband, Hades.

Pomegranate Symbolism

In many cultures both the pomegranate itself and various objects that represent it symbolize abundance and fertility. The red precious gemstone garnet is an aluminum silicate that derives its name from its resemblance to the seed of the pomegranate. When worn as jewelry, garnet symbolizes fecundity, and it is one of the traditional gifts from a husband to his wife on the occasion of their second wedding anniversary. In the Christian church, the fruit itself and references to it are often used to stand for the Resurrection, immortality, royalty, and fertility.

In ancient Anatolia (a region of modern Turkey), the pomegranate was a sacred fruit of paradise. There it was believed that scattering pomegranate fruit inside the house of a newlywed bride would make her marriage long-lasting and productive, as well as making the family rich, with many children who will have long life.

In Rome, the goddess Juno was often shown holding a pomegranate as a symbol of marriage. In heraldry, the pomegranate was the badge of Catherine of Aragon, first wife of English king Henry VIII.

literature and art until the 17th century. Flemish painter Peter Paul Rubens (1577–1640) and Italian sculptor Gian Lorenzo Bernini (1598–1680) both created representations of her in the early 1620s. In the 19th century poets such as A. C. Swinburne (1837–1909) and painters such as Dante Gabriel Rossetti (1828–1882) and Frederick Leighton (1830–1896) drew on her myth in numerous works. In the 20th century the myth was attractive to a wide range of women writers, including American H. D. (Hilda Doolittle) (1886–1961) and Canadian Margaret Atwood (born 1939).

DEBORAH LYONS

Bibliography
Bulfinch, Thomas. *Bulfinch's Mythology.* New York: Barnes & Noble, 2006.
Howatson, M. C. *The Oxford Companion to Classical Literature.* New York: Oxford University Press, 2005.

SEE ALSO: Demeter; Hades; Zeus.

PHOBOS

Phobos, Greek god of fear, was the son of Aphrodite, the goddess of sensual love and beauty, and her lover Ares, the self-centered, drunken, and dim-witted god of war. Phobos's twin brother was Deimos, or dread. Phobos's name is the root of the modern word *phobia*.

Above: A fresco from the House of Saints and Martyrs in the Roman city of Pompeii depicts Aphrodite with her lover Ares. Their twins, Phobos and Deimos, inherited their father's warlike nature.

Phobos shared with most of Ares' other children a terrible reputation that always preceded him. There are few occasions when Phobos plays a major role in mythology, but there are numerous references to his presence in ancient Greek literature, such as in Hesiod's (fl. 800 BCE) epics *Theogony* and *Shield of Heracles,* and also in Homer's (c. ninth–eighth century BCE) epic the *Iliad*.

Some mythographers suggest that Ares was originally a death god before he became the god of war. He underwent this transition because ancient Greeks were empire builders, constantly battling to extend their territory, and contemporary Greek culture associated death with war. The role of a death god differed little from a war god. However, the underworld, where the dead reside, became such a vast and overcrowded place after so many wars and deaths that governing the dead souls came to require a dedicated god. Later, after further differentiation, Hades became ruler of the underworld and Ares became associated exclusively with war. A further tie between Ares and death lies in the fact that Phobos and Deimos (Fear and Terror) and Ares' sister, Eris (Strife), appear in Greek mythology as death demons as well as war demons. In one myth, soul-eating underworld spirits known as the Keres make their first appearance in Greek mythology on the battlefield in the company of Phobos, Eris, and other war demons allied with Ares. Mythographers also argue that ancient Greeks followed the Babylonian custom of giving gods' names to planets. They passed the red planet belonging to the Babylonian death god Nergal to Ares, god of war, thus forging a relationship between death and war in Ares' character. The red planet is now known as Mars, for the Roman god of war.

Other children of Ares

Most of Ares' children were terrible in some way: they were often dangerous, belligerent, and unruly. Cycnus, for example, beheaded passing strangers and stacked the heads to make a temple that he dedicated to his father. Another son of Ares was Diomedes, who met with a gruesome death. He was king of the Bistones, a warlike tribe that lived in the ancient Greek region of Thrace. He kept four horses that he chained up and fed with human flesh.

Sacrifices to Phobos

In several Greek myths heroes and heroines sacrifice to Ares and his children, including Phobos, to improve their chances of victory in battle. Appeasing Phobos was seen to be a way of winning his favor so that opponents might suffer from the fear and panic that he could inflict upon them. In one myth the Amazon warrior Oreithyia sacrificed to Ares before she led an attack on Attica, where Theseus held captive her sister Antiope. To improve his chances in battle, Theseus was advised by an oracle to sacrifice to Phobos. After a four-month battle during which Antiope was slain, Theseus finally defeated the Amazons and Oreithyia retreated, to die of grief at her sister's death.

The Macedonian king and general Alexander the Great (356–323 BCE) also sacrificed to Phobos. Greek biographer Plutarch (c. 46–120 CE) reports that the sacrifice took place in the presence of a seer during a secret ritual the night before the battle of Arbela (331 BCE). Plutarch also mentions a sanctuary of Phobos in Sparta, which was closed during rare times of peace.

Left: The remains of a stone relief dating to the fifth century BCE depicting Queen Antiope of the Amazons and her abductor the Greek hero Theseus. He sacrificed to Phobos before defending Attica from Antiope's furious sister Oreithyia.

Diomedes died at the hands of Heracles, who had to tame the horses for his eighth labor. To calm and control the animals, Heracles fed Diomedes to them. The Amazon queen Penthesileia was a powerful and merciless daughter of Ares who led an army to defend Troy during the Trojan War. In some Greek myths Meleager is another of Ares' sons. He was the hero who killed a ravenous boar sent by the goddess of hunting, Artemis, who was angry that Oeneus, king of the Aetolians (who is sometimes credited as Meleager's father), had not sacrificed to her. During the Calydonian boar hunt, Meleager marshaled a band of men to hunt the beast and finally killed it himself. Harmonia was exceptional among Ares and Aphrodite's children. She was beautiful and virtuous and married Greek hero Cadmus; together they established the city of Thebes. Their wedding was so important that the gods attended and brought them gifts. In another version of the myth

Harmonia is a Naiad (water nymph) who is Ares' lover. The product of their union is the Amazons, a race of warrior women who live apart from men and fearlessly defend their way of life.

Phobos in mythology

In one myth Phobos features with another of Ares' sons, Kyknos, a renowned thief and highway bandit. The pair lay in wait for pilgrims traveling to Apollo's shrine at Pytho, beheaded them, and then stole the sacrificial oxen that the pilgrims were bringing to Apollo. One day, when the Greek hero Heracles approached the region in a chariot driven by his nephew Iolaus, they came upon another chariot in which Kyknos and his father Ares were riding with the twins Phobos and Deimos as their charioteers. (In some versions of the myth Phobos and Deimos are not charioteers for their father Ares, but are his horses, Fear and Terror). Kyknos took an instant dislike to Heracles and saw an opportunity to rid the world of the hero.

Heracles and Kyknos leaped from their chariots and began fighting. During the duel Heracles managed to sever two of Kyknos's neck tendons with his spear. As Kyknos fell mortally wounded, his enraged father jumped from

Phobos in the Stars

Ancient Greeks and later the Romans adopted astrology as a system to predict the future. The study of the position and movement of the planets was taken so seriously that astrologers often held important offices in the government, influencing politics with their advice. Astrology replaced more basic predictive systems such as reading the entrails of animals. It closely reflected contemporary pantheons so that Mars, the Roman counterpart of Ares, was associated with the red planet of the same name. Astronomy, the scientific study of the stars, adopted these Roman names and uses others from classical mythology to label new stars that are discovered.

In mid-August 1877 astronomers discovered two moons orbiting Mars. They were named Phobos and Deimos, the gods Fear and Dread, who were the sons of Mars, or Ares in Greek mythology. These names have proved ominous. The larger moon, Phobos, is so close to Mars that the planet's gravitational field is slowly claiming it. Scientists predict that, in 50 million years or so, Phobos will either crash to Mars' surface or shatter into a ring of debris circling the planet.

Above: An image of Phobos, one of the moons of the planet Mars, taken by a probe in 1978. The moon was named for the Greek god of fear, and son of Ares.

the chariot and continued the fight. The war god's spear struck hard against the shield of his opponent, knocking Heracles off balance. Tasting victory, Ares drew his sword and rushed to the kill. Heracles, however, managed to thrust his own spear deep into Ares' thigh and threw him to the ground. Phobos and Deimos leaped forward to snatch their injured father away and then fled to Olympus. Local Pythians eventually buried the body of Kyknos, but Apollo ordered the Anaurus River to wash away his grave, since he had attacked so many of his devotees and stolen their offerings.

Elsewhere in Greek mythology Phobos is represented metaphorically: he is not a personification of fear but fear itself. He is often referred to as an incapacitating fear that is free-floating, ungrounded, arising out of nowhere, illogical, and irrational. Ancient Greeks, especially soldiers during a battle, might feel the presence of Phobos and invoke his name to describe a fear that caused a rout or a terrified withdrawal. The feeling of fear associated with Phobos became a term described by his name, *phobos*. It has much in common with panic, which ancient Greeks called a *phobos panikos*, a *phobos* inflicted by the god of shepherds, Pan. Ancient Greeks sometimes viewed *phobos* as the result of the *mastix*, a whip or a metaphorical scourge that imposed mastery over animals but could also madden and disorder humans.

Modern phobias

All known phobias have their root in *phobos*. Some examples are phobophobia, fear of fear; claustrophobia, fear of enclosed spaces; agoraphobia, fear of open spaces; xenophobia, fear of strangers; aichomophobia, fear of being touched by a pointed object, whether a spear or an index finger; hagiophobia, fear of being around holy persons or objects; and cremnophobia, fear of falling off a cliff. Modern medical dictionaries list more than two hundred types of phobias.

Although Phobos was not a great deity in Greek mythology, the negative connotations of his name, many of which still exist today, ensure that he is one of the most enduring gods in the Greek pantheon.

KATHLEEN JENKS

Bibliography

Bulfinch, Thomas. *Bulfinch's Mythology.* New York: Barnes & Noble, 2006.

Gardner, Jane F. *Roman Myths.* Austin, TX: University of Texas Press, 1993.

Homer, and Robert Fagles, trans. *The Iliad.* New York: Penguin, 2009.

Howatson, M. C. *The Oxford Companion to Classical Literature.* New York: Oxford University Press, 2005.

SEE ALSO: Apollo; Ares; Artemis; Mars; Pan.

PLUTUS

In ancient Greek mythology, Plutus was the god of abundance or wealth and the personification of riches (Greek: *ploutos*). He is sometimes confused with Pluton, another name for Hades, god of the dead.

According to Greek epic poet Hesiod (fl. 800 BCE), Plutus was born in Crete, the son of Demeter, goddess of fruitfulness, and Iasion, a mortal son of Zeus who was later killed by the king of the gods. The symbolism of this union seems to represent a "sacred marriage" between deity and mortal, making the earth fertile. In art, Plutus is sometimes represented as a child with a cornucopia, a horn filled to overflowing with fruits of the earth. While Plutus principally symbolized the riches of agricultural produce, by extension he became the god of every form of wealth. Proverbially in Greece, wealth was blind, and that is how the god first appears in the play *Plutus*, a comedy by Aristophanes (c. 450–c. 388 BCE). He soon recovers his sight, however, and sets about enriching only those who deserve him.

There was no religious cult of Plutus, but the child Plutus played a part in the Eleusinian Mysteries, where he was represented with Demeter and Persephone at the moment of their reunion, the time when fertility returned to the earth.

What's in a name

The similarity of the names Plutus and Pluton is unlikely to be accidental. The god of the dead was also sometimes depicted with a cornucopia. Many people regarded him as a giver of wealth because wealth comes from the earth, and it is to the earth that all mortals return when they die. Connected with this notion is the idea that humans have to be reconciled with the dead in order to prosper. The dead must be at peace for new life to go forward, and this idea is extended to the god of the dead. The Greeks propitiated their dead by giving them *meiligmata*, "soothing offerings." Pluton was sometimes known as Meilichios, meaning "soothed" or "soothing." Ancient Greeks sacrificed to Meilichios in the hope of having their luck improve, thus restoring prosperity and ending poverty and deprivation. The link between wealth and death was maintained in the art and literature of the Christian period. In *Paradise Lost*, English poet John Milton (1608–1674) remarks: "Let none admire [wonder] that riches grow in hell: that soil may best deserve the precious bane [poison]."

JAMES M. REDFIELD

Above: Plutus not only bestowed wealth, he also protected it. This bas-relief depicts him repelling scavenging birds from a vineyard.

Bibliography

Hesiod, and M. L. West, trans. *Theogony* and *Works and Days*. New York: Oxford University Press, 2008.

Howatson, M. C. *The Oxford Companion to Classical Literature*. New York: Oxford University Press, 2005.

SEE ALSO: Demeter; Hades; Persephone.

POMONA

Pomona was the Roman goddess of fruit (*poma*), especially apples and pears. She was famous for her devotion to her orchards and for her chastity. The main story attached to her revolves around her eventual seduction by the nature god Vertumnus.

Above: This 19th-century tapestry by Edward Burne-Jones (1833–1898) and William Morris (1834–1896) depicts Pomona holding a branch from an apple tree.

The story of Pomona and Vertumnus is told by Roman poet Ovid (43 BCE–17 BCE) in his *Metamorphoses*. According to Ovid, Pomona dwelled in Latium in the days of King Proca and was more beautiful than any other woman who lived there. However, Pomona did not want to have anything to do with love. No faun or satyr could seduce her. Even the fertility god Priapus tried and failed. However, one nature god, Vertumnus, fell so madly in love with Pomona that he became determined to make her his wife.

The seduction of Pomona
Vertumnus was the Roman god of the changing seasons, and as such could take on any shape he wanted. He used this ability to spy on Pomona. Sometimes he turned into a farmer's son and, carrying a heavy basket on his shoulders, walked by the vegetable garden where Pomona worked. At other times he came to her orchard as a fruit farmer, a cattle herder, or a fisherman. In these various guises he watched the goddess as she tended to her orchard.

Eventually, in an attempt to win her hand, Vertumnus adopted a different disguise. Transforming himself into the shape of an old woman, he approached Pomona's garden. He first complimented her on the beauty of the apples that hung from the trees in her orchard, and then he told her that the most beautiful thing in the garden was Pomona herself. Vertumnus pointed to an elm tree around which a vine was attached. He explained to the nymph how the tree and the vine complemented one another and how the vine needed the tree to support it.

"And yet, Pomona," Vertumnus went on, "you haven't learned a thing from the lesson of the elm and the vine. You, who are so beautiful, will attach yourself to no-one. Worse, you run away from love, while all the people in your surroundings—gods, demigods, even mortals—are in love with you. Listen to me, an old woman who cares about you more than anyone. Choose a husband. And choose the best—Vertumnus."

Vertumnus went on to list the reasons why he would make such a good husband. From the safety of his disguise he gave Pomona a detailed description of Vertumnus's good looks and his ability to change shape at will. He went on to describe to Pomona the god's love of nature and gardens. Most important of all, he told the goddess about Vertumnus's undying and absolute love for her. Finally, he told her that she should beware the wrath of Venus, goddess of love. In order to illustrate the dangers of incurring the goddess's anger, Vertumnus told Pomona the story of Iphis and Anaxarete.

Above: Vertumnus and Pomona, *by Dutch artist Adriaen van de Velde, is one of the most famous depictions of the pair's courtship.*

Iphis and Anaxarete

The son of a poor widow, Iphis fell in love with a rich and beautiful girl named Anaxarete. Day after day, he went to the gate of her home and begged the servants to give her his love letters. The staff did what he asked, but still Anaxarete would have nothing to do with him. At long last Iphis gave up. Unable to win her love, he tied a rope to the gate and hanged himself. Before he did so, however, he prayed to the gods that he would become famous because of his suffering.

A few days later the funeral procession took Iphis's body past the house of Anaxarete. This was the moment for Venus's revenge. Anaxarete, who heard the wailing and weeping outside her house, went to the window to look at the procession. However, when she saw the body of Iphis on the bier, her gaze froze. The blood drained from her body. She tried to walk away, but she could not—she stood riveted before the window. Anaxarete's body gradually turned to stone to match her heart.

Once he had completed his story, Vertumnus asked Pomona if her heart too was made of stone. He then threw off his disguise and revealed himself in his true form. Pomona, won over by his charm and eloquence, agreed to become his lover.

Historians know very little about Pomona other than the details preserved in the story recorded by Ovid. However, it is known that she had a sanctuary, the Pomonal, some 12 miles (19 km) outside Rome on the road to Ostia. Pomona had no holidays on the Roman calender and is therefore believed to have had only movable feasts, which could take place on various dates.

Pomona in art

There are no surviving representations of Pomona from ancient Greek or Roman art. In later art, however, Pomona is often depicted with Vertumnus. Among the best known representations of the pair are two paintings by 17th-century Dutch artists. Both works are entitled *Vertumnus and Pomona* and show Vertumnus courting the goddess while disguised as an old woman. One is by Adriaen van de Velde (1636–1672); the other is by Paulus Moreelse (1571–1638). Pomona is also depicted in a group sculpture by French artist Camille Claudel (1864–1943).

FEYO SCHUDDEBOOM

Bibliography

Bulfinch, Thomas. *Bulfinch's Mythology.* New York: Barnes & Noble, 2006.

Ovid, and A. D. Melville, trans. *Metamorphoses.* New York: Oxford University Press, 2008.

SEE ALSO: Priapus.

POSEIDON

Poseidon was the Greek god of the sea. He was known for both his violent temper and his tendency to bear long grudges—the Greek hero Odysseus was just one mythical character to suffer because he had offended the god. Like his brother Zeus, Poseidon had a voracious sexual appetite and fathered a large number of children. Many of the myths attached to him revolve around the tragic consequences of his violent pursuit of mortals.

There are various theories about the origins of Poseidon. The god was worshiped as Poseidon Heliconius by the Ionians, a race of people who migrated from mainland Greece to western Asia around 1000 BCE. Some scholars have suggested that, if this name was derived from that of Mount Helicon in Boeotia, Poseidon might originally have been a sky god. Poseidon's characteristic trident, or three-pointed spear, could once have been a thunderbolt. The god's connection with bulls and horses, on the other hand, suggests an association with fertility. His name is probably derived from the Greek for "husband of Da," that is, flowing water. This would suggest that Poseidon was a version of a common Indo-European god associated with rivers and other water sources.

Whatever his origins, it is as the fearsome ruler of the seas that Poseidon is best known today. According to Greek poet Hesiod (fl. 800 BCE), Poseidon was one of the six children of the Titans Rhea and Cronus. When Poseidon and his siblings were born, their mother Rhea had to watch in horror as her husband ate their children. Cronus had heard a prophecy from his mother, the earth goddess Gaia, that one of his children would kill him. However, Rhea managed to save Zeus, her youngest child, by giving Cronus a stone to swallow in his place and hiding the boy in a cave on Crete. When Zeus grew up, he forced his father to vomit up all the divine children. Together, Zeus and his brothers Hades and Poseidon got their revenge on Cronus by driving him away and taking over his kingdom. Lots were drawn to determine who would take over the various parts of

Right: A depiction of Poseidon from a sixth-century-BCE Greek dish. Poseidon is carrying his most famous attribute, the trident.

God of Earthquakes

As well as being god of the sea, Poseidon was also the god of earthquakes. The Greek poet Homer (c. ninth–eighth century BCE) uses various titles to reflect this aspect of his personality. One of these titles is *Gaieochos*, which means "holder of the earth." This title reflects the idea that the sea encircled the earth, holding it in its place. Another epithet that Homer uses to describe him is *Enosichthon*, which means "earth shaker." Certain areas of Greece are badly afflicted by earthquakes, and in ancient times these regions were often home to Poseidon cults. One was the Isthmus of Corinth, where the Isthmian games were held every two years in honor of the god; another was Helice in Achaea. According to Greek geographer Strabo (c. 64 BCE–c. 23 CE), the city was devastated by an earthquake and a tidal wave in 373 BCE. Both were said to be the work of Poseidon.

Cronus's realm. Zeus became ruler of sky and earth, Hades of the underworld, and Poseidon of the sea.

Other authors offer alternative versions of Poseidon's parentage. One variation has Rhea putting a young horse in Poseidon's place, saving him from being swallowed, as she later saved Zeus. In this story Poseidon's association with horses goes back to the very earliest point in his life. Another myth says that Poseidon was thrown into the sea by his father and then went on to rule his watery habitat.

Poseidon and Amphitrite

Poseidon's wife was the sea nymph Amphitrite. According to one story, when Poseidon first courted her, Amphitrite fled from him. Poseidon sent all the sea creatures in pursuit of her. Eventually Delphinus, the dolphin, found her and pleaded on the god's behalf. Amphitrite was eventually won over by the dolphin's persuasive powers and agreed to marry the god. As a reward, Poseidon placed the dolphin in the sky as a constellation. Other accounts of the origins of the marriage show a darker side to the sea god's nature, saying that Poseidon carried the nymph off, raped her, and made her his wife against her will.

In ancient art Poseidon was depicted as handsome, bearded, and fierce, a figure very much like his brother Zeus. Like his brother, Poseidon was an unfaithful husband and betrayed his wife on numerous occasions. For example, he chased after Demeter while the grain goddess was searching the earth for her stolen daughter, Persephone. Demeter transformed herself into a mare, but Poseidon took the form of a stallion and raped the goddess. The

coupling produced both a daughter, Despoina, and a magical horse, Areion. Later Areion came into the possession of the Greek hero Heracles.

Many of the recipients of Poseidon's sexual attentions suffered greatly because of them. One was a beautiful young girl named Caenis, whose story is told by Roman poet Ovid (43 BCE–17 BCE) in his *Metamorphoses*, a collection of stories in which the main figures undergo some form of transformation. Poseidon raped the girl and then offered her any gift that she named. Caenis asked that she be turned into a man so that she should never endure such an ordeal again. Poseidon granted her wish, transforming her into a man named Caeneus, giving him the additional gift of invulnerability. Caeneus was later involved in the battle between the centaurs and the Lapiths, a people who lived in Thessaly. The battle occurred at a wedding feast, and Caeneus's gift of invulnerability enabled him to kill many of the centaurs. Eventually, however, they hammered him into the ground with tree trunks.

Another figure whose life was blighted by her sexual liaison with Poseidon was Medusa, a beautiful woman who made love to the sea god in Athena's temple. According to one version of Medusa's story, recorded by Greek writer Apollodorus (fl. 140 BCE), Athena was so incensed that she transformed Medusa into a hideous monster. The vain Medusa was particularly proud of her beautiful head of hair, so Athena turned it into a mass of writhing snakes. Medusa's head was so ghastly to see that all who set eyes on her were transformed into stone. Athena's persecution of Medusa did not end with the transformation, however. Much later she helped the Greek hero Perseus kill the monster.

Children of Poseidon

Poseidon and Amphitrite had several children, the most notable of whom was the sea god Triton, who was a man from the waist up and a fish from the waist down and who blew a horn made from a conch shell. By blowing this shell Triton was able to calm the seas. Triton also appears in the story of Jason and the Argonauts, swimming beside the *Argo* and leading the ship to safety. However, like his father, Triton had a darker side and was said to attack boats and rape women bathing in the sea.

Poseidon also had many children with other goddesses and women, most notably the earth goddess Gaia. One of the pair's most famous offspring was the giant Antaeus, who ruled over Libya. The Greek hero Heracles came to the country as part of his search for the garden of the

Above: This statue of Poseidon by Greek sculptor Calamis dates to the fifth century BCE. It was recovered off the coast of Greece in 1928.

Erechtheus

Erechtheus was a mythical hero and king of Athens. According to legend, he was the son of the earth goddess Gaia and was raised by the goddess Athena. Erechtheus defended the city of Athens against the Thracian king Eumolpus. This king was Poseidon's son and ancestor of the priests of Eleusis. Despite the patronage of his father, Eumolpus died at the hands of Erechtheus. In revenge, Poseidon drove Erechtheus into the earth with a blow of his trident.

Erechtheus is often confused with his father, Erichthonius, also a king of Athens. Both kings were often conflated with Poseidon and were worshiped at their own cult sites. The Athenians built a temple to Erechtheus, the Erechtheum, on the Acropolis. One of the temple's altars was jointly dedicated to both Erechtheus and Poseidon.

Hesperides, the location of the golden apples of immortality. Gaia had originally given the miraculous apple tree to Zeus and Hera at their marriage. Antaeus challenged everyone who came to his land to a wrestling match. He inevitably won the contests, and he used the skulls of his defeated opponents to decorate the temple of his father, Poseidon. The secret of Antaeus's success lay in the fact that whenever a part of his body touched the ground, he gained strength through contact with his mother, Gaia. However, Heracles overcame him by hoisting him into the air and crushing him until he perished.

Scylla and Charybdis

Another fearsome offspring of Gaia and Poseidon was Charybdis, a giantess who was cast into the ocean by Zeus. Charybdis was chained to the seabed. Three times each day she sucked the water above her downward, causing a giant whirlpool to appear on the ocean's surface. The whirlpool was so strong that any ship caught in it was certain to be destroyed. To make matters worse, Charybdis lived in the Straits of Messina, which separate Italy and Sicily. The other side of the straits was the home of the six-headed sea

Below: In this woodcut, Greek hero Odysseus is depicted sailing between Scylla and Charybdis. Both sea monsters came into existence as a result of Poseidon's lustful behavior.

Above: Perseus and Andromeda *by Rutilio Manetti (1571–1639). Andromeda sits chained while the sea monster sent by Poseidon approaches.*

monster Scylla. Scylla lived in a cave halfway up a cliff and would reach down and seize sailors as their ships went past. All travelers who passed through the straits thus faced an unenviable choice. In order to give one of the monsters a wide berth, they would be forced to sail close to the other, putting themselves in mortal danger.

There are various stories that attempt to explain Scylla's origins. One of them says that Scylla was originally a beautiful maiden, the daughter of Crateis, usually identified with Hecate, the goddess of witchcraft. When Poseidon tried to court Scylla, Amphitrite flew into a rage. The betrayed wife was so furious that she threw a potion into Scylla's bath that turned the luckless maiden into a sea monster. This story makes Scylla another unfortunate victim of Poseidon's uncontrolled lust, just like Medusa and Caenis.

Either purposefully or unintentionally, Poseidon was responsible for most of the monsters who dwelled in the already dangerous waters of the sea. He could easily be offended and was capable of inflicting terrible punishments on mortals who slighted him. For example, Cassiopeia, queen of Ethiopia, once boasted that she was more beautiful than any of the Nereids, the sea nymphs who were daughters of another sea god, Nereus. The Nereids were so offended that they asked Poseidon to punish Cassiopeia. First, Poseidon sent a tidal wave that flooded

her land. Then he sent a sea monster to attack her people. When the queen and her husband, Cepheus, consulted an oracle to see how they could rid their land of its plight, they were told that they would have to sacrifice their daughter Andromeda to the sea beast. The king and queen tried to do so, chaining Andromeda to a rock, but the girl was saved at the last minute by the hero Perseus.

Poseidon and Odysseus

Once a mortal had offended Poseidon, he or she could not expect the crime to be either forgiven or forgotten. The sea god's most famous longstanding quarrel was with Odysseus. The Greek hero gained Poseidon's enmity by gouging out the eye of the god's son, the giant Cyclops Polyphemus. Odysseus and his men, on their way home from the Trojan War, had entered the giant's cave and stolen food from him. Polyphemus retaliated by shutting the hero and his crew in the cave with a great stone and proceeding to eat the sailors, one at a time. Odysseus craftily got Polyphemus drunk, then drove a wooden stake into the giant's single eye. Tricking Polyphemus by hiding under the giant's sheep as they passed through the cave door, Odysseus and his men sped away in their ship.

Above: This terra-cotta relief from the fourth century CE shows *Amphitrite, wife of Poseidon, riding a sea monster.*

Polyphemus roared out curses after them and begged his father, Poseidon, to grant him a favor. He begged that Odysseus should never make it back to his beloved homeland, or that, if he did, then he should do so without either his ship or his men, having suffered many torments on his travels. Poseidon granted Polyphemus's request and proved to be a persistent adversary for Odysseus, unleashing a series of violent storms that almost cost the hero his life. Odysseus managed to survive only with the help of another deity, the goddess Athena, who protected and guided him on his travels.

The rivalry of Poseidon and Athena

Poseidon and Athena were often adversaries in Greek mythology. Many years earlier, the two deities had vied for the position of divine ruler of Athens and Attica. The two deities demonstrated their powers by creating magical gifts for the Athenians. Poseidon struck a stone with his trident, and a saltwater spring erupted from the place where the trident hit the rock. Athena, meanwhile, touched the earth with her spear, and an olive tree grew. Cecrops, the king of Athens, judged that Athena's gift was more useful and built a temple to her on the Acropolis, the central hill in Athens. The king's decision drove Poseidon into a fury, and the sea god sent a flood to punish the Athenians. In order to appease the god, they built another temple, dedicated specifically to him, in the center of their city. The legend of the contest remained popular with Athenians for centuries. Greek travel writer Pausanias (143–176 CE) claimed that he was shown the mark where Poseidon's trident struck the rock.

Poseidon clashed with two other deities over the possession of regions. According to Pausanias, the sea god vied with Hera over the region of Argos. When the river gods Inachus, Cephissus, and Asterion ruled in favor of Hera, Poseidon once again flew into a rage. In spite, he dried up the three gods' rivers, causing the region to be barren. Poseidon also competed with the sun god Helios for the city of Corinth. In this case Helios was granted supremacy over the city itself, while Poseidon was allowed to rule the isthmus on which it was located.

As well as the sea, Poseidon was also associated with bulls and horses (see box, page 246). In two famous myths,

Poseidon Hippion—God of Horses

Even though he was the god of the sea, the animal with which Poseidon was most closely associated was the horse. He was sometimes known as Poseidon Hippion—*hippos* is the Greek work for the animal. There are many myths that associate Poseidon with horses. Roman poet Virgil (70–19 BCE) claimed that Poseidon created the first horse by striking the earth with his trident. A more famous equine creation of Poseidon was the winged horse Pegasus. The Gorgon Medusa was pregnant by Poseidon when she was beheaded by Greek hero Perseus. The pair's offspring—Pegasus—sprung fully formed from her neck. Poseidon also gave the immortal horses Xanthus and Balius to Peleus, the father of Greek hero Achilles.

Horses were often sacrificed to Poseidon. Greek writer Pausanias wrote that in the region of Argolis, horses were drowned in a river as an offering to the god.

Right: This Greek silver coin from the third century BCE depicts the winged horse Pegasus.

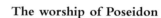

bulls sent by Poseidon from the sea were the cause of great tragedy. King Minos of Crete had prayed to the sea god to send him a fabulous bull, which he would immediately sacrifice. Poseidon sent a bull so beautiful Minos could not bear to give it up. He decided to use the bull to enrich his herd and sacrificed another in its place. Poseidon went into a rage. He caused Pasiphae, Minos's wife, to fall in love with the bull. Daedalus, the court artist, created the lifelike form of a cow for Pasiphae to hide in so that the creature could have intercourse with her. The offspring of their union was a monster, the Minotaur, that was a source of tragedy for many years.

Another bull sent from the sea by Poseidon brought tragedy to the life of Hippolytus, the son of Athenian hero Theseus. Theseus's wife, Phaedra, fell in love with her young stepson, and when he rejected her advances, she committed suicide, claiming that Hippolytus had tried to rape her. Theseus was so angry that he called on Poseidon to avenge him. The sea god promptly sent a bull from the sea to the beach where Hippolytus was driving his chariot. The bull so terrified Hippolytus's horses that he was thrown from his chariot and dragged to his death by his horses' reins.

The worship of Poseidon

The Greeks were a nation of seafarers and, as such, treated Poseidon with great reverence. The fact that his name appears frequently on Linear B tablets found at Mycenae shows that he was worshiped at a very early stage of Greek history. Linear B was a form of script that was used between 1400 and 1150 BCE. Classical sources show that Poseidon was also widely worshiped in later times. For example, in his *Guide to Greece*, Pausanias lists numerous temples that were dedicated to the god. Among the most notable were those at Athens, Argos, Sparta, and the islands of Tenís and Achaea. The finest example of a temple to Poseidon to still exist today is probably that at Sounion in Attica, a region of central Greece. The building was constructed sometime between 450 and 440 BCE and is made of marble. The partially destroyed frieze on one side of the building is believed to show a fight between Athena and Poseidon for control of Attica.

The most famous festival held in honor of Poseidon was the Isthmian Games. The games were held on the Isthmus of Corinth, which was believed to come under the divine

Above: The temple of Poseidon at Sounion, Greece. Built in the fifth century BCE, the building is the best preserved temple to the sea god to still exist.

protection of the god. The Isthmian Games were first held in the sixth century BCE and consisted of athletic events as well as poetry and music contests. A number of sacrifices were made to Poseidon. Among the animals sacrificed were the two most closely associated with the sea god—horses and black bulls.

Poseidon in art

In Roman times, Poseidon came to be identified with the god Neptune. Both Poseidon and his Roman equivalent have been widely represented in art. One of the most famous ancient statues of Poseidon still to exist is by fifth-century-BCE sculptor Calamis. The statue was recovered from the sea off the coast of Artemisium in Greece in the early 20th century. It stands almost 7 feet (2.1 m) tall.

Since Calamis's day, there have been many sculptures of Poseidon and Neptune. The representations of the god invariably depict him as bearded and muscular and usually carrying his most famous attribute, the trident. Because of his association with water, statues of Poseidon are often found in fountains. Possibly the most famous of such statues is that found in the Trevi Fountain in Rome. It was created by Niccoló Salvi (1697–1751). It depicts the sea god in a chariot drawn by horses. Another famous statue is one by Italian sculptor Bartolommeo Ammannati (1511–1592). It stands in the Piazza della Signoria in the city of Florence, Italy.

The sea god has also been a popular subject for painters. Among the most famous paintings to depict Poseidon or Neptune are *Triumph of Neptune and Amphitrite* by Nicolas Poussin (1594–1665); *Jupiter, Neptune, and Pluto* by Caravaggio (1573–1610); and *Neptune Creates the Horse* by Jacob Jordaens (1593–1678).

BARBARA GARDNER

Bibliography

Homer, and Robert Fagles, trans. *The Odyssey.* New York: Penguin, 2009.

Pausanias, and Peter Levi, trans. *Guide to Greece.* New York: Viking Press, 1984.

SEE ALSO: Athena; Cronus; Neptune; Triton; Zeus.

PRIAPUS

In Greek mythology, Priapus was a god of sex. He was associated particularly with fertility rites, and his responsibilities included protecting crops and gardens from animals, birds, and thieves. In art and literature, Priapus is usually portrayed as a grotesque little man with a disproportionately large phallus.

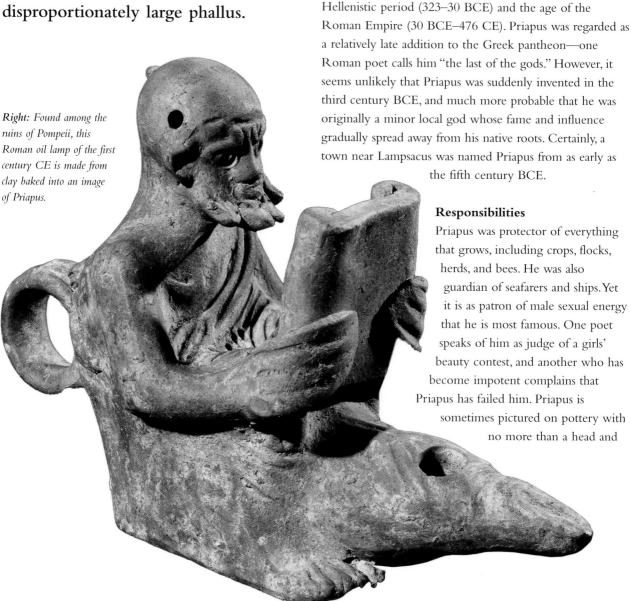

Right: Found among the ruins of Pompeii, this Roman oil lamp of the first century CE is made from clay baked into an image of Priapus.

According to the most common version of the story of Priapus, he was the son of Dionysus and Aphrodite. Aphrodite went to Lampsacus, a Greek city on the Hellespont, to bear the child. While she was in labor, Hera, jealous of her fertility, laid her hand on Aphrodite and caused the baby to be born with a large phallus. Aphrodite was so appalled by this defect that she wanted nothing to do with her son. She abandoned him on the mountains, where he was raised by shepherds who became the first to honor him as a symbol of fertility.

The oldest literary sources of the legend date from the Hellenistic period (323–30 BCE) and the age of the Roman Empire (30 BCE–476 CE). Priapus was regarded as a relatively late addition to the Greek pantheon—one Roman poet calls him "the last of the gods." However, it seems unlikely that Priapus was suddenly invented in the third century BCE, and much more probable that he was originally a minor local god whose fame and influence gradually spread away from his native roots. Certainly, a town near Lampsacus was named Priapus from as early as the fifth century BCE.

Responsibilities

Priapus was protector of everything that grows, including crops, flocks, herds, and bees. He was also guardian of seafarers and ships. Yet it is as patron of male sexual energy that he is most famous. One poet speaks of him as judge of a girls' beauty contest, and another who has become impotent complains that Priapus has failed him. Priapus is sometimes pictured on pottery with no more than a head and

Above: This Roman bas-relief from the first century CE showing Priapus among the vines is a reminder that Priapus was not just a sex god: he was also a guardian of crops.

sexual organs. His image also appears mounted on square stone pillars. These are known as herms because they were originally used to depict the god Hermes. The link between Priapus and Hermes is that they were both protectors of boundaries. In some versions of the legend, Priapus is even said to be the child of Hermes by Aphrodite. This parentage links Priapus with another god of sexual energy, Hermaphroditus. (Accounts of Priapus's parentage vary widely: sometimes his mother is not Aphrodite but a nymph; his father is also given as Adonis and even Zeus.)

Links with Pan

Priapus's rejection at birth by his mother links him with Pan, who was also a god of flocks and herds. Like Pan, Priapus was honored with all-night festivals, and he was occasionally said to have acted jointly with Pan. Although Priapus had shrines dedicated to him in some cities, and in others there were statues of him by the harbor, he did not belong to any formalized civic pantheon, except perhaps at Lampsacus, where he seems to have received special honors as a native son. Priapus was, like Pan, a god of the country people, of gardeners and shepherds. Unlike Pan or the satyrs, however, he had no

animal features; he was almost invariably entirely human— except that very occasionally he was depicted as a rooster or with a rooster's head.

In the Hellenistic and Roman periods most artistic representations of Priapus were rough, unsophisticated images carved from fig wood. Since that material is easily perishable, no such artifacts survive, but they are extensively described by poets. Sometimes they were set up on the shore by fishers, but most often they appeared in gardens. They evidently looked less like traditional works of sculpture and more like scarecrows or Halloween jack-o'-lanterns. Crude and somewhat ridiculous, they were intended to keep out intruders and strangers and to protect believers from evil spirits. Country people would cut any branch of a tree that resembled a phallus, carve a rough face on it, and set it up in their garden, decorating it with wreaths of flowers and sometimes a splash of red paint. There it would ward off disease, bad weather, and especially thieves. Among the ancient bynames for Priapus were Gardenkeeper and Fruitguard.

Priapus in Art and Literature

Priapus is commonly represented naked or holding garden produce in his cloak, which he raises to reveal his phallus. The House of the Vettii at Pompeii, Italy, contains both a painting of Priapus weighing his phallus against a sack of coins and a fountain statue of the god spurting water from his organ.

In *Astronomica*, Hyginus, a Roman author of the first century CE, tells the story of a disagreement between Priapus and an ass about the relative sizes of their sexual organs. Priapus wins the argument and beats the ass to death. In *Fasti* by Roman poet Ovid (43 BCE–17 CE), Priapus is attracted to the nymph Lotis. He creeps up on her as she sleeps, but just as he is about to climb on top of her a donkey wakes her with its braying. This story inspired the painting *Feast of the Gods* by Venetian Giovanni Bellini (c. 1430–1516). Among other famous representations of the god are drawings of a sacrifice to him by Venetian Jacopo de' Barbari (1440–1516) (left) and of his birth by French artist Nicolas Poussin (1594–1665). There is also a bronze sculpture of Priapus by Spanish artist Pablo Picasso (1881–1973).

Left: Sacrifice to Priapus *by Jacopo de' Barbari. The drawing shows women—one of whom holds an infant—making an offering at the altar of the god.*

Sacrificial ass

Priapus's sexuality was distorted and awkward, always somewhat ludicrous and generally unsuccessful. According to one story, he was attempting to ravish a sleeping nymph when a donkey brayed and awakened her. Priapus was always linked with asses (see box), probably because they symbolized lechery and were associated with sexual potency. At Lampsacus donkeys were sacrificed to Priapus; this seems to be the only ritual in which a donkey was thought to be an appropriate sacrificial animal.

In the early Common Era, Priapus underwent some odd transformations. Some Gnostics—members of a second-century religious movement who believed that the human spirit could be released from its bondage in the physical body—worshiped Priapus as the primary god, protector of all creation. His status was thus raised to the level of Eros. However, Priapus evidently retained his traditional role with country people, and early Christians inveighed against him as a source of dissolute behavior. Yet vestiges of worship remained. In Scotland in the 13th century CE, a lay Cistercian brother put up a statue of Priapus in order to put an end to an epidemic among the cattle. Today in the Mediterranean region, representations of sexual organs, in the form of amulets or gestures, are widely believed to be protective, especially against the evil eye—this is the cult of Priapus without the name.

Priapus was one of the few Greek deities who was quite differently regarded by country folk and city dwellers. The former revered him as a powerful guardian of their property and interests, while the latter saw him principally as a bawdy figure of fun.

James M. Redfield

Bibliography

Bulfinch, Thomas. *Bulfinch's Mythology.* New York: Barnes & Noble, 2006.

Howatson, M. C. *The Oxford Companion to Classical Literature.* New York: Oxford University Press, 2005.

See also: Aphrodite; Dionysus; Eros; Hera; Hermaphroditus; Hermes; Pan.

PROMETHEUS

Prometheus was a Titan, son of the Titan Iapetus and the Oceanid Clymene. In some myths Prometheus was the creator of humankind; in others he was their benefactor and champion. This latter role has led some scholars to compare him to other culture-bearer deities, such as the Aztec god Quetzalcoatl.

According to some versions of the myth, Prometheus fashioned mortal men from clay, animating them with a spark of Aether (the divine upper air). Some writers claimed that the oddly shaped Pindus Mountains in north-central Greece were the remains of his work. The legend that Prometheus formed mortals in his own image explains why he always had the interests of mortals at heart.

In another version, Prometheus was involved in the re-creation of the human race. Zeus had become angry with the way people were ignoring the gods and tending only to their own interests. He flooded the world and destroyed most of it. Only two mortals survived the great flood: Deucalion, the son of Prometheus, and his wife Pyrrha, daughter of Epimetheus (brother of Prometheus). On Prometheus's instructions, the mortal couple built a boat and rode over the waves. Finally the waters subsided and Deucalion and Pyrrha touched land at Mount Parnassus, a place the ancient Greeks considered to be at the center of their known world. Prometheus advised them to consult the oracle of Gaia, the Great Earth Mother. She instructed them to "throw the bones of their mother" over their shoulders. Deciding that rocks were the bones of the earth,

Right: An anonymous artist sculpted this version of Prometheus's face, which forms part of a relief found on a building in the ancient Greco-Roman city of Aphrodisias (in modern Turkey).

they hurled rocks behind them. As the rocks fell they took human form: thus did Deucalion and Pyrrha restore men and women to the earth.

Prometheus came into conflict with Zeus on several occasions. Their first dispute arose over a sacrificial ritual. At an early gathering of men and gods, Prometheus divided up the meat of the sacrificial offering. He put the meat and hide in one pile, and the bones and fat in another, covering the first with the stomach of the sacrificial ox, and the other with its gleaming fat. Then he asked Zeus to choose which portion he wanted. Zeus chose the gleaming pile of bones and fat, but became angry when he discovered that Prometheus had deceived him. Zeus determined to punish both Prometheus and mortals for this trick.

Etiological Myths

An explanation of a ritual custom that specifically examines its mythological origin is called an etiological myth. Some etiological myths claim to explain the cause of natural occurrences such as earthquakes or a particular detail of the appearance of an animal, such as spots on a leopard. Others attempt to link more recent ceremonies and rituals to the mythological past. The trick that Prometheus performs at the sacrifice to the gods forms an important part of an ancient Greek religious ritual: it is because of Zeus's choice that humans forever after burned the bones and fat on the altars of the gods and kept the meat for their own meal and the hide for their own clothing. The custom established by the deceitful trick can be explained etiologically: the gods enjoy the aroma of the sacrifice (the burning fat makes an attractive smell) and are aware that men are making offerings to them, and mortals can enjoy the meat and eat it in communion with the divinities.

As punishment Zeus decided to take fire away from men, who were the only gender that then existed. It was now difficult for mortals to enjoy their meat cooked, and it was hard for them to keep warm. It was also impossible for them to make metal implements for war. Prometheus took pity on the mortals. Stealing fire back from Mount Olympus, he returned it to them. To accomplish this theft Prometheus hid a flame in a hollow fennel stalk, a plant that has a tissuey substance inside that can keep a fire smoldering. Once fire was again back in mortals' hands, humankind could return to a better life in a more comfortable world.

When Zeus saw fire gleaming on earth, his anger grew, and he determined to punish both men and their benefactor. For men he created woman. He ordered the smith god Hephaestus to design the first woman, Pandora, a "beautiful evil" to disturb and distract men. Pandora was given a jar of evils, and Zeus offered her to Prometheus's brother, Epimetheus. Charmed by the beautiful gift, Epimetheus forgot his brother's warning: never accept a gift from the gods. Epimetheus learned too late that Pandora's curiosity would urge her to open the jar and let loose all manner of sorrows and sickness into the world. Only Hope remained in the jar: now humankind had ills but no hope to conquer them. Pandora's descendants were women who tormented and distracted men with their sexuality.

Prometheus, whose name means "forethought," knew in advance of his actions what punishment he would suffer.

Zeus bound him to a rock, where each day an eagle would peck at his liver and each night his liver would regenerate, so that his pain was endless. Nevertheless he persisted in his defiance of Zeus's rule and in his concern for humankind: he taught mortals all the arts of civilization. In *Prometheus Bound*, a play by Aescyhylus (525–456 BCE), the character of Prometheus proclaims:

[Men] at first seeing, looked in vain,
hearing, they did not hear,
but like to the forms of dreams
they muddled through their long life entirely by chance.

Prometheus taught men to build houses, to domesticate animals, to sail ships, and to measure the rotation of the seasons by using the stars. He also instructed them how to mine for metals, understand mathematics, practice medicine, and interpret oracles and dreams.

According to Aeschylus, Prometheus received several visitors while suffering the torment of the eagle. Oceanus came by to urge him to yield to Zeus, but Prometheus refused. A chorus of Oceanids arrived to keep him company below his rocky confinement. And the virgin priestess Io, another victim of divine wrath, came racing past Prometheus in her vain attempt to escape a stinging gadfly sent by Zeus's jealous wife, Hera. Io had been changed into a cow, either by Zeus himself to deceive Hera or by Hera in revenge for her husband's affair with the mortal woman; Hera then sent the gadfly to torment the transformed maiden. In some versions, Prometheus shared the power of his forethought with Io. He describes a journey to her in which she will cross from Europe to Asia over a strait of water now known as the Bosporos ("cow crossing") in Turkey. Prometheus tells her that she will finally arrive in Egypt, escape from the gadfly, and by the touch of Zeus bring forth a son who will be the ancestor of a new race—the Egyptians.

Prometheus's secret

To further torment Zeus, Prometheus taunted him with a secret that he refused to reveal. There was a female being courted by Zeus who was destined to have a son mightier than his father. Since Zeus enjoyed courting many females—some that were divine and powerful, some that were divine but with lesser power (nymphs), and others that were mortal—suddenly the amorous god was limited in his pursuits. Prometheus refused to reveal the identity of the woman, so Zeus determined that Prometheus would stay chained to the mountains. In some versions, Zeus was so angry about Prometheus's secret that he sent a thunderbolt that hurled the Titan and his rock into darkest Tartarus (the lowest level of the underworld). There he remained for a long time; when he emerged into the light once more, he was still imprisoned in the mountains.

Each day Prometheus concealed his secret, the eagle devoured his liver. In time, Prometheus told Zeus the name of the dangerous lady. It was the sea nymph Thetis, a nymph whom Zeus had eyed amorously. To avoid Prometheus's prophecy, Zeus declared that Thetis would marry a mortal—Peleus was that man. Their son was the mighty Achilles, who overshadowed his father Peleus in fame and was considered to be among the greatest mortal warriors alongside Ajax and Hector.

Since Prometheus had yielded to Zeus and revealed his secret, Zeus laid aside his anger. He sent his son Heracles

to kill the eagle and ordered that the chains be removed from the Titan. To thank Heracles, Prometheus told him how to accomplish his 11th labor; he advised Heracles to send Atlas to pluck the golden apples from the garden of the Hesperides for him. Then he told Heracles that he should agree to hold up the world while Atlas gathered the apples. The plan worked. Upon his return Atlas was tricked into taking the world back upon his shoulders, and Heracles left with the apples.

Prometheus was at last free. After Prometheus's release he realized the dangers of defying Zeus, and the tyranny of Zeus became more moderate.

Below: A bronze statue of Prometheus carrying a lighted torch stands in Rockefeller Plaza, New York City. American sculptor Paul Manship (1885–1966) designed and built the effigy in 1934.

Prometheus in other myths

Prometheus also played a role in several other myths. In some accounts he uses an ax to split Zeus's head, allowing Athena to be born (in other versions it is the smith god Hephaestus who wields the ax). Prometheus shared with Hephaestus the Temple of Hephaestus, called the Hephaesteion, which overlooked the Agora in Athens. In ancient Greece it was unusual for two divinities to share a temple, but here it made sense that two gods associated with fire were worshiped together. Around the temple were the shops of the bronze workers, who labored under the guidance of Prometheus and Hephaestus. Prometheus himself was celebrated annually by ancient Greeks with a

Perpetual Punishment

For stealing fire from Olympus, Zeus devised a terrible punishment for Prometheus. He ordered his servants Force, Might, and Hephaestus to chain (or in some versions of the myth to impale) the Titan to the sheer heights of the Caucasus Mountains. To add to this lonely torment, Zeus sent his bird, the eagle, to eat the Titan's liver each day. Each night the liver regenerated. The Titan was imprisoned like this and suffered constant pain until he was released.

The punishment that Zeus devised for Prometheus was not a random one. Ancient peoples believed that the liver, not the heart, was the seat of the emotions. When the eagle ate Prometheus's liver, the punishment was appropriate to the crime: Zeus decided that the Titan loved mortals too much, so the god attacked the place where his passion arose. The nightly regeneration of the liver was also appropriate, since the liver is the one organ in the human body to have the power to regenerate itself. It is not known if the ancients knew this or if the myth was devised because the Titan was immortal and it kept his suffering continual. In any case, Zeus created an effective punishment for the Titan who stood up against him.

Left: This 18th-century statue was sculpted by French artist Nicolas Sebastien Adam (1705–1778). It shows Prometheus bound by chains to a rock while an eagle devours his liver.

Below: In this 19th-century painting by German artist Karl Lehmann (1814–1882), distressed Oceanids surround the rock to which Prometheus is chained and keep him company while he endures Zeus's punishment.

Modern Prometheus

Mary Wollstonecraft Shelley (1797–1851) wrote a story derived from the Prometheus myth. *Frankenstein, or, The Modern Prometheus*, presents Frankenstein, a young medical student, who creates a new creature from parts of human cadavers he finds in cemeteries and dissecting rooms. The new "man" he creates experiences different emotions from love to anger, and eventually becomes disillusioned with life and kills his creator. Unlike Prometheus, Frankenstein is not immortal, and his act of "creation" is not motivated by Promethean concern for the human race. He acts from an interest in science, life, and death.

Above: In Bride of Frankenstein *(1935) American actor Boris Karloff (1887–1969) played the role of Frankenstein's monster— a character that was inspired by the myth of Prometheus.*

torch race around the Agora. Scholars argue that the flaming torch symbolized the fennel stalk in which Prometheus stored the fire that he returned to mortals.

In post-classical times, Prometheus came to be seen not only as the champion of mortals but as a rebel against a tyrant. Some people used the example of Prometheus's defiance in the face of Zeus's brutality to represent a method of reacting to different kinds of tyranny.

Prometheus's story was retold by English poet Percy Bysshe Shelley (1792–1822). In his long romantic poem, *Prometheus Unbound*, Shelley described a world that thrived on the kind of compassion that Prometheus showed toward humankind in Greek mythology.

In another interpretation of the myth, *Prometheus Misbound,* a story by French writer André Gide (1869–1951), the Titan becomes a symbol of proper action in a meaningless world. In Gide's story Prometheus's acceptance of the eagle demonstrates how to create a purpose in life. In this version Prometheus is imprisoned in a jail cell and the Titan allows the eagle to devour his liver and his body until he is thin enough to slip through the bars of his cell and the eagle is strong enough to carry him away. At the end of *Prometheus Misbound*, Prometheus invites his friends to a dinner party and serves the roasted eagle as the main course. The metaphorical message contained in Gide's story is that a devouring passion will lead to a better life.

Prometheus, whose name reveals his prophetic powers, remains a symbol of rebellion against oppression. Some argue that the myth of Prometheus undermines the position of women in society, but others claim that the high level of civilization mortals achieved through the gifts and teaching of Prometheus far outweighs any complaints made against his myth. In art and elsewhere, Prometheus is still associated with themes such as wisdom and creative grandeur.

KARELISA HARTIGAN

Bibliography

Apollodorus, and Robin Hard, trans. *The Library of Greek Mythology.* New York: Oxford University Press, 2008.

Bulfinch, Thomas. *Bulfinch's Mythology.* New York: Barnes & Noble, 2006.

Cotterell, Arthur. *Oxford Dictionary of World Mythology.* Oxford: Oxford University Press, 1986.

Graves, Robert. *The Greek Myths.* New York: Penguin, 1993.

Howatson, M. C. *The Oxford Companion to Classical Literature.* New York: Oxford University Press, 2005.

SEE ALSO: Atlas; Hephaestus; Hera; Zeus.

PROTEUS

In Greek mythology, Proteus was one of several minor sea gods. He could foresee the future, but he would not help humans without coercion.

Proteus is usually described as a very old, bearded man. He lived either on or near Pharos, an island in the Mediterranean Sea off the coast of Egypt. As a sea god, Proteus could guide and protect ships, and sailors prayed to him to keep them safe. He also looked after herds of seals belonging to Poseidon, the preeminent sea god. Proteus is often said to have been one of the 6,000 children of the Titan Oceanus and his sister Tethys, but there is no general agreement about the identity of his father—in some tales Proteus is described as a son of Poseidon.

Proteus was an "old man of the sea"—he was extremely wise, knew everything, and could predict the future and reveal what was going on in other places. However, he did not like sharing his knowledge. Humans who wanted to ask him questions had first to bring him under their control. This was difficult, for Proteus had an infinite capacity to change his shape. According to Roman poet Ovid (43 BCE–17 CE) in *Metamorphoses*, Proteus could turn himself into any plant or animal he chose, or into stone, running water, or fire. The only way to overpower him was to hold him tightly, whatever he changed into, until at last he resumed his true shape of an old man. Then, and only then, would Proteus give the victor the benefit of his prophetic counsel.

Like Proteus, Thetis was a minor sea deity. She too could change shape, and the only way to control her was to hold

Below: In addition to being the home of Proteus, Pharos was the site of a great lighthouse, one of the Seven Wonders of the Ancient World.

PHAROS

PROTEUS

her tightly. Both Zeus and Poseidon loved Thetis, but neither would marry her because an oracle had foretold that her firstborn son would be mightier than his father—Zeus, in particular, was terrified of the possible consequences of creating someone stronger than himself. Proteus suggested that Thetis marry Peleus, a mere mortal who was king of the Myrmidons in Thessaly (a region of east-central Greece).

Thetis thought that Peleus was beneath her, and she resisted marrying him by changing her shape. Peleus decided to ask the gods for advice. He poured wine into the sea as an offering, and Proteus came to help him. He told Peleus that to win control over Thetis, he must hold her firmly, whatever she changed into, until she resumed her original shape. Peleus succeeded in doing this, and the marriage went ahead. Their son was the hero Achilles.

Menelaus and Aristaeus

After the Trojan War, Menelaus was returning home to Sparta when his fleet was blown off course and stranded at Pharos. Before long his men began to run out of food. Proteus's daughter, Eidothee, took pity on Menelaus and told him the secret of how he could force Proteus to help him. She helped Menelaus and three of his men to hide under sealskins while Proteus was counting his herd. When the old sea god finally lay down to sleep, the men jumped out of their hiding places, took hold of him, and held him firmly, even though he turned himself into a lion, a snake, a panther, a boar, running water, and a huge tree. Finally Proteus gave in—he turned back into his true form and agreed to answer Menelaus's questions. Proteus told the hero that he must make offerings to Zeus before he could get home. He also told Menelaus that his brother Agamemnon had been murdered, and that Odysseus was trapped by Calypso on the island of Ogygia. Menelaus recounts his adventures with Proteus to Telemachus, Odysseus's son, in the *Odyssey*, an epic poem by Homer (c. ninth–eighth century BCE).

Another mythological character who managed to win control over Proteus was Apollo's son Aristaeus, a beekeeper. When the gods killed his bees as punishment for courting Eurydice and unwittingly causing her death, he sought out Proteus in Pharos and tied him down while he was sleeping in the afternoon. The sea god then advised Aristaeus that the only way to expiate his crime was by

sacrificing 12 cows. Three days after Aristaeus had carried out the old man's instructions, a swarm of bees flew out of one of the carcasses. Aristaeus bred this new strain of bees and was restored to his livelihood.

Old men of the sea

Many other cultures and mythologies feature sea gods who are portrayed as old men. The Celtic old man of the sea, for example, is Lir or Llyr; the Nordic version is Njörd. The theme of the magical ability to change shape is also found throughout mythology. In the case of Proteus, it may be connected to his role as a sea god, reflecting the changing and unpredictable nature of the sea itself. In modern English, the adjective *protean* is used to describe anyone or anything that can change its appearance or shape quickly and easily.

ANNA CLAYBOURNE

Bibliography

Homer, and Robert Fagles, trans. *The Iliad* and *The Odyssey*. New York: Penguin, 2009.

Ovid, and A. D. Melville, trans. *Metamorphoses*. New York: Oxford University Press, 2008.

SEE ALSO: Apollo; Nereus; Thetis; Zeus.

QUIRINUS

Quirinus is one of the most complex deities in the Roman pantheon. Unlike many other Roman gods, there are no known myths attached to him and he had little distinct personality of his own. However, the rituals attached to his worship formed an important part of the state religion of Rome.

Some historians believe that Quirinus was originally worshiped by the Sabines, an ancient Italian people who lived to the east of the Tiber River and were absorbed by the Romans in the third century BCE. This theory is based on the writings of Roman scholar Varro (116–27 BCE). However, many historians dispute this claim and argue that this theory was based on the mistaken association of the name of Quirinus with that of Cures, the chief Sabine city. Unlike gods such as Jupiter and Mars, Quirinus did not become identified with an equivalent Greek deity. Because of this, we have no body of myths involving him. Little was known about his appearance or personality, although we do know that he was sometimes depicted as a bearded man dressed in clerical clothes.

Quirinus's importance lies in the fact that he was one of only three gods served by a major flamen, the name given to a member of the oldest and most sacred of the Roman priestly colleges. Some scholars believe that the name derives from the same Indo-European source as the Sanskrit word *Brahman,* the name given to the priest class of ancient India. The post of flamen dates to the archaic era. The archaic era was the earliest period of Roman culture, stretching from around 1000 BCE to the beginning of the Roman Republic in 509 BCE. The flamen of Jupiter, the flamen of Mars, and the flamen of Quirinus are often called the priests of the "archaic triad." Each of the three divinities had his own special area of concern. Jupiter presided over legal and religious affairs, Mars's sphere of influence was war and the protection of the state, while

Right: A banquet scene from a Roman fresco found in the town of Pompeii, Italy. The ancient Romans looked to Quirinus to ensure an abundant harvest. The god had to be appeased if the city was to have a plentiful supply of food.

Left: The remains of Trajan's forum, built on the Quirinal Hill, Rome. The hill was named for Quirinus and was once the site of a temple dedicated to him.

Quirinus was concerned with the fruitfulness of the harvest and the overall well-being of the citizens.

Once a year, the three flamens, or flamines, came together at the shrine of Fides (the goddess of good faith), which was on the Capitoline Hill in front of the great Temple of Jupiter Optimus Maximus. Roman historian Livy (59 BCE–17 CE) describes the ritual, whose origin he attributes to the second Roman king, Numa Pompilius (c. 715–673 BCE). According to Livy, Numa "established the annual ritual of Fides and set it down that the flamines should go in a two-horse hooded carriage to the goddess's chapel, and that they should wrap their hands up to their fingers in preparation for making sacrifice as a sign that Good Faith must be kept." At the ritual's conclusion, the flamens unwrapped and clasped each other's hands in a gesture of agreement. This pledge was a symbolic act meant to mark the union of the three gods' spheres of influence and assure the gods' protection of the city of Rome.

Quirinus and the myrtle tree

The temple of Quirinus on the Quirinal Hill (also named for the god) was completed in 325 BCE. Roman poet Ovid (43 BCE–17 CE) describes the temple as being shaded by a large grove of trees. Pliny the Elder (23–79 CE) wrote that in front of the temple there grew two sacred myrtle trees. One was called the patricians' myrtle and the other, the plebeians'. The patricians and the plebeians were the two classes of citizens in Rome. According to Pliny, when the patricians were dominant in the state, their tree flourished but the plebeians' myrtle shriveled. When the plebeians grew stronger, the patrician myrtle began to fail and the plebeians' tree grew vigorously.

The flamen of Quirinus appeared on at least three other occasions during the Roman liturgical year. During the Consualia, a festival held on August 21, he made sacrifices at the underground altar of Consus, the god of the stored harvest. At the Robigalia (on April 25), the flamen performed a sacrifice meant to protect the crops from disease. Finally, at the Larentalia (on December 23), the priest of Quirinus made a public sacrifice to Acca Larentia, the mythical benefactress of Rome, who was sometimes said to be the stepmother of Romulus and Remus. Quirinus himself was sometimes identified with Romulus, the deified founder and first citizen of Rome. According to Livy, when Romulus died he ascended to heaven and became Quirinus.

Another festival, the Quirinalia (on February 17), belonged specifically to Quirinus, though there is no direct mention of his flamen in its rites. This festival was popularly known as the Feast of Fools. It allowed those "foolish" Romans who no longer knew their proper curia (city ward) to have a catch-up day on which they could perform rites connected to the making of bread. These rituals had been carried out earlier by the 30 Roman curiae in separate ceremonies on days posted by the chief officer of each group.

DANIEL P. HARMON

Bibliography

Turcan, Robert, and Antonia Nevill, trans. *The Gods of Ancient Rome: Religion in Everyday Life from Archaic to Imperial Times.* New York: Routledge, 2001.

SEE ALSO: Jupiter; Mars.

SATURN

Originally an ancient Roman god of agriculture, Saturn later became identified with Cronus, the Greek god who fled to Italy after he had been dethroned as ruler of the universe by Zeus. Saturn gave his name to a day of the week and to a planet of the solar system.

The pre-Roman god on whom Saturn is based may well have been an Etruscan agricultural deity. The origin of his name, *sator*, is thought to be the Etruscan word for "sower of seed." Saturn is usually depicted holding a farming implement. In many versions of the legend he is the husband of Ops and the father of Picus, another agricultural god. Other versions, however, place greater emphasis on his similarities to Cronus, and so make him the father of Jupiter, Juno, Ceres, Pluto, and Neptune. (Cronus's children were the equivalent Greek deities—respectively, Zeus, Hera, Demeter, Hades, and Poseidon.) When Saturn was banished from Mount Olympus, the home of the gods, by his son Jupiter, he took refuge in Latium, Italy, where the hospitable Janus shared his throne with the newcomer. Saturn established the village of Saturnia on the Capitoline Hill across the Tiber from Janus's settlement and introduced agriculture and winemaking to the district.

According to the most popular tradition, Saturn and his consort Ops—later identified with Rhea—were widely worshiped in Rome in the Golden Age, an idealized preclassical period during which there was thought to have

Below: This painting of Saturn forms part of Allegory of Divine Providence *by Italian artist Pietro da Cortona (1596–1669).*

Ops

Saturn's consort, Ops, is thought to have been assimilated into Roman mythology from an existing agricultural goddess of the ancient Sabine people of Italy. The Sabines believed that Ops could be invoked simply by touching the earth. Her festival on August 25, which was known in Latin as the Opeconsivia, was based on a ceremony that dated from no later than the early period, about 500 BCE, when Rome had kings. The Opeconsivia was traditionally held in a shrine within the Regia, the ancient royal palace, where the high priest of the cult, veiled in white, officiated with Ops's priestesses at a harvest ceremony that celebrated and gave thanks for the safe storage of the state's crops by Rome's king and his daughters.

In her other role as wife of Consus, Ops was worshiped as goddess of, among other things, horse racing, secret deliberations, sound advice, and the harvest. There are no surviving legends that feature both Consus and Saturn—there seems to have been no suggestion of adultery or even that Ops married Consus after Saturn had disappeared. The two stories probably originated in different parts of Rome or its territories: in the days before writing, those who knew one version would probably never have heard the other.

been universal peace, justice, and plenty. Saturn gave the people their first laws and taught them how to cultivate the soil. In art Saturn is often depicted with a scythe and billhook, implements used in grape growing, and he is often credited not just with introducing winemaking but also with inventing it.

Temple

During the reign of the last king of Rome, Tarquinius Superbus (ruled 534–510 BCE), work began on a temple to Saturn at the foot of the Capitoline Hill. The building was dedicated in 497 BCE. It was later used as Rome's treasury (Saturni Aerarium). The Tables of Law and Senate decrees were also kept there. The foundations of this temple and eight pillars still remain at the western end of the Forum.

In legend, Saturn disappeared from Rome at the end of the Golden Age: why he left and where he went, no one knows. Yet his cult did not decline: on the contrary, he was worshiped with even greater enthusiasm in his absence, probably as an expression of a desire to return to the good old days. For the greater part of each year the feet of the statue of Saturn in his temple were swathed in wool bandages to prevent the god from running away. The strapping was removed, however, and the effigy carried through the streets during the Saturnalia, the god's festival in December that developed into the most important social event of the Roman year.

Below: The second largest planet in the solar system is named Saturn for the Roman god of agriculture.

Saturnalia

The Saturnalia was a winter solstice carnival that commemorated Saturn's Golden Age, when freedom and equality reigned and violence and oppression were unknown. It probably began as a harvest celebration invoking blessings for winter-sown crops and encouraging the sun to return. It lost its rustic roots and changed radically, however, when it was adopted by city dwellers.

Originally the Saturnalia was a one-day festival, but when it was transplanted to an urban environment it began to stretch over several days, during which courts, schools, and shops were closed, executions and military exercises put on hold, and the streets thronged with merrymakers. Gambling was permitted, along with ribald speech and a wide range of dances, some suggestive, many lewd. All social distinctions were suspended for the duration of the Saturnalia as a reflection of the humane equality associated with Saturn's Golden Age. Masters and slaves changed places, and some moral codes were relaxed. There was much feasting and ceremonial exchanges of gifts—usually candles, small clay dolls, sprigs of holly, and wax fruits. A carnival king or prince (Saturnalicius Princeps) was chosen by lot from slaves or criminals and given full power to reign over the festivities. This "king" wore the ears of an ass, a tradition that developed from a confusion between Saturn and Egypt's ass-god, Seth. Saturn was said to have had a club made of holly. Thus, at the end of the festivities, the king would undergo a mock execution in which he was beaten with sprigs of the plant.

Originally the Saturnalia was held on December 19. When Julius Caesar (100–44 BCE) reformed the Roman calendar, the festival was moved two days earlier to December 17, but soon spread to include the following day. Later, December 19 and 20 became the Opalia, dedicated to Saturn's consort, Ops. To this four-day festival, Emperor Caligula (ruled 37–41 CE) added a fifth day, *dies juvenales*, honoring the city's youth. Eventually, the carnival expanded to a full seven days, December 17 to 23.

Left: This 12th-century carving on the walls of Ferrara Cathedral, Italy, depicts two revelers celebrating the Saturnalia.

By about the third century of the Common Era the Saturnalia had lost much of its former religious significance and become an all-purpose midwinter festival. It regained its spiritual aspect only after it was replaced in the calendar by the Christian festival of Christmas.

Darker aspect

The midwinter Saturnalia was a time of abundant food and wine, and boisterous behavior. In this manifestation, Saturn was a god of joy and plenty. He had another, less pleasant, aspect, however: the Saturn of astrology was the grim ruler of the sign of Capricorn, which begins at the winter solstice and runs through the first half of Janus's month, January. This Saturn was a dour lord of time and a stern, inflexible taskmaster. The English word *saturnine* is used to describe one who is grave or gloomy.

Saturn's consort

In addition to the Opalia, Ops was also honored as the wife of the earth god Consus with a festival held annually on August 25, the Opeconsivia (see box, page 262). As the mother of Jupiter, she was also honored with her son in the temple on the Capitoline Hill in Rome.

KATHLEEN JENKS

Bibliography

Bulfinch, Thomas. *Bulfinch's Mythology.* New York: Barnes & Noble, 2006.

Gibbon, Edward. *The Decline and Fall of the Roman Empire.* New York: Modern Library, 1983.

Turcan, Robert, and Antonia Nevill, trans. *The Gods of Ancient Rome: Religion in Everyday Life from Archaic to Imperial Times.* New York: Routledge, 2001.

SEE ALSO: Cronus; Hades; Hestia; Janus; Juno; Jupiter; Neptune; Plutus; Poseidon; Vesta; Zeus.

SELENE

Selene was the Greek goddess of the moon—she was sometimes considered to be the moon itself. Her name means "she who gleams." Selene and her sister Eos (the dawn) and their brother Helios (the sun) were the children of the Titans Theia and Hyperion. In some myths Selene was the wife of Helios and in others she was his daughter. She was a descendant of Gaia (the earth) and Uranus (the heavens) and is often counted among the primary, elemental powers in the universe, along with other nature deities such as Night and Ocean.

The moon was a powerful force in ancient Greek thought: its different phases set the rhythm for nature and gave order to the Greek calendar of festivals. The Carneia, for example, a great annual festival at Sparta, always concluded under the full moon. The time of the waxing moon was thought particularly favorable to growth and to any new enterprises; the new moon therefore was believed to be the best time to get married. According to fifth-century-BC poet Empedocles, the waning moon indicated the time when women experienced the menstruation cycle. The moon was also believed to have been the cause of madness. This belief endures in the word *lunacy,* from the Latin word *luna,* which means "moon." The moon's power of control also endures in the expression *moonstruck,* which describes the state of a deranged person. A gem called moonstone, meanwhile, was a protection against this affliction; amulets

Right: This third-century-CE sculpture is of the Greek goddess Selene. A crescent symbol is set upon her head, indicating her aspect as moon goddess.

Above: Selene is depicted in this third-century-CE Roman mosaic with the crescent moon behind her. She is about to wake her lover Endymion from his sleep.

to protect against evil were also made in the form of the moon or with one of its many names inscribed on them. Some ancient Greeks considered the moon to be the source of dew, so in various myths Herse ("dew") was the daughter of Selene. Plutarch (c. 46–120 CE) reported that moonlight threw young children into convulsions; that those who fell asleep in moonlight awoke stunned and hardly able to get up; that moonlight rotted wood; and that childbirth was easiest during the full moon—leading Selene to be worshiped as a goddess of childbirth.

Greek philosopher Plato (c. 428–c. 348 BCE) asserted that all humankind bowed down to the rising and setting sun, and to the moon. However, there is little evidence that Greek worship of the moon was practiced before the Roman Empire (30 BCE–476 CE), when it became an aspect of many goddesses. This is in contrast to western Asia at that time, where moon goddesses were leading figures in pantheons. Men, the Phrygian moon goddess, for example, was worshiped in many places in Anatolia (modern Turkey.)

There is a hymn dedicated to Selene in a collection known as the Homeric Hymns (scholars dispute that Homer [c. ninth–eighth century BCE] wrote these hymns, suggesting instead that they merely echoed his style). In the hymn Selene is described as a winged deity, crowned with gold, rising in her shining garments from the ocean and driving her horse-drawn chariot across the sky as "a portent and a sign to mortals." In visual art she is also frequently represented in motion, riding on a horse or sometimes on a goat (a creature traditionally associated with Hecate, goddess of magic and the underworld), or driving a chariot drawn by horses or by bulls. On the base of the great statue of Zeus at Olympia, carved by Greek sculptor Phidias (fl. c. 490–430 BCE), Selene is depicted riding on a horse opposite Helios, who is in his chariot. Selene's emblem is the crescent, which she wears most often on or behind her head; sometimes she stands upon it.

Selene's lovers

Selene was thought of as a desirable and fertile young woman, and there are a number of accounts of her sexual adventures. According to one myth, Pan, the god of shepherds, seduced Selene. He gave her a gift of a fine sheep's fleece, then he and Selene shared a cave on Mount Lycaon in Arcadia. At Nemea, home of the Nemean Games, Selene was known as the mother of the local goddess Nemea, who had created the fearsome Nemean Lion—a monster Heracles had to kill and skin for his first labor. A traditional myth in Athens recounted that Selene had a child by Zeus named Pandia. According to the genealogy of Athens, Pandia was the wife of Antiochus, a local hero who gave his name to one of the 10 Athenian tribes. Pandia was also the name of an Athenian festival held in honor of Pandia and her father, Zeus. In another myth Selene was the mother of Musaeus, a legendary Greek bard. One of two legendary seers was thought to be the father, either Eumolpus or Antiphemus.

The most famous of Selene's lovers, however, was Endymion. In one version of the myth he is said to have been herding cattle when Selene took him for her lover. Most versions agree that he was in an eternal sleep inside a cave, however. In some versions the youth pursued the goddess Hera, and his eternal sleep was a punishment from Zeus, who was Hera's brother and husband; in another version Zeus offered him the privilege of choosing how he was to die, and he selected eternal sleep; in another account Selene fell in love with Endymion and asked Zeus to give him immortality and eternal youth, so Zeus put him into an eternal sleep. Once Endymion was asleep, Selene occasionally visited the cave and roused him to make love. Ancient Greeks believed that when the moon was eclipsed, Selene was in the cave with Endymion. They had 50 daughters who were often interpreted as the 50 lunar months of the four-year cycle that governed many of the great festivals—for example, the Olympic Games.

Endymion was frequently represented in art, most notably as the subject of a long poem by John Keats (1795–1821) titled *Endymion*. The myth of Endymion inspired many 19th-century artists and is also a popular theme of modern painting and poetry.

Selene and magic

Some ancient peoples believed the moon was inhabited by spirits; neo-Platonists believed that the moon was the "other earth" where purified souls go when they die. Selene was also a patron of magic and witchcraft; magic herbs, for example, were usually collected and dried by moonlight. It was a familiar popular belief as early as the classical period that witches could bring the moon down from the sky. Selene is invoked in ancient witchcraft, particularly in love magic; Hellenistic and Roman authors associated her with the goddess of magic, Hecate. She is invoked along with Hecate at the beginning of a Hellenistic poem on love magic by Theocritus (c. 310–250 BCE) in which the refrain is: "Take thought for my love, and whence it comes, Lady Moon."

Witches

Various definitions of witches and witchcraft have been put forward by anthropologists. Today, a witch is generally seen as a woman who has supernatural powers and uses them for evil purposes. However, men have also been seen as capable of practicing witchcraft. Similarly, at various times in history, witches have been believed to be able to use their powers for good as well as evil. Also, although witches have been widely persecuted, especially in Europe, in many ancient cultures they held important positions in society.

The persecution of witches arose from early religious policies enacted by the Roman Catholic and other Christian churches toward the end of the Roman Empire. Many religious doctrines at this time taught that both women and nature religions were evil and dangerous. The term *pagan*, which initially referred to rural Romans, came to be used derisively to describe all non-Christians.

From the 12th century CE onward, the Roman Catholic Church attempted to enforce orthodoxy throughout Europe. It took great steps to stamp out all non-Christian religious practices, which were universally denounced as witchcraft. Some sources record that during witchhunts and the Spanish Inquisition (1233–1734), more than 150,000 people were accused of practicing witchcraft and burned to death—a period known as the Burning Times.

Witchcraft reemerged during the late 18th century in a secretive form, and it still exists today. Scholars, poets, and writers, such as William Butler Yeats (1865–1939), drew extensively upon Celtic, Greek, and Roman mythology in their works, invoking deities such as Isis, Hecate, and Selene.

Above: The moon had an important role in witchcraft, and in this illustration it oversees a witch dance.

One book on magic begins: "Come to me, dear mistress, three-faced Selene." In art Selene has often been represented as part of a triad. For example, Selene, Helios, and Eos were represented in the form of a body with three heads. Another book prescribes making a magic image of Selene—from potter's clay, sulfur, and the blood of a spotted goat—as an effective love charm. In texts about magic Selene sometimes sends dreams to people in their sleep.

Selene was involved in mysteries—rites that were performed to initiate people into a cult or to explain different stages of life, such as sexual maturity, marriage, and death. Roman politician Cicero (106–43 BCE) called Selene the mother of the Orphic Dionysus, who was often celebrated in mysteries. Selene played some part in the mysteries at Eleusis, where it was recorded that a representation of Selene was given by the Eleusinian priest and placed on the altar.

Left: This glazed plate is decorated with an illustration of Selene mounted on a podium, surrounded by her worshipers.

Other moon goddesses

By a process called syncretism, attributes from some deities were passed on to other deities. Often this occurred when one empire defeated another and an old pantheon was replaced by a new set of gods. Deities were not usually forgotten or made entirely obsolete, but were assimilated into the new pantheon and adopted new names. Sometimes conquest was not necessary to start this process, but a cultural shift would cause one deity to be favored over another. In this way Greeks replaced Selene and worshiped Artemis as moon goddess. Likewise Romans worshiped Diana as moon goddess after Luna lost favor. Originally Luna was the equivalent of Selene.

Scholars suggest that changes in Selene's identity originated in the fifth century BCE, and they point to Aeschylus's plays as a source: in one play Selene is the child of Zeus and Leto, who were usually the parents of Artemis. Artemis also appears in some representations with the crescent on her head, a symbol that was usually associated with Selene. Mostly the changes are attributed to Greek and Roman writers during the Roman Empire who consistently refer to Artemis and Diana as moon goddesses and give little mention to Selene. Thus in the play *The Golden Ass* by Apuleius (c. 124–c. 170 CE), the hero prays to "the Moon goddess, sole sovereign of mankind" and begs for her help, whether she calls herself Ceres, Venus, Artemis, or Proserpina. She appears to him and tells him she is Nature, the universal mother, also known as Pessinuntica, Mother of the gods, Artemis, Aphrodite, Proserpina, Dictynna, Corn Mother, Juno, Bellona, Rhamnubia, Queen of Heaven, and in Egypt by her real name, which is Isis. Luna or Selene thus becomes one of the many names for the goddess of the moon.

JAMES M. REDFIELD

Bibliography

Aeschylus, and Philip Vellacott, trans. *Prometheus Bound and Other Plays*. London: Penguin, 1973.
Apuleius, and Joel C. Relihan, trans. *The Golden Ass*. Indianapolis, IN: Hackett, 2007.

SEE ALSO: Artemis; Diana; Dionysus; Eos; Gaia; Hecate; Helios; Juno; Pan; Uranus; Venus; Zeus.

THETIS

Thetis, a Nereid, was the mother of Achilles, the greatest warrior in Greek mythology. Her role in Achilles' story, and in other myths, reveals her as an archetypal mother figure.

The 50 daughters of the sea god Nereus and the sea nymph Doris were known as the Nereids. The beautiful Nereids lived in the Aegean Sea, which they guarded while also protecting sailors from harm. For example, they helped the Greek Argonauts sail safely past

the twin dangers of the monster Scylla and the whirlpool Charybdis on their way back from Colchis, where they had won the Golden Fleece. Thetis was the best known of the Nereids, and was exceptionally beautiful. In addition, like her father Nereus and the sea god Proteus, she had the ability to change shape into whatever she wanted.

Marriage to a mortal

Both Zeus, the king of the gods, and Poseidon, the most powerful sea god, loved Thetis. However, when the goddess Themis foretold that the Nereid would have a son who would be more powerful than his father, they left her alone—neither deity wanted a son who might overthrow him. Instead, the gods decided that Thetis should marry Peleus, king of Phthia in northeast Greece. Thetis, repelled by the idea of marrying a mere mortal, resisted Peleus by changing her shape. However, the king prayed to the gods for help and learned from Proteus that to control Thetis he must hold her tightly, whatever form she took. Peleus heeded this advice and won Thetis's hand in marriage.

Thetis and Peleus's wedding set in motion the chain of events that led to the Trojan War. They invited all the gods and goddesses to the celebration, except for the unpleasant Eris, goddess of discord. Eris turned up regardless and threw a golden apple among the crowd, marked, "To the fairest." The goddesses Aphrodite, Athena, and Hera, each thinking herself the fairest, fought over the apple. Eventually they asked the Trojan prince Paris to judge for them. He chose Aphrodite, who rewarded him with the love of Helen, the most beautiful woman in the world. Helen, however, was already married to the Greek king Menelaus. When Paris ran away with her, the Greeks declared war on Troy.

Thetis and Achilles

Soon after marrying Peleus, Thetis gave birth to their son, Achilles. She loved him dearly and could not bear the thought that, since the child's father was mortal, he might not live forever like her. She also knew that her son was fated to die in battle at Troy, but desperately wanted to

Left: This portrait of Zeus and Thetis was painted by French artist Jean-Auguste-Dominique Ingres (1780–1867).

Above: This painting, by 18th-century French artist Antoine Rogat Borel, depicts Thetis immersing Achilles in the Styx River.

prevent this outcome. Thetis tried to burn away Achilles' mortality in a fire, but she was disrupted by Peleus, who thought she was murdering their child. Furious at her husband's intervention, Thetis returned to live in the sea. In another account, told by Roman poet Statius (45–96 CE), Thetis made Achilles invulnerable by dipping him in the underworld Styx River. The boy retained a weak spot, however: his heel, which his mother had held while dipping him in the water.

Despite her return to the sea, Thetis never stopped watching over her son. When Achilles was nine, the seer Calchas predicted that the Greeks could not win the Trojan War unless Achilles fought with them. So Thetis disguised her son as a girl and took him to the island of Scyros, where she hoped he would be well hidden. Her plan failed: the Greeks discovered him, and Achilles set off for Troy.

Thetis often intervened in the Trojan War to support her son—interventions that were described by Greek poet Homer (c. ninth–eighth century BCE) in his epic the *Iliad*. When Achilles argued with the Greek general Agamemnon and withdrew from the fighting, Thetis persuaded Zeus to give the Trojans the upper hand to teach the general a lesson. As a result of Achilles' refusal to fight, his friend Patroclus went into battle disguised as Achilles, only to be killed by the Trojan Hector. Patroclus's death spurred

Achilles to rejoin the war, but Hector had stolen his armor from his dead companion's body. Thetis went to Hephaestus, the blacksmith of the gods, and asked him to make new armor for her son. Finally, when Achilles was killed by Paris, Thetis and the other Nereids rose out of the sea and came to Troy to mourn him.

Mother figure

Besides being Achilles' doting mother, Thetis cared for other gods and heroes when they needed her. For example, when Hera threw Hephaestus from heaven in her disgust at his lameness, Thetis and the goddess Eurynome rescued him. When Dionysus, god of wine, dived into the sea after being chased by a mortal, Thetis comforted him.

Thetis was an example of a typical character found in myths—the loving mother figure. Her story also explores the concept of destiny and whether it can be altered. Greek mythology contains many instances of people trying to avoid the fate predicted for them, but somehow, as in the case of Achilles, it almost always comes true.

ANNA CLAYBOURNE

Bibliography

Hamilton, Edith. *Mythology: Timeless Tales of Gods and Heroes.* New York: Grand Central, 2011.
Homer, and Robert Fagles, trans. *The Iliad.* New York: Penguin, 2009.

SEE ALSO: Dionysus; Hephaestus; Nereus.

TITANS

In Greek mythology the Titans were the first generation of gods to come into being after the creation of the basic features of the cosmos. For a time they ruled the universe. However, they were ultimately overthrown by their successors, the Olympians.

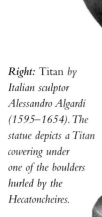

Right: Titan by Italian sculptor Alessandro Algardi (1595–1654). The statue depicts a Titan cowering under one of the boulders hurled by the Hecatoncheires.

According to Greek poet Hesiod (fl. 800 BCE), who wrote an account of the origins of the universe in his epic poem *Theogony*, the first entity to come into being was Chaos, a great void into which all matter would subsequently be fitted. It was followed by Gaia (the earth), Eros (love), and Tartarus. Tartarus was a dark place located far beneath the earth that would later serve as a great prison for gods and other immortal beings who could not be killed. Gaia, who was personified as a goddess, then gave birth to Pontus (the oceans), Ourea (the mountains), and Uranus (the sky). After she had created the basic physical characteristics of the world, Gaia then mated with Uranus to create a whole generation of actual beings. These were the 12 Titans and six monsters: the three Cyclopes and the three Hecatoncheires (or Hundred-Handed Ones). The Cyclopes were one-eyed giants, while the Hecatoncheires were creatures with 50 heads and 50 pairs of arms each. There were six male and six female Titans. In order of birth, the brothers were Oceanus, Coeus, Crius, Hyperion, Iapetus, and Cronus; the sisters were Theia, Rhea, Themis, Mnemosyne, Phoebe, and Tethys. Some of the offspring of the first generation were also generally considered as belonging to the Titans, in particular Prometheus, son of Hyperion, and Atlas, son of Iapetus.

The overthrow of Uranus

Uranus, the first ruler of the world, was a cruel king and a jealous father. He prevented his children from being born, forcing them back into the depths of Gaia's womb. Gaia was appalled by this, so she created a sickle made of adamant (an unbreakable stone, often identified with diamond) and suggested to her children that they punish Uranus for his outrageous behavior. All were too frightened to speak, with the exception of the youngest son, Cronus, who offered his help. Cronus and Gaia set up an ambush for Uranus as he returned to Gaia as usual at nightfall. While Uranus lay on Gaia, Cronus came out from hiding and castrated his father with the sickle, tossing his testicles into the sea. From the blood spilled during this act, the Giants were born.

As a result of this uprising, the Titans became rulers of the universe. From them came all subsequent generations of gods. The most important of the Titans' offspring were the children of Cronus and Rhea, a group of gods that would later be known as the Olympians, after their home on Mount Olympus.

The Olympians had a troubled entry into the world. Cronus proved to be just as bad a father as Uranus had been. Whenever Rhea gave birth to a child, Cronus swallowed the infant whole. He did this because he feared that one of his children would overthrow him, just as he had overthrown his own father. Finally, Rhea gave birth to Zeus, whom she hid from Cronus. The child grew up in hiding on the island of Crete. When Zeus reached maturity, he conspired with his mother, Rhea, and his grandmother, Gaia, and together they gave Cronus a potion that forced him to disgorge all the children he had swallowed.

The Titanomachia

After he had been reunited with his brothers and sisters— the gods Hades and Poseidon and the goddesses Hera, Demeter, and Hestia—Zeus led the Olympians in a great battle against Cronus and the other Titans to determine who would rule the universe. All but two of the Titans fought against the Olympians:

Right: Titan Struck by Lightning *by French sculptor François Dumont (1688–1726). Zeus's thunderbolts were important weapons in the battle between the Titans and the Olympians.*

only Oceanus and Prometheus joined the side of Zeus. The clash, known as the Titanomachia, lasted for 10 years. The two sides were evenly matched, but the tide of the war turned in favor of the Olympians when Zeus enlisted the help of the Cyclopes and the Hecatoncheires, who had been imprisoned in Tartarus by Cronus. Zeus killed Campe, the monster that guarded these creatures, and freed them. In gratitude both the Cyclopes and the Hecatoncheires joined the war on the side of Zeus. The Hecatoncheires used their great strength to hurl huge boulders at the Titans. The Cyclopes, meanwhile, helped the Olympians by making a trident for Poseidon, a cap of invisibility for Hades, and thunder and lightning for Zeus. The Olympians used these gifts in their struggle and eventually vanquished the Titans.

All but one of the Titans who had fought against Zeus were banished to Tartarus, where they were confined for the rest of eternity. The sole exception was Atlas,

Above: Fall of the Titans *by Peter Paul Rubens (1577–1640) depicts the final stages of the Titanomachia.*

whose special punishment was to hold up the heavens on his shoulders. The punishment inflicted on the Titans greatly angered Gaia, who persuaded the Giants to rise up against the Olympians. The result was another mighty conflict, the Gigantomachia, which the Olympians won only with the help of the mortal hero Heracles.

The ancient Greeks saw the Titanomachia and the Gigantomachia as two stages of the same struggle, a conflict between modern forces of order and an old regime of a more brutal, primitive, and disorderly kind. It is characteristic of the difference between the Titans and the Olympians that a key element in the defeat of Cronus and the Titans was cunning and intelligence. When Cronus demanded his latest newborn child from Rhea, she deceived him by handing him a rock wrapped in swaddling clothes. Similarly, Cronus was tricked into drinking the potion that brought all his children back into the world. The defeat of Cronus was thus a triumph of subtlety and cunning over brute force and ignorance.

Mounts Olympus and Othrys

According to Hesiod, when the battle took place between the Titans and the gods, the two sides were based on different mountains. The Titans lived on Mount Othrys, while Zeus and his siblings dwelled on Mount Olympus. Both mountains are real. Olympus is situated in northern Greece, just west of the Gulf of Thérmai, while Othrys lies around 75 miles to the south. Of the two mountains, Olympus is by far the higher. It stands at 9,570 feet (2,917 m). By contrast, Othrys is only 5,663 feet (1,726 m) high.

The ancient Greeks believed that Mount Olympus was at the center of their country, which was, in turn, at the center of the world. Because Olympus seemed to reach the clouds, the Greeks equated its summit with heaven. According to Greek epic poet Homer (c. ninth–eighth century BCE), "many-peaked Olympus" was in a state of perpetual calm, undisturbed by storms or rain. The chief gods and goddesses met there to settle the affairs of humans. Each of the main Greek gods and goddesses was assigned a dwelling place along Olympus's slopes.

Children of the Titans

Right: This marble statue from the third century BCE depicts the Titan Themis, who was the mother of both the Horae (the seasons) and the Moirai (the Fates).

Among them, the 12 Titans produced thousands of offspring. Many of them were important figures in Greek mythology in their own right. Iapetus, for example, was the father of Prometheus, Epimetheus, and Atlas. Prometheus gave humankind the gift of fire, while Epimetheus was responsible for introducing sorrow and disease to the world by accepting from Zeus the gift of the woman Pandora. As a punishment for his part in the Titanomachia, Atlas was condemned to carry the weight of the heavens on his shoulders for eternity. The descendants of Epimetheus and Prometheus also played significant roles in Greek myth. Deucalion, son of Prometheus, and Pyrrha, daughter of Epimetheus, were the only humans to survive the great flood, and were thus the ancestors of the entire human race. Their son Hellen was the first Greek.

Other Titans were the ancestors of major natural phenomena. Oceanus, the oldest of the Titans, was father of 3,000 river gods and 3,000 water nymphs. All of the major rivers of Greece were said to be his sons. Crius was the grandfather of the four winds: Zephyrus, Boreas, Notus, and Eurus; while Hyperion married his sister Theia to produce the sun god Helios, the moon goddess Selene, and Eos, goddess of the dawn. Two of the female Titans mated with Zeus to produce other important phenomena: Themis gave birth to both the Horae (the seasons) and the Moirai (the Fates), while Mnemosyne (Memory) begat the nine Muses.

The Titanomachia in art

The Titanomachia and the Gigantomachia were represented on numerous monuments in Greece. An important example was the gold and ivory statue of Athena, sculpted by Phidias (fl. c. 490–430 BCE), which stood inside the Parthenon on the Acropolis in Athens. The Gigantomachia was represented on the inside of the warrior goddess's great shield. Also depicted in this work were the battle fought by the Olympians against the Amazons (the Amazonomachia), an image of which was carved on the outside of the shield, and the Olympians' battle against the centaurs (the Centauromachia), which appeared on the goddess's sandals. Like the Titans and Giants, the Amazons and the centaurs were forces of disorder. Thus they were threats to both the Olympian regime and the human world. Depictions of the Titanomachia and the Gigantomachia frequently featured the goddess Athena. An illustration of Athena fighting in the wars featured prominently on versions of a famous robe that were woven every four years and paraded through the streets of Athens as part of her great city festival, the Panathenaia.

Zagreus and the Titans

One famous myth involving the Titans is the story of the young god Zagreus, who was slain and dismembered by them and later reborn as the Olympian deity Dionysus. Zagreus was worshiped by the adherents of the mystery cult Orphism. The main source for Zagreus's story is the *Dionysiaca*, an epic poem written in the fifth century CE by Nonnus, a Greek writer who lived in Panopolis, Egypt.

During the Titanomachia the goddess Demeter hid her daughter Persephone in a cave for safety. However, she was found by Zeus, who took the form of a snake and raped her. Persephone became pregnant and later gave birth to a son, Zagreus. The infant son of Zeus immediately took his place on his father's throne and began to play with Zeus's thunderbolts. However, Zeus's wife, Hera, was consumed with jealousy and persuaded the Titans to kill Zagreus.

Disguising their faces with chalk, the Titans came to Mount Olympus and attacked the child. Zagreus responded by changing into many different shapes, taking on the appearance of his father Zeus, the Titan Cronus, a newborn baby, a lion, and a bull. However, these efforts could not save him. The Titans killed the infant, cut his body to shreds, and ate the pieces. One part of Zagreus's body remained, however: the heart. Zeus took it and turned it into a potion, which he gave to his mortal lover Semele. Semele drank the potion and in due course became pregnant. Zagreus was thus born again, this time as the god of wine, Dionysus.

In a slight variation on the usual account of the Titanomachia, the Orphics believed that Zeus then struck the Titans with his thunderbolts, turning them to dust. Humankind was created from the ashes. According to Orphic mythology, this accounted for the good and evil that was present in every human being. The evil was derived from the ashes of the bodies of the wicked Titans, while the good came from the remnants of the body of Zagreus that they had eaten.

Another famous depiction of the struggles was found in Pergamon, a city in Asia Minor (part of modern Turkey). There, King Eumenes II (ruled c. 197–c. 160 BCE) built the Altar of Zeus, a monument to national pride and Pergamene achievement. The friezes that decorated the altar depicted the deeds of Telephus, the mythic founder of the city, and the great battles of the Titanomachia and the Gigantomachia. Here again the Titans and Giants symbolized disruption and disorder, standing in contrast to their successors, the Olympian gods, who represented power, success, and civilization.

Etymology and significance

Scholars are divided as to the derivation of the name *Titan*. Some believe it comes from the Greek verb *titaino*, meaning "to stretch" or "to strain," because the Titans had to exert themselves so much in order to overthrow Uranus. Other accounts, however, suggest that the word *Titan* comes from the verb *tino*, meaning "to punish," because the Titans punished the wickedness of their father and would themselves be punished in turn.

At one time, many historians believed that the Titans were the gods of the peoples who lived in the Balkan Peninsula before the Greek-speaking Indo-Europeans migrated there. According to this theory, the Titanomachia could be seen as a mythic account of how the Olympian gods of the Greeks took over from the pre-Greek Titans. This interpretation has largely been rejected, however. An almost identical sequence of events has been identified in the mythologies of other parts of the Mediterranean and western Asia. It seems likely that the similarities are due to the fact that Greek culture was profoundly influenced by contacts with Mesopotamian culture.

In modern English the noun *titan* and the adjective *titanic* have come to be used to describe almost anything that is exceptionally large or overpowering. Hence, what was in its time the largest passenger steamship ever built was named *Titanic*. *Titan* is also the name given to an important series of U.S. rockets, some of which have been used to power NASA's space probes. The largest moon of the planet Saturn, meanwhile, is also called Titan. A number of Saturn's other large moons—Tethys, Rhea, Iapetus, Hyperion, and Phoebe—are named for individual members of the first generation of Titans, while three of Saturn's smaller moons—Atlas, Prometheus, and Epimetheus—are named for members of the next generation of Titans.

ANTHONY BULLOCH

Bibliography

Graves, Robert. *The Greek Myths*. New York: Penguin, 1993.
Hesiod, and M. L. West, trans. *Theogony* and *Works and Days*. New York: Oxford University Press, 2008.

SEE ALSO: Atlas; Cronus; Dionysus; Gaia; Mnemosyne; Oceanus; Prometheus; Uranus; Zeus.

TRITON

According to ancient Greek poet Hesiod (fl. 800 BCE), Triton was the son of Poseidon, god of the sea, and of Amphitrite, the sea queen. One myth claims that he lived with his parents in a golden palace at the bottom of the sea, and that he slept on a bed of sponges.

Triton was one of several minor Greek sea deities, including Nereus, Phorcys, Proteus, and Glaucus. Some of these sea gods assumed human form, but Triton was represented as a sea monster. He had a man's upper body and a head, which was usually bearded, and a long fish tail—occasionally this was divided into two flukes.

Triton is sometimes associated with centaurs, since in some Roman art he is represented with the forelegs of a horse. In Roman poetry Triton is well known for the hollow conch shell which he blows like a trumpet; the sound of his conch could drive back the waves, raise rocks and islands, and even frighten the giants when they were at war with the gods. In the *Aeneid* by Virgil (70–19 BCE), Triton was so proud of his musical talent that he became jealous of Misenus, the trumpeter of the Roman hero Aeneas. As Aeneas's ship approached the Bay of Naples, Triton drowned Misenus.

There are two versions of a traditional myth about Triton. According to one version, women from Tanagra in Boeotia came down to the sea for purification before the rites of Dionysus, god of wine. As they swam there, Triton disturbed them. They called to Dionysus for help, and he fought and defeated Triton. According to the other version,

Below: Swiss artist Arnold Böcklin (1827–1901) painted the sea god Triton aiding a Nereid. At right, a cupid appears in pursuit of the couple.

Right: Triton is represented drinking from his conch shell in this famous fountain in Rome, Italy, sculpted by Italian artist Gian Lorenzo Bernini (1598–1680).

Right: Triton is represented drinking from his conch shell in this famous fountain in Rome, Italy, sculpted by Italian artist Gian Lorenzo Bernini (1598–1680).

Triton lay in ambush on the coast of Tanagra, waiting for cattle to be driven along the shore. He seized some of the animals as they passed; he also attacked small boats. The citizens of Tanagra placed a bowl of wine by the shore and Triton was attracted by the smell; he drank the wine and fell asleep by the sea. A man then came with an ax and cut off his head. Legend has it that in Hellenistic times the headless body of Triton was displayed at a temple in Tanagra.

In another myth Triton is associated with Libya and with a great Libyan lake that the Greeks called Lake Tritonis. Pindar (c. 522–c. 438 BCE) recounts that Jason and the Argonauts arrived there after a tidal wave swept their ship inland. Triton disguised himself as a local king called Euphemus and, welcoming the sailors, gave them a clod of earth as a gift. Greek historian Herodotus (c. 484–425 BCE) claimed that Triton received a golden tripod from the Argonauts, and that in return he showed them the way out of the lake to the sea. On the way to the sea, Triton took the clod of earth from the Argonauts and dropped it into the sea—it became the island of Thera. In this legend the magical creation of Thera may reflect how the Greeks colonized Libya: they used Thera as a stepping stone to reach the mainland. Herodotus mentions that on the island there was a sanctuary and an altar that were dedicated to Triton, but there remains little evidence of worship of Triton elsewhere. Scholars speculate that it is possible that Herodotus received his version from Greeks in Libya, who attributed qualities of a local deity to Triton.

Triton in art

In Etruscan, Hellenistic Greek, and Roman art and literature (and occasionally in earlier examples), Triton is often pluralized; a similar process happened with Cupid, Roman god of love, who was often transformed into a number of figures called cupids. In some forms of art, and especially in mosaics, tritons are depicted with Poseidon or other marine deities; and numerous tritons sometimes appear alongside cupids.

In Athenian art a frequent representation including Triton portrays an incident for which there is no literary source: a struggle between Triton and Heracles. Heracles had been charged to obtain the golden apples of the Hesperides for his 11th labor. He had to subdue the sea god Nereus so that he could learn the way to the garden of the Hesperides, where the golden apples grew. Heracles' struggle with Nereus is represented a number of times in early art. From the mid-sixth century BCE onward, however, Nereus was replaced by Triton. In some examples, Nereus appears as a third character in the scene—as a witness to the battle. Some scholars suggest that cultural changes brought about by migration or invasion could have been responsible for introducing new deities, or replacing older gods and goddesses. It is uncertain why Athenian artists substituted Triton for Nereus, however.

For Romans, tritons became a frequent pictorial motif in mosaics, cameos, sculptured reliefs, terra-cottas, bronzes, and most other media. Some representations of tritons were female. In Etruscan art tritons were sometimes depicted as male and female members of couples.

Although Triton is rarely mentioned in mythology, he was always considered to be a personification of the waves and the power of the ocean.

JAMES M. REDFIELD

Bibliography
Hesiod, and M. L. West, trans. *Theogony* and *Works and Days.* New York: Oxford University Press, 2008.
Virgil, and Robert Fagles, trans. *The Aeneid. New York:* Penguin, 2009.

SEE ALSO: Eros; Poseidon.

TYCHE

Tyche was the Greek goddess of chance and was known as Fortuna by the Romans. According to Greek poet Hesiod (fl. 800 BCE), Tyche was the daughter of the Titans Oceanus and Tethys, although other writers claimed that Zeus (king of the gods) was her father.

The ocean has always been notoriously unpredictable, and its mythological inhabitants shared in its fickle nature. Tyche, whose name can be translated as "chance," "fortune," "fate," "success," "destiny," or "luck," belonged to a small group of deities such as Eros (god of love) whose names described their functions. While Tyche was recognized as a goddess fairly early, her personality did not develop until quite late, during the Hellenistic period (323–30 BCE). At that time cities and officials adopted Tyche as their patron deity, and people made dedications and sacrifices at her shrines.

Tyche was associated primarily with good luck. She was depicted as a female wearing a turreted crown and carrying a horn of plenty in one hand and a ship's rudder in the other. The crown of city walls symbolized the fact that she directed cities' destinies, the horn represented the prosperity she brought, and the rudder symbolized fortune. Tyche's rise in popularity after the classical period (in Athens this was about 479–338 BCE) signified the extent to which the Greeks believed that chance governed their lives.

The role of fate in the Greek world

Like most people, the Greeks desired to understand their world, both to control it and to render it less arbitrary and frightening. The Olympian gods were the earliest systematic attempt to account for everyday events.

Tyche was the default explanation for anything that was not attributable to these deities. It was no contradiction for *Tyche* to mean both "chance" and "fate." In Greek thought, fate was unstoppable. Fortune was the revelation

Above: Archaeologists date the construction of this colossal stone head of Tyche to c. 50 BCE. It stands on the slope of Mount Nimrod in Turkey.

of that fate, and destiny was the fulfillment of that fortune. When fortune was beneficial, it was called luck or success, and when not, it was chance.

Tyche in literature

While early writers sometimes personified Tyche as a goddess, most of the time they referred to an impersonal *tyche*. One of the earliest mentions of Tyche was in the 12th Olympian ode of Greek poet Pindar (c. 522–c. 438 BCE), which celebrated an athletic victory. In the poem

catastrophe. She was often addressed euphemistically, as if by naming her "kindly" or "savior" she might be persuaded to bring good luck instead of bad.

Greek comic dramatist Menander (c. 342–c. 292 BCE) called Tyche a blind goddess, although this description may have referred more to her indiscriminate ways than to her physicality. Tyche delivers the prologue in Menander's play *The Shield*, announcing that she plans a surprise ending.

Hellenistic historian Polybius (c. 200–c. 118 BCE) used Tyche to explain otherwise inexplicable historical events. Tyche also presided over human affairs in Greek novels, which date from the Roman period (after 30 BCE). In these, Tyche personified the chaotic world: pirate raids, slavery, shipwrecks, mistaken identities, and chance occurrences. The novels are equally ambivalent about how to cope with Tyche. In some, another god overrides her mischief; others reduce her to the expression "by chance." Tyche represented the unknown, and people alternately appeased and disparaged her as human hopes rose and fell.

Philosophical approaches to Tyche

Greek philosopher Plato (c. 428–c. 348 BCE) identified Tyche as the spontaneous cause of divine actions, and his pupil Aristotle (384–322 BCE) conceived of her impersonally as spontaneity itself. The philosophical schools that grew out of Platonic and Aristotelian thought, notably Stoicism and Epicureanism, dealt particularly with the problem of chance. The Stoics defined Tyche as "a cause unclear to human understanding," suggesting that her workings would be logical to a higher intelligence. The Epicureans adopted a mechanistic view of the universe— in their view there was no such thing as chance, and even seemingly random occurrences could be explained by the movement of matter.

There were three famous ancient Greek statues of Tyche, now lost—two by Praxiteles (370–330 BCE) and one by Eutychides (third century BCE).

KATHERYN CHEW

Pindar called Tyche the daughter of Zeus, unlike Hesiod's genealogy, which made Tyche and Zeus cousins. Perhaps Pindar wished to imply that Zeus had some sway over Tyche, and that the universe was under his control and was not subject to the whims of chance.

Tyche was entirely absent from the epics of Greek poet Homer (c. ninth–eighth century BCE), simply because there was no need for a goddess of chance in Homer's world—everything in his stories developed under the careful providence of other deities.

In the Greek dramas, Tyche occasionally engineered unexpected outcomes—an unforeseen reprieve or a sudden

Bibliography

Bulfinch, Thomas. *Bulfinch's Mythology.* New York: Barnes & Noble, 2006.
Howatson, M. C. *The Oxford Companion to Classical Literature.* New York: Oxford University Press, 2005.

SEE ALSO: Oceanus; Zeus.

TYPHON

In Greek mythology, Typhon was the youngest son of Gaia. He was also the personification of volcanic forces.

Typhon was the youngest son of Gaia (Earth) and Tartarus (the underworld). Fire shone forth from his eyes, red-hot lava poured from his gaping mouths, and he made every kind of noise—sometimes he spoke articulately like a human, but at others he bellowed like a bull, roared like a lion, barked like a dog, or hissed like a snake. Whatever his form of utterance, his voice made the mountains echo. Typhon terrorized the universe, and he would have conquered it if Zeus had not intervened and struck him with a thunderbolt. There followed a long battle between them during which the sea boiled and the mountains melted like metals in a foundry. At length Zeus cast Typhon down into Tartarus. In this way the eternal rule of Zeus over the universe was finally established. In some versions of the myth, Typhon was confined after his defeat either in the land of the Arimi in Cilicia (the eastern Mediterranean coastal region of Asia Minor, part of modern Turkey), under Mount Etna in Sicily, or in other volcanic regions, where he was the cause of eruptions. Typhon was thus the personification of volcanic forces. Among Typhon's children by his wife, Echidna, were Cerberus, the three-headed hound of hell; the multiheaded Hydra of Lerna; the Chimaera; and the Sphinx. Typhon was also father of dangerous winds (typhoons), and he was identified by later writers with Egyptian god Seth.

Embellished accounts

The earliest description of Typhon (or Typhoes) occurs in the *Theogony* by Greek poet Hesiod (fl. 800 BCE). Nearly seven centuries later Apollodorus (fl. 140 BCE) tells essentially the same story with additional details. Typhon, he says, was the largest child of Gaia. From the thighs upward he had the form of a man, but he was taller than mountains and his head sometimes touched the stars. From the thighs downward he had the shape of two enormous vipers. He also had wings and tangled hair that streamed from his head and chin. When Typhon began to throw rocks at heaven, the gods fled to Egypt and turned themselves into animals. (This is probably intended to explain the animal form of Egyptian deities.) Zeus attacked Typhon with a sickle, but Typhon wrested the weapon from his grip and used it to cut out the tendons of Zeus's hands and feet. He then dragged Zeus off and imprisoned him inside a cave. Hermes and Pan together recovered the tendons and healed Zeus, who this time came after Typhon in a chariot drawn by winged horses. The Fates tricked Typhon by

Below: The painting encircling this Greek vase from the seventh or sixth century BCE depicts Typhon. Both sides of the vase are shown.

Above: A typhoon photographed from space. The name Typhon *comes from Greek* typhon, *meaning "violent whirlwind."*

offering him food that they told him would make him invulnerable but which in fact weakened him. Zeus then took his chance and drove Typhon across the sea to Sicily. There Zeus piled Mount Etna on top of the monster; the smoke and fire emitted by the volcano were thought to be the thunderbolts with which Zeus subdued him. Thus Typhon lives on—he was never destroyed, merely subjugated. He remains a force of chaos and destruction, and may be held in check only for as long as Zeus's peace is preserved—the price of order is eternal vigilance. Of the many other authors who have written about the Typhon legend, the most famous are Greek playwright Aeschylus (525–456 BCE) and Roman poet Ovid (43 BCE–17 CE).

Typhon and the struggle between Zeus and Hera

Another version of the story, dating from at least the sixth century BCE, makes the birth of Typhon an episode in the endless marital strife between Zeus and his consort Hera. When Zeus gave birth to goddess Athena on his own, Hera was angry. She wanted to prove that she could do anything

Zeus could do, so she alone produced Typhon, and his brother Hephaestus. Since Athena had no father, and Typhon had no mother, they were antithetical figures—always opposed to each other. In one early Greek myth Athena showed her courage above all other gods by single-handedly defending Mount Olympus when it was attacked by Typhon. All the other gods fled in terror, but Athena battled with the monster while at the same time goading her father, Zeus, into action. Eventually Zeus plucked up his courage and returned to the fray, striking the monster with his thunderbolts. In this account it was Athena, not Zeus, who threw Mount Etna on top of Typhon, crushing the monster underneath.

James M. Redfield

Bibliography

Bulfinch, Thomas. *Bulfinch's Mythology.* New York: Barnes & Noble, 2006.

Hesiod, and M. L. West, trans. *Theogony* and *Works and Days.* New York: Oxford University Press, 2008.

Ovid, and A. D. Melville, trans. *Metamorphoses.* New York: Oxford University Press, 2008.

See also: Athena; Gaia; Hermes; Pan; Zeus.

URANUS

For the ancient Greeks, Uranus, the personification of the sky, was the first ruler of the universe. He was the father and grandfather of many of the most important gods in the Greek pantheon.

According to the Greek creation myth, elucidated by the poet Hesiod (fl. 800 BCE), Uranus was predated by four beings: Chaos (the void), Gaia (the earth), Tartarus (the region far below the earth), and Eros (sexual love). From Chaos came the basic cyclical divisions of time, Erebus (Darkness), Nyx (Night), Aether (Brightness), and Hemera (Day); but it was Gaia who created the primary physical divisions of the world: Pontus (the oceans), Ourea (the mountains), and Uranus (the sky).

Father and grandfather of a pantheon

Once he was brought into being, Uranus became the first all-powerful ruler in the universe and the ultimate procreator. He lifted himself up into the sky by day, but at night came back down to lie on Gaia, his mother. Their union resulted in a number of children, from whom were descended all the generations of gods and other creatures who wielded power in the universe. Uranus and Gaia were the parents of the 12 Titans: Oceanus, Coeus, Crius, Hyperion, Iapetus, Theia, Rhea, Themis, Mnemosyne, Phoebe, Tethys, and Cronus. In addition, they produced the three gigantic, one-eyed Cyclopes—Brontes, Steropes, and Arges—and the three Hecatoncheires (Hundred-Handed Ones)—Briareos, Cottus, and Gyges. Each of the latter had a hundred arms and 50 heads.

Below: The Mutilation of Uranus *by Italian artist Giorgio Vasari (1511–1574). Vasari's painting shows Uranus's son Cronus wielding the sickle that he used to sever his father's genitals.*

Left: A spectrograph of Uranus provides an enhanced impression of the planet's blue-green color that associates it with the sky.

A heavenly host

Many of Uranus's descendants reflected his association with the heavens. The children of the Titan Hyperion and the Titaness Theia were Helios (Sun), Selene (Moon), and Eos (Dawn), while Hyperion himself was also sometimes identified as the sun. Another Titan, Astraeus, was closely connected with the sky at both day and night—Astraeus's name means "Starry," and his children were the North, South, East, and West Winds, as well as all the stars. The Titan Coeus and the Titaness Phoebe had a daughter, Leto, and, through her, two grandchildren, the Olympian deities Artemis and Apollo. Artemis had a close association with the moon, and was sometimes identified with Selene, while her brother was linked to the sun in his guise as Phoebus Apollo (the Shining One). Even Uranus's monstrous offspring the Cyclopes had heavenly associations, revealed by their names: Brontes ("Thunderer"), Steropes ("Lightner") and Arges ("Flashing").

Furthermore, despite Uranus's role as a primal figure, associated with a stage in the creation of the universe that was full of elemental and crude beings, he was the father of a number of divinities who represented order and creativity. Through his daughter Mnemosyne (Memory) he was the grandfather of the nine Muses, who inspired every form of creativity. His granddaughter Urania was the Muse of astronomy. Through the Titaness Themis he was the grandfather of some of the most powerful principles of regularity in the world: the three Horae (Seasons) and the three Moirai (Fates).

As in many other cosmologies from the Mediterranean and western Asia, therefore, the first generative pair in the Greek account of creation were Earth and Sky. The nature of Uranus's coupling with Gaia supports the suggestion that the deity's name is connected to the ancient Greek word for dew: Uranus descended on Earth, bringing the sky's moisture—dew, mist, and rain—that fertilized the ground.

Naming the Planets

Modern astronomers have drawn heavily on Greek mythology to find appropriate names for the planets and other important bodies in the solar system, and Uranus—the third-largest planet in the solar system—is no exception. Uranus, which was discovered in 1781, is the seventh planet in order of distance from the sun. Appropriately for a planet named for the Greek personification of the sky, Uranus appears blue-green, the result of the absorption of red light by methane gas in its atmosphere.

In 2004 a group of astronomers believed that they had discovered a new planet, located around 8 billion miles (13 billion km) from Earth. However, other scientists argued that, at a mere 1,100 miles (1,800 km) in diameter, the discovery only merited the term *planetoid*. The name astronomers gave to their sighting continued a broadening of tradition to include nonclassical mythology. This name was Sedna, for the Inuit sea goddess. In myth, Sedna's wild temper and voracious appetite led her parents to take her out to sea in a boat and cast her overboard. So desperate was Sedna to hold on to the boat that her father was forced to sever her fingers, one by one, to make her let go. She then sank to the bottom of the ocean, which became her domain. The cold world Sedna inhabited made her name an appropriate choice for the object orbiting in the farthest icy reaches of the solar system.

Sons against fathers

Uranus, however, had no love for his children. On the contrary, he was a forceful, autocratic figure who was unwilling to contemplate any challenge to his position and so hated his offspring. He refused to allow his children even to be born and instead held them back inside Gaia. She was unable to bear the pain caused by this act of suppression and decided to take action against her partner. She created a sickle out of adamant and urged her children to use it in rebellion against their father. All of them were too afraid to do so—with the sole exception of Gaia's youngest son, Cronus, who agreed to lie in ambush one night and attack his father.

As day turned into night, Uranus returned as usual to settle on Gaia. He was set upon by Cronus, who, reaching out with his left hand and wielding Gaia's sickle in his right, cut off his father's genitals and flung them into the sea. By this act of violence Uranus was deposed by Cronus, who released all his brothers and sisters from Gaia's womb. Consequently, the Titans replaced their parents as the dominant generation of gods. However, Cronus took after his father, both in the tyranny of his rule and in his fear of being overthrown by the children his wife Rhea bore him—a fear that led him to swallow each child after its birth. In the end, however, Cronus was deposed by his children, just as Uranus had been. Uranus himself was only too happy to participate in the downfall of his rebellious son. He advised his daughter Rhea on strategies to ensure that her son Zeus survived to adulthood and to make Cronus release the children he had swallowed, thus providing Zeus with much-needed allies.

While the castration of Uranus signified the end of his reign, it also resulted in the creation of several new divinities. From the combination of Uranus's genitals and the elemental waters of the sea into which they were thrown came the beautiful love goddess Aphrodite. Drops of blood from Uranus's castration that fell on Gaia also led her to produce three other sets of beings. The first were the three Furies—Alecto, Megaera, and Tisiphone—whose role, appropriately in view of their origin, was to exact vengeance on crimes of violence committed within families. Second were the Giants, huge and hideous creatures who mounted an unsuccessful rebellion against the Olympian gods, a battle known as the Gigantomachy. Third and finally, the mingling of Uranus's blood with Gaia produced the Meliads, the nymphs of ash trees. In addition, according to one tradition, the sickle that Cronus threw away after the attack on his father fell to the earth, where it formed the Greek island of Corcyra (modern Corfu).

Rivalry and violence

The graphic violence that features in the story of Uranus's overthrow by Cronus seems to have shocked some of the ancient Greeks themselves. The philosopher Plato (c. 428–c. 348 BCE), for instance, suggested that the account should be censored and withheld almost entirely from the young. However, the central motif of violence and castration is not uniquely Greek. In Anatolia (part of modern Turkey), the creation myth that the Hittites adopted

Left: An 18th-century engraving of Cronus by Italian artist Giovanni Cavattoni. Gaia's sickle is depicted at the Titan's feet.

The Uranus Myth and Social Taboo

To a modern audience the phenomenon of incest is a striking feature in each of the first three generations of the Greek gods. However, it should be remembered that Uranus was essentially an elemental figure, and that he and Pontus were the first distinctive males to be created by Gaia. Although Uranus was technically a son of Earth—despite being created without the aid of a male partner—the act of mother–son incest at this stage in the cosmogony was regarded by the ancient Greeks as the inevitable consequence of taking a single entity as the starting point for all of creation.

In general, however, incest was held by the ancient Greeks to be a social taboo—as it remains today in virtually all societies. The taboo is seen clearly in the story of Oedipus, who unwittingly married his mother, Jocasta. The actions of both son and mother when they discovered their true relationship speak loudly of the stigma attached to incest: Jocasta hanged herself, and Oedipus gouged out his own eyes.

Left: Mnemosyne *by English artist Dante Gabriel Rossetti (1828–1882). Mnemosyne was one of the many offspring of Uranus and Gaia. She was the mother of the nine Muses.*

from the Hurrian people told how the father god Kumarbi attacked his master, the creator god Anu, by biting off Anu's testicles. Anu's seed grew inside Kumarbi until he gave birth to three children, including the weather god Teshub, who overthrew his father. The underlying pattern of events of the Greek and Hittite myths is strikingly similar, and some scholars believe that some kind of common ancestry may well link the two accounts.

Separating Earth from Sky

Greek mythology, like that of many other ancient cultures, regarded the earth and the sky as the two primary sources for the rest of creation, and the separation of this pair was a critical step in the cosmogony of the world. Some scholars believe that the separation occurred with Gaia's creation of Uranus, an act of parthenogenesis (self-reproduction) that created Sky as an entity distinct from Earth. Other scholars argue that it was Cronus who caused the division between the heavens and the earth when he castrated his father—so preventing Uranus from lying on Gaia and fertilizing her.

The separation of the earth and sky finds a strong parallel in Egyptian mythology. The Egyptians believed that their sky deity, Nut, was female; in contrast, Geb (Earth)

Above: The southern coastline of the Greek island of Corfu. According to myth, Corfu was formed when Cronus discarded the sickle that he had used to castrate Uranus, and it fell to the earth.

was male. Nut married Geb and bore him four children. In one version of the story, however, the deities' father, Shu, god of air, had to separate the couple because they were holding on to one another so tightly that none of their children could emerge. Once the sky was pried away from the earth, over which it formed an arch, the next generation of gods could come forth. However, unlike his Greek counterpart, the Egyptian earth deity grieved after his parting from the sky. The Egyptians believed that Geb's distress at the loss of Nut was the cause of earthquakes.

Uranus in Roman myth

Roman mythology gives a much less prominent role to the process of cosmogony and the early stages of the creation of the universe, but it does attribute a similar role to Uranus, who is identified as a sky god, born of elemental parentage early in the history of the universe. Unlike the Greek account, however, the Roman Uranus does not emerge from an act of parthenogenesis and instead has two parents, the Titans Oceanus and Tethys. These parents themselves represent a major difference from the Greek version made famous by Hesiod, who counted Oceanus and Tethys among the offspring of Uranus and Gaia.

Another difference between the accounts is that, according to Roman beliefs, Uranus was the brother of the earth goddess Tellus. In the Roman story, Uranus and Tellus were the earliest divine couple, who gave birth to the gods Jupiter (the equivalent of the Greek Zeus), Vulcan (the Greek god was Hephaestus), and Venus (the Greek goddess was Aphrodite) without an intermediate generation.

In Roman relief sculpture and sarcophagi, Uranus sometimes appeared representing the firmament of heaven, often paired with Tellus in scenes representing the glory of the Roman Empire. The deity was also depicted in specific myths, such as in the Judgment of Paris, the creation of man by Prometheus, and the fall of Helios's son Phaethon.

ANTHONY BULLOCH

Bibliography

Hesiod, and M. L. West, trans. *Theogony* and *Works and Days*. New York: Oxford University Press, 2008.

March, Jenny. *Cassell's Dictionary of Classical Mythology*. London: Cassell, 2001.

Storm, Rachel. *The Encyclopaedia of Eastern Mythology*. London: Lorenz Books, 1999.

Turcan, Robert, and Antonia Nevill, trans. *The Gods of Ancient Rome: Religion in Everyday Life from Archaic to Imperial Times*. New York: Routledge, 2001.

SEE ALSO: Aphrodite; Apollo; Cronus; Fates; Furies; Gaia; Muses; Nyx; Titans; Zeus.

VENUS

Venus was the Roman goddess of love. From at least as early as the fourth century BCE she was identified with Greek goddess Aphrodite. Almost all of the myths attached to the Roman goddess were inherited from her Greek counterpart.

Left: The Capitoline Venus, by an unknown Roman artist, is based on an earlier statue of Aphrodite by Greek sculptor Praxiteles (370–330 BCE).

Venus was the lover of Mars, the Roman war god who was identified with the Greek Ares, and the wife of Vulcan, the equivalent of the Greek Hephaestus. Another important relationship Venus enjoyed was with a Trojan prince named Anchises. The goddess fell in love with the mortal when she saw him tending his flocks on Mount Ida, and she eventually bore him a son, Aeneas. According to myth, Aeneas grew up to found the city of Rome. As Aeneas's mother, Venus enjoyed a special place in the Roman pantheon.

However, for all the importance attached to her, the origins of the Roman Venus still remain unclear. There is no evidence of her in the earliest Roman religious calendars, and, unlike a number of the old Roman gods, she had no flamen (a type of priest dedicated entirely to the worship of a single deity). Two Roman writers, Marcus Terentius Varro (116–27 BCE) and Ambrosius Theodosius Macrobius (fl. c. 400 CE), remark upon her absence in archaic religious sources. This lack of evidence has led many scholars to conclude that Venus was not an early Roman divinity at all.

The oldest existing representation of Venus is an engraving on a mirror found in the ancient Italian city of Praeneste (present-day Palestrina). It dates from the second half of the fourth century BCE, and the goddess is labeled Venos, an archaic spelling of *Venus*. She is seated to the left of Jupiter; to his right is Proserpina, the goddess of the dead. The three gods are grouped around a small ornamental box, the burial chest of Venus's young lover, Adonis. Jupiter has been called in to arbitrate the

Above: Birth of Venus *by Sandro Botticelli (1445–1510) depicts the goddess rising from the waves. Like most myths about Venus, the story of her birth was originally told about her Greek counterpart, Aphrodite.*

competing claims of the two goddesses, both of whom are in love with Adonis. Venus wants Adonis to live with her, while Proserpina claims him for the underworld. Jupiter's compromise is to allow Adonis to spend four months of every year with Venus, four months with Proserpina, and four months to do as he pleases. The compromise distresses Venus, who in the engraving covers her face with her cloak. Thus the very first visual image of Venus is a reference to a myth that was originally attached to the Greek Aphrodite, evidence that the two goddesses were synonymous from a very early age.

Venus, goddess of gardens

The first explicit mention of Venus in Roman literature dates from around the mid-third century BCE, when author Gnaeus Naevius (c. 270–c. 199 BCE) used her name symbolically to stand for green vegetables. This association was echoed in the second century BCE, when comic writer Titus Maccius Plautus (c. 254–184 BCE) referred to Venus as the protector of gardens. Varro wrote that vegetable growers made August 19 a holiday "because on that date a temple was dedicated to Venus and gardens were sacred to her." In his summary of the work of first-century-CE scholar Marcus Verrius Flaccus, Sextus Pompeius Festus (second or third century CE) explicitly states that gardens were under the watchful protection of Venus. These passages might seem to suggest that Venus was originally a Roman goddess of gardens. This theory has largely been rejected by modern scholars, however. Some have suggested that the fact that statues of Venus graced Roman gardens may indicate that her physical beauty was thought to have the power to draw out the life-giving forces of growth. According to this interpretation, Venus's role as the protective goddess of gardens would have been secondary to her primary role as goddess of love.

Venus's rise in status can be seen in the number and magnificence of the temples that were established in her

The Name of Venus

Since the publication in 1954 of *La Religion Romaine de Vénus,* a study by academic Robert Schilling, scholars have tried to establish the meaning of the goddess's name as revealed through a cluster of Latin words related to *Venus.* The Latin verb *venerari* means "to venerate or solicit the good will of a god." The noun *veneratio* denotes "the act of worship, or veneration." The noun *venia* denotes a "kindly or charming disposition" and often "forgiveness" sought through worship of the gods. The term *venenum* refers to an herb or potion—especially a love charm—used for medicinal or magical purposes. An underlying meaning in all these words is "charm," perhaps even "magical charm." When a Roman "venerated" a god or goddess, he intended to capture the deity's good will (*venia*) and to "charm" the deity, thus winning the god's or goddess's assent to his prayer.

Left: One of the brightest objects in the night sky, the planet Venus was named for the Roman goddess of love.

honor from the middle of the Republican period (509–31 BCE) onward. The first temple of Venus in Rome was erected in 295 BCE by politician Quintus Fabius Maximus. It stood near the Circus Maximus. According to Roman writer Livy (59 BC–17 CE), it was paid for by fines levied on Roman matrons convicted of adultery. There the goddess was worshiped as Venus Obsequens, a name that suggests she looked favorably on peoples' prayers. The temple was dedicated on August 19 during the Rustic Vinalia, a wine festival that was originally associated purely with Jupiter but was eventually shared with Venus. Venus gradually took on an expanded role in Roman festivals, from which she had originally been absent, and came to be closely associated with Jupiter.

Venus of Mount Eryx

Venus's close relationship with the father of the gods was strengthened in 215 BCE when Quintus Fabius Maximus (d. 203 BCE), the grandson of Quintus Fabius Maximus, dedicated a temple to Venus on the Capitoline Hill. The new temple was built close to the great sanctuary of Jupiter Optimus Maximus. The dedication day of Venus's temple was April 23, a date that coincided with the Earlier Vinalia, another wine festival that was originally sacred to Jupiter alone. The new Capitoline temple housed the cult of Venus of Mount Eryx. The cult, which had been imported from Sicily, incorporated both Greek and Phoenician elements and emphasized pleasure and fertility. In Sicily the cult had flourished among the Elymians, a people who considered themselves, like the Romans, to be Trojan immigrants. The importation of the cult thus emphasized the ties between Aeneas, Venus, and Rome. In contrast to the Sicilian rites, however, the rituals carried out in the new temple in Rome were performed with decorum and reserve.

A second Roman sanctuary of Venus Erycina (from Eryx, modern Erice in Sicily) was dedicated by Porcius Licinius in 181 BCE outside the Colline Gate. It was renowned for its elegant temple and surrounding colonnade. Both Ovid (43 BCE–17 CE) and Plutarch (c. 46–120 CE) described the rituals performed at the new temple, which were closer in spirit to those celebrated on Mount Eryx.

The foundation story of the temple of Venus Verticordia ("Venus the Changer of Hearts"), built on the slope of Rome's Aventine Hill in 114 BCE, emphasizes the

Above: The Temple of Venus in the ground of the villa of Emperor Hadrian. The temple dates from the first century BCE.

goddess's respect for chastity. The sanctuary was built as an act of atonement for the moral lapse of three vestal virgins who had broken their vow of chastity. A woman named Sulpicia, judged to be the most virtuous matron of Rome, was selected to dedicate the goddess's cult statue. The foundation myth of the Venus Verticordia cult expresses the traditionally Roman character of the goddess, which contrasts with the more eastern, Greek and Phoenician, nature of the Venus of Mount Eryx. It seems likely that the character of the Roman Venus was largely formed in the Latin religious sanctuary near the city of Lavinium (modern Pratica di Mare), where she was worshiped in association with Aeneas.

A number of Roman statesmen took steps to be associated with either Venus or her Greek predecessor. In the early first century BCE the general Lucius Cornelius Sulla (138–78 BCE) assumed the nickname Epaphroditus ("Beloved of Aphrodite") to assert that he was her favorite. In 55 BCE another Roman general, Pompey the Great

(106–48 BCE), dedicated a temple to Venus Victrix ("Venus, Granter of Victory") on the Campus Martius. Later, Roman general and political leader Julius Caesar (100–44 BCE) built a temple to Venus Genetrix ("Venus the Mother"). The inference was that Venus was the mother of both Caesar's family and the Roman people as a whole. Caesar's successor as emperor and adopted son, Augustus (63 BCE–14 CE), allotted Venus a place in the temple of Mars. Later, Emperor Hadrian (76–138 CE) supervised the construction of the Temple of Venus and Roma. The temple was dedicated on April 21, the traditional date for the founding of Rome. The choice of this date strengthened the identification of Venus with Rome itself.

DANIEL P. HARMON

Bibliography

Scheid, John, and Janet Lloyd, trans. *An Introduction to Roman Religion*. Bloomington, IN: Indiana University Press, 2003.

Turcan, Robert, and Antonia Nevill, trans. *The Gods of Ancient Rome: Religion in Everyday Life from Archaic to Imperial Times*. New York: Routledge, 2001.

SEE ALSO: Aphrodite; Jupiter.

VESTA

Vesta was the Roman goddess of the hearth, the equivalent of the Greek goddess Hestia. Vesta featured in few myths, but she was an important member of the Roman pantheon. Her worship was a central feature of Roman life.

Vesta was the daughter of the fertility god Saturn and his wife Ops, goddess of abundance and wealth. Vesta was the sister of five major Roman deities: Ceres, Plutus, Juno, Neptune, and Jupiter. Unlike her siblings, Vesta appeared in very few stories. One of the few myths to involve her also features Priapus, a minor Roman deity associated with sexuality. Vesta was famous for her chastity. Knowing this, the ever lustful Priapus crept up on her while she was sleeping, hoping to take her by surprise and rape her. However, Vesta was awoken by the braying of the donkey owned by the old satyr Silenus. Thanks to this intervention, Vesta managed to escape from Priapus and preserve her virginity. From that moment on, Vesta was associated with donkeys.

The worship of Vesta

Vesta was one of the more mysterious goddesses of the Roman pantheon. Scholars do not know much about her roots, except that originally Romans worshiped her privately in their own homes. However, the nature of Vesta's cult changed and eventually she was worshiped at a state level. The transformation is attributed to Roman king Numa Pompilius (c. 715–673 BCE), who elevated her status and assigned Rome's safety to her care.

Every Roman household dedicated its hearth to Vesta, and a number of domestic rituals were held in her honor. For example, newborn babies were carried around the family hearth to mark their arrival into the world. Every meal began and ended with an offering to Vesta, usually in the form of the first and last drink of wine.

However, rituals were not restricted to domestic hearths. Every Roman town or city also had a public hearth. The hearth fire of every new colony was kindled with coals brought from the home city of the new arrivals. The flames of Vesta's sacred hearth fires were not allowed to go out. These fires symbolized the spiritual heart of the cities.

In Rome, the sacred fire was kept in the Temple of Vesta (or Aedes Vesta) in the Forum Romanum. The forum was located just to the north of the Palatine Hill, one of the seven hills of Rome. Historians believed that a succession of temples was built on this site. The one that remains today dates from 191 CE, when Julia Domna (c. 167–217 CE), wife of Roman emperor Septimius Severus (c. 145–211 CE), ordered its restoration. She had 20 columns built around the central circular room and the outer walls decorated with half columns. The sacred hearth burned at the very center of the building, where it was tended by six priestesses known as the vestal virgins. According to legend, this flame was first ignited in the seventh century BCE during the reign of Numa Pompilius. It represented Rome's security and prosperity. Every year on March 1 the fire was ceremoniously renewed. The sacred fire in Vesta's temple burned until 394 CE, when the temple was closed by Emperor Theodosius (347–395 BCE) as part of a purge of all non-Christian cults.

The Temple of Vesta played an important role in the festival of Vestalia, which lasted for a week, beginning on June 7 and ending on June 15. Normally, the inner sanctum of the temple could only be visited by the vestal virgins. However, on the first day of the festival it opened its doors to all female citizens of Rome. The women visited the temple barefoot and made offerings to the goddess. On the last day of the festival, the vestal virgins ritually cleansed the temple.

The vestal virgins were the only female priests within the Roman religious system. They came under the protection of the Pontifex Maximus (the high priest of Rome), and were led by the Virgo Vestalis Maxima, the most senior vestal virgin. Girls were selected to be vestal

Right: The Vestal Virgin *by German artist Alois Schram (1864–1919). The vestal virgins, priestesses who dedicated their lives to Vesta, played an important role in Roman religion.*

VESTA

Above: The Vestal Virgins *by Hector Leroux (1829–1900). The painting depicts a ceremony being carried out at the Temple of Vesta in the Forum Romanum.*

Portrayal in Art

Although few ancient representations of Vesta survive today, scholars believe that she was usually depicted as a stern woman wearing a long dress with her head covered. She was seen as being regal and removed. Her personality stood in contrast to that of other Roman deities, who were more human in nature, and whose exploits involved interaction with mortals. The absence of stories and myths involving the goddess may account for the paucity of paintings and statues depicting her.

Although Vesta herself is not particularly widely represented in art, her attendants, the vestal virgins, have been a relatively more popular subject. One of the most famous depictions of one of Vesta's priestesses is *Herm of a Vestal Virgin*, a marble bust by Italian sculptor Antonio Canova (1757–1822). The bust has a sparse appearance that reflects the strict morality of the order—the white of the marble suggests the vestal virgin's purity. The priestess is depicted gazing coldly into the distance with a scarf wrapped around her hair.

virgins between the ages of six and ten. The girls were chosen by the Pontifex Maximus and came from distinguished patrician families—the patricians were the wealthier of the two classes of Roman citizens, the other class being the plebeians. Vestal virgins served for 30 years: the first 10 years as novices, the next 10 years as vestal virgins proper, and the last 10 years as tutors to the younger priestesses. After 30 years of service, they were released from their vow of chastity and allowed to marry.

The vestal virgins enjoyed privileges that other Roman women did not. They could own their own property, for example. They also had special front-row seats at games—all other women were relegated to the back rows. However, if a vestal virgin broke her vow of chastity, she could expect a harsh punishment. The blood of vestal virgins could not be spilled, so transgressors were buried alive. The offender's lover was flogged to death. The live burials took place at the Campus Sceleratus ("evil field"), located outside the Servian Wall that surrounded Rome. These executions were infrequent, but several did occur.

Vestal virgins in myth

One of the most famous mythical vestal virgins was Rhea Silvia, daughter of King Numitor of Alba Longa, who was dethroned by his brother Amulius. Amulius ordered the Pontifex Maximus to choose his niece for service to Vesta;

House of the Vestal Virgins

From the sixth century BCE until the end of the fourth century CE, Vesta's priestesses lived together in the House of the Vestal Virgins (or Atrium Vestae). The House of the Vestal Virgins was located behind the Temple of Vesta, between the Palatine Hill and the Regia (the residence of the kings of Rome). Together, the Temple of Vesta, the House of the Vestal Virgins, the Regia, and another building called the Domus Publica formed a complex where all the religious duties of the king were carried out. Scholars believe that the king's wife and daughters administered the cult of Vesta until Rome became a republic.

An older House of the Vestal Virgins, smaller than the present ruins, was aligned on an east–west axis. It consisted of a front room that ran the full width of the house on the north side and six separate rooms in the back. This floor plan was maintained for over five centuries, until 64 CE, when the building was destroyed by fire. The ruins that are visible today are the remains of the building that was built after the fire. The new house was larger and had three levels. Scholars believe the vestal virgins' private rooms were on the first floor. The house contained statues of former vestal virgins. After the suppression of all non-Christian cults in 394 CE, the vestal virgins were forced to leave the complex, and the sacred fire was extinguished.

Right: The remains of the House of the Vestal Virgins in Rome. The statues depict former vestal virgins and date from around the beginning of the third century CE.

he had learned from an oracle that Rhea Silvia's children would threaten his power. Rhea Silvia served Vesta faithfully as a vestal virgin, until one day she was raped by Mars, Roman god of war. In due course, Rhea Silvia gave birth to twin boys, Romulus and Remus. Fearing the prophecy, Amulius abandoned the boys on the Tiber River. However, they survived and grew up to overthrow Amulius and found the city of Rome.

Another famous mythical vestal virgin was Julia Flammia, who was chosen to be a virgin when she was nine years old. The only memento she possessed from her childhood was her mother's plain agate necklace. One day, while the young priestess was tending the sacred fire, the necklace broke and the beads fell into the flames. Julia fished them out with an iron rod and discovered that the stones had become the color of the fire. The Romans used this myth to explain the origins of carnelian, a red semiprecious stone.

ALYS CAVINESS

Bibliography

Gardner, Jane F. *Roman Myths.* Austin, TX: University of Texas Press, 1993.

Scheid, John, and Janet Lloyd, trans. *An Introduction to Roman Religion.* Bloomington, IN: Indiana University Press, 2003.

Turcan, Robert, and Antonia Nevill, trans. *The Gods of Ancient Rome: Religion in Everyday Life from Archaic to Imperial Times.* New York: Routledge, 2001.

SEE ALSO: Hestia.

ZEUS

In Greek mythology, Zeus was supreme god of the cosmos, which he ruled from Mount Olympus. Ancient Greeks believed he was god of justice, because he could look down from the heavens and see everything that people did. His special bird was the eagle, king of birds. As god of the sky, Zeus sent rains down on the earth. His favorite weapon was the thunderbolt.

Below: Zeus sits on his throne amid the other Olympian gods in a frieze on a civic building in Athens, Greece.

Zeus did not start out as supreme ruler of the universe—he had to win that position from his father, Cronus, and wrest his power from Titans and earthborn Giants. Once he had gained the divine throne, however, Zeus became the unchallenged leader of the Olympians, the major divinities of the Greek world for more than 600 years.

According to tradition, Cronus, a Titan, overcame his father Uranus and was determined to remain in power. When Cronus learned that he was destined to be overthrown by his son, he took drastic steps to prevent the prophecy from coming true. Every time his, wife, Rhea gave birth to a child, Cronus swallowed the infant. When he had devoured two sons, Poseidon and Hades—and in some versions of the legend also three daughters, Hestia, Demeter, and Hera—Rhea turned to her mother, Gaia, for help in thwarting her husband. Together they came up with a plan.

The Age of Zeus

Zeus is an ancient deity, but historians were not sure quite how early he was worshiped until archaeological excavations beneath the foundations of a house at Palaikastro in the northeast corner of Crete uncovered the altar of a temple dedicated to the Greek god. Within the earthworks they found evidence of cult practices that had continued from the eighth century BCE until the Roman conquest of the island in 67 BCE. In the surrounding area they uncovered an inscription, broken in many pieces, that contained a hymn to Zeus, and several antefixae (carved ornaments on a roof) in the shape of lion heads. The Cretan sanctuary is thought to have been plundered by Christians at the end of the fourth century CE.

When Rhea gave birth to her third son, Zeus, she gave Cronus a stone wrapped in a baby blanket, which he at once swallowed. Rhea meanwhile hid the real baby in a cave on Mount Dicte (or Mount Ida) on the island of Crete. There the goat Amaltheia gave him milk, and the Curetes—a brotherhood of Cretans—banged their bronze shields to conceal the baby's crying. Thus did Zeus escape his father and grow to manhood in secrecy.

When Zeus came of age, he conspired with Rhea or Gaia to give Cronus a drug that forced him to disgorge all the children he had swallowed. The divine offspring emerged fully grown from their father's stomach, and they all immediately joined Zeus in a battle against Cronus and the other Titans. Only two Titans sided with Zeus: Prometheus and Oceanus. The Cyclopes (one-eyed giants) and the Hecatoncheires (three giant sons of Uranus and Gaia who each had 100 arms and 50 heads) were dug up from the earth, in which Uranus had buried them, and they also fought alongside Zeus. In a war that lasted 10 years, the Titans were defeated and sent down below the earth to Tartarus. Zeus then divided the world among his brothers. Claiming the sky for himself, he allotted the sea to Poseidon and the underworld to Hades.

Before the new deities could assume power, however, they had to fight one more battle. Gaia, angry that the Giants had been given no portion of the world, roused them to battle against Zeus. After another 10-year struggle, Zeus and his brothers defeated the Giants, as well as Typhon, a monster created by Gaia. Depending on different

Left: Olive groves on the slopes of Mount Ida in Crete. It was here that Zeus was brought up in secret.

versions of the myth, either Typhon was imprisoned by Zeus under Mount Etna, a volcano in Sicily, or thrown into Tartarus. Once the Titans, the forces of barbarism, and the Giants, the agents of unrestrained violence, had been defeated, a new pantheon could take over the universe. They settled on Mount Olympus, and hence became known as the Olympians.

Versatile god

In the Greek pantheon Zeus was originally a sky god, a weather deity who sent rain and who, when angry, hurled lightning and thunderbolts. On Mount Olympus he gathered the clouds about his throne and watched the actions of mortals on earth. In time, his role developed and he became the guiding deity for various aspects of civilized life in ancient Greece. When Greeks took oaths, they swore to Zeus; and it was Zeus who made sure that both parties kept their word. Thus Zeus upheld law and justice among men. He was invoked as the god of marriage, Zeus Teleios; and in times of need, he was a savior, Zeus Soter. He was also god of guests, Zeus Xenios (see box, page 297).

Above: This painting by French artist Nicolas Poussin (1594–1665) shows the infant Zeus being fed with milk from the goat Amaltheia.

In art, Zeus is almost always pictured as a strong and fit male, usually with a beard. He often holds in his hand a thunderbolt and carries a shield made of goatskin. This was known as his aegis: in modern English, "to be under someone's aegis" means to be under his or her protection. In time Zeus lent his aegis to his favorite daughter, Athena, and it became a regular part of her attire. In images of Zeus seated on his throne, his bird, the eagle, appears perched on the god's scepter. Oak trees, towering into the sky, were sacred to Zeus. At Dodona in northwestern Greece, the rustling of oak leaves was said to tell the word of Zeus. Priests resided there to interpret these rustlings.

Amorous god

Zeus was an amorous god, and there are numerous legends about his affairs with gods and humans. Although they make great stories—they involve many disguises and subterfuges to escape detection—the tales also have symbolic significance. Since in the polytheistic belief system

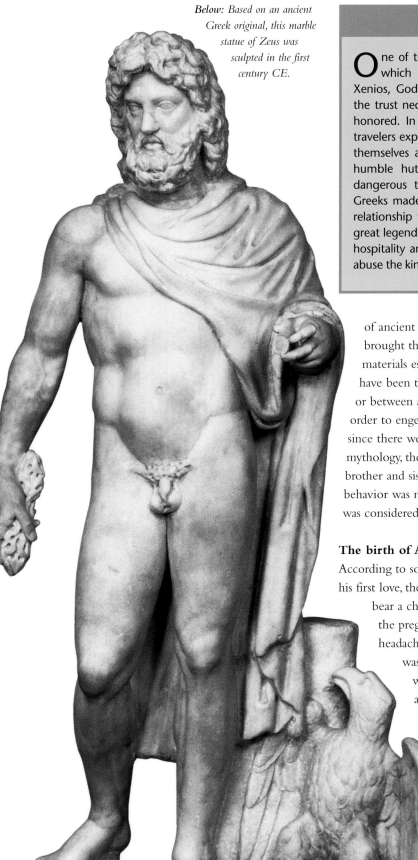

Below: Based on an ancient Greek original, this marble statue of Zeus was sculpted in the first century CE.

Hospitality

One of the most important human activities over which Zeus presided was hospitality. As Zeus Xenios, God of Guest-Friendship, he made sure that the trust necessary between host and guest was fully honored. In a world without regular hotels or inns, travelers expected to be taken in wherever they found themselves at the end of the day, whether it was a humble hut or a regal palace. Since it may be dangerous to let a stranger into one's house, the Greeks made sure that this temporary but important relationship was protected by their chief god. Many great legends of Greek mythology turn on violations of hospitality and the vengeance brought on those who abuse the kindness of the host or the trust of the visitor.

of ancient Greece there was no single deity who brought things to life, many of the beings, forces, and materials essential to human existence were believed to have been the product of unions between two deities or between a deity and a mortal. Zeus would mate in order to engender what the world needed. In early days, since there were few male and female figures in Greek mythology, these alliances were often made between brother and sister or others who were closely related. This behavior was not tolerated by Greeks among mortals but was considered acceptable for the early gods.

The birth of Athena

According to some stories, when Zeus found out that his first love, the Titan Metis (Thought), was destined to bear a child mightier than its father, he swallowed the pregnant mother. Zeus then developed a headache that could be relieved only when his skull was split with an ax. While versions vary as to who wielded the ax, nearly every account agrees that, once the blow was landed, it was Athena, fully developed and armed, who sprang from the head of Zeus. Others reject the Metis story and have Athena herself claiming that she had no mother. In these versions, she sprang from Zeus's head as a tangible representation of her father's divine thought. Athena was her father's favorite child. She shared with him not only his aegis but also the secret of where he kept the thunderbolts and

Right: This marble frieze showing the marriage of Zeus and Hera stands on the wall of a temple at Selinunte, an ancient Greek city in Sicily.

how to use them. As goddess of wisdom and creative crafts, it is appropriate that Athena should have appeared from the head of the king of gods and men.

Zeus also made alliances with other Titan females. Themis, daughter of Uranus and Gaia, bore him the Horae, three goddesses who made the seasons change. Their names were Eunomia (Good Order), Dike (Justice), and Eirene (Peace). She also gave birth to the three Fates, Clotho, Lachesis, and Atropos. From Zeus's alliance with Mnemosyne, goddess of memory, were born the nine Muses—Calliope, Clio, Erato, Euterpe, Melpomene, Polyhymnia, Terpsichore, Thalia, and Urania. The offspring of Zeus's affair with Leto, daughter of Coeus and Phoebe, were sun god Apollo and goddess of hunting Artemis.

Zeus mated with lesser divinities as well. From his liaison with the sea nymph Eurynome were born the three Graces, whom Greek poet Hesiod (fl. 800 BCE) named Aglaiea (Splendor), Euphrosyne (Joy), and Thalia (Bloom). On another occasion the nymph Maia caught Zeus's roving eye; from their union Hermes was born. Zeus was on the point of having an affair with Thetis, but just in time Prometheus warned him that any child the sea nymph bore would be more powerful than his father. To prevent being part of this outcome, Zeus married Thetis off to the mortal Peleus; she later gave birth to Achilles.

Formidable wife

Zeus's wife or consort was his sister, Hera. Through her marriage to Zeus she became an important goddess who looked after the lives of married women. With Zeus she produced at least three children: Hebe, goddess of youth; Eileithyia, goddess of childbirth; and Ares, god of war. While some say there was a fourth child of the union, Hephaestus, god of fire, the more common version is that Hera produced him on her own as a reprisal against Zeus for his solo creation of Athena. However, unlike Athena, Hephaestus was born lame: his legs were deformed, and his body misshapen. Disgusted by her son's appearance, and angry at her own ineptitude, Hera threw Hephaestus off Mount Olympus, and he landed on the island of Lemnos. According to other accounts, however, it was not Hera who expelled Hephaestus but Zeus himself. Either way, fire was needed in the Greek world, and so was its patron deity. Hephaestus was restored to Mount Olympus, and there he married Aphrodite, goddess of love.

In addition to goddesses and nymphs, Zeus was attracted to many mortals. One of the first human females he pursued was Europa, daughter of Agenor, king of Tyre. In order to get close to her, Zeus turned himself into a beautiful white bull and pranced into the meadow where Europa and her sisters were tending the family herd. Fascinated by the fine animal, Europa climbed on its back. At once the bull dashed into the sea and carried the princess off to Crete. There he revealed his true identity and intentions. In time Europa gave birth to Minos—according to tradition, the Minoan culture on Crete is named for him. Two other children were also born from this couple: Rhadamanthys, who after his reign of Phaistos on Crete became a judge in the underworld, and the third son, Sarpedon. Stories of Sarpedon vary: in one of the best known he went off to Asia Minor (modern Turkey) to rule over the people of Lycia.

Io, a priestess of Hera, was another mortal who attracted Zeus. She was lured by the god into a grove outside the city of Argos. In some versions of the myth, when Hera caught sight of the two lovers, she immediately turned Io into a white cow. In others it was Zeus who changed Io into a cow that Hera then asked to have for her own. In either case, Io remained a cow and Hera sent Argus, a 100-

eyed giant, to watch over her. Hermes, assigned by Zeus to rescue Io, lulled all of Argus's eyes to sleep with music and then cut off his head. Argus became a peacock or, in another version, his eyes were transplanted by Hera onto the peacock's tail. When Io was rescued, Hera sent a stinging gadfly to torment her. The cow girl fled across the Bosporus, the strait between Europe and Asia in modern Turkey, a place whose name means "cow crossing." Io went on to Egypt, where Zeus finally restored her to human form. From his touch she gave birth to a son, Epaphus, who would become the founder of the Egyptian race.

Alcmene of Thebes was also ravished by Zeus, even though she had just married Amphitryon, son of Alcaeus, king of Tiryns, a town in the eastern Peloponnese. Alcmene told her new husband that she would not go to his bed until he had avenged wrongs done to her brothers. While Amphitryon was off on this mission, Zeus came to Alcmene's bed in the form of Amphitryon himself.

Alcmene, thinking her husband was safely home, agreed at last to sleep with him. She was shocked when later that night her true mortal husband returned. As a result of the double union, Alcmene gave birth to two children: Iphicles, son of Amphitryon, and Heracles, son of Zeus. Hera did everything in her power to destroy this child of her husband's, but every time Heracles escaped her plots.

Zeus and Danae, Leda, and Semele

There was nothing a mortal could do to resist the attentions of Zeus. Acrisius, king of Argos, had been warned by the Delphic oracle that his daughter Danae would give birth to a son who would one day kill his grandfather. In an effort to prevent the omen from coming to pass, Acrisius immediately imprisoned his daughter in an underground chamber made of bronze with only a small aperture for light and air. No man could come in, and she could not go out. As Danae mourned the loss of her freedom, she noticed a strange, sunny glow creeping through the window. Gradually the glow coalesced into a shower of gold, and then into the form of Zeus. He was attracted to the imprisoned girl and determined to be her lover. Danae naturally felt little loyalty to her father at this point and saw no reason why she should not have an affair with this handsome divinity. Later she gave birth to a son, Perseus. Acrisius shut mother and child into a chest and threw it into the sea. The chest was washed ashore, and Perseus grew to manhood on the island of Seriphos. When he returned to Argos to take part in athletic contests there, his throw of the discus went wide and struck Acrisius among the watching bystanders. Thus did Perseus kill his grandfather, and thus was destiny fulfilled. Some stories say that Perseus lived on to establish the citadel at Mycenae.

The most unusual story of Zeus and a mortal woman is that of his relationship with Leda, queen of Sparta. This time the god embarked on his seduction in the form of a large white swan. As a result of her union with the swan, Leda laid either one or two eggs. From these hatched two daughters, Helen and Clytemnestra, and two sons, Castor and Pollux. Helen and Pollux were children of Zeus; Clytemnestra and Castor were fathered by Leda's mortal husband, Tyndareos.

Semele, daughter of Cadmus, king of Thebes, also attracted Zeus's interest. The god appeared to her as a mortal lover. Hera, aware of her husband's infidelity, disguised herself as Semele's maid and persuaded the princess to ask her lover to reveal his true power. Having promised Semele that he would answer any request, Zeus was compelled to show his true form. While demonstrating his lightning, he unleashed a bolt which consumed Semele in its flames. Zeus snatched the unborn child from her ashes and sewed it into his own thigh. In time the baby was born from the thigh of Zeus. Dionysus was thus a god of double birth whose mortality had been burned away in Zeus's fire. In all of Greek mythology, Dionysus was the only child of a union between mortal and god who was immortal and fully divine.

Divine power

Not all stories of Zeus concern the god's amatory adventures. Many tell of his unrivaled power. In the conflict for supremacy between Zeus and the Titans, Prometheus supported Zeus and for a time was his chief counselor. Later, over the question of how to apportion a sacrificial animal justly between the gods and humans, he devised

a plan by which humans received the choicest parts. Angered, Zeus denied humanity the gift of fire proposed by Prometheus, fearing that its use for making tools and weapons would cause mortals to consider themselves the equals of the gods. Prometheus, however, stole fire from the hearth of Zeus and carried it to Earth in a fennel stalk. (In another version of the legend, Prometheus took fire from the forge of Hephaestus.)

As punishment Zeus ordered Prometheus to be chained to a rock on Mount Caucasus, where he underwent the daily torment of an eagle devouring his liver, which grew back each night. Throughout his ordeal Prometheus taunted Zeus with a secret, known only to him: that the goddess Thetis, who was being courted by Zeus, would give birth to a son who would grow up to be mightier than his father. In fact, this mortal was the Greek hero Achilles, who grew up to be a greater warrior than his mortal father Peleus.

In another legend, Zeus ordered the creation of a woman to plague Prometheus and all men. Pandora was endowed with alluring graces and furnished with a magic jar (Pandora's box). Suspecting trickery, Prometheus refused to accept her, but his brother Epimetheus gladly took her

Above: The remains of the great temple of Olympian Zeus still stand in Athens. The building originally had 104 columns.

as his wife. Succumbing to temptation, Pandora opened the jar, whereupon all the evils and diseases that came to afflict mortals were released. By the time the jar was closed, only Hope remained inside, so humans had ills but no hope.

In another story, Zeus grew angry when Asclepius, son of Apollo and god of healing, brought a mortal back to life. He hurled Asclepius down to the realm of the dead. Although Asclepius was later returned to the earth so that he could continue curing humans, he never ascended Mount Olympus because he was too busy serving mortals as divine physician.

Zeus ruled from Mount Olympus but had sanctuaries in many parts of Greece. The most famous of these was at Olympia in the western Peloponnese, where the Olympic Games were held in his honor every four years. Athletes competed in honor of Zeus for a crown of olive leaves. The men offered their best gift, their physical ability, to the god whose rule was supreme. Greeks used the span between Olympic festivals as their dating system: events in Greek history were measured in Olympiads, four-year periods from 776 BCE. The stadia where the contests were held became the standard unit of measurement: distances between cities were measured not in miles but in stadia,

units of approximately 600 feet (185 m). For the temple to Zeus at Olympia, Greek sculptor Phidias (fl. c. 490–430 BCE) carved a statue from gold and ivory measuring 42 feet (12.8 m) in height. It was one of the Seven Wonders of the Ancient World. Athletic contests were also held in Zeus's honor at Nemea, near Corinth, every two years. At Nemea the athletic events were similar to those at Olympia, only here the winner won a crown made of the soft dark green leaves of watercress.

Karelisa Hartigan

Bibliography

Aeschylus, and A. Shapiro and P. Burian, eds. *The Oresteia.* New York: Oxford University Press, 2010.

Bulfinch, Thomas. *Bulfinch's Mythology.* New York: Barnes & Noble, 2006.

Hesiod, and M. L. West, trans. *Theogony* and *Works and Days.* New York: Oxford University Press, 2008.

Homer, and Robert Fagles, trans. *The Iliad.* New York: Penguin, 2009.

Howatson, M. C. *The Oxford Companion to Classical Literature.* New York: Oxford University Press, 2005.

See also: Aphrodite; Ares; Asclepius; Athena; Cronus; Demeter; Dionysus; Fates; Gaia; Graces; Hades; Hebe; Hephaestus; Hera; Hermes; Hestia; Mnemosyne; Muses; Poseidon; Prometheus; Thetis; Titans; Typhon; Uranus.

PRONUNCIATION GUIDE

Using the Pronunciation Guide

A syllable rendered in large capital letters indicates that the syllable should be stressed. Where two syllables are stressed in a single word, large capital letters indicate where the main emphasis should fall, while small capital letters indicate the position of the secondary emphasis.

Achelous	AK-e-LOW-us
Achilles	a-KIL-eez
Actaeon	ak-TEE-on
Adonis	a-DON-nis
Aegir	A-jeer
Aeneas	ee-NEE-ass
Agamemnon	ag-uh-MEM-non
Ajax	AY-jaks
Alcestis	al-SES-tis
Andromeda	AN-DROM-eh-da
Anemoi	a-NEE-moy
Antigone	an-TIG-o-nee
Aphrodite	af-ro-DIE-tee
Apollo	a-POL-o
Arachne	a-RAK-nee
Ares	AIR-eez
Ariadne	ar-i-AD-nee
Artemis	AHR-te-mis
Asclepius	as-KLEP-ee-us
Astarte	as-TAR-tay
Atalanta	at-a-LAN-tuh
Ate	AY-tee
Athena	a-THEE-na
Atlas	AT-las
Atreus	AY-tree-us
Attis	AT-is
Bacchus	BAK-us
Bellerophon	bell-AIR-o-fon
Britomartis	brit-O-mar-tis
Cadmus	KAD-mus
Callisto	ka-LIS-toe
Calypso	ka-LIP-so
Cassandra	ka-SAN-dra

Castor	KAS-ter
Circe	SIR-see
Clytemnestra	kly-tem-NES-tra
Cronus	KRO-nus
Cupid	KEW-pid
Cyclops	SI-klops
Daedalus	DED-a-lus
Danae	DAY-nigh
Daphne	DAF-nee
Demeter	dem-MEE-ter
Deucalion	dew-KAY-lee-on
Diana	die-AN-a
Diomedes	die-oh-MEE-deez
Dionysus	die-oh-NIGH-sus
Dis	DIS
Dryads	DRY-adz
Electra	ee-LEK-tra
Endymion	en-DIM-ay-on
Eos	EE-os
Erichthonius	er-IK-tho-nee-us
Eros	EER-os
Europa	you-RO-pa
Faunus	FAW-nus
Gaia	GUY-er
Galatea	gal-a-TEE-a
Ganymede	GAN-ee-meed
Hades	HAY-deez
Hebe	HEE-bee
Hecate	HEK-a-tee
Hecuba	HEK-u-ba
Helios	HE-lee-os
Hephaestus	hef-EYE-stus
Hera	HER-a
Heracles	HER-a-kleez
Hermaphroditus	her-maf-ro-DI-tus
Hermes	HUR-meez
Hero	HE-ro
Hesperides	hes-PER-e-deez
Hestia	HES-ti-a
Hippolyte	hip-POL-i-tee
Hippolytus	hip-POL-i-tus
Hypnos	HIP-nos
Icarus	IK-a-rus

Idomeneus	i-DOM-en-ay-us	Pasiphae	pa-SIF-aye
Iphigeneia	IF-i-jay-NEE-uh	Patroclus	pah-TROW-klus
Janus	JAY-nus	Peleus	PE-lee-us
Jason	JAY-son	Pelops	PEE-lops
Juno	JOO-no	Penates	pe-NAY-teez
Jupiter	JOO-pi-ter	Penelope	pen-EL-o-pee
Laocoon	lay-O-koon	Persephone	pur-SEF-o-nee
Laomedon	lay-O-may-don	Perseus	PUR-see-us
Lares	LAIR-eez	Phaethon	FAY-thon
Leda	LEE-da	Philoctetes	fil-ok-TEE-teez
Leto	LEE-tow	Phobos	FO-bos
Lycaon	lie-KAY-on	Pleiades	PLEE-uh-deez
Maenads	may-NADS	Plutus	PLOO-tus
Medea	me-DEE-a	Pollux	POL-luks
Memnon	MEM-non	Pomona	po-MO-na
Menelaus	MEN-ay-lay-us	Poseidon	po-SY-don
Mercury	MUR-cure-ee	Priam	PRY-am
Midas	MY-das	Priapus	PRY-a-pus
Minerva	min-ER-ver	Prometheus	pro-MEE-thee-us
Minos	MY-nos	Proteus	PRO-tee-us
Mnemosyne	nem-OS-i-nee	Psyche	SY-kee
Momos	MO-mus	Pygmalion	pig-MAY-lee-on
Morpheus	MOR-fee-us	Remus	REE-mus
Muses	MYOU-ses	Rhea Silvia	REE-uh sil-VEE-uh
Myrmidons	MUR-me-donz	Romulus	ROM-you-lus
Myrrha	MER-ra	Satyrs	SAY-ters
Narcissus	nar-SIS-us	Selene	sel-EE-nee
Nemesis	NEM-e-sis	Sibyl	SIB-il
Neptune	NEP-tune	Silenus	si-LEE-nus
Nereus	NER-ee-ous	Sisyphus	SIS-e-fuss
Nestor	NES-tor	Tantalus	TAN-ter-lus
Nike	NY-kee	Tiresias	tie-REE-see-us
Nyx	NIKS	Theseus	THEE-see-us
Oceanus	o-SEE-a-nus	Thetis	THEE-tis
Odysseus	o-DISS-ee-us	Tithonus	ti-THO-nus
Oedipus	E-di-pus	Triton	TRY-ton
Orestes	o-RES-teez	Troilus	TROY-lus
Orion	o-RI-on	Tyche	TY-kee
Orpheus	OR-fee-us	Typhon	TY-fon
Paeon	PEE-on	Uranus	YOOR-un-us
Pan	PAN	Venus	VEE-nus
Pandora	pan-DOOR-uh	Vesta	VES-ta
Paris	PA-ris	Zeus	ZOOS

MAJOR PANTHEONS

GREECE

OLYMPIAN DEITIES

Aphrodite: goddess of love and beauty. She was married to the smith god Hephaestus, although she took numerous lovers, including Adonis and Ares.

Apollo: god of prophecy and divination, and patron of music and the arts. Apollo provided humans with laws and a sense of community.

Ares: son of Zeus and Hera; god of war. During battles he rode in a chariot wielding a sword and was accompanied by his sons Phobos and Deimos.

Artemis: virgin goddess of hunting and protector of the wilderness and unmarried women. She was also worshiped as the goddess of childbirth. Her parents were Zeus and Leto.

Athena: goddess of wisdom, crafts, and war. She taught mortals to use the plow and invented the trumpet.

Demeter: goddess of corn and cultivation. Hades stole her daughter Persephone and held her in the underworld for four months of the year.

Dionysus: son of Zeus and Semele; he was the god of wine, vegetation, and human emotion. He was rescued unborn from the ashes of his incinerated mother and was sewn into Zeus's thigh, from which he eventually was born.

Hades: god of the underworld and lord of the dead. Hades was married to Persephone, whom he abducted and tricked into living with him for four months of the year.

Hephaestus: god of fire and metalworking who fashioned armor for the gods. He was born lame and was mocked by the other gods for his disability. Hephaestus was the husband of Aphrodite.

Hera: queen of the gods and goddess of women and marriage. She was married to Zeus and occupied herself restricting his extramarital exploits.

Hermes: messenger god and god of boundaries. He was one of the youngest gods, and was worshiped by those who had to cross a boundary, such as shepherds and heralds. He escorted the dead to the underworld.

Hestia: virgin goddess of the hearth. Hestia was responsible for maintaining harmony in the home and in cities.

Persephone: goddess of agriculture and the underworld. The daughter of Zeus and Demeter, she was taken to the underworld by her uncle, Hades, and forced to stay there for four months of the year.

Poseidon: god of the sea, known for his fearsome temper. He was capable of creating violent storms. Poseidon was often depicted holding a trident.

Zeus: supreme god of the cosmos and of justice. He was married to Hera, but his sexual appetite was unequalled; he took many lovers and fathered many children.

TITANS

Atlas: uncle to the parents of the human race. He was father of the Pleiades, and the Hyades, and according to some sources, the Hesperides. He is famous for the punishment inflicted upon him by Zeus—to hold the heavens on his shoulders.

Coeus: husband of Phoebe and father of Leto; often associated with intelligence.

Crius: grandfather of the four winds and all the stars. He married Eurybia, and was the father of Astraeus, Pallas, and Perses.

Cronus: youngest of the first generation of Titans. He castrated his father, Uranus, and saved his mother, Gaia, from agony by releasing his brothers and sisters from her

womb. Cronus married his sister Rhea, and was the father of the Olympian deities Hestia, Demeter, Hera, Hades, Poseidon, and Zeus.

Helios: god of the sun who brought light to the world by driving his chariot across the sky.

Hyperion: husband and brother of Theia and father of Helios, Selene, and Eos.

Iapetus: father of Atlas, Epimetheus, and Prometheus.

Leto: by Zeus, the mother of Apollo and Artemis. She gave birth to the two deities on the floating island of

Partial Family Tree of Ancient Greek Deities

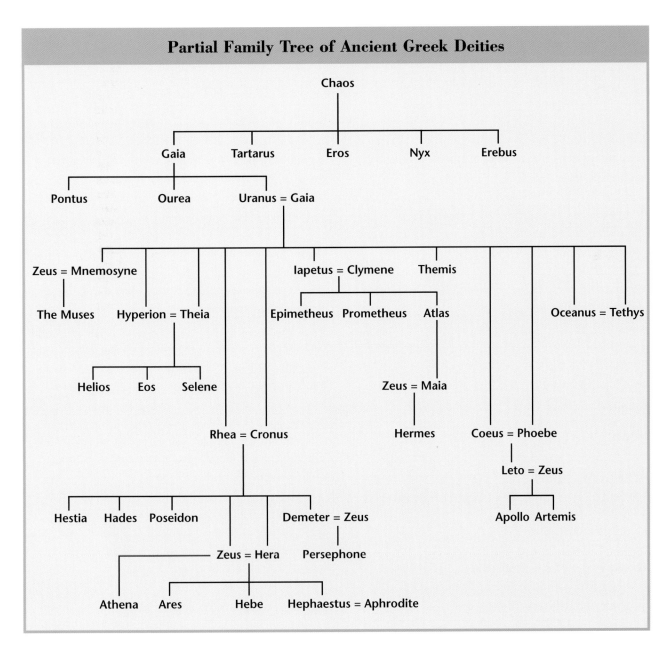

Delos. She had traveled there to escape the wrath of Zeus's jealous wife, Hera.

Mnemosyne: Titan who was widely associated with the power of memory. By Zeus, she was the mother of the Muses, goddesses who provided inspiration to artists.

Oceanus: eldest of the Titans, and god of the river that Greeks believed surrounded the earth. He married his sister Tethys and by her was the father of the Oceanids, three thousand water nymphs.

Phoebe: mother of Leto and Asteria by her brother Coeus. She was the grandmother of Apollo, who took the name Phoebus Apollo in her honor.

Prometheus: either the creator of humankind or its champion. Prometheus stole fire from the gods and gave it to humans. His punishment was to endure daily an eagle eating his liver while he was chained to a rock.

Rhea: mother of the Olympian gods Hestia, Demeter, Hera, Hades, Poseidon and Zeus. Rhea married her brother Cronus.

Tethys: Titan who married her brother Oceanus. By him, she was the mother of the Oceanids—the three thousand nymphs of the waters and land.

Theia: mother of Helios, Selene, and Eos. Theia married her brother Hyperion.

Themis: goddess of justice, law, and order. By Zeus, she was the mother of the Horae (seasons) and the three Fates. She presided over the assemblies of the gods.

ROME

Apollo: god of prophecy and patron of the arts who shared his name with his Greek equivalent. He was the guardian of shepherds and the god of healing. He came to be associated with the sun.

Bacchus: god of wine whose Greek equivalent was Dionysus. He was later known to Romans as Liber, the god of vegetation, fertility, theater, and of all wild nature. His worshipers included the satyrs.

Ceres: earth goddess whose Greek equivalent was Demeter. She was patroness of agriculture, especially of fruit and grain. When she shut herself away in grief at the abduction of her daughter Proserpina, the world became barren until Proserpina returned.

Consus: god of grain storage; husband of Ops, goddess of plenty. Because grain was stored in holes underneath the earth, so was Consus's altar. He was later worshiped as god of secret counsels.

Cupid: god of love and the son of Venus; closely identified with Amor. He was the equivalent of the Greek Cupid and was the lover of Psyche. He carried a bow that shot love-inducing arrows.

Cybele: earth goddess and mother of the gods; goddess of fertility and wild nature. Her consort was the god of vegetation, Attis. Cybele was identified with the Greek mother of the gods, Rhea.

Diana: goddess of women and childbirth, hunting, and the moon. She was identified with Artemis and later worshiped by slaves who sought refuge in her temples.

Dis: god of the underworld; another title for Pluto. Dis was the equivalent of the Greek Hades.

Flora: goddess of flowers, fertility, and spring. One myth recounted that she was originally a nymph called Chloris, but was transformed into a goddess when she was kissed by the West Wind, Zephyrus.

Fortuna: goddess of fortune and good luck; she was originally a goddess of fertility and blessing worshiped largely by mothers. Her Greek equivalent was Tyche.

Furiae: the Furies; avenging goddesses who pursued criminals through life and beyond death. They were born from the drops of blood shed on the Earth, Gaia, when Cronus castrated his father Uranus.

Juno: chief goddess whose Greek equivalent was Hera; sister and wife of Jupiter. One of the Capitoline Triad, Juno was goddess of marriage and childbirth. She was the mother of Mars and Minerva.

Jupiter: chief god, known as Optimus Maximus ("best and greatest"); the equivalent of the Greek Zeus. Originally

Jupiter was worshiped as a sky and weather god. He was the husband of Juno and the father of Minerva.

Lares: guardian spirits that protected houses, fields and crossroads. They were usually portrayed as dancing youths carrying drinking cups.

Mars: god of war whose Greek equivalent was Ares. He may originally have been a guardian of crops. He was the father by Rhea Silvia of the twins Romulus and Remus, the founders of Rome.

Mercury: messenger of the gods; god of commerce and guardian of merchants and travelers. He shared many attributes with his Greek equivalent Hermes, except that Mercury was also father by the nymph Lara of the guardian spirits called the Lares.

Minerva: goddess of wisdom, arts and crafts, and war. She was daughter of Jupiter and Juno and one of the Capitoline Triad. Her Greek equivalent was Athena, whose attributes she shared.

Neptune: god of the sea; originally an Italian god of fresh water. He was identified with the Greek god Poseidon. The Romans also worshiped him as Neptune Equester, god and patron of horse racing.

Ops: goddess of plenty; wife of Consus. She was identified with the Greek goddess Rhea and was also said to be the wife and sister of Saturn. She was worshiped with Ceres as the protector of harvests.

Quirinus: god associated with the fruitfulness of the harvest; later identified with the deified Romulus. One of the Roman hills, the Quirinalis, was named for him.

Saturn: god of agriculture who taught humans the benefits of civilization. He was identified with the Greek god Cronus and was the husband of Ops. From his name came the word *Saturday*.

Tellus: ancient earth goddess, later identified with Cybele. Her Greek equivalents were Gaia and Ceres and she was mother of the personification of rumor, Fama.

Venus: goddess of love, beauty, grace, and fertility. She was the equivalent of the Greek goddess Aphrodite and was the daughter of Jupiter. Her lovers included Mars, Vulcan, and Adonis.

Vesta: virgin goddess of the hearth and its fire who was the equivalent of the Greek goddess Hestia. Her cult was at first followed in private homes but became a state cult; vestal virgins maintained a fire in her temple on the Palatine Hill in Rome.

Vulcan: god of fire, especially the destructive fire of volcanoes; invoked to prevent fires. He was the equivalent of the Greek smith god Hephaestus.

FURTHER READING AND RESOURCES

Aeschylus, and A. Shapiro and P. Burian, eds. *The Oresteia.* New York: Oxford University Press, 2010.

Agha-Jaffar, Tamara. *Demeter and Persephone: Lessons from a Myth.* Jefferson, NC: McFarland and Company, 2002.

Alberti, Leon Battista, and Virginia Brown, ed. *Momus.* Cambridge, MA: Harvard University Press, 2003.

Apollodorus, and Robin Hard, trans. *The Library of Greek Mythology.* New York: Oxford University Press, 2008.

Apollonius Rhodius, and R. Hunter, trans. *Jason and the Golden Fleece.* New York: Oxford University Press, 2009.

Apuleius, and Joel C. Relihan, ed. *The Tale of Cupid and Psyche.* Indianapolis, IN: Hackett, 2009.

Apuleius, and Joel C. Relihan, trans. *The Golden Ass.* Indianapolis, IN: Hackett, 2007.

Barber, Antonia. *Apollo and Daphne: Masterpieces of Greek Mythology.* Los Angeles: Paul Getty Museum Publications, 1998.

Beard, Mary, John North, and Simon Price. *Religions of Rome.* New York: Cambridge University Press, 1998.

Bremmer, J. N., and N. M. Horsfall. *Roman Myth and Mythography.* London: University of London Institute of Classical Studies, 1987.

Bulfinch, Thomas. *Bulfinch's Mythology.* New York: Barnes & Noble, 2006.

Bulfinch, Thomas. *Myths of Greece and Rome.* New York: Penguin, 1998.

Burr, Elizabeth, trans. *The Chiron Dictionary of Greek and Roman Mythology: Gods and Goddesses, Heroes, Places, and Events of Antiquity.* New York: Chiron Publications, 1994.

Calame, Claude, and Daniel W. Berman, trans. *Myth and History in Ancient Greece.* Princeton, NJ: Princeton University Press, 2003.

Camus, Albert, and Justin O'Brien, trans. *The Myth of Sisyphus.* London: Penguin, 2000.

Clauss, Manfred, and Richard Gordon, trans. *The Roman Cult of Mithras.* New York: Routledge, 2001.

Cotterell, Arthur. *Oxford Dictionary of World Mythology.* Oxford: Oxford University Press, 1997.

Craft, M. Charlotte. *Cupid and Psyche.* New York: William Morrow and Company, 1996.

Crudden, Michael, trans. *The Homeric Hymns.* New York: Oxford University Press, 2002.

Dumézil, Georges, and Philip Krapp, trans. *Archaic Roman Religion.* Baltimore, MD: Johns Hopkins University Press, 1996.

Edwards, Ruth B. *Kadmos the Phoenician: A Study in Greek Legends and the Mycenean Age.* Amsterdam: Hakkert, 1979.

Euripides, and Peter Burian and Alan Shapiro, eds. *The Complete Euripides,* 5 vols. New York: Oxford University Press, 2009–2010.

Farnaux, Alexandre, and David J. Baker, trans. *Knossos: Searching for the Legendary Palace of King Minos.* New York: Harry N. Abrams, 1996.

Finley, M. I. *The World of Odysseus.* New York: New York Review of Books, 2002.

Foley, Helene P. *The Homeric Hymn to Demeter.* Princeton, NJ: Princeton University Press, 1994.

Frazer, James George. *The Golden Bough.* New York: Oxford University Press, 2009.

Garber, Marjorie, and Nancy J. Vickers, eds. *The Medusa Reader.* New York: Routledge, 2003.

Gardner, Jane F. *Roman Myths.* Austin, TX: University of Texas Press, 1993.

Gibbon, Edward, and H.-F. Mueller, ed. *The Decline and Fall of the Roman Empire*. New York: Modern Library, 2003.

Goldsworthy, Adrian. *The Complete Roman Army*. New York: Thames and Hudson, 2003.

Graves, Robert. *The Greek Myths*. New York: Penguin, 1993.

Guerber, H. A. *The Myths of Greece and Rome*. New York: Dover Publications, 1993.

Guirand, Félix, ed. *Larousse Encyclopedia of Mythology*. London: Hamlyn, 1983.

Hamilton, Edith. *Mythology*. New York: Grand Central, 2011.

Harding, Anthony. *The Mycenaeans and Europe*. San Diego: Academic Press, 1984.

Hesiod, and M. L. West, trans. *Theogony* and *Works and Days*. New York: Oxford University Press, 2008.

Homer, and Robert Fagles, trans. *The Iliad*. New York: Penguin, 2009.

Homer, and Robert Fagles, trans. *The Odyssey*. New York: Penguin, 2009.

Horace, and David West, trans. *The Complete Odes and Epodes*. New York: Oxford University Press, 2008.

Howatson, M. C. *The Oxford Companion to Classical Literature*. New York: Oxford University Press, 2005.

Hughes, Dennis D. *Human Sacrifice in Ancient Greece*. New York: Routledge, 1991.

Kerenyi, Karl, and Ralph Manheim, trans. *Eleusis*. Princeton, NJ: Princeton University Press, 1991.

Komar, Kathleen L. *Reclaiming Klytemnestra*. Champaign, IL: University of Illinois Press, 2003.

Macgillivray, Joseph Alexander. *Minotaur: Sir Arthur Evans and the Archaeology of the Minoan Myth*. New York: Hill and Wang, 2000.

March, Jenny. *Cassell's Dictionary of Classical Mythology*. London: Cassell, 1998.

Matyszak, Philip. *Chronicle of the Roman Republic*. New York: Thames and Hudson, 2003.

McLaren, Clemence. *Inside the Walls of Troy*. New York: Atheneum, 1996.

O'Neill, Eugene. *Three Plays: Desire under the Elms, Strange Interlude, Mourning Becomes Electra*. New York: Vintage Books, 1995.

Ovid, and A. D. Melville, trans. *Metamorphoses*. New York: Oxford University Press, 1998.

Pausanias, and Peter Levi, trans. *Guide to Greece*. New York: Viking Press, 1984.

Pindar, and Richard Stoneman, trans. *The Odes: And Selected Fragments*. New York: Everyman's Library, 1998.

Pinsent, John. *Greek Mythology*. London: Hamlyn, 1982.

Plato, and G. M. A. Grube, trans. *Republic*. Cambridge, MA: Hackett Publishing, 1992.

Plato, and James H. Nichols, Jr., trans. *Gorgias and Phaedrus*. Ithaca, NY: Cornell University Press, 1998.

Pomeroy, Sarah B. *Goddesses, Whores, Wives, and Slaves: Women in Classical Antiquity*. New York: Schocken Books, 1995.

Race, William H., ed. *Pindar: Olympian Odes, Pythian Odes*. Cambridge, MA: Harvard University Press, 1997.

Rose, Carol. *Giants, Monsters, and Dragons*. New York: Norton, 2000.

Rosenberg, Donna. *World Mythology: An Anthology of the Great Myths and Epics*. New York: McGraw-Hill, 2001.

Scheid, John, and Janet Lloyd, trans. *An Introduction to Roman Religion*. Bloomington, IN: Indiana University Press, 2003.

Scullard, H. H. *Festivals and Ceremonies of the Roman Republic*. Ithaca, NY: Cornell University Press, 1981.

Sirracos, Constantine. *History of the Olympic Games*. Long Island City, NY: Seaburn Books, 2000.

Sophocles, and Christopher Perry, ed. *Philoctetes*. London: Cambridge University Press, 1969.

Sophocles, and Judith Affleck and Ian McAuslan, eds. *Oedipus Tyrannus*. Cambridge University Press, 2003.

FURTHER READING AND RESOURCES

Sophocles, and Robert Fitzgerald, trans. *The Oedipus Cycle: Oedipus Rex, Oedipus at Colonus, Antigone.* San Diego, CA: Harcourt, 2002.

Turcan, Robert, and Antonia Nevill, trans. *The Gods of Ancient Rome.* New York: Routledge, 2001.

Ulansey, David. *The Origins of the Mithraic Mysteries.* New York: Oxford University Press, 1991.

Virgil, and Robert Fitzgerald, trans. *The Aeneid.* New York: Vintage, 1990.

West, Martin L., ed. *Homeric Myths, Homeric Apocrypha, Lives of Homer.* Cambridge, MA: Loeb Classical Library, 2003.

Wilk, Stephen R. *Medusa: Solving the Mystery of the Gorgon.* New York: Oxford University Press, 2000.

Wiseman, T. P. *Catullus and His World: A Reappraisal.* Cambridge: Cambridge University Press, 1985.

Wiseman, T. P. *Remus: A Roman Myth.* New York: Cambridge University Press, 1995.

FOR YOUNGER READERS

Bolton, Lesley. *The Everything Classical Mythology Book: Greek and Roman Gods, Goddesses, Heroes, and Monsters from Ares to Zeus.* Avon, MA: Adams Media Corporation, 2002.

Colum, Padraic. *The Children's Homer: The Adventures of Odysseus and the Tale of Troy.* Mineola, NY: Dover Books, 2004.

Colum, Padraic. *The Golden Fleece and the Heroes Who Lived before Achilles.* New York: Random House, 2010.

Connolly, P. *The Ancient Greece of Odysseus.* New York: Oxford University Press, 1998.

Day, Nancy. *Passport to History: Your Travel Guide to Ancient Greece.* Minneapolis, MN: Runestone, 2001.

Evslin, Bernard. *Heroes, Gods, and Monsters of the Greek Myths.* Minneapolis, MN: Sagebrush Educational Resources, 1999.

Fleischman, Paul. *Dateline: Troy.* Cambridge, MA: Candlewick Press, 2006.

Green, Jen. *Ancient Greek Myths.* New York: Gareth Stevens, 2010.

Homer, retold by Geraldine McCaughrean. *The Odyssey.* New York: Puffin Books, 1997.

Hull, Robert E. *World of Ancient Greece: Religion and the Gods.* Danbury, CT: Franklin Watts, 2000.

Innes, Brian. *Myths of Ancient Rome.* Austin, TX: Raintree Steck-Vaughn, 2001.

James, Simon. *Eyewitness: Ancient Rome.* New York: Dorling Kindersley, 2000.

Lively, Penelope. *In Search of the Homeland: The Story of the Aeneid.* New York: Delacorte Press, 2001.

Low, Alice. *The Macmillan Book of Greek Gods and Heroes.* New York: Maxwell Macmillan International, 1994.

McCaughrean, Geraldine. *Greek Myths.* New York: Margaret K. McElderry Books, 1993.

McCaughrean, Geraldine. *Roman Myths.* New York: Margaret K. McElderry Books, 2001.

McLaren, Clemence. *Aphrodite's Blessings: Love Stories from the Greek Myths.* New York: Atheneum Books, 2002.

Múten, Burleigh. *Goddesses: A World of Myth and Magic.* Barefoot Books, 2003.

Osborne, Mary Pope. *Favorite Greek Myths.* New York: Scholastic Press, 1991.

Pearson, Anne. *Eyewitness: Ancient Greece.* New York: Dorling Kindersley, 2000.

Ross, Stewart. *Ancient Greece: The Original Olympics.* New York: Peter Bedrick Books, 1999.

Schomp, Virginia. *Myths of the World: The Ancient Greeks.* New York: Benchmark, 2008.

Schomp, Virginia. *Myths of the World: The Ancient Romans.* New York: Benchmark, 2009.

Sharman-Burke, Juliet. *Stories from the Stars: Greek Myths of the Zodiac.* New York: Abbeville Kids, 1996.

INTERNET RESOURCES

The Age of Fable: Thomas Bulfinch
Electronic version of the 1913 edition of Bulfinch's compilation of myths, including Greek and Roman myths.
www.bartleby.com/bulfinch

Digital Librarian: Mythology
A collection of links to sites that are useful to students of mythology.
www.digital-librarian.com/mythology.html

Encyclopedia Mythica
Encyclopedia of mythology, folklore, and legends from around the world. The site is divided geographically, with Greece and Rome included in the section for Europe.
www.pantheon.org

Etymological Dictionary of Classical Mythology
A site that lists modern words and terms derived from figures or episodes from classical mythology.
http://library.oakland.edu/information/people/personal/kraemer/edcm/contents.html

Forum Romanum
The site, dedicated to Roman literature, contains works by a vast number of Roman authors in the form of both original Latin texts and English translations.
www.forumromanum.org

God Checker
Aimed largely at younger users, this humorous site contains descriptions of the gods of a variety of ancient civilizations, including Greece and Rome.
www.godchecker.com

Gods, Heroes, and Myth
This general site for world mythology contains particularly comprehensive lists of Greek and Roman mythology.
www.gods-heros-myth.com

The Golden Bough: A Study in Magic and Religion
Electronic version of the 1922 edition of James Frazer's *The Golden Bough*, a study in comparative mythology.
www.bartleby.com/196

Greek Mythology Link
Extensive site that includes maps, timelines, and biographies of all the major characters in Greek mythology.
www.maicar.com/GML

Internet Classics Archive
Collection of English translations for ancient texts, primarily works written by Greek and Roman authors such as Apollodorus, Pausanias, and Ovid.
http://classics.mit.edu/index.html

The Mystica
This site that provides information on world mythology features sections on Greek mythology, Roman mythology, and Greco-Roman mythology.
www.themystica.org/mythical-folk/info/topics.html

MythHome
Comprehensive site that covers all the major pantheons, including ancient Greece and Rome, with material organized by culture, time, and theme.
www.mythome.org/mythhome.htm

Mythography
This site is dedicated to Greek, Roman, and Celtic mythology and includes extensive links to other relevant print and online resources.
www.loggia.com/myth/myth.html

Mythweb
Aimed primarily at younger users, this site provides a basic introduction to Greek mythology, including the Olympian deities and the major myths.
www.mythweb.com

Olga's Gallery: Ancient Greek and Roman Myths
This catalog of paintings that depict scenes from classical mythology allows the user to select a Greek deity or hero and then view a selection of paintings that feature him or her.
www.abcgallery.com/mythindex.html

Theoi Project: A Guide to Greek Gods, Spirits, and Monsters
This comprehensive site features extensive lists of Greek mythological figures and explores Greek mythology in classical literature and art.
www.theoi.com

Windows to the Universe
This site, aimed at younger users, includes information about the relationships between space and mythology. Material related to Greece and Rome is included in the Classical Mythology section.
www.windows2universe.org/mythology/mythology.html

INDEX

PICTURE CREDITS